America's
TEST KITCHEN

America's
TEST KITCHEN

Cooking
for Two

2011

THE YEAR'S BEST RECIPES CUT DOWN TO SIZE

BY THE EDITORS OF
AMERICA'S TEST KITCHEN

PHOTOGRAPHY BY
CARL TREMBLAY, KELLER + KELLER, AND DANIEL J. VAN ACKERE

AMERICA'S TEST KITCHEN
17 Station Street, Brookline, MA 02445

Library of Congress Cataloging-in-Publication Data
The Editors at America's Test Kitchen

AMERICA'S TEST KITCHEN COOKING FOR TWO 2011:
The Year's Best Recipes Cut Down to Size

1st Edition

Hardcover: $35 US
ISBN-13: 978-1-933615-78-3   ISBN-10: 1-933615-78-8
1. Cooking. 1. Title
2011

Manufactured in the United States of America

10 9 8 7 6 5 4 3 2 1

Distributed by America's Test Kitchen
17 Station Street, Brookline, MA 02445

EDITORIAL DIRECTOR: Jack Bishop
EXECUTIVE EDITOR: Elizabeth Carduff
EXECUTIVE FOOD EDITOR: Julia Collin Davison
SENIOR EDITORS: Lori Galvin and Suzannah McFerran
ASSOCIATE EDITORS: Kate Hartke, Adelaide Parker, and Dan Souza
TEST COOKS: Rebecca Morris, Christie Morrison, and Kate Williams
EDITORIAL ASSISTANT: Alyssa King
DESIGN DIRECTOR: Amy Klee
ART DIRECTOR: Greg Galvan
ASSOCIATE ART DIRECTOR: Matthew Warnick
STAFF PHOTOGRAPHER: Daniel J. van Ackere
ADDITIONAL PHOTOGRAPHY: Keller + Keller and Carl Tremblay
FOOD STYLING: Marie Piraino and Mary Jane Sawyer
PRODUCTION DIRECTOR: Guy Rochford
SENIOR PRODUCTION MANAGER: Jessica Lindheimer Quirk
SENIOR PROJECT MANAGER: Alice Carpenter
PRODUCTION AND TRAFFIC COORDINATOR: Kate Hux
ASSET AND WORKFLOW MANAGER: Andrew Mannone
PRODUCTION AND IMAGING SPECIALISTS: Judy Blomquist, Heather Dube, and Lauren Pettapiece
COPYEDITOR: Barbara Wood
PROOFREADER: Jeffrey Schier
INDEXER: Elizabeth Parson

PICTURED ON THE FRONT COVER: Zucchini, Tomato, and Ricotta Tarts (page 139)
PICTURED OPPOSITE TITLE PAGE: Baked Ziti with Sausage (page 102)
PICTURED ON BACK OF JACKET: Classic Chicken Pot Pies (page 61), Easiest-Ever Pulled Pork (page 20), Chicken in a Pot with Red Potatoes and Carrots (page 201), and Summer Berry Snack Cakes (page 269)

Contents

THE SMART SHOPPER'S GUIDE

MAKING THE MOST OF THE RECIPES IN THIS BOOK

LET'S FACE IT—WASTING FOOD IS AN ISSUE MOST OF us struggle with, but when you're cooking for two, it's an even bigger problem. Sure, there are some stores where you can buy loose leafy greens or a handful of Brussels sprouts, but usually you're stuck with pre-packaged produce sold in large quantities. The same is true of canned goods and many other items used in everyday recipes. So what's the solution to this problem? Careful planning and shopping. To that end, we've prepared this guide to key ingredients, both perishable and canned, that are used throughout the book. So if you're making one recipe with half a head of cauliflower or half a can of chickpeas, you can see which other recipes in the book call for them so you don't have to toss the extras.

STOCKING THE COOKING-FOR-TWO KITCHEN

IN GENERAL, WHEN YOU'RE COOKING FOR TWO, you really don't need special equipment—the usual battery of pots, pans, knives, and tools will work just fine. (Although if your kitchen isn't stocked with smaller skillets—8- and 10-inch—or a small saucepan, you'll need them for certain recipes in this book.) But for some scaled-down entrées and desserts, we found we needed small baking dishes, pie plates, and more; even a small slow cooker, although not required, came in handy for our scaled-down slow-cooked recipes. Fortunately, this equipment is inexpensive and widely available both online and at many retail stores. Plus, when it comes to things like ramekins and small tart pans and pie plates, you'll never need more than two (and sometimes just one will suffice). Here's a list of the cookware that we found most useful for the recipes in this book.

SMALL BAKING DISHES

A small baking dish, such as this 8½ by 5½-inch ceramic dish (with straight sides no higher than 2 inches to expose the surface of the food), came in handy when we wanted to scale down our Eggplant Casserole (page 137). For our petite yet decadent Tiramisù (page 284), we reached for an even smaller 3-cup baking dish (measuring approximately 7¼ by 5¼ inches). Note that dishes of a comparable size or of a different material can be used.

GRATIN DISHES

To make two individual Baked Zitis with Sausage (page 102), we needed a pair of 2-cup gratin dishes (measuring approximately 9 by 6 inches), although dishes of comparable size could be used instead.

RAMEKINS

Ramekins are handy for making both savory and sweet dishes. In our testing, we found that 5-ounce ramekins were the perfect size for making petite but rich Chocolate Pots de Crème (page 283), and 12-ounce ramekins were ideal for making our Classic Chicken Pot Pies (page 61).

SMALL SLOW COOKER

Although a standard 6-quart slow cooker works fine for the slow-cooker recipes in this book—and we've devoted a whole chapter to slow-cooking for two—we found a 3- to 3½-quart oval slow cooker easier to maneuver, clean, and store.

MINI LOAF PANS

We find mini loaf pans (which measure approximately 5½ by 3 inches) incredibly useful in the for-two kitchen. They're ideal for individual lasagnas, such as our White Spinach Lasagna (page 104), and scaled-down quick breads, such as our Cheddar Cheese Bread (page 259).

SMALL CAKE PAN

With a 6-inch round cake pan, you can make a perfectly sized cake for two (see our Apple Upside-Down Cake on page 267).

SMALL PIE PLATE

We found that a 6-inch pie plate works perfectly when you want to bake a pie that serves two (see our Sweet Cherry Pie on page 275 and Key Lime Pie on page 278).

SMALL TART PANS

When you want to make individual tarts, like our Zucchini, Tomato, and Ricotta Tarts (page 139), two 4-inch tart pans (with removable bottoms) hold just the right amount of crust and filling.

SMALL BUNDT PANS

These 1-cup pans are ideal for making two scaled-down Summer Berry Snack Cakes (page 269).

PAN-ROASTED THICK-CUT FISH FILLETS

CHAPTER 1

EVERYDAY MAIN DISHES

STEAK TIPS WITH MUSHROOM-ONION GRAVY

STEAK TIPS SMOTHERED IN MUSHROOM AND ONION gravy are classic pub fare, appearing on menus across the country. While this dish always beckons with its promise of juicy meat and hearty, satisfying flavors, it's often disappointing, with chewy, overcooked beef swimming in either a thin, flavorless brown sauce or a thick sludge of salty gravy. That's because many cooks cut the beef too small and it overcooks in the blink of an eye, or they turn to flavor-sacrificing shortcuts like canned cream of mushroom soup or dried onion soup mix. It wasn't hard to picture a better version—one that featured tender, meaty pieces of steak covered in a sauce enriched with fresh mushrooms and onions, and didn't include canned soup in the ingredient list.

Before we got into specific ingredients, we settled on a basic framework for the recipe. To keep our steak tips in the realm of streamlined weeknight supper, we decided to keep the cooking to a single skillet. We would first sear the beef and set it aside, then build the gravy, and finally add the meat back to the gravy to cook through. Besides convenience, this method would ensure that our dish had lots of meaty, rich flavor. Searing the meat would leave the skillet full of crusty browned bits, known as fond, providing a flavorful base for the sauce. Adding the partially cooked beef to the gravy and simmering until it cooked through would allow the flavors to mingle and build depth.

With our path laid out, the next task was finding the right beef for the job. Though you occasionally find the dish made with tender, richly flavored, expensive cuts like strip steak, rib-eye steak, and tenderloin, we didn't want to pay top dollar for a midweek meal for two. We turned instead to cheaper cuts: flank steak, round steak, and, of course, the most common choice, sirloin steak tips (also known as flap meat), cut from the sirloin area between the cow's short loin and back legs. This beefy cut has a wealth of internal marbling that melted into the coarse muscle fibers of the steak, adding tenderness when the meat was cooked to medium-rare. Flank steak made a suitable substitute if steak tips were unavailable but wasn't nearly as meaty-tasting, and round steak lacked intramuscular fat, easily turning bland, dry, and chalky after simmering in the gravy. Steak tips, which can easily be purchased in small quantities (12 ounces proved just right for two people), were ideal for this dish.

When it came time to prepare the steak, we wanted to develop a flavorful, well-seared crust yet leave the interior slightly underdone, so it wouldn't turn chewy and tough when returned to the pan to simmer with the gravy. We experimented with cutting the meat into various sizes to see which would cook best. Eventually, we settled on fork-friendly 1½-inch chunks, which were large enough that they could develop plenty of browned crust yet didn't cook through too quickly.

For the richest, most tender tips possible, we decided to marinate the meat briefly in soy sauce, one of the test kitchen's proven methods for beefing up steak flavor and juiciness. (The salty soy draws juice out of the steak, and then the reverse happens as the soy, along with the moisture, flows back in, bringing flavor deep into the meat.) A 30-minute soak in the soy sauce and a quick sear produced incredibly beefy steak tips, with a substantial crust and plenty of fond left behind. With a rich flavor base now encrusting the pan, we figured the rest would be gravy.

Up to this point, we had been adding a little vegetable oil to the pan and starting the sauce with a quarter of a pound of sliced white mushrooms and a single sliced onion. The flavor of the finished gravy proved more mild than meaty, so we tried increasing the amount of mushrooms. Even after doubling the amount, the flavor was still lacking. We tried portobellos, which provided an earthiness to the dish, but they were costly and, unless we scooped out their black gills, they left the gravy unappealingly gray and murky. Looking beyond fresh mushrooms, we tried adding some dried porcini to the pan along with the white mushrooms. While their texture was only subtly perceptible, the porcini contributed the intense mushroom flavor we were after.

Our next consideration was the liquid component of the sauce. Homemade broth was out of the question; this was a weeknight meal, after all. Instead, we were making do with store-bought beef broth—a beefy but mild alternative—so we decided to try adding some flavor enhancers. We tested Worcestershire sauce, tomato paste, red wine, and soy sauce. Tasters felt lukewarm about each addition, which seemed to overpower the beefy flavor rather than enhance it.

Then we stumbled upon a better way to boost the gravy's flavor. To cook the mushrooms in the same pan that we used to cook the beef, we needed to make sure they released moisture quickly enough to dissolve the flavorful fond before it burned. When we added the

STEAK TIPS WITH MUSHROOM-ONION GRAVY

white mushrooms, onion, and porcini mushrooms (along with a pinch of salt) and immediately covered the pan, the mushroom and onion juices starting flowing more quickly than with heat alone. Once the vegetables had "deglazed" the pan, we pulled off the cover and continued to sauté them until they were deeply browned, their liquid had cooked off, and even more browned bits clung to the pan. We now had a triple-header for flavor: a classic meat fond compounded by both mushroom and onion fond. With big beefy flavor in abundance, we focused on thickening our sauce and adding some final touches.

Stirring cornstarch into the skillet seemed like an easy way to thicken the broth into gravy, but it created a gelatinous sauce that reminded tasters of bad cafeteria food. Sprinkling in flour after the mushrooms had browned was equally simple but much more effective in creating a rich, lump-free gravy. As a finishing touch, we added some minced garlic and minced fresh thyme, which accented the woodsy flavor of the mushrooms nicely.

After we prepared yet another batch and gently simmered the meat and gravy together for five minutes to meld their flavors, tasters declared this dish finished—and far better than anything they'd ever been served in a pub.

Steak Tips with Mushroom-Onion Gravy
SERVES 2

Steak tips, also known as flap meat, are sold as whole steak, cubes, and strips. To ensure evenly sized chunks, we prefer to purchase whole steak tips and cut them ourselves. Serve over Simple White Rice (page 26) or egg noodles.

- 12 **ounces sirloin steak tips, trimmed and cut into 1½-inch chunks (see note)**
- 2 **teaspoons soy sauce**
  Salt and pepper
- 4 **teaspoons vegetable oil**
- 8 **ounces white mushrooms, trimmed and sliced thin**
- 1 **small onion, halved and sliced thin**
- ⅛ **ounce dried porcini mushrooms (about 2 tablespoons), rinsed and minced**
- 1 **garlic clove, minced**
- ¼ **teaspoon minced fresh thyme or pinch dried**
- 1 **tablespoon unbleached all-purpose flour**
- 1 **cup beef broth**
- 1 **tablespoon minced fresh parsley**

1. Combine beef, soy sauce, and ½ teaspoon pepper in medium bowl. Cover and refrigerate at least 30 minutes or up to 1 hour.

2. Heat 2 teaspoons oil in 10-inch skillet over medium-high heat until just smoking. Brown beef on all sides, 3 to 6 minutes; transfer to plate.

3. Add remaining 2 teaspoons oil, white mushrooms, onion, porcini mushrooms, and pinch salt to skillet, cover, and cook over medium heat until mushrooms are very wet, about 3 minutes. Uncover, scrape up any browned bits, and continue to cook until vegetables are browned and thick fond forms on bottom of skillet, 3 to 6 minutes longer.

4. Stir in garlic and thyme and cook until fragrant, about 30 seconds. Stir in flour and cook for 30 seconds. Stir in broth, scraping up any browned bits, and bring to simmer.

5. Return browned beef, with any accumulated juice, to skillet and simmer over medium-low heat until beef registers 130 degrees on instant-read thermometer, 3 to 6 minutes. Off heat, season with salt and pepper to taste, sprinkle with parsley, and serve.

NOTES FROM THE TEST KITCHEN

OUR FAVORITE TRADITIONAL SKILLET
We use our skillets all the time, for everything from searing steaks to braising chicken to cooking pasta. While nonstick skillets can be purchased at a reasonable price (see page 74), traditional skillets can cost anywhere from $30 to $150 or more. Preliminary tests of traditional skillets confirmed our suspicion that cheap was not the way to go, but how much do you really need to spend? We tested eight pans from well-known manufacturers. All of the pans tested had flared sides, and most had uncoated stainless steel cooking surfaces, which we prize for promoting a fond (the browned, sticky bits that cling to the interior of the pan when food is sautéed, which help flavor sauces).

We concluded that medium-weight pans (not too heavy and not too light) are ideal—they brown food beautifully and are easy to handle. These pans have enough heft for heat retention and structural integrity, but not so much that they are difficult to manipulate. For its combination of excellent performance, optimum weight and balance, and overall ease of use, the **All-Clad Stainless Steel Fry Pan**, which comes in 8-inch ($75), 10-inch ($85), and 12-inch ($125) sizes, was the hands-down winner.

WEEKNIGHT BEEF STEW

IT'S EASY TO SEE WHY MANY HOME COOKS STEER clear of beef stew when not cooking for a crowd. Good beef stew requires that the cook cut a large roast, prep numerous vegetables, then simmer the whole mass with broth for hours until the meat is tender—a ritual that yields rich sauce and tender beef but can take all day and requires loads of knife work. We wanted a richly flavored, hearty beef stew that cooked in a fraction of the time (ideally, less than an hour) and yielded just enough for two (no week's worth of leftovers allowed). Since we knew our choice of beef would dictate cooking time, and likely pose the biggest challenge, we started there.

Normally, we would turn to boneless chuck-eye roast for beef stew. Cut from the shoulder of the cow, this roast is intertwined with a tough network of sinew and collagen that requires hours of gentle heat to break down. In beef stew, chuck roast not only melts into tender, well-textured bites, it also provides body and flavor. Given our strict time constraints (and because we didn't need so much meat), we turned to a very different cut of beef, namely, a quick-cooking steak. After rounding up the usual suspects—strip, rib eye, tenderloin, flank, and steak tips (also known as flap meat)—we prepared several batches of stew to see which one would most closely approximate the flavor and body of chuck roast.

After cutting each steak into bite-size pieces, we browned them in a large saucepan and removed them before building a basic stew with onion, carrot, potato, garlic, beef broth, and a small amount of red wine. Once the carrot and potato were tender, we stirred in the browned beef to warm through. We tasted the various steaks side by side and quickly noticed a dividing line. On one side of the fence sat the strip, rib-eye, and tenderloin steaks, which didn't provide the rich meatiness that our beef stew needed. Flank steak and steak tips fared much better. With their moderate amount of connective tissue and intense beefiness, they did a fine job of mimicking stew meat. In the end, steak tips triumphed for their slightly superior meaty flavor.

While we had successfully prepared beef stew in a fraction of the time it takes to make traditional versions, we still had to work on the stew's flavor, which lacked the complexity of long-cooked stew. To address the flavor issue, we prepared another batch of beef stew and found that searing the beef in two batches provided more fond and meaty flavor while adding only a few extra minutes to our cooking time. After sautéing the vegetables, we added a teaspoon of tomato paste, which added depth of flavor. Although an unusual ingredient for beef stew, some minced anchovy, which we've used to amp up beefy dishes in the past, seemed a good inclusion; half a fillet provided rich, earthy flavor and complexity. Any more, though, and the anchovy called attention to itself. When it was time to add the browned beef, we also stirred in some soy sauce, which the test kitchen has found can contribute big meaty flavor. Our stew now tasted surprisingly rich and beefy, considering that it had simmered for a mere 15 minutes. Happy with the way our super-fast stew for two was shaping up, we addressed a few lingering issues.

To compensate for the lack of body, we found it easiest to stir in a tablespoon of flour after softening the aromatics. Now we had a slightly thickened broth. Frozen peas added color, and some fresh minced thyme and a bay leaf served to round out all the flavors in our quick, yet richly flavored, weeknight beef stew.

Weeknight Beef Stew
SERVES 2

Steak tips, also known as flap meat, are sold as whole steak, cubes, and strips. To ensure evenly sized chunks, we prefer to purchase whole steak tips and cut them ourselves. Be careful not to overcook the beef in step 4 or it will taste dry.

- 12 **ounces sirloin steak tips, trimmed and cut into ½-inch pieces (see note)**
  Salt and pepper
- 4 **teaspoons vegetable oil**
- 1 **carrot, peeled and sliced ¼ inch thick**
- 1 **small onion, minced**
- 2 **garlic cloves, minced**
- 1 **teaspoon tomato paste**
- ½ **anchovy fillet, rinsed and minced**
- ½ **teaspoon minced fresh thyme or ⅛ teaspoon dried**
- 1 **tablespoon unbleached all-purpose flour**
- 3 **tablespoons dry red wine**
- 1½ **cups beef broth**
- 1 **small Yukon Gold potato (about 6 ounces), peeled and cut into ½-inch pieces**
- 1 **bay leaf**
- ¼ **cup frozen peas**
- 1 **teaspoon soy sauce**

1. Pat beef dry with paper towels and season with salt and pepper. Heat 2 teaspoons oil in large saucepan over medium-high heat until just smoking. Brown half of beef on all sides, 3 to 6 minutes; transfer to plate. Repeat with remaining beef and remaining 2 teaspoons oil; transfer to plate.

2. Add carrot and onion to fat left in pan and cook over medium heat until softened, about 5 minutes. Stir in garlic, tomato paste, anchovy, and thyme and cook until fragrant, about 30 seconds. Stir in flour and cook for 1 minute.

3. Stir in wine, scraping up any browned bits. Stir in broth, potato, and bay leaf and bring to simmer. Cover, reduce heat to medium-low, and simmer until carrot and potato are tender, 15 to 20 minutes.

4. Remove bay leaf. Return browned beef, with any accumulated juice, to pan. Stir in peas and soy sauce and continue to cook until stew is heated through, about 2 minutes (do not overcook beef). Off heat, season with salt and pepper to taste and serve.

NOTES FROM THE TEST KITCHEN

THE BEST LARGE SAUCEPAN

A large saucepan is an essential piece of cookware. When cooking for two, you can use this versatile pot for many tasks, including making soups and stews and cooking vegetables and side dishes. To find out if brand matters, we tested eight models, all between 3 and 4 quarts in size. They were all fully clad pans, meaning that the pan's metal layers extend from the cooking surface up the sides of the pan (as opposed to pans with a disk bottom). We tested the pans for sauté speed, ability to heat evenly, and user-friendliness. The most important quality turned out to be slow, even heating, but user-friendliness also played a huge role. Some pans were too heavy and had awkwardly shaped handles, which made the pots hard to move when full. Other pans had sharply angled corners, which were hard to reach into with a whisk. Our favorite saucepan was the **All-Clad Stainless 4-Quart Saucepan**, $194.99 (shown), which boasts a stellar cooking performance and is sturdily constructed. But, if you're on a budget, we also liked the Cuisinart MultiClad Unlimited 4-Quart Saucepan, which is our best buy at $69.99.

BEEF SATAY WITH PEANUT DIPPING SAUCE

SLICES OF MARINATED BEEF WOVEN ONTO BAMBOO skewers and briefly grilled are a traditional Southeast Asian favorite known as satay. Fortunately for us, this traditional street food offering migrated across the ocean. At its best, satay boasts tender meat with a sweet yet salty flavor, and the accompanying dipping sauce, usually highlighted with the flavor of peanuts, provides a bold and spicy counterpoint. But more often than not, beef satay is tough and dry, and the dipping sauce pasty and dull. We thought beef satay would make the perfect casual dinner for two, so we set out to bring it indoors (with the help of our broiler) but still keep the flavors exotic and the meat tender.

Starting with the beef, we surveyed the local butcher counter for possibilities. We decided to focus on cuts that we commonly turn to for marinating and skewering—sirloin steak tips and round, skirt, flank, and blade steaks. We decided to test them all. To provide intense, direct heat, comparable to that of a grill, we turned to the broiler. We gathered a pile of wooden skewers—they tend to be thinner than metal skewers and so wouldn't produce large, gaping holes in the meat—and began preparing our first batch of satay, cutting the meat into ¼-inch strips.

The various cuts of meat produced substantially different textures. Round steaks were dry and chewy, and we immediately cut them from contention. The sirloin steak tips and blade steak both tasted great, but their small size made it tough to slice them into long strips. Both the skirt steak and flank steak were easy to slice—especially after we let the meat firm up in the freezer for 15 minutes. Because skirt steak can be difficult to find and is a bit more expensive, flank steak was our pick.

For the most tender meat possible, we knew we had to slice the flank steak against the grain before we threaded the meat onto the skewers. We started by cutting 8 ounces of steak into two halves, with the grain, and then sliced each half into ¼-inch strips against the grain. A quick pounding between two sheets of plastic wrap brought our strips down to an ideal ⅛ inch thick and prevented the cooked meat from becoming tough and chewy (we found this method far easier than slicing the meat so thin from the outset). The thin pieces were easy enough to weave onto the skewers, and we found that leaving a small portion of the skewer exposed made for a nice "handle" on our casual dinner. To protect the exposed portion of the skewers when they were in the oven, we covered the ends with foil; this way, they wouldn't burn or catch fire. In less than 10 minutes under the broiler, our thin slices of flank steak were perfectly cooked.

Having found the right cut of meat and the best way to prepare it, we focused next on adding flavor with a simple marinade. Researching a variety of traditional recipes, we noted that most were based on a combination of fish sauce and raw sugar. Without an easy supply of raw sugar, we substituted brown sugar, which has a richer, deeper flavor than granulated sugar, and tested various amounts of fish sauce until tasters were happy. We found that a substantial amount of brown sugar (4 teaspoons) was key to both flavor and even browning, and 1 teaspoon of fish sauce added seasoning without fishiness.

In the spirit of experimentation, we then tried adding flavors we had encountered in other recipes, such as coconut milk, lime juice, sriracha (an Asian chili sauce), hot sauce, and an array of fresh herbs. Coconut milk dulled the beef's natural flavor, and the tart, acidic flavor of lime juice tasted unpleasant once cooked. Sriracha added a pleasant, spicy heat without the sour, vinegary flavor that hot sauce contributed. Cilantro and sliced scallions tasted soapy when mixed into the marinade, but tasters liked their fresh flavor and color, so we saved these for the dipping sauce.

Marinating the beef for more than one hour made the thin slices mushy, but less than 30 minutes didn't give the meat long enough to pick up the flavors of the marinade. Within this range, our skewers were full-flavored and moist. Now we could focus on the peanut sauce.

While many recipes we found called for breaking out the blender to make a smooth puree of peanuts, garlic, and whole spices, we found that blending such a small amount of ingredients was not worth the effort—especially when we found a suitable substitute in creamy peanut butter. To spice things up, we tried whisking in

a range of flavorings. In the end, the same ingredients used in the marinade—fish sauce, sriracha, and brown sugar—also tasted good in the peanut sauce. To round out the sauce, we added lime juice for a welcome burst of tart acidity, and raw garlic for a robust background note. The sauce was slightly thick and pasty at this point, but thinning it out with hot water solved the problem. Now our dipping sauce had the perfect consistency and exotic, bright flavors—the perfect match for our sweet yet spicy beef satay.

Beef Satay with Spicy Peanut Dipping Sauce
SERVES 2

To make slicing the steak easier, freeze it for 15 minutes. You will need ten to fourteen 12-inch wooden skewers for this recipe.

SATAY

- 8 ounces flank steak, trimmed (see note)
- 4 teaspoons brown sugar
- 1 teaspoon fish sauce
- 1 teaspoon sriracha

DIPPING SAUCE

- 2 tablespoons creamy peanut butter
- 2 tablespoons hot water
- 1½ teaspoons fresh lime juice
- 1½ teaspoons sriracha
- 1 teaspoon fish sauce
- ¾ teaspoon brown sugar
- 1 garlic clove, minced
- 1 tablespoon minced fresh cilantro
- 1 scallion, sliced thin

1. FOR THE SATAY: Following photos on page 12, slice steak in half with grain, then crosswise on bias into ¼-inch-thick pieces. Place pieces of meat in single layer between 2 sheets of plastic wrap and pound to ⅛-inch thickness.

2. Mix brown sugar, fish sauce, and sriracha together in medium bowl. Stir in meat to coat, cover, and refrigerate at least 30 minutes or up to 1 hour.

3. FOR THE DIPPING SAUCE: Meanwhile, whisk peanut butter, water, lime juice, sriracha, fish sauce, brown sugar, and garlic together in bowl until smooth. (Sauce can be refrigerated in airtight container for up to 3 days.) Sprinkle with cilantro and scallion; set aside.

4. Position oven rack 6 inches from broiler element and heat broiler. Pat meat dry with paper towels and weave onto wooden skewers, 1 piece per skewer. Lay skewers on aluminum foil–lined baking sheet and cover skewer ends with strip of foil. Broil until meat is browned, 6 to 9 minutes, flipping halfway through. Serve with dipping sauce.

NOTES FROM THE TEST KITCHEN

MAKING BEEF SATAY

1. Using a chef's knife, slice the steak in half lengthwise with the grain. Then slice the steak halves across the grain on the bias into ¼-inch-thick pieces.

2. Place the steak slices between two sheets of plastic wrap and pound to ⅛-inch thickness.

3. After marinating the steak pieces, weave them onto the skewers, one per skewer, until each strip is secure.

4. Cover the ends of the skewers with aluminum foil to keep them from burning.

SKILLET-GLAZED PORK CHOPS

BONELESS PORK CHOPS ARE NOTHING IF NOT convenient. Available straight from the supermarket meat case, they cook quickly and pair well with a tangy glaze. So what's the problem? All too often, by the time these ultra-lean cuts brown, they have turned leathery and dry and become curled from the high heat of the pan. And instead of offering a bright spot amid a dinner-time disaster, the glaze is either too sweet or hasn't been reduced enough to coat the meat. We wanted deeply browned, juicy chops and a well-balanced glaze—and we hoped these goals were not incompatible.

We tackled the curling problem first. This issue was easily solved by making a few slashes through the fat and silver skin before cooking our chops; this stopped the meat from bowing as the silver skin cooked and contracted. Finding the right cooking method, however, proved more difficult. We began by trying two gentle cooking methods found in our research. First, we started the chops in a cold pan and then slowly heated them until cooked through. For another test, we poached the chops in a simple maple glaze. Not surprisingly, both methods produced pale gray chops. (In its favor, poaching did at least keep the chops moist and tender.)

Although these tests bombed, they confirmed what we had suspected from the get-go: We would have to sear the chops to develop both a dark crust and rich flavor. Searing at a high temperature causes proteins on the surface of the meat to brown, creating hundreds of new flavor compounds. In addition to affecting the flavor of the meat itself, searing leaves flavorful browned bits in the pan, an important building block for a robust glaze. But searing comes at a price—the risk of overcooking our chops would be even greater.

In our next test, we closely monitored the pan as we seared two chops until browned on the first side. We then flipped the chops and—taking a cue from our failed poached chops—poured in a mixture of maple syrup and chicken broth. We let the chops simmer gently until cooked through. While the chops themselves were now tender, moist, and well browned (on one side at least), and stayed flat in the pan, the glaze was a disaster. Besides being overly sweet and lacking

SKILLET-GLAZED PORK CHOPS

any complexity, the glaze hardly clung to the pork and instead just ran off the sides of our chops.

Putting aside the flavor issues for the time being, we tried a battery of tests using various amounts of maple syrup and chicken broth in an attempt to get the consistency just right. To our surprise, we had a difficult time lining up the pork and glaze cooking times. Sometimes we got an overreduced, candylike glaze coating underdone chops; other times the chops cooked through before the glaze had time to thicken.

For a more foolproof method, we tried cooking the chops completely, removing them from the pan to rest briefly, then reducing the glaze in the empty skillet until properly thickened, which took but a few minutes. To coat the chops in the glaze, all we needed to do was to return them to the skillet just before serving. Now we had complete control over both elements of the dish. To ensure that the chops stayed moist, we reduced the heat to medium-low when cooking them on their second side. Happy with our method, we focused on bringing the flavors of the glaze into balance.

Although it was now the proper consistency, our working glaze of maple syrup and chicken broth tasted overly chicken-y and far too salty. Given that we had ample meaty fond left in the skillet after cooking the chops on both sides, we wondered if we needed the chicken broth at all. Tasters were begging for some

acidity to cut the sweetness of the maple syrup, so we tried to kill two birds with one stone and swapped out the chicken broth in favor of cider vinegar. This glaze was much improved but still lacked complexity. Scanning the pantry shelves, we landed on another ingredient that works well with sweet sauces, Dijon mustard. Just 1½ teaspoons provided brightness and depth of flavor. A final addition of minced fresh thyme lent an earthy background note.

After glazing our way through pounds of pork, we had finally achieved our goal: well-browned, juicy, perfectly glazed pork chops for two.

Skillet-Glazed Pork Chops
SERVES 2

If the pork is "enhanced," do not brine. If brining the pork, do not season with salt in step 1.

- 2 **(6- to 8-ounce) boneless center-cut pork chops, ¾ to 1 inch thick, trimmed, sides slit (see page 152), brined if desired (see note; see page 18)**
  Salt and pepper
- 3 **tablespoons maple syrup**
- 2 **tablespoons cider vinegar**
- 1½ **teaspoons Dijon mustard**
- ½ **teaspoon minced fresh thyme or ⅛ teaspoon dried**
- 2 **teaspoons vegetable oil**

1. Pat chops dry with paper towels and season with salt and pepper. Combine maple syrup, vinegar, mustard, and thyme in small bowl and set aside.

2. Heat oil in 10-inch skillet over medium-high heat until just smoking. Brown chops well on one side, 3 to 5 minutes. Flip chops, reduce heat to medium-low, and continue to cook until chops register 140 to 145 degrees on instant-read thermometer, 6 to 9 minutes. Transfer chops to plate, tent loosely with foil, and let rest while preparing glaze.

3. Add maple syrup mixture to skillet, scraping up any browned bits, and simmer over medium heat until thick and syrupy, 2 to 4 minutes. Return chops, with any accumulated juice, to skillet and continue to simmer, flipping frequently, until coated in glaze, 1 to 2 minutes longer. Serve.

NOTES FROM THE TEST KITCHEN

ENHANCED OR UNENHANCED PORK?

Because modern pork is remarkably lean and therefore somewhat bland and prone to dryness if overcooked, a product called "enhanced" pork has overtaken the market. In fact, it can be hard to find unenhanced pork. Enhanced pork has been injected with a solution of water, salt, sodium phosphate, sodium lactate, potassium lactate, sodium diacetate, and varying flavor agents to bolster flavor and juiciness; these enhancing ingredients add 7 to 15 percent extra weight. After several taste tests, we have concluded that although enhanced pork is indeed juicier and more tender than unenhanced pork, the latter has more genuine pork flavor. Some tasters also picked up artificial, salty flavors in enhanced pork. It can also leach juice that, once reduced, will result in overly salty sauces. We prefer natural pork, but the choice is up to you.

PORK CUTLETS WITH MUSTARD-CIDER SAUCE

ON PAPER, A PACKAGE OF SUPERMARKET PORK cutlets offers everything the time-pressed cook could want in a weeknight meal: thrift, almost no preparation, and dinner on the table in minutes. However, things aren't always as they seem—the benefits of pork cutlets are just about always outweighed by the fact that a single package usually contains uneven, oddly shaped specimens, which ensures uneven cooking and dry, stringy, pale results. We wanted to make the most of convenience but still have moist, tender cutlets encased in a nicely browned crust.

To prevent lean meat from drying out, we usually turn to brining, so we began by giving our packaged ¼-inch-thick cutlets a 30-minute soak in salted water. After a quick sauté in a 12-inch skillet (they were too wide to cram into a 10-inch skillet), our cutlets were definitely moist and tender, and they were well seasoned, too. But now we had a new problem on our hands. Brining had worked too well—the retained moisture kept the meat so wet that it steamed, cooking the cutlets all the way through before they even had a chance of browning. What we needed was some way to trigger browning while the meat exterior was still wet.

Thinking of other ways to jump-start the browning, we considered sugar, which caramelizes at a lower temperature than protein. We wondered if sprinkling the cutlets with a bit of sugar before adding them to the pan would have any effect. It did—the cutlets browned much faster. On a roll, we wondered if we could get the meat to brown even more.

The only other element we could tinker with was the cooking fat. We'd been using olive oil, but we figured that if we included some butter, which contains sugars and milk proteins, we might be able to boost browning. (Butter alone wasn't feasible; with its low smoke point, it burned too easily over the relatively high heat we needed for searing.) Half a tablespoon of butter heated in our skillet with a tablespoon of oil not only deepened the browning on the cutlets but left us enough flavorful browned bits in the skillet for a pan sauce.

Still, perfectly cooked though they were, our cutlets lacked one critical element: deep meaty taste. We headed back to the supermarket and scanned the butcher's case for something that would provide richer pork flavor. Tenderloin—the thin, tapered muscle that runs along the opposite side of the spine from the larger loin muscle—was one option. But while its texture would be more supple than that of our cutlets, this cut has even less flavor.

Taking another look at the possible cuts, we wondered if a section from the blade end (the end closest to the front of the pig) might work. Since the blade-end section contains only a small portion of meat from the

---

NOTES FROM THE TEST KITCHEN

CUTTING RIBS INTO CUTLETS

1. Slice each rib lengthwise to create two (or three) cutlets, each about ⅜ inch wide.

2. Place the cutlet between two sheets of plastic wrap and pound to an even ¼-inch thickness.

THE BEST MEAT POUNDER

Flattening a pork or chicken cutlet takes a steady hand and the right tool; otherwise, your dinner is likely to be ragged around the edges. We recently tested five models of meat pounders to see which one worked best. Overall, we preferred pounders with vertical handles, as they offered the best leverage and control. The offset-handled pounders garnered criticism for the way the heel of the pounding disk could dig into the meat. We also liked models that were heavy (our winner weighs almost 2 pounds) and had a large surface area. The **Norpro Grip-EZ Meat Pounder**, $17.50, came out on top, providing the right combination of control and force to produce nearly flawless cutlets.

SAUTÉED PORK CUTLETS WITH MUSTARD-CIDER SAUCE

lean loin and plenty of flavorful darker red meat from the hog's fattier shoulder, it boasts far richer flavor. While slicing cutlets from a whole blade-end roast is an option when cooking cutlets for a family, we needed only 12 ounces for two servings. An easier (albeit unusual) option occurred to us: boneless country-style spare ribs. A common choice for braising or grilling, these meaty ribs combine a large portion of the flavorful shoulder meat with minimal connective tissue and only a bit of bland loin (and occasionally none at all).

As an added bonus, because the ribs are sold portioned into thin pieces, which are available in small packages, they required little work to be fashioned into cutlets for two. It was a simple matter of trimming each rib of external fat, slicing it lengthwise into two or three pieces less than ½ inch wide, and gently pounding each of them into ¼-inch-thick cutlets.

After just four minutes total in a hot skillet, these cutlets cooked up exactly as we'd hoped: tender, juicy, and flavorful on the inside, with a deep brown crust. All that was left was to whip up a couple of pan sauces. Tasters wholeheartedly approved of one featuring mustard and cider as well as a variation with lemon juice and capers.

Sautéed Pork Cutlets with Mustard-Cider Sauce

SERVES 2

If the pork is "enhanced" (see page 14 for more information), do not brine. If brining the pork, do not season with salt in step 1. Look for ribs that are about 3 to 5 inches long. If your ribs are more than 5 inches long, cut them in half crosswise before slicing them lengthwise to ensure more evenly sized cutlets.

- **12 ounces boneless country-style pork ribs, trimmed of excess fat, cut and pounded into cutlets (see page 15), brined if desired (see note; see page 18) Salt and pepper**
- **½ teaspoon sugar**
- **1 tablespoon olive oil**
- **1 tablespoon unsalted butter, cut into 2 pieces**
- **1 shallot, minced**
- **½ teaspoon unbleached all-purpose flour**
- **¼ cup low-sodium chicken broth**
- **¼ cup apple cider**
- **¼ teaspoon minced fresh sage, parsley, or thyme**
- **2 teaspoons whole-grain mustard**

1. Adjust oven rack to middle position and heat oven to 200 degrees. Pat cutlets dry with paper towels and season with salt and pepper. Sprinkle sugar evenly over each cutlet. Heat oil in 12-inch skillet over medium-high heat until just smoking. Add 1 piece butter, let melt, and quickly add cutlets. Cook cutlets until browned on both sides, 2 to 4 minutes. Transfer cutlets to large plate and keep warm in oven while making sauce.

2. Add shallot to fat left in skillet and cook over medium heat until softened, about 1 minute. Stir in flour and cook for 30 seconds. Whisk in broth, cider, and sage and bring to boil. Reduce heat to low and simmer until slightly thickened, 2 to 3 minutes.

3. Off heat, whisk in mustard, remaining 1 piece butter, and any accumulated juice from pork. Season sauce with salt and pepper to taste, spoon over pork, and serve.

VARIATION

Sautéed Pork Cutlets with Lemon-Caper Sauce
Follow recipe for Sautéed Pork Cutlets with Mustard-Cider Sauce, substituting ¼ cup white wine for apple cider. Substitute 2 tablespoons rinsed capers, 1 teaspoon grated lemon zest, and 1 teaspoon fresh lemon juice for mustard in step 3.

CRANBERRY-ROASTED PORK TENDERLOIN

JUICY, SUCCULENT PORK LOIN PAIRED WITH CRANberry sauce makes quite the showstopper on an elegant dining room table. But when you're cooking for two, a whole pork loin means a whole lot of leftovers, and a holiday-style dinner generally entails hours of labor. We sought to downsize this festive classic, and the work involved in pulling it off, so we could still enjoy the combination of tender pork and brightly flavored cranberry sauce anytime.

A single pork loin roast can weigh anywhere from 2 pounds to 3 pounds or more—enough to serve at least six. With this large cut out of the equation, we turned to a more suitably sized roast—pork tenderloin. As its name suggests, pork tenderloin is a supremely tender muscle that runs alongside the loin. And, as a tenderloin averages about 12 ounces, it provides just the right amount of meat for two.

As we were researching this dish, we came across a recipe that called for roasting a pork loin at a relatively high temperature (450 degrees) in a sauce of canned cranberry sauce, chicken broth, and vinegar. While we

NOTES FROM THE TEST KITCHEN

BRINING 101

Both poultry and pork are lean, and in some preparations they can cook up dry. The salt in a brine changes the structure of the muscle proteins and allows them to hold on to more moisture when exposed to heat. In a sample test, tasters had no trouble picking out brined pork chops versus chops left untreated. Though we leave brining optional, if you have the time it will give you juicier meat in recipes like our Skillet-Glazed Pork Chops (page 14) and Roasted Chicken Breasts (page 63).

TO BRINE: Follow the amounts in the chart and dissolve the salt (we use table salt) in the water in a container or bowl large enough to hold the brine and meat. Submerge the meat completely in the brine. Cover and refrigerate, following the times in the chart (do not overbrine or the meat will taste too salty). Remove the meat from the brine, rinse, and pat dry with paper towels. The meat is now ready to be cooked.

Note that kosher poultry and enhanced pork should not be brined because they've already been treated with salt. Brining will only make the meat unpalatably salty.

POULTRY OR MEAT	COLD WATER	SALT	TIME
Chicken			
2 (12-ounce) bone-in, skin-on split chicken breasts	1 quart	¼ cup	30 minutes to 1 hour
2-4 (6-ounce) bone-in, skin-on chicken thighs	1 quart	¼ cup	30 minutes to 1 hour
Game Hens			
2 (1¼- to 1½-pound) Cornish game hens	2 quarts	½ cup	30 minutes to 1 hour
Pork			
12 ounces boneless country-style pork ribs	1 quart	2 tablespoons	30 minutes to 1 hour
2 (6- to 8-ounce) boneless center-cut pork chops	1 quart	2 tablespoons	30 minutes to 1 hour
1 (12-ounce) pork tenderloin	1 quart	2 tablespoons	30 minutes to 1 hour

suspected this simple sauce would need some help, we liked the simplicity of the method, which required one pan and no searing (because the sauce is so potent, it apparently negates the need for searing). We weren't sold, so we cooked up two tenderloins—searing one and skipping that step with the second roast. And to accommodate the smaller size of the roasts, we turned the temperature down to 400 and finessed the cooking time, to just over 15 minutes. Both roasts were good, but even more surprising was that the unseared roast was a bit juicier—no doubt because it had spent less time in the hot pan. Unseared roasts usually sport a dull gray exterior, but here, the ruby-red color of the glaze masked any dull gray color of the roast's exterior. With an easy method paving our way to a satisfying pork roast dinner, we moved on to working on the sauce's flavors.

The majority of cranberry sauce recipes found in our research called for little more than jellied cranberry sauce and, as such, produced a sauce with a flat, sweet flavor and thin texture. Our working sauce, which added chicken broth and vinegar to the mix, was OK, but not as complex as it could be. To boost both texture and flavor, we swapped in whole-berry cranberry sauce for the jellied stuff. To further boost cranberry flavor, we tried cranberry juice in place of the chicken broth. This sauce was already a big improvement, but it still tasted a bit one-note. For balance, we turned to items we'd seen in other recipes. Baking spices were overwhelming; strips of orange peel were too much work. Bottled barbecue sauce was too smoky, but a mix of ketchup, Dijon mustard, and vinegar cut through the sweetness nicely and gave the sauce some interest. Garlic and thyme rounded out the flavors, but there was still something missing.

We tried stirring in fresh cranberries but found their flavor unpleasantly sharp; besides, it can be tough to find fresh cranberries in the middle of summer, and we wanted this to be a recipe that could be prepared year-round. Seeking a more pleasant pucker and easy availability, we tossed in dried cranberries instead and waited to see what would happen. The berries plumped in the sauce and added bright pockets of tart chew. With a final addition of some brown sugar, the sauce snapped into focus. We now had a dish that was fit for company, but perfect for two.

Cranberry-Roasted Pork Tenderloin

SERVES 2

If the pork is "enhanced" (see page 14 for more information), do not brine. If brining the pork, do not season with salt in step 2. Use whole-berry cranberry sauce, not jellied cranberry sauce. Do not use unsweetened cranberry juice in this recipe.

- 1 tablespoon unsalted butter
- 1 garlic clove, minced
- 1 teaspoon minced fresh thyme or ¼ teaspoon dried
- ½ cup whole-berry cranberry sauce (see note)
- ½ cup cranberry juice (see note)
- ¼ cup dried cranberries
- 1 tablespoon ketchup
- 1 teaspoon Dijon mustard
- 1 teaspoon brown sugar
- ½ teaspoon white vinegar
- 1 (12-ounce) pork tenderloin, trimmed, brined if desired (see note; see page 18)
- Salt and pepper

1. Adjust oven rack to upper-middle position and heat oven to 400 degrees. Melt butter in 10-inch ovensafe nonstick skillet over medium heat. Stir in garlic and thyme and cook until fragrant, about 30 seconds. Stir in cranberry sauce, cranberry juice, dried cranberries, ketchup, mustard, brown sugar, and vinegar and bring to boil. Reduce heat to medium-low and simmer until slightly thickened, about 5 minutes.

2. Pat pork dry with paper towels, season with salt and pepper, and nestle into skillet with sauce, curling it as needed to fit. Transfer skillet to oven and roast until tenderloin registers 140 to 145 degrees on instant-read thermometer, 16 to 20 minutes, flipping pork halfway through. Transfer pork to carving board, tent loosely with foil, and let rest for 10 minutes.

3. Meanwhile, season sauce with salt and pepper to taste, transfer to serving bowl, and cover to keep warm. Slice pork and serve, passing sauce separately.

EASIEST-EVER PULLED PORK

IT TAKES A LOT OF PATIENCE TO MAKE BARBECUED pulled pork. Generally the process is as follows: Rub a large, fatty, tough pork shoulder (from the upper part of the front leg) with a potent spice blend, refrigerate the meat for a few hours to let the spices work their magic, smoke the meat over coals and wood for another two hours, and finish off with three hours in the oven (plus resting time). In total, it takes about 10 hours. During that slow process, the collagen and fat in the meat melt until the pork is so tender it collapses into smoky shreds with the merest touch of a fork. The recipe yields plenty of succulent pork for sharing with friends, but what if you're a party of two? Neither 10 hours nor hauling out the grill seems worth it. We wanted to make pulled pork for a pair. That meant bringing it indoors and finding a way to streamline this traditionally slow food.

The reduction in yield and time meant first and foremost that we'd need a smaller cut than the pork shoulder. We went right to lean cuts, which cook quickly. Indeed, pork tenderloin, center-cut chops, and rib chops performed as promised. The meat was tender, but it was so lean it lacked the silky texture and shreddable consistency of proper barbecue. In search of well-marbled cuts that were still suitably small, we hit on country-style ribs and bone-in blade chops, which are actually shoulder chops, pork shoulder's next-door neighbor. Both produced tender, richly flavored meat that shredded into classic-looking barbecue. Though it was a close contest, blade chops eventually triumphed for their slightly superior texture when shredded. After a few tests, we determined that two 8- to 10-ounce bone-in blade-cut chops yielded just the right amount of barbecue for two soft hamburger buns. Having cleared one hurdle, we turned to tackling the cooking method.

To effectively tenderize this well-marbled, tough cut indoors, we considered roasting and braising. Roasting just dried out the pork. Braising, however, showed promise. We first browned the chops in a large saucepan, added some liquid (just water for the time being), then covered the pot and slid it into a 300-degree oven. About an hour and a half later, the meat was shreddable; the low, slow moist heat had worked to break down the fat and collagen.

Now we worked on refining the braising liquid, which would cook down in the oven and be used to coat the meat. For our next test, after browning the chops, we added classic barbecue ingredients to the pan: ketchup, cider vinegar, and brown sugar. The results weren't all that we'd hoped—tasters wanted more kick.

What these chops needed was a spice rub similar to the one we use for a full pork shoulder. A coating of paprika, cumin, salt, pepper, and brown sugar did just the trick. To get even more flavor into the meat, we cut the chops off the bone and into strips. This provided more surface area for the spice rub to cling to. To round out the sauce, we softened an onion and a chopped slice of bacon (for barbecue smokiness) in the pan before stirring in minced garlic and some red pepper flakes. This batch had it all: tender, silky pork imbued with smoke and spice. Best of all, this indoor barbecue for two was on the table in less than two hours.

NOTES FROM THE TEST KITCHEN

PREPARING PORK CHOPS FOR PULLED PORK

1. Keeping the knife as close to the bone as possible, cut the meat off the bone. Discard the bone.

2. Trim excess large sections of fat from the meat.

3. Slice the meat into 1-inch-thick strips.

Easiest-Ever Pulled Pork

SERVES 2

It is important to trim away any large sections of fat to prevent the final dish from being overly greasy. Serve with dill pickle chips and coleslaw.

    2 (8- to 10-ounce) bone-in blade-cut pork chops
       (see note)
    1 tablespoon brown sugar
 1½ teaspoons paprika
  ½ teaspoon ground cumin
       Salt and pepper
    4 teaspoons vegetable oil
    1 small onion, minced
    1 slice bacon, chopped fine
    1 garlic clove, minced
  ⅛ teaspoon red pepper flakes
  ¼ cup cider vinegar
    2 tablespoons ketchup
    2 soft hamburger buns

1. Adjust oven rack to lower-middle position and heat oven to 300 degrees. Following photos, cut chops away from bones, trim large sections of fat, and slice meat into 1-inch-thick strips. Combine 1 teaspoon brown sugar, paprika, cumin, ¼ teaspoon salt, and ½ teaspoon pepper in bowl. Pat pork dry with paper towels and rub with spice mixture.

2. Heat 2 teaspoons oil in large ovensafe saucepan over medium heat until just smoking. Add half of pork and brown on all sides, 1 to 3 minutes; transfer to plate. Repeat with remaining pork and remaining 2 teaspoons oil; transfer to plate.

3. Add onion and bacon to fat left in pan and cook until softened, about 5 minutes. Stir in garlic and red pepper flakes and cook until fragrant, about 30 seconds. Stir in vinegar, ketchup, and remaining 2 teaspoons brown sugar, scraping up any browned bits, and bring to simmer. Return browned pork, with any accumulated juice, to pan. Cover, transfer pan to oven, and cook until dinner fork slips easily in and out of pork, about 1½ hours.

4. Transfer pork to carving board, let cool slightly, and shred into bite-size pieces following photo on page 71. Return pork, with any accumulated juice, to pan and toss to coat with sauce. Serve on buns.

EASIEST-EVER PULLED PORK

PORK TACOS WITH MANGO SALSA

GROUND BEEF TACOS WITH ALL THE FIXINS—shredded cheese, lettuce, and chopped tomato—might be your typical taco night fare, but what if you're looking to change things up? Enter *tacos al pastor*, warm corn tortillas filled with slow-cooked chile-rubbed pork, chopped onions, a few sprigs of cilantro, and a squeeze of fresh lime. The problem is that the recipe relies on slow-cooked pork shoulder. We wanted our taco night for two to be fuss-free, so we turned to quick-cooking ground pork. Our aim? Infuse the meat with the same smoky flavor as the long-cooked version.

To start, we addressed chile flavor. Most authentic versions of tacos al pastor use a combination of hard-to-find dried chiles and a laundry list of spices. While dried chiles, such as anchos and chipotles, probably would have worked well, we didn't want to spend an hour soaking and rehydrating them. Instead, we opted for chipotle chiles in adobo sauce, which provided a smoky, open-fire flavor along with some subtle lingering heat.

We sautéed a small amount of shallot with the chipotle chiles to give our taco filling an aromatic base, then stirred in the ground pork. A generous handful of minced cilantro added bold citrusy notes, and a couple of teaspoons of lime juice enlivened the flavors in the sauce and stayed true to the flavor profile of the authentic dish.

For a fresh topping, tasters demanded a brightly flavored salsa. We considered a few tropical fruit options, such as papaya and pineapple, but in the end, tasters preferred mango; a single mango was the right amount for our salsa. To keep our shopping list concise and echo the flavor profile of the filling, we included minced shallot, cilantro, and lime juice in our salsa. Now it had all the bright, fresh flavor it needed.

We divided our pork filling among six warm corn tortillas (three per person), topped it with our mango salsa, and garnished it with shredded Monterey Jack cheese. Tasters agreed that we were close, but the filling lacked cohesiveness. On the suggestion of one colleague, we opted to stir the shredded cheese directly into the filling when we made our next batch of tacos. Problem solved—the cheese melted into the pork, lending it flavor and creaminess and unifying the filling ingredients.

As we watched tasters devour our pork tacos with mango salsa, we knew taco night was back and better than ever.

NOTES FROM THE TEST KITCHEN

CUTTING MANGO FOR SALSA

1. Cut a thin slice from one end of the mango so that it sits flat on the cutting board.

2. Resting the mango on the trimmed bottom, cut off the skin in thin strips from top to bottom, using a sharp paring, serrated, or chef's knife.

3. Cut down along each side of the flat pit to remove the flesh.

4. Trim around the pit to remove any remaining flesh. The mango flesh can now be chopped into smaller pieces.

Pork Tacos with Mango Salsa

SERVES 2

If you can find ground pork only in a 1-pound package, see page 23 for a recipe to use up the leftover ground pork.

- 1 large mango (about 1 pound), peeled, pitted, and cut into ¼-inch pieces (see photos)
- ¼ cup minced fresh cilantro

1 shallot, minced

4 teaspoons fresh lime juice

Salt and pepper

2 teaspoons vegetable oil

1 teaspoon minced chipotle chile in adobo sauce

12 ounces ground pork

1 ounce Monterey Jack cheese, shredded (about ¼ cup)

6 (6-inch) corn tortillas, warmed (see page 203)

Lime wedges, for serving

1. Combine mango, 2 tablespoons cilantro, half of shallot, 2 teaspoons lime juice, ⅛ teaspoon salt, and ⅛ teaspoon pepper in medium bowl.

2. Heat oil in 10-inch skillet over medium heat until shimmering. Add remaining shallot, chipotle chiles, and ¼ teaspoon salt and cook until softened, about 5 minutes. Stir in pork and cook, breaking meat up with wooden spoon, until pork is no longer pink, about 5 minutes.

3. Off heat, stir in remaining 2 tablespoons cilantro, remaining 2 teaspoons lime juice, and cheese and season with salt and pepper to taste. Spoon small amount of pork filling into center of each tortilla, top with mango salsa, and serve with lime wedges.

USE IT UP: GROUND PORK

Breakfast Sausage

MAKES 2 PATTIES

Make sure not to overcook the sausage or it will taste tough and dry.

4 ounces ground pork

1 teaspoon maple syrup

1 small garlic clove, minced

⅛ teaspoon dried sage

⅛ teaspoon dried thyme

⅛ teaspoon cayenne pepper

⅛ teaspoon salt

⅛ teaspoon pepper

½ slice high-quality white sandwich bread, crusts removed, torn into small pieces

1 tablespoon whole milk

1 teaspoon vegetable oil

1. Spread out pork in bowl and sprinkle with maple syrup, garlic, sage, thyme, cayenne, salt, and pepper. Mash bread and milk together in small bowl to form paste, then add to pork. Using your hands, gently fold flavorings into pork, then shape into two round patties.

2. Heat oil in 8-inch nonstick skillet over medium heat until shimmering. Add patties and cook until well browned on both sides, 3 to 4 minutes per side. Let drain on paper towel–lined plate for 1 minute. Serve.

CAJUN RED BEANS AND RICE

BEANS AND RICE ARE A COMBINATION CONSUMED the world over. Though this simple yet satisfying supper exists in many permutations, one of our favorite renditions is Cajun red beans and rice. The beans are paired with slices of spicy sausage, which infuses the dish with smoky, spicy flavor. White rice provides the perfect counterpoint to the potently flavored beans and sausage. While we have lots of experience cooking big pots of beans, we wondered what challenges we would encounter when preparing a smaller quantity.

We started with the legumes and asked ourselves whether canned or dried would be preferable. When beans are a supporting player—say, in a salad—we find that canned beans work well, providing decent flavor and texture. But for a dish in which they would be a major player, dried beans were the way to go. After some diligent research, we found that New Orleans cooks reach for a specialty local dried red kidney bean, which offers tender skins and ultra-creamy interiors when cooked. But given that we needed only 6 ounces of beans to feed two (considering that our meal also included sausage and rice), mail-order legumes were out of the question. A few recipes suggested using "small red beans" (also called Mexican red beans), common in Caribbean and Latin American cooking. Luckily, these beans were readily available at the supermarket.

Back in the test kitchen, we prepared two batches of beans, one kidney and one small red, rehydrating them in water overnight, then simmering them for a few hours in a large saucepan. Hands down, tasters preferred the batch made with small red beans, praising the smooth interior texture and the yielding yet still-intact skins, versus the "mealy" texture and chewy

CAJUN RED BEANS AND RICE

skins of the kidney beans. For even better texture, we brined the beans overnight in salt water, a technique that also seasons them through and through.

As we were gauging the beans' texture and flavor, we noticed that the amount of simmering liquid would need some finessing. While we were able to scale down the amount of beans by about a third (from 1 pound of beans to serve six to 6 ounces of beans to serve two), we couldn't cut back on the cooking liquid (just water for now) using the same ratio. A single pound of beans typically requires somewhere around 9 cups of cooking liquid, but when we trimmed the liquid to just 3 cups, the beans were underdone and there was no moisture left in the pan for the sauce. We eventually settled on 6 cups of liquid, which gave us well-cooked, tender beans. Next up, we tackled the meat.

Authentic recipes for Cajun red beans include as many as three different pork products, among them sausage, ham, and pork shoulder. We wanted a similar depth of flavor without the fuss of buying three different types of meat. The sausage part was easy. Andouille is the usual choice, and just 3 ounces of this coarse-textured, heavily smoked link seasoned with garlic and spices provided depth and complexity. Many recipes also call for tasso: pork coated thickly with spices, onion powder, and garlic powder, then hot-smoked until it resembles jerky. Diced and browned, it lends a peppery kick to the dish. Since it's as difficult (if not more so) to find outside Louisiana as specialty dried beans, we searched for a substitute. After a few tests, we found that the flavor could be approximated with a single slice of bacon combined with paprika, black pepper, and cayenne. We saved the garlic and onion (both fresh) for our aromatics.

Finally, some New Orleans cooks consider pickled pork shoulder (pickle meat) a mandatory component. Again, we had no hope of finding this obscure product outside Louisiana, so, on a whim, we tried replacing it with vinegar. Granted, this simple substitute doesn't exactly replicate the flavors of pickle meat, but it worked well enough. Just ½ teaspoon of red wine vinegar added to the pot about an hour into cooking and a few splashes added right before serving provided all the right brightness to balance the dish's meatiness.

At this point, we wondered if we could use a more flavorful cooking liquid. Until now, we'd been using water, but we thought replacing it with chicken broth might be better. Store-bought broth did add some complexity to the beans, but it also lent too much chicken flavor and made the dish too salty, especially given that we already had our sausage and bacon going into the pan. We eventually settled on a ratio of 1 part broth to 2 parts water.

We now looked to the aromatics to round out the flavors of the dish. Many Cajun recipes, including beans and rice, start out with sautéed green pepper, onions, and celery—a slight variation on the French *mirepoix* (which swaps peppers for carrots). We found all three to be crucial for achieving the right depth of flavor. Adding a minced garlic clove helped the flavors pop in our homey, hearty red beans and rice.

Cajun Red Beans and Rice

SERVES 2

For the starch from the beans to thicken the cooking liquid, it is important to maintain a vigorous simmer in step 2. Kielbasa can be substituted for the andouille.

- 6 ounces dried small red beans (about 1 cup), picked over, rinsed, and salt-soaked (see page 25)
- 1 slice bacon, chopped fine
- 1 small onion, minced
- 1 celery rib, minced
- 1 small green bell pepper, stemmed, seeded, and chopped fine
- 1 garlic clove, minced
- ½ teaspoon paprika
- ¼ teaspoon minced fresh thyme
- 1 bay leaf
  Pinch cayenne pepper
  Salt and pepper
- 4 cups water
- 2 cups low-sodium chicken broth
- 3 ounces andouille sausage, halved lengthwise and sliced ¼ inch thick (see note)
- ½ teaspoon red wine vinegar, plus extra for seasoning

- 1 recipe Simple White Rice (recipe follows)
- 2 scallions, sliced thin
  Hot sauce (optional)

1. Drain beans thoroughly, discarding soaking liquid, and rinse well. Cook bacon in large saucepan over medium heat until browned and almost fully rendered, 5 to 8 minutes. Stir in onion, celery, and bell pepper and cook until softened, about 5 minutes.

2. Stir in garlic, paprika, thyme, bay leaf, cayenne, and ¼ teaspoon pepper and cook until fragrant, about 30 seconds. Stir in beans, water, and broth and bring to boil over high heat. Reduce heat and simmer vigorously, stirring occasionally, until beans are just soft and liquid begins to thicken, 45 to 60 minutes.

3. Stir in sausage and vinegar and continue to cook until liquid is thick and beans are fully tender and creamy, about 25 minutes longer. Remove and discard bay leaf; season with salt, pepper, and vinegar to taste. (Beans can be cooled and refrigerated in airtight container for up to 2 days.) Serve over rice, sprinkling with scallions and passing hot sauce separately, if desired.

Simple White Rice

SERVES 2

You will need a small saucepan with a tight-fitting lid to make this recipe.

- 1 teaspoon vegetable oil
- ¾ cup long-grain rice, rinsed (see page 118)
- 1¼ cups water
- ¼ teaspoon salt

1. Heat oil in small saucepan over medium heat. Stir in rice and cook until edges of grains begin to turn translucent, about 2 minutes. Stir in water and salt, increase heat to high, and bring to boil. Reduce heat to low, cover, and simmer until all liquid is absorbed, 18 to 22 minutes.

2. Off heat, uncover saucepan and place clean kitchen towel folded in half over it, then replace lid. Let rice stand for 10 minutes, then fluff with fork and serve.

CHICKEN PAPRIKASH

CHICKEN PAPRIKASH IS A CLASSIC HUNGARIAN DISH that has been popular in this country for decades. It features tender chicken in a velvety sauce potently flavored with paprika and enriched by sour cream—or at least that's how we imagined it. In reality, chicken paprikash is often a plate of bland, flabby-skinned chicken mingling with limp vegetables and draped in a sauce that is harsh, gritty, or curdled (thanks to the dairy) and tastes nothing of paprika. We were determined to get this dish back on track, so that we had both tender bites of chicken and a creamy, vibrantly flavored sauce.

The first round of testing confirmed that bone-in, skin-on chicken pieces were key, and we determined that 1½ pounds of chicken served two amply. Searing the skin in a 10-inch skillet and then scraping up the browned bits, also known as fond, gave the sauce a rich chicken flavor. The bones added body to the sauce and kept the chicken moist. But braising, the common method used to prepare this dish, turned the skin flabby and the sauce greasy. One taster pointed out that because the chicken would be served coated in sauce, the skin could be removed once it had contributed its flavor during the browning step. Indeed, no one missed it, and removing it meant the grease was history.

Next, we tackled the vegetables. Onions and red bell peppers are common, but we found recipes that used other ingredients. We tested a few alternatives: Mushrooms turned slimy, carrots added unwanted bulk, and green bell peppers were unpopular. All detracted from the sweetness and creaminess of the sauce. In the end, tasters agreed that lightly caramelized onions and red peppers, bolstered by some minced garlic, tasted best.

NOTES FROM THE TEST KITCHEN

ALL ABOUT PAPRIKA

Some cooks think of paprika as merely a garnish for deviled eggs, but we use it in a number of recipes for both color and flavor. So where does paprika come from? In truth, there is no single paprika pepper. The powdered spice we call paprika comes from a variety of peppers that range in intensity and flavor from the sweetest bells to the hottest chiles to smoked peppers. This accounts for the different kinds of paprika you might see at the market. We use sweet paprika in Chicken Paprikash, which is the traditional choice; smoked paprika and hot paprika are also commonly available.

Preventing the sauce from curdling proved to be a simple matter of stirring in the sour cream off the heat. The real challenge, we soon realized, would be to enhance the paprika flavor yet keep the sauce silky. We initially tested 2 teaspoons of paprika in our paprikash; tasters admired the dish's vibrant red color but found the paprika flavor elusive, at best. When we scaled all the way up to 2 tablespoons, we could finally taste the paprika. However, now it was harsh and felt somewhat gritty. Nonetheless, we wanted the dish to taste like its namesake spice, so we used the full 2 tablespoons and set about finding a way to counter the bitterness and grit.

In our research, we unearthed a recipe for goulash (Hungarian beef stew) that called for pureeing cooked, jarred red peppers to add creaminess and flavor to the sauce. In theory, this would allow us to reduce the amount of paprika yet retain a sweet roasted pepper flavor. But because we were creating just two servings of chicken paprikash, we didn't want to break out the blender to pulverize a tiny amount of jarred red peppers. Perhaps a store-bought puree was the solution.

Hungarians use a product called paprika cream (essentially a concentrated paste of red peppers) in a number of dishes to add flavor and creaminess. While this specialty ingredient is nearly impossible to find stateside, it got us thinking about a different vegetable paste that is readily available at the supermarket: tomato paste. As little as 1 teaspoon of sweet, smooth tomato paste tempered the bitterness of the paprika. And we found that increasing the amount of tomato paste to a full tablespoon not only resulted in better flavor, but it also gave the sauce enough body to mask the grittiness, while at the same time boosting the dish's deep crimson color. To ensure that our sauce would cling to the chicken, we stirred in a small amount of flour with the tomato paste, before adding ¾ cup of chicken broth (just enough liquid to braise the chicken). After the chicken was cooked through, we set it aside to rest and stirred in ⅓ cup of sour cream (any more than that, and the pepper flavor we had worked so hard to achieve was dulled). Finally, we returned the chicken to the skillet and turned it to coat with the sauce.

Served over hot buttered egg noodles, chicken paprikash—with its tender chicken and richly flavored sauce—was a Hungarian tradition we were glad to be taking part in.

Chicken Paprikash

SERVES 2

If using kosher chicken, do not brine. If brining the chicken, do not season with salt in step 1. Low-fat sour cream can be used in this recipe. See page 178 for a recipe to use up the leftover sour cream. Serve over egg noodles.

- 1½ **pounds bone-in, skin-on split chicken breasts, trimmed (see page 63) and cut in half, and/or chicken thighs, trimmed, brined if desired (see note; see page 18)**
  Salt and pepper
- 2 **teaspoons vegetable oil**
- 1 **onion, minced**
- 1 **red bell pepper, stemmed, seeded, and sliced into ¼-inch strips**
- 2 **tablespoons paprika**
- 1 **garlic clove, minced**
- 1 **tablespoon tomato paste**
- 1 **tablespoon unbleached all-purpose flour**
- ¾ **cup low-sodium chicken broth**
- ⅓ **cup sour cream (see note)**

1. Pat chicken dry with paper towels and season with salt and pepper. Heat oil in 10-inch skillet over medium-high heat until just smoking. Brown chicken on both sides, about 10 minutes; transfer to plate. When chicken is cool enough to handle, remove and discard skin.

2. Stir onion and bell pepper into fat left in skillet and cook over medium heat until softened, about 5 minutes. Stir in paprika and garlic and cook until fragrant, about 30 seconds. Stir in tomato paste and flour and cook for 1 minute. Whisk in broth, scraping up any browned bits, and bring to boil.

3. Return browned chicken, with any accumulated juice, to skillet, cover, and simmer over low heat until breast pieces register 160 to 165 degrees and/or thighs register 175 degrees on instant-read thermometer, 20 to 25 minutes.

4. Transfer chicken to plate, tent loosely with foil, and let rest for 5 minutes. Meanwhile, off heat, stir sour cream into sauce until incorporated and season with salt and pepper to taste. Return chicken to pan, turn to coat with sauce, and serve.

BATTER-FRIED CHICKEN

THERE ARE DOZENS OF WAYS TO FRY A CHICKEN, but one appealing method has practically disappeared: batter-frying. In the 19th century, recipes for it were common. Chicken parts were dipped in a batter not unlike pancake batter and either shallow- or deep-fried in lard. Modern versions of this recipe that we found sounded simple enough—flour, salt, egg, and milk or buttermilk—and promised a delicate, fantastically crunchy coating encasing moist, nicely seasoned chicken. Depressingly, the coatings these recipes produced were a disappointment. They were soft and doughy, and most of the time the batter burned before the chicken was cooked through. We set out to develop a recipe that solved these problems. And since part of the challenge of frying chicken is the multiple batches required—it's messy, the timing can be tricky, and constant monitoring of the oil temperature is necessary—we figured frying chicken for two would be a much simpler affair.

Most recipes we found started with breaking down a whole chicken—which is way too much meat for two people. Instead, we zeroed in on chicken parts. Bone-in breasts are a natural pick when cooking for two because they are easy to purchase in small quantities. Cutting the breasts in half crosswise created four evenly sized pieces that would cook quickly.

Before we tackled the batter, we needed to decide on a frying technique. Recipes were divided between deep- and shallow-frying. We tried both methods and there was no contest: Shallow-frying didn't require heating up quarts of oil, so it won out. As for cooking oil, we like both vegetable oil and peanut oil because of their high smoke points and neutral flavor. After testing a range of cooking vessels, we settled on a large saucepan. With its narrow diameter and straight sides, our saucepan helped us keep the amount of oil to a minimum—just 1½ cups. But because we weren't deep-frying, we knew we'd have to slowly lower the chicken pieces into the oil to prevent the batter from touching the bottom of the pot and sticking.

Frying method and chicken parts in hand, we turned to the batter. Looking over the failed recipes that we'd tried, we had a hunch the egg in the batter was contributing to the soggy, soft coating. Taking out the egg did make the coating crisper, but it did nothing to solve the issue of overbrowning. Wondering if the milk sugars in the dairy were causing the batter to burn, we put in a call to our science editor, who confirmed our suspicions. When wet batter hits hot frying oil, the moisture in the batter vaporizes, leaving behind the solids that adhere to the chicken. In this case, the sugars in the milk solids were browning too fast.

Obviously, we needed liquid of some sort to turn the flour mixture into batter. We tried beer, club soda (which is sometimes used in tempura batter), and water. Even light beers added too much of their own flavor, and club soda was no better than plain water. Choosing the easiest (and cheapest) path, we settled on tap water and moved on to the other elements of our batter.

Starting with ½ cup of flour, we stirred in water, salt, and plenty of pepper. We really weren't sure how thick the batter was supposed to be, so we opted for the consistency of pancake batter to be sure it would stick to the chicken. The results were promising. After 10 minutes of frying, the batter hadn't burned (always a good sign), and by the time the chicken was cooked through, the exterior was a pretty golden brown. But the texture was more of a thick carapace than the thin, crispy coating we were after.

We thinned the batter with more water than we had used before. For crispness, we turned to cornstarch, and after testing varying amounts, we replaced half of the flour with an equal amount of cornstarch. This mixture produced a crisper, more delicate coating, but some tasters still found it overly dense. Back in the pantry, we wondered if baking powder might add the lift and lightness we were after. Along with this leavener, we stirred in some paprika and cayenne for flavor. We dunked the chicken into the batter to coat it thoroughly, let the excess batter drip off (now the coating was so thin you could see through it), and carefully lowered the chicken into the hot oil.

Some 15 minutes later, the chicken looked amazing, and a single bite confirmed that we'd hit the mark. The meat was juicy yet cooked through. The picture-perfect, golden-brown crust snapped and crackled, and tasters loved its pleasant peppery bite. Just as we'd hoped, our batter-fried chicken was incredibly crispy. But even better, it was a snap to make for two.

Batter-Fried Chicken

SERVES 2

We use a saucepan with an 8-inch diameter for this recipe; if your pan is wider, you may need more oil to reach the ½-inch depth. If using kosher chicken, do not brine. If brining the chicken, do not season with salt in step 2. Be sure to lower the chicken slowly into the oil in step 3 to prevent the batter from sticking to the bottom of the pan.

- ¼ **cup unbleached all-purpose flour**
- ¼ **cup cornstarch**
- ½ **teaspoon baking powder**
- ¼ **teaspoon paprika**
- ⅛ **teaspoon cayenne pepper**
  Salt and pepper
- ½ **cup cold water**
- 1½ **cups vegetable oil or peanut oil (see note)**
- 2 **(12-ounce) bone-in, skin-on split chicken breasts, trimmed (see page 63), cut in half, and brined if desired (see note; see page 18)**

1. Whisk flour, cornstarch, baking powder, paprika, cayenne, ½ teaspoon salt, and ½ teaspoon pepper together in large bowl. Whisk in 6 tablespoons water until smooth. (Batter should be just thinner than pancake batter; if too thick, stir in remaining 2 tablespoons water, 1 tablespoon at a time, as needed.) Refrigerate until ready to use (but no longer than 1 hour).

2. Pour oil into large saucepan until it measures ½-inch depth. Heat oil over medium-high heat until it registers 375 degrees on instant-read thermometer. When oil is hot, pat chicken dry with paper towels and season with salt.

3. Whisk batter to recombine, add chicken, and toss to coat. Using tongs, remove chicken from batter, one piece at a time (allowing excess to drip back into bowl), and slowly add to oil (to prevent sticking).

4. Fry chicken for 1 minute to set coating. Gently flip chicken and continue to fry, adjusting burner as necessary to maintain oil temperature between 300 and 325 degrees, until chicken is deep golden brown and registers 160 to 165 degrees on instant-read thermometer, 10 to 18 minutes, flipping chicken halfway through. Transfer chicken to wire rack set over rimmed baking sheet and let rest for 5 minutes before serving.

CHICKEN CORDON BLEU

CHICKEN CORDON BLEU, AN ELEGANT DISH OF breaded and fried chicken breasts stuffed with ham and Swiss cheese, rose to popularity in the United States in the 1960s when all things French were in vogue. Although chicken cordon bleu isn't truly of French origin—there are variations in other cultures and countries—it nonetheless became a symbol of refined taste and a mainstay at fashionable dinner parties. But nowadays, you're more likely to encounter it as a tired selection at wedding halls, where caterers have the time and staff to pound, stuff, and roll. We thought chicken cordon bleu deserved better, so we set out to create a foolproof version that would make a sophisticated dinner for two. And since we were making only two servings (not enough for a whole banquet hall), we hoped the procedure would be much easier.

Traditionally, chicken breasts are butterflied, pounded, mounded with ham and cheese, rolled tightly, coated in bread crumbs, and fried in lots of oil. We hoped to streamline the recipe (avoiding, among other things, the hassle and mess of deep-frying) but retain the dish's spectrum of textures—crunchy, crispy coating, tender chicken, and gooey, cheesy interior. Following several recipes for baked chicken cordon bleu, we meticulously pounded and rolled a number of chicken breasts. However, we had a problem with the cheese melting out of the seams. We arranged stuffed breasts in casserole dishes. These bundles steamed, and the breading peeled off (a good thing, as it turned out, because the coating was soggy, pale, and disagreeable). Next, we tried cooking the breasts on baking sheets. By the time the crumbs browned, the chicken had dried out.

Clearly, the challenges we faced had to do with the construction of the dish. The more we pounded the butterflied chicken breasts, the more uneven and ragged they got. When we tried to enclose the cheese and ham, the breasts pulled apart, the ham broke through, and the insides spilled out. The rolls kept unrolling, and if we secured them with toothpicks or twine, they were difficult to bread. We were losing patience when we found a recipe that instead called for cutting a pocket in the breasts and placing the filling in it. This method proved far easier, so we put down the mallet and at the same time switched from sliced to shredded

cheese, which melted better. It didn't take us long to realize that two large (8 ounces each) chicken breasts were easier to stuff than smaller specimens. Even so, we still had issues.

The cheese still wouldn't stay put. We blocked the opening of the pocket with a slice of ham, but it failed to make a tight seal, plus the elegant cordon bleu turned homely—there was no pretty ham-and-cheese swirl when we cut into it. We tinkered with batch after batch before finally devising an easy, dependable method: We simply sprinkled the shredded cheese on the ham slices, then rolled the ham into cylinders and tucked two cylinders into each chicken breast.

We then floured each stuffed breast, dipped it into an egg wash, and rolled it in fresh bread crumbs. To avoid having to break out the food processor to make less than a cup of bread crumbs, we switched to panko, which provided much better texture than regular store-bought bread crumbs. Tossed with melted butter and toasted, these crumbs added color and some crispness to the chicken. But everybody missed the richness and deep crunch of the topping of the deep-fried chicken cordon bleu. We suspected we could turn up the crunch level on our bread crumbs, but with what? At the grocery store, we scoured the snack aisle, looking for something that would pack more of a wallop. We filled our cart and returned to the test kitchen, crumbling, in turn, corn crisps, potato chips, and cheese crackers with the panko. In each instance, tasters were lukewarm. But we hit the jackpot with Ritz crackers; when mixed with the panko, the Ritz cracker crumbs boasted a buttery richness and baked up crunchy. With the proper stuffing method and a promising coating in hand, we addressed our last challenge: baking the breasts.

For testing purposes we'd been baking the chicken on a rimmed baking sheet, but the crumbs on the bottom unfailingly emerged sodden. We elevated the chicken on a wire rack set over the baking sheet to let any juice drip away—a moderate improvement. Next, we fiddled with oven temperatures and rack positioning as we tried to achieve moist chicken, melted cheese, and crispy golden crumbs simultaneously. Eventually, we discovered we could have it all by starting the chicken on the lowest rack of a 450-degree oven (this made escaping moisture evaporate quickly) and finishing it on the middle rack at a somewhat lower temperature

CHICKEN CORDON BLEU

STUFFING CHICKEN CORDON BLEU

1. Top each slice of ham with ¼ cup of shredded cheese and roll into a tight cylinder.

2. Using a paring knife, cut into the thickest part of the chicken breast to create a deep pocket about 3 to 4 inches wide.

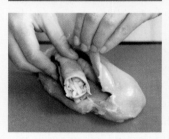

3. Stuff each pocket with two ham-and-cheese rolls and press the seams together. Then refrigerate the chicken for at least 20 minutes before breading.

THE BEST BLACK FOREST HAM

In Germany, Black Forest ham is a traditional regional specialty produced according to strict regulations. The dark exterior comes from smoke as well as a mixture of salt and spices, including garlic, sugar, and juniper berries, and the curing and smoking process can take up to three months. In North America, however, the hams are usually cured quickly by brining. The smoke flavor is often artificial, and the exterior is painted with caramel coloring. We compared German Black Forest ham ($17.95 per pound) with four brands of domestic ham (ranging from $5 to $10 per pound). Not surprisingly, German-made Black Forest ham was outstanding, whereas some domestic imitators tasted like "processed," "rubbery" canned ham. But when we used the sliced hams to make our Chicken Cordon Bleu, the smoked, paper-thin slices of the imported ham dried out and the rich flavor was "overpowering." For this recipe, we preferred a domestic ham, **Dietz & Watson Black Forest Smoked Ham**, which had "good ham flavor" and "balance." If you do have the imported ham, save it to savor on its own.

(400 degrees) without using the wire rack at all. All that was left to do was adjust the seasonings.

We added a tablespoon of Dijon mustard to the egg wash for extra flavor and then tested various combinations of cured pork (ham, prosciutto, Canadian bacon) and cheese (shredded Swiss, Emmenthaler, Gruyère). We decided on smoky Black Forest ham and mellow, nutty Swiss. Our cordon bleu for two had it all: tender, moist chicken; a gooey, cheesy center; rich, salty flavor from the ham; and a crispy crust to top it all off.

Chicken Cordon Bleu

SERVES 2

To help prevent the filling from leaking, use large (8-ounce) chicken breasts and thoroughly chill the stuffed breasts before breading. We like Black Forest ham in this recipe.

- 4 thin slices deli ham (about 4 ounces) (see note)
- 4 ounces Swiss cheese, shredded (about 1 cup)
- 2 (8-ounce) boneless, skinless chicken breasts, trimmed (see note)
  Salt and pepper
- 12 Ritz crackers, finely crumbled
- ¾ cup panko bread crumbs
- 3 tablespoons unsalted butter, melted
- ⅓ cup unbleached all-purpose flour
- 1 large egg
- 1 tablespoon Dijon mustard

1. Adjust oven racks to lowest and middle positions and heat oven to 450 degrees. Following photos, top each ham slice with ¼ cup cheese and roll tightly; set aside. Pat chicken dry with paper towels. Cut deep pocket in thickest part of breast and stuff each breast with 2 ham-and-cheese rolls. Season chicken with salt and pepper, cover, and refrigerate for at least 20 minutes.

2. Meanwhile, toss crackers and panko with melted butter and bake on rimmed baking sheet on middle rack, stirring occasionally, until light brown, 3 to 5 minutes. Let crumbs cool slightly.

3. Place flour in shallow dish. Beat egg and mustard together in second shallow dish. Spread cooled crumb mixture in third shallow dish. Dredge one stuffed chicken breast lightly in flour and shake off excess. Coat in egg mixture, allowing excess to drip off, then dredge in crumbs, pressing to adhere. Transfer chicken to clean baking sheet. Repeat with remaining stuffed chicken breast. (Uncooked stuffed and breaded chicken can be refrigerated in airtight container for up to 24 hours.)

4. Bake on lowest rack until bottom of chicken is golden brown, about 10 minutes. Move baking sheet to middle rack, reduce oven temperature to 400 degrees, and bake until chicken is golden brown and registers 160 to 165 degrees on instant-read thermometer, 18 to 24 minutes. Transfer to platter and let rest for 5 minutes before serving.

THAI CHICKEN WITH BASIL

TAKEOUT MIGHT SEEM LIKE AN EASY SOLUTION TO "What's for dinner?" when cooking for two. But besides the obvious cost, delivery has another downside: leftovers. We wanted to bring Thai takeout home, without having to dial up a local establishment, and set out to re-create one of our favorite dishes, chicken with basil, for two. Our version would be replete with tender chicken and exotic, heady, spicy flavors.

Traditionally, the dish goes something like this: Chicken is finely chopped with a pair of cleavers, then it's cooked with a big handful of hot basil in oil flavored with garlic, shallots, and fiery Thai chiles, then the dish is finished with splashes of fish sauce and Thai-style oyster sauce plus a bit of sugar. As opposed to Chinese stir-fries, which are cooked over intense heat, Thai chicken is prepared over medium to low heat, which allows the oil to become infused with flavor before the chicken is even added; this step ensures that the whole dish has a bright, clean flavor defined by the aromatic, grassy basil and a perfect balance of heat and sweetness. Although it sounds simple in theory, the potential pitfalls are numerous. Unevenly cooked aromatics can leave the dish with a bitter, burnt flavor or a raw-tasting harshness. Mincing raw chicken by hand is manageable with two heavy cleavers—but a downright chore with only a chef's knife. Moreover, the dish's signature ingredient, hot basil, is nearly impossible to find in this country. We'd have to come up with some suitable substitutions as we strove to bring this exciting stir-fry to the table.

We knew that infusing the oil with aromatics was essential to developing complex layers of flavor, so our first task was to develop a foolproof method. We'd already burned our first attempt: two finely chopped Thai chiles, a clove of garlic, and a thinly sliced shallot cooked in a tablespoon of vegetable oil. We thought that adding extra vegetable oil to our 10-inch nonstick skillet (the skillet's flat bottom was better suited to a Western-style burner than a wok's curved bottom) might help them cook more evenly, and it did. But we had to use a full 3 tablespoons of oil to make a difference, which made the dish greasy. Turning down the heat would almost certainly lead to more even results; we reasoned that if we also started in a completely cold skillet, we'd even further increase our chances of success. We dialed back the oil to 1 tablespoon and added it and the aromatics to a cold skillet before turning on the heat. After a few minutes of stirring, our aromatics had cooked to a perfectly even shade of golden brown. Next up, the chicken.

We didn't want to injure ourselves attempting the two-cleaver chopping method, so we tried having a go with store-bought ground chicken. Unfortunately, it was ground much too fine and cooked up into a mealy, mushy texture. We've used the food processor before for chopping meat, so we decided to give it a shot here. We were happy to find that this yielded chicken with the coarser texture of hand-chopped meat that we were looking for. Dark meat was more forgiving but contained fatty stringy bits, so we decided to stick with tender breast meat, bearing in mind that we'd have

---

NOTES FROM THE TEST KITCHEN

ALL ABOUT FISH SAUCE
Fish sauce is a salty, amber-colored liquid made from salted, fermented fish. When used in small amounts, it adds a well-rounded, salty flavor to sauces, soups, and marinades. Because most supermarkets don't carry a wide selection of fish sauce, we recommend buying whatever is available. Fish sauce will keep indefinitely without refrigeration.

THAI CHICKEN WITH BASIL

to be careful not to overcook it. Since we were pulling the processor out anyway, we used it to chop the garlic and chiles, further streamlining the dish.

Traditionally, Thai chicken with basil is prepared over medium-low heat. We expected this low-temperature method to work well with our lean breast meat. We added all of the meat to the skillet in a single batch, stirring it constantly to promote even cooking. This test resulted in slightly dry meat. In our next trial, to further guarantee moist meat, we added a teaspoon of fish sauce to the food processor as we chopped the chicken, then let the mixture rest for a brief 15 minutes in the refrigerator. Because of its high concentration of salt, the fish sauce acted as a brine, seasoning the meat and helping it retain moisture as it cooked. Now we had tender bites of chicken. With our basic method in order, we moved on to the sauce.

With no access to Thai-style oyster sauce, we'd been substituting Chinese-style oyster sauce. Unfortunately, the thicker consistency and heavier flavors of the Chinese version were weighing down the dish. But simply decreasing the amount didn't work; with less oyster sauce, the dish went from overloaded to lacking complexity. Then we thought about a Thai table condiment that diners often add to their dishes to brighten the overall flavor: white vinegar. Although it isn't traditionally cooked into the dish, adding a mere ½ teaspoon balanced the heaviness of the oyster sauce and brought a big boost of brightness. While we were in the business of brightening flavors, we made an unconventional move, and decided to set aside some of our raw garlic-chile mixture to be added to the sauce at the end of cooking. The combination of fresh and cooked aromatics was an instant hit with tasters. Only one problem remained: incorporating the flavor of the basil.

Unlike sweet Italian basil or even Thai basil, which is available in some specialty markets, hot basil has a robust texture that can stand up to prolonged cooking, giving it plenty of time to release its distinctive aroma into the chicken. Simply substituting Italian basil doesn't work: Add it anytime before the last minute of cooking and it becomes wilted and slimy. But when it spends only a short time in the skillet, it doesn't offer nearly enough flavor. We needed a way to keep the leaves bright green and fresh-tasting, while at the same time lending the dish a deep basil flavor.

Then it clicked: We were already infusing the oil to deliver garlic, chile, and shallot flavor to the chicken, so why not do the same with the basil? We gave it a try, chopping half a cup of basil leaves along with the chiles and garlic, then cooking them all together. Chopped this fine and cooked for so long, the basil readily released its flavor into the dish, and the small pieces did not suffer from the sliminess that plagued the larger leaves. To add fresh texture and bright green color, we stirred in an additional ½ cup of whole basil leaves right before serving. Now our dish was infused with a deep basil flavor and rich complexity—not bad for 20 minutes of work (delivery would have taken twice as long).

Thai Chicken with Basil

SERVES 2

For a mild version of the dish, remove the seeds and ribs from the chiles. If fresh Thai chiles are unavailable, substitute 2 serranos or 1 medium jalapeño. Serve with Simple White Rice (page 26).

- 1 cup fresh basil leaves, tightly packed
- 2 green or red Thai chiles, stemmed (see note)
- 1 garlic clove, peeled
- 2½ teaspoons fish sauce, plus extra for serving
- 1½ teaspoons oyster sauce
- 1½ teaspoons sugar, plus extra for serving
- ½ teaspoon white vinegar, plus extra for serving
- 1 (8-ounce) boneless, skinless chicken breast, trimmed and cut into 2-inch pieces
- 1 shallot, sliced thin
- 1 tablespoon vegetable oil
   Red pepper flakes, for serving

1. Pulse ½ cup basil, chiles, and garlic in food processor until finely chopped, 10 to 12 pulses, scraping down workbowl as needed. Transfer 1½ teaspoons basil mixture to small bowl and stir in 1½ teaspoons fish sauce, oyster sauce, sugar, and vinegar; set aside. Transfer remaining basil mixture to 10-inch nonstick skillet.

2. Without washing food processor bowl, pulse chicken and remaining 1 teaspoon fish sauce in food processor until meat is coarsely chopped, 6 to 8 pulses. Transfer to medium bowl and refrigerate for 15 minutes.

3. Stir shallot and oil into basil mixture in skillet. Cook over medium-low heat, stirring constantly, until garlic and shallot are golden brown, 5 to 8 minutes. (Mixture should start to sizzle after about 1½ minutes; if it doesn't, adjust heat accordingly.)

4. Stir in chicken and cook over medium heat, breaking up chicken with wooden spoon, until only traces of pink remain, 2 to 4 minutes. Add reserved basil–fish sauce mixture and cook, stirring constantly, until chicken is no longer pink, about 1 minute. Stir in remaining ½ cup basil leaves and cook, stirring constantly, until basil is wilted, 30 to 60 seconds. Serve immediately, passing extra fish sauce, sugar, vinegar, and red pepper flakes separately.

HONEY-ROASTED CORNISH GAME HENS

FEW DINNERS ARE AS APPEALING AS A WHOLE roasted chicken, an enticing centerpiece with moist, juicy meat and lightly browned skin. Unfortunately, a whole bird is usually off the table when it comes to supper for two, as it means at least a day or two of leftovers. But we wanted to enjoy the comforting flavors and tender meat of a roasted bird, so we decided to downsize and replaced the chicken with Cornish game hens. To bump up the flavor of the game hens' mild meat, we chose to include a honey-flavored glaze, for a sweet yet savory flavor profile.

Inexpensive and quick-cooking, Cornish game hens are ideal when cooking for two—each diner gets his or her own bird and so is able to enjoy both light and dark meat. But having made game hens in the past, we knew we'd have to look out for the potential pitfalls. As is true when roasting chicken, the white meat and dark meat cook at different rates. But because of the diminutive nature of game hens, it can be a challenge to brown and lightly crisp the skin before the meat dries out. With these concerns in mind, we headed into the test kitchen to develop a foolproof cooking method.

A roasting pan might be the go-to equipment for other (read: larger) birds, but it would completely ruin our game hens—the high sides would shield the small birds from the heat of the oven, and the reduced airflow would prevent essential browning. We decided to use a baking sheet with a wire rack set inside; the hot air could now circulate freely around the two birds. Next, we gave the birds some space on the wire rack. Just as chicken pieces won't brown if overcrowded in a skillet, Cornish hens won't brown if arranged too close together. To ensure even cooking, we also knew we'd need to rotate the birds during cooking; this kept the breast meat moist and juicy. Because Cornish hens are in the oven for such a relatively short time, we settled on one turn, from breast side down to breast side up, instead of multiple turns. After testing a range of temperatures, we settled on 400 degrees for the first portion of cooking, then cranked the oven up to 450 degrees for the last few minutes of cooking to ensure rich color. This combination of temperatures encouraged browning, but it also kept the meat moist and juicy. Now we needed to work on the flavor profile.

Starting simply, we tried coating the hens liberally with warm honey (which was much easier to spread than cool honey) before roasting. This technique led to burnt, flabby skin as the honey caramelized long before the birds were cooked through. In addition, the honey flavor was almost nonexistent. Waiting to coat the hens with honey halfway through cooking wasn't much better. What if we combined the honey with butter, to make a compound butter of sorts? We rubbed our honey butter on top of and under the skin of the birds, but we found that it oozed onto the baking sheet and burned. It was clear from our tests that the honey had to be added later in the process.

For our next test, we simply seasoned the birds with salt, pepper, and a little paprika, which added nice color and flavor, and roasted them breast side down until the backs turned golden brown, which took about 25 minutes. Cooked this way, the breasts were protected from the heat while the longer-cooking dark meat got a head start. After flipping the hens breast side up, we brushed on a simple mixture of honey and cider vinegar (our earlier tests had told us we needed something acidic to cut through the sweetness of the honey). About 25 minutes later, our hens were perfectly done, but most of the glaze was sitting on the bottom of the baking sheet and burning. To thicken the glaze, we added a little cornstarch; now the glaze stayed put during roasting. These Cornish hens were tender, moist, and bursting with honey flavor. But even when thickened, some of the honey mixture dripped off the roasting birds. Instead of lamenting this loss, we decided to take advantage of the situation to make a complementary sauce.

To the mixture in the baking sheet we added water and chicken broth. This worked to deglaze the pan drippings during the last few minutes of roasting (if we added the water and chicken broth any earlier, the moisture caused the skin to get soggy). While the hens rested, we reduced this liquid on the stovetop, then thickened it with a little more cornstarch so it had some body. Finished with more honey and vinegar, and a bit of butter and thyme for richness and depth, our sauce reinforced the intense flavors of the glaze.

After about an hour of cooking, we had on our hands two well-browned, honey-infused roasted game hens— and we were sure there'd be no leftovers.

Honey-Roasted Cornish Game Hens
SERVES 2

If using kosher game hens, do not brine. If brining the hens, omit the salt in step 1. To save on dishes, use the same saucepan to reduce the sauce in step 6 that you used to simmer the glaze in step 3; there is no need to wash the saucepan before using it in step 6.

  Salt and pepper
½ teaspoon paprika
2 (1¼- to 1½-pound) Cornish game hens, giblets removed, brined if desired (see note; see page 18), wings tucked (see page 200)
5 tablespoons honey
5 teaspoons cider vinegar
½ cup plus 2 teaspoons water
1 teaspoon cornstarch
½ cup low-sodium chicken broth
½ teaspoon minced fresh thyme
1 tablespoon unsalted butter

1. Adjust oven rack to middle position and heat oven to 400 degrees. Combine ¾ teaspoon salt, ¼ teaspoon pepper, and paprika in small bowl.

2. Pat hens dry with paper towels and rub salt mixture under skin and over outside of each hen. Lay hens, breast side down, on wire rack set inside rimmed baking sheet. Roast until backs are golden brown, about 25 minutes.

3. Meanwhile, bring ¼ cup honey and 1 tablespoon vinegar to simmer in small saucepan over medium-high heat. Whisk together 2 teaspoons water and ½ teaspoon cornstarch in small bowl, then whisk into pan. Continue to simmer glaze until thickened, 1 to 2 minutes. Remove from heat and cover to keep warm.

4. Remove hens from oven and brush backs with one-third of glaze. Flip hens breast side up and brush with half of remaining glaze. Continue to roast for 15 minutes longer.

5. Remove hens from oven and increase oven temperature to 450 degrees. Pour remaining ½ cup water and broth into baking sheet. Brush hens with remaining glaze and continue to roast until glaze is spotty brown and breasts register 160 to 165 degrees and thighs register 175 degrees on instant-read thermometer, 5 to 10 minutes longer. Transfer hens to plate and let rest for 10 minutes.

6. Pour baking sheet juice into small saucepan, let settle for 5 minutes, then remove as much fat as possible from surface using large spoon. Stir in remaining 1 tablespoon honey and thyme and bring to simmer over medium-high heat. Cook until sauce is reduced to ½ cup, 2 to 6 minutes.

7. Whisk together remaining ½ teaspoon cornstarch and remaining 2 teaspoons vinegar in small bowl, then whisk into pan. Continue to simmer sauce until thickened, 1 to 2 minutes. Off heat, whisk in butter and season with salt and pepper to taste. Serve hens, passing sauce separately.

CATFISH IN CARAMEL SAUCE

ONE OF THE MOST POPULAR SOUTHERN VIETNAMESE "home-style" dishes is catfish simmered in a caramel sauce. The sauce is made from a mixture of sugar and water that is cooked until it becomes slightly bitter, at which point more water is added, along with fish sauce and other seasonings, to create a slightly thin, caramel-flavored sauce. This combination of hearty catfish and sweet, salty caramel sauce is uniquely satisfying and an easy way to turn a few humble ingredients into an exotic entrée. We set out to create a catfish dinner for two, for a bold and exciting new addition to the weeknight repertoire.

To get our bearings, we made one of the recipes that we came across in our research. This recipe called for cooking sugar and water to a caramel directly in the skillet in which the fish and other sauce ingredients would cook. As is often the case when making caramel, the sugar crystallized. But the recipe wasn't a total failure—we liked its straightforward method of cooking everything in a single skillet.

To prevent the sugar from hardening, we borrowed a technique that we use when making caramel for desserts. We poured the water into the skillet first and then gently sprinkled the sugar evenly over the water. By evenly distributing the sugar, we were able to eliminate the need to stir the mixture before it caramelized, which helped keep the sugar from crystallizing on the sides of the skillet. After a few tests, we determined that a traditional 10-inch skillet was the right cooking vessel to use, as the dark surface of a nonstick pan made it difficult to judge the color of the caramel.

Next, we tested using dark brown sugar, light brown sugar, and granulated sugar. Both of the brown sugars left a cloyingly sweet aftertaste and lacked any complexity. White sugar, on the other hand, was clean-tasting and gave us the nutty caramel flavor we sought. With our caramel in place, we turned to the other ingredients in the sauce.

Garlic is a common addition, and tasters liked a hefty three cloves. Vegetable oil and pork fatback are the two types of fat typically used in this dish. It didn't make sense to seek out fatback when we needed just a few tablespoons, so we went with vegetable oil alone. This move worked well, as the neutral flavor of the oil didn't compete with the caramel or the fish. We mixed the garlic with the vegetable oil, then poured the mixture into the caramel to cook and release its flavors.

The remaining question was how much fish sauce to add. Knowing that a little goes a long way, and wanting to keep the careful balance of salty and sweet that is the hallmark of this dish, we tried amounts ranging from 1 tablespoon to ½ cup. After a few rounds of testing, we settled on 5 teaspoons of fish sauce as the perfect balance to the ¼ cup of sugar in the caramel. Our sauce was just about finished, but we decided to add a good dose of pepper to give the sauce a spicy dimension.

Finally, we focused our attention on the catfish. All of the recipes we came across called for catfish steaks with the skin on, but these aren't available in most supermarkets, so we settled on the more readily available skinless catfish fillets, which we cut crosswise into manageable 2-inch-wide pieces. We encountered a huge span of cooking times in the recipes we researched, so we decided to test the entire range. We cooked the fish for 10 minutes, 30 minutes, and two hours. Contrary to what we thought from years of experience cooking fish in the test kitchen, the fish that cooked for two hours, while a bit mealy, was still acceptable. The fish cooked for 10 minutes hadn't spent enough time in the pan to acquire the flavor of the sauce, but we found that a cooking time of 25 to 30 minutes was just long enough for the sauce to thicken and the fish to absorb the sauce's complex flavors.

Finished with cilantro leaves and scallions, our catfish in caramel sauce thrilled our tasters. After just one bite, they were hooked.

Catfish in Salty-Sweet Caramel Sauce
SERVES 2

Trout, tilapia, or hybrid striped bass can be substituted for the catfish; avoid flaky white fish such as cod or haddock. If your fillets have skin on them, follow the instructions on page 39 to remove it. For an accurate measurement of boiling water, bring a full kettle of water to a boil, then measure out the desired amount. Serve with Simple White Rice (page 26).

- **3**   garlic cloves, minced
- **2**   tablespoons vegetable oil
- **2**   tablespoons cold water
- **¼**   cup sugar
- **⅓**   cup boiling water (see note)
- **5**   teaspoons fish sauce
- **¾**   teaspoon pepper
- **12**   ounces skinless catfish fillets (about 3 medium fillets), sliced crosswise into 2-inch-wide pieces (see note)
- **⅓**   cup loosely packed fresh cilantro leaves
- **3**   scallions, green parts only, sliced thin on bias

1. Stir garlic and oil together in small bowl and set aside. Pour cold water into 10-inch skillet and sprinkle evenly with sugar. Cook water-sugar mixture over medium heat, gently swirling pan as needed (do not stir), until sugar melts and mixture turns dark amber, 8 to 12 minutes.

2. Stir in garlic mixture and cook until fragrant, about 30 seconds. Off heat, slowly whisk in boiling water; be careful as sauce will sizzle and steam. Return skillet to medium heat and stir in fish sauce and pepper.

3. Lay fish in skillet, skinned side up, without overlapping and bring to simmer. Simmer gently until fish is tender and sauce is thick and syrupy, 25 to 30 minutes, gently flipping each piece halfway through.

4. Transfer fish to platter and pour sauce over top. Sprinkle with cilantro and scallions and serve.

BROILED SALMON WITH SALSA

WE LOVE SALMON'S NATURALLY RICH FLAVOR, AND when it's broiled, the textural contrast between the crisp, golden crust and the moist flesh underneath is unbeatable. And thanks to its almost-certain availability at the fish counter, salmon is a great option when cooking for two. Unfortunately, this fish's popularity has resulted in a glut of forgettable recipes that produce soggy skin and overcooked flesh, often drowned in a heavy sauce. We wanted to come up with a foolproof broiled salmon recipe that consistently delivered succulent flesh topped with a crisp, flavorful crust. We also wanted to come up with a fresh-tasting garnish that would accentuate and balance the flavor of the fish, not overpower it.

Of the recipes we tested, those in which the fish was topped with a spice rub showed the most promise in terms of bold flavor and a satisfying crust. After some initial testing, we settled on a combination of coriander, ginger, garlic powder, salt, and pepper. Tasters were happy with the flavor of the rub, but in the short amount of time the fish needed to cook through using our broiling method (just under 10 minutes), there was little crust to speak of, and the spice rub was a bit dry and powdery.

We needed something to help speed up the caramelization. Surveying the contents of our pantry, we hit on granulated sugar, which has the power to accelerate browning and encourage caramelization. After one test, we found that granulated sugar didn't provide enough flavor, so we moved on to brown sugar. Tasters agreed they liked the balancing, slightly maple-y sweetness the brown sugar added to the bold spice rub, but they were not satisfied with the level of caramelization—the crust

wasn't as crisp as we'd hoped, and the spices still tasted powdery.

Moving on to other sweeteners, we considered honey next. We brushed the salmon lightly with honey, sprinkled on the spices (we kept a touch of brown sugar for flavor), and placed the salmon under the broiler—finally, we saw some progress. The honey caramelized quickly under the broiler, and better yet, it helped solve the problem of the powdery spices. As the honey bubbled under the heat, it quickly cooked the spices, creating a unified caramelized crust. We tested various amounts of honey and settled on a single teaspoon per salmon fillet. Any more than that, and the honey pooled and ran off the salmon, taking our spice rub with it. To make the honey easier to spread, we mixed a small amount of water with it. Because the quantities were so small, we found we didn't need to heat the honey to mix it; all we had to do was stir the water (just ¼ teaspoon) right into the honey.

We had made real progress, but we were still troubled by a few powdery pockets where the spice rub had not cooked in the honey. We had assumed that the salmon skin, which contains some fat, would provide enough oil to lubricate the spices and help them cook. Brushing the tops of our fillets with olive oil just served to disrupt the even layer of spices, so we had to find another solution. That's when one of our colleagues handed us a canister of vegetable oil spray.

BROILED SALMON WITH PINEAPPLE SALSA

Sure enough, a light spritz did the trick. Our salmon was now a deep golden color, with a flavorful crisp crust and moist fish beneath.

Finally, we turned our attention to accompaniments. We wanted to top the fish with something fresh and light to balance the salmon's richness without stealing the spotlight, and we came up with a few quick salsas that were both easy and flavorful. We started with pineapple and added a bit of jalapeño for a kick. Lime juice added punch and acidity, and cilantro added a fresh finish. We developed a second salsa with mango in lieu of the pineapple, and a third with honeydew.

Broiled Salmon with Pineapple Salsa

SERVES 2

We find it easiest to buy fresh pineapple that has already been peeled and cored. To make this dish spicier, add the chile seeds. If your fillets have skin on them, follow the instructions on page 39 to remove it.

SALSA

- 4 ounces peeled and cored fresh pineapple (see note), chopped medium (about ¾ cup)
- 1 scallion, sliced thin
- ½ jalapeño chile, stemmed, seeded, and minced (see note)
- 2 teaspoons fresh lime juice
- 1 teaspoon minced fresh cilantro
  Salt and pepper

FISH

- 2 teaspoons honey
- ¼ teaspoon water
- ½ teaspoon brown sugar
- ½ teaspoon ground coriander
- ¼ teaspoon ground ginger
- ¼ teaspoon garlic powder
- ¼ teaspoon pepper
- ⅛ teaspoon salt
- 2 (6-ounce) skinless center-cut salmon fillets, about 1½ inches thick (see note)
  Vegetable oil spray

1. FOR THE SALSA: Combine all ingredients in bowl and season with salt and pepper to taste.

2. FOR THE FISH: Position oven rack 6 inches from broiler element and heat broiler. Stir honey and water together in bowl. In second bowl, combine brown sugar, coriander, ginger, garlic powder, pepper, and salt.

3. Pat fish dry with paper towels and place, skinned side down, on aluminum foil–lined rimmed baking sheet. Brush each fillet with honey mixture. Sprinkle spice mixture evenly over fish and gently press to adhere. Coat tops of fillets with vegetable oil spray.

4. Broil until salmon is golden, center of thickest part of fillets is still translucent when cut into with paring knife, and thickest part of fillets registers 125 degrees on instant-read thermometer, 6 to 9 minutes. Serve with salsa.

VARIATIONS

Broiled Salmon with Mango Salsa
Follow recipe for Broiled Salmon with Pineapple Salsa, substituting ½ mango, peeled and chopped medium (see page 22), for pineapple.

Broiled Salmon with Honeydew and Radish Salsa
You can substitute cantaloupe for the honeydew melon.

Follow recipe for Broiled Salmon with Pineapple Salsa, substituting ¾ cup chopped honeydew melon for pineapple, 2 chopped radishes for jalapeño, and 2 teaspoons fresh lemon juice for lime juice.

USE IT UP: JALAPEÑO CHILE

Jalapeño-Garlic Butter
MAKES ¼ CUP

To make the butter spicier, add the chile seeds. Serve on toasted bagels or warm cornbread, or use it to give grilled chicken, fish, or even baked potatoes a flavor boost. The butter can be refrigerated in an airtight container for up to 1 week.

- 4 tablespoons (½ stick) unsalted butter, softened
- ½–¾ jalapeño chile, stemmed, seeded, and minced (see note)
- 1 small garlic clove, minced
- ¼ teaspoon salt
- ¼ teaspoon pepper

Thoroughly mix all ingredients together in small bowl.

PAN-ROASTED THICK-CUT FISH FILLETS

PAN-ROASTED FILLETS OF THICK-CUT HALIBUT, COD, and other kinds of white fish have become fixtures on the menus of virtually every restaurant. And for good reason: When well executed, the cooking method used—pan-roasting—yields moist, white pieces of tender, flavorful fish with a chestnut-brown crust. But try to replicate these results at home, and you'll most likely end up with overbaked fillets. The problem is that recipes for pan-roasted fish require keen attention and a practiced hand—that is, the skill of an experienced restaurant chef, not the busy home cook who's also managing another dish or two for a well-rounded dinner. Our goal was simple: We wanted a foolproof recipe for producing two succulent, well-browned, thick-cut fish fillets, for a simple seafood supper.

From our initial tests, we knew we needed fillets at least an inch thick; thinner fillets ended up overcooked by the time they achieved a serious sear. Since skin-on fillets are not always available, we started our testing with skinless fillets. We carefully patted them dry to minimize the risk of sticking, then seasoned them with salt and pepper. To cook two fillets at a time with ample room for flipping, a 10-inch skillet was a must.

Armed with the right fish and the right pan, we started with a popular technique used in restaurants to achieve a good crust: Sear the fish on one side in a blazing-hot skillet, flip it, then add a big pat of butter to the pan and repeatedly baste the fish as it cooks. A few burned fingers later, we realized that spooning hot butter in a sizzling skillet for anything more than a minute is impractical at home, so we switched to a safer method: Sear in a hot pan, flip, then transfer the pan to a hot oven to cook the fish through. We'd have to shelve the butter and find another way to add flavor.

To figure out how hot the pan needed to be, we seared fish at every temperature, noting texture, appearance, and flavor. No matter what we did, the results were problematic. If we added the fish to the pan just as the oil started to smoke, we could produce an attractive and flavorful sear in about three minutes, but we also got a tough, dried-out interior. Starting in a cooler pan or cooking for less time left the fish tender but failed to develop the crust. For now, a compromise would have to work. We scaled back the sear to a light golden brown, which we accomplished in about 1½ minutes.

As for the oven, a few tests told us that 425 degrees was the way to go. Any hotter, and the fish dried out before it cooked through. Any cooler, and the cooking time increased, while flavor and texture remained the same. In a 425-degree oven, it took just under 10 minutes for the fillets to turn opaque. We found it best to err on the side of undercooking (just a touch translucent at the center) to preserve as much moisture as possible. Despite having tested our way through 20-odd pounds of various fillets, we thought our fish still lacked the flavor—and the visual appeal—of restaurant-style seared fish. The problem was that to develop serious flavor, we needed plenty of browning, but for texture, we couldn't let the fish get too hot. Part of the solution might be to increase the rate of browning. But what if we also insulated the fish at the same time, to protect it against drying out? Many recipes call for dusting the fillets with flour before searing. It sounded promising, and at first it seemed to work—the proteins and sugars in the flour contribute to browning, so the coated fish developed a flavorful crust much faster than uncoated fish, and in fact, these were the best fillets yet. But the flour lent a pasty texture to the crust. We ran into the same problem no matter what starch we tried: flour, cornmeal, cornstarch, potato starch, potato flour, and rice flour.

Thinking back to how we used honey to encourage caramelization in our Broiled Salmon with Pineapple Salsa (page 41), we decided to try granulated sugar, hoping it would accelerate browning and encourage caramelization. We dusted our fillets with a touch of sugar, placed them in the hot skillet, and crossed our fingers. We knew we were on the right track when the fish had a well-browned crust just a minute later. Tasting it after it came out of the oven confirmed our observation—the fish was well browned, flavorful, and, most important, tender. Best of all, not one taster noticed any sweetness; they just remarked on how good the fish looked and tasted, especially with a squeeze of lemon or a piquant relish.

Pan-Roasted Thick-Cut Fish Fillets
SERVES 2

Thick white fish fillets with a meaty texture, like haddock, sea bass, cod, or halibut, work best in this recipe. If your fillets have skin on them, follow the instructions on page 39 to remove it. Because most fish fillets differ in thickness, some pieces may finish cooking before others; be sure to immediately remove from the pan any fillet that reaches 135 degrees. The fish can be served on its own or with Green Olive, Almond, and Orange Relish or Roasted Red Pepper, Hazelnut, and Thyme Relish (recipes follow).

2 (6- to 8-ounce) skinless white fish fillets,
   1 to 1½ inches thick (see note)
   Salt and pepper
¼ teaspoon sugar
2 teaspoons vegetable oil
   Lemon wedges, for serving

1. Adjust oven rack to middle position and heat oven to 425 degrees. Pat fish dry with paper towels and season with salt and pepper. Sprinkle ⅛ teaspoon sugar evenly over skinned side of each fillet.

2. Heat oil in 10-inch ovensafe nonstick skillet over high heat until just smoking. Place fillets in skillet, sugared sides down, and press down lightly to ensure even contact with pan. Cook until browned, 1 to 1½ minutes. Using two spatulas, flip fillets and transfer skillet to oven.

3. Roast fillets until centers are just opaque and register 135 degrees on instant-read thermometer, 7 to 10 minutes. Serve immediately with lemon wedges.

Green Olive, Almond, and Orange Relish
MAKES ABOUT ¾ CUP

If the olives are marinated, rinse and drain them before chopping. The relish can be refrigerated in an airtight container for up to 1 day.

¼ cup slivered almonds, toasted (see page 240)
¼ cup pitted green olives, coarsely chopped (see note)
1 small garlic clove, minced
½ teaspoon grated orange zest plus
   2 tablespoons fresh orange juice
2 tablespoons extra-virgin olive oil
2 tablespoons minced fresh mint
1 teaspoon white wine vinegar
   Salt and pepper

Pulse almonds, olives, garlic, and orange zest in food processor until nuts and olives are finely chopped, 10 to 12 pulses. Transfer to bowl and stir in orange juice, olive oil, mint, and vinegar. Season with salt and pepper to taste and spoon over fish before serving.

Roasted Red Pepper, Hazelnut, and Thyme Relish
MAKES ABOUT ¾ CUP

We prefer the flavor of smoked paprika in this recipe, but sweet paprika can be substituted in a pinch; the flavor profile will be different. The relish can be refrigerated in an airtight container for up to 1 day.

¼ cup hazelnuts, toasted (see page 240)
   and skinned (see photos)
¼ cup jarred roasted red peppers, rinsed, dried,
   and coarsely chopped
1 small garlic clove, minced
¼ teaspoon grated lemon zest plus
   2 teaspoons fresh lemon juice
2 tablespoons extra-virgin olive oil
2 tablespoons minced fresh parsley
½ teaspoon minced fresh thyme
⅛ teaspoon smoked paprika (see note)
   Salt and pepper

Pulse hazelnuts, red peppers, garlic, and lemon zest in food processor until finely chopped, 10 to 12 pulses. Transfer to bowl and stir in lemon juice, olive oil, parsley, thyme, and paprika. Season with salt and pepper to taste and spoon over fish before serving.

NOTES FROM THE TEST KITCHEN

SKINNING HAZELNUTS

1. After toasting the hazelnuts, transfer them to a clean kitchen towel. Rub the warm nuts together in the towel to scrape off as much of the brown skin as possible.

2. Open the towel and discard the skins that have come away from the nuts (note that a few patches of skin may remain).

THAI RED CURRY WITH SHRIMP, BELL PEPPER, AND SNAP PEAS

CHAPTER 2

ONE–DISH SUPPERS

BRAISED BEEF SHORT RIBS

FEW DISHES ARE AS EMINENTLY SATISFYING AS A plate of braised, beefy short ribs, nestled in a rich, velvety sauce and piled next to tender carrots and potatoes infused with the flavor of the meat. But while we love dining on short ribs in restaurants and pubs, the cooking time required prevents them from showing up on the dining room table in our own homes. Most recipes call for browning the ribs, braising them in the oven with the vegetables for hours until tender, then resting the ribs in the braising liquid overnight so that the rendered fat solidifies into an easy-to-remove layer. Although some recipes suggest skipping the overnight rest and skimming the fat with a spoon, short ribs simply give off too much fat for this method to be effective. We wanted to bring this restaurant favorite home, but in order to make braised short ribs a viable option for two, we had to ditch the overnight rest.

Our first task was to choose the correct ribs. Butchers typically divide the ribs into sections about 10 inches square and 3 to 5 inches thick. Cutting the ribs between the bones and into lengths of between 2 and 6 inches yields what butchers call "English" style, a cut typically found in European braises. Cutting the meat across the bone yields the "flanken" cut, more typically found in Asian cuisines. Because English-style short ribs are easier to find, we focused our attention there.

The first step in most braises is browning the meat. Searing adds color and flavor, but in this case it also presents an opportunity to rid the ribs of some of their excess fat. But why not get rid of the fat before the ribs even went into the pan? Before searing, we trimmed the hard, waxy surface fat from 2½ pounds of bone-in English-style short ribs, leaving only a thin layer behind. Then, trading in our Dutch oven for a large saucepan, we browned the ribs and proceeded with the usual protocol.

This first test provided an important clue as to how to reduce the fat further. Short ribs contain a layer of fat and connective tissue between the meat and the bone. Once fully cooked, this layer shrinks into a tough, chewy strip called "strap meat" that we found unattractive and mostly inedible. To get rid of that strip would mean cutting the meat off the bone and serving the ribs boneless. Maybe we didn't need the bones at all.

For our next test, we prepared the ribs as we had been doing (with bones intact), but we also prepared a batch with the bones cut off. We were shocked by the difference in the amount of fat rendered—the bone-in batch produced nearly ¾ cup of fat, while the boneless batch produced a mere 2 tablespoons. Removing the bones (and the fat between the bones and meat) nearly solved the greasy sauce problem (a quick trip through a fat strainer rid us of the remaining fat). As for flavor, tasters found little difference between the bone-in and boneless braising liquids. But the dish with cooked bones did come out differently in another way: It had significantly more body, which came from the connective tissue attached to the bone that had broken down during cooking. Looking for an easy way to achieve that rich texture, minus the bones, we experimented with gelatin, which we sometimes use to give body to sauces. In the past, we've found that while both cornstarch and flour offer plenty of thickening power when it comes to sauces, they don't offer the supple texture—similar to that of connective tissue when it breaks down—that gelatin can provide. Sprinkling just ½ teaspoon into the sauce a few minutes before serving delivered a similar supple texture, without the grease. Now, with no use for the bones, we were able to switch to 1¼ pounds of boneless short ribs and shave off some prep time.

At this point, we looked to ramp up the richness of the sauce (which was all beef broth up to now) and add our vegetables. After searing and removing the meat, we sautéed an onion in the leftover browned bits and then stirred in a few big flavor hitters: tomato paste, garlic, and an anchovy—an ingredient that, when used judiciously, brings depth of flavor without drawing attention to itself. Next, we deglazed the pan with some red wine. To cook off its harsh, boozy flavor, we simmered it until it was reduced by half.

For the vegetables, two carrots and a single large potato proved ample for two diners. The vegetables absorbed rich, meaty flavor from the sauce, while offering up sweetness and body. After returning the browned ribs to the pot, we set the cover on top and transferred the pot to a 300-degree oven to gently simmer. About 2½ hours later, we had ultra-tender short ribs and perfectly cooked vegetables. We now strained and defatted the only slightly fatty braising liquid before reducing the sauce to a silky consistency. After stirring in the gelatin, we sprinkled some minced parsley over the sauce for a last-minute burst of freshness. Our braised beef short ribs didn't take nearly as long as traditional recipes, but they were still as richly flavorful and tender.

Braised Beef Short Ribs with Potato and Carrots

SERVES 2

If boneless ribs are unavailable, substitute 2½ pounds of bone-in English-style beef short ribs with at least 1 inch of meat above the bone. To remove the meat from the bone, see the photo on page 235. Serve with egg noodles.

1¼ pounds boneless beef short ribs, trimmed (see note)
   Salt and pepper
2 teaspoons vegetable oil
1 onion, halved and sliced thin
1 anchovy fillet, rinsed and minced
1 teaspoon tomato paste
2 garlic cloves, peeled
¾ cup dry red wine
2 carrots, peeled and cut into 2-inch chunks
1 cup beef broth
1 sprig fresh thyme
1 bay leaf
1 large Yukon Gold potato (about 12 ounces), peeled and cut into 2-inch chunks
1 tablespoon cold water
½ teaspoon unflavored powdered gelatin
2 tablespoons minced fresh parsley

1. Adjust oven rack to lower-middle position and heat oven to 300 degrees. Pat beef dry with paper towels and season with salt and pepper. Heat oil in large saucepan over medium-high heat until just smoking. Brown beef on all sides, 8 to 10 minutes; transfer to plate.

2. Add onion to fat left in pan and cook over medium heat until softened and lightly browned, 5 to 7 minutes. Stir in anchovy and tomato paste and cook until beginning to brown, about 2 minutes. Stir in garlic and cook until fragrant, about 30 seconds. Stir in wine, scraping up any browned bits, and simmer until reduced by half, 5 to 7 minutes.

3. Stir in carrots, broth, thyme, and bay leaf. Return browned beef, with any accumulated juice, to pan and bring to simmer. Cover, transfer pan to oven, and cook for 75 minutes, flipping meat halfway through.

4. Stir in potato and continue to cook until dinner fork slips easily in and out of meat and potato is tender, 45 to 60 minutes longer.

5. Place water in small bowl and sprinkle gelatin on top; let stand for 5 minutes. Transfer meat, carrots, and potato to serving platter and tent loosely with foil. Strain cooking liquid through fine-mesh strainer into fat separator, pressing on solids to extract as much liquid as possible; discard solids. Let braising liquid settle for 5 minutes, then return defatted liquid to saucepan. Simmer liquid vigorously over medium-high heat until reduced to ¾ cup, 5 to 7 minutes.

6. Off heat, stir in gelatin mixture and parsley. Season sauce with salt and pepper to taste, pour over meat, and serve.

STRIP STEAK WITH CORN AND BLACK BEAN SALAD

PAN-SEARING IS A GREAT WAY TO COOK STEAK— with just a hot pan and a little oil, you can create a crusty, well-seared exterior and tender, juicy interior. And it's an ideal technique when cooking for two; since enough steak for two fits perfectly in one skillet, there's no need to fuss with multiple batches. Plus, while the skillet is out, it's easy enough to come up with a simple side to round out dinner. We set out to create a perfectly browned pan-seared steak, matched by a flavorful yet simple side dish—all cooked in a skillet.

We tested a number of cuts of beef but eventually settled on strip steak, an extremely flavorful cut that's a favorite in the test kitchen. We found that one large 12-ounce strip steak provided the right amount of meat for two people. With the cut settled, we turned our attention to the proper cooking technique. For a perfectly seared steak, we found that a high-quality, heavy skillet was important for even heat distribution; a 10-inch skillet was just the right size. Using the right level of heat was also key; to achieve the perfect crust, we found that the skillet should be heated until just smoking before adding the steak. If the skillet was not hot enough, the steak cooled the pan down and it ended up stewing or steaming rather than searing. Once the steak was placed in the skillet, we made sure not to move it as this could cause the steak to release liquid, which impedes browning. Achieving a deep brown crust on the first side took three to five minutes, then we flipped the steak, reduced the heat, and continued cooking until it was medium-rare, another five to seven minutes. To prevent overcooking, we found it was best to always undercook the steak a bit to allow for what is referred to as carryover cooking as the steak rested.

We now had a nicely cooked steak—browned with a crust on the outside and a rosy interior—but tasters thought it could use a flavor boost. Up to this point we'd simply sprinkled the steak with salt and pepper before searing. How else could we impart flavor? We first considered salting the steak for an extended period of time—a technique often used in restaurants, and a technique we use to both impart seasoning and keep lean poultry and pork moist—but we wanted to keep this dish simple, and salting requires advance planning. But what about a spice rub, which delivers big flavor in a short amount of time? After we experimented with various combinations of salt and spices, tasters favored a bold mixture of chili powder, cumin, coriander, oregano, garlic powder, pepper, and salt. Many recipes for spice rubs call for toasting the spices first before using them, but we found this step to be unnecessary. The intense heat of the skillet did the toasting for us.

The spice rub was now creating an excellent crust on our steak with plenty of flavor, but it also caused us to pay a bit more attention to the heat level of the pan—the spices could quickly burn if we weren't careful and paying close attention. Reducing the heat in the pan as needed to avoid burning the spices was an extra degree of care that we did not mind adding to ensure that our steak was both flavorful and perfectly cooked every time.

Taking a bite of our spice-rubbed steak, we thought that a refreshing salad would be an ideal accompaniment, providing a welcome contrast in both flavor and texture. Keeping with the Southwestern theme of our spice rub, we toasted some corn in the skillet before searing the steak—a move that intensified the flavor of the corn—and combined it with some black beans, bell pepper, scallion, jalapeño, garlic, cumin, lime juice, and cilantro. In record time, we had created a simple and flavorful meal for two—and we didn't have a huge pile of dishes to tackle afterward.

Spice-Rubbed Strip Steak with Toasted Corn and Black Bean Salad

SERVES 2

If desired, ¾ cup frozen corn, thawed and thoroughly patted dry, can be substituted for the fresh corn; the cooking time will be the same. Be sure not to stir the corn when cooking in step 1 or it will not brown well. To make this dish spicier, add the chile seeds. We prefer this steak cooked to medium-rare, but if you prefer it more or less done, see our guidelines in "Testing Meat for Doneness" on page 149. See page 119 for a recipe to use up the leftover black beans and page 41 for a recipe to use up the leftover jalapeño chile.

SALAD

- 1 teaspoon vegetable oil
- 1 ear fresh corn, husk and silk removed, kernels cut from cob (about ¾ cup; see page 50)
- ¾ cup drained and rinsed canned black beans
- 1 red bell pepper, stemmed, seeded, and chopped fine
- 1 scallion, sliced thin
- ½ jalapeño chile, stemmed, seeded, and minced (see note)
- 2 tablespoons fresh lime juice
- 2 tablespoons minced fresh cilantro
- 2 garlic cloves, minced
- ¼ teaspoon ground cumin
- Salt and pepper

STEAK

- ½ teaspoon chili powder
- ½ teaspoon ground cumin
- ¼ teaspoon ground coriander
- ¼ teaspoon dried oregano
- ¼ teaspoon garlic powder
- ¼ teaspoon salt
- ¼ teaspoon pepper
- 1 (12-ounce) boneless strip steak, about 1¼ inches thick
- 2 teaspoons vegetable oil

1. FOR THE SALAD: Heat oil in 10-inch nonstick skillet over medium-high heat until shimmering. Add corn and cook, without stirring, until well browned and toasted, 5 to 7 minutes. Transfer corn to medium bowl and let cool. Wipe out skillet with wad of paper towels.

SPICE-RUBBED STRIP STEAK WITH TOASTED CORN AND BLACK BEAN SALAD

2. Stir black beans, bell pepper, scallion, jalapeño, lime juice, cilantro, garlic, and cumin into corn and season with salt and pepper to taste. Cover and refrigerate until flavors meld, about 15 minutes.

3. FOR THE STEAK: Meanwhile, combine chili powder, cumin, coriander, oregano, garlic powder, salt, and pepper in small bowl. Pat steak dry with paper towels, then rub spice mixture evenly over steak.

4. Heat oil in skillet over medium-high heat until just smoking. Carefully lay steak in skillet and cook until well browned on first side, 3 to 5 minutes, reducing heat if spices begin to burn. Flip steak, reduce heat to medium, and continue to cook until center of steak registers 125 degrees on instant-read thermometer (for medium-rare), 5 to 7 minutes longer.

5. Transfer steak to carving board, tent loosely with foil, and let rest for 5 minutes. Slice steak into ¼-inch-thick pieces and serve with corn and black bean salad.

VARIATION

Spice-Rubbed Strip Steak with Cherry Tomato and Black Bean Salad

Although yellow bell pepper is visually appealing here, red pepper can be used in its place.

Follow recipe for Spice-Rubbed Strip Steak with Toasted Corn and Black Bean Salad, omitting step 1. Substitute 6 ounces cherry tomatoes (about 1 cup), quartered, for corn, 1 yellow bell pepper for red bell pepper, and ¼ cup minced red onion for scallion and garlic in step 2.

NOTES FROM THE TEST KITCHEN

CUTTING CORN KERNELS FROM THE COB

Standing the corn upright inside a large bowl, carefully cut the kernels from the cob using a paring knife.

SHEET PAN BEEF STIR-FRY

WHEN YOU'RE COOKING FOR TWO, THE PREP FOR stir-fry suppers is a snap. After a little chopping, the meat hits the heat, followed by the vegetables, then the two are tossed together in a potently flavored sauce and served over rice. But we wondered if we could make this dish even easier—allowing us some time to walk away from the stove rather than standing over a skillet.

In the test kitchen, we have found a large, flat cooking surface (such as a 12-inch nonstick skillet, our stir-fry pan of choice) to be crucial to stir-fries. As we considered oven-appropriate alternatives to the skillet, a sheet pan came to mind—in addition to having the largest flat surface of any piece of cookware, it is relatively thin (compared to a skillet or roasting pan) and transfers heat quickly. We wondered if it might work to simply spread out our stir-fry ingredients on a sheet pan, throw it into a hot oven, and walk away.

Most stir-fries start with a protein; for our stir-fry, we decided to go with beef. We chose flank steak as the optimal cut—it is widely available, has a nice beefy flavor, and, when sliced thinly against the grain, is tender. Although we usually marinate the steak in a simple combination of soy sauce and Chinese rice cooking wine when making traditional stir-fries, we opted to skip this step—without intense stovetop heat to rapidly drive off liquid, we knew we would need to keep moisture to a minimum for our oven stir-fry.

Because everything would go into the oven at once, we needed to choose vegetables that would cook at the same rate as the beef and cut them appropriately. After a few preliminary tests we found that sliced red bell pepper worked well—it cooked quickly and added visual appeal. Snap peas paired well with the bell pepper, cooked at the same rate, and retained their bright green color and signature crunch.

With the protein and vegetables ready to go, we tackled the cooking. Broiling would provide plenty of intense heat, but it would also require almost as much hands-on time as a traditional stir-fry; since the heat comes mostly from the top, we would need to stir every few minutes to ensure even cooking. Instead, we tossed the beef and vegetables with oil, salt, and pepper, spread the mixture on a sheet pan, and slid it into a very hot (500-degree) oven. The stir-fry ingredients cooked through in less than 15 minutes, but the moisture hadn't fully evaporated in that time, resulting in limp vegetables and pale meat sitting in a pool of liquid.

What if we started with a hot pan? We set an oven rack to the lowest position (closest to the heat source) and put the sheet pan on the rack while the oven heated. When the pan was hot, we carefully but quickly scattered the vegetables and meat on top and were met with an encouraging sizzle. This batch was a huge improvement—the direct contact with the hot surface drove off some moisture immediately and jump-started cooking. In just under 10 minutes, the vegetables and meat were nicely cooked and had achieved a little browning, and there were no pools of liquid.

Next we considered the aromatics. In our traditional stir-fry technique, aromatics (typically minced garlic, ginger, and scallions) are added toward the end of cooking and briefly sautéed. To mimic this process, we first tried tossing the aromatics with the hot meat and vegetables as soon as they came out of the oven. The residual heat wasn't sufficient to tame the garlic and ginger, and tasters found their flavors raw and harsh. We had better luck adding them to the stir-fry before cooking. Sliced scallion, however, was best when added at the end as a garnish.

Finally we tackled the sauce. Continuing with our easy, stovetop-free mode of operation, we turned to the microwave. After we put the stir-fry in the oven, our plan was to microwave the sauce in a big bowl until it was hot and just the right glazy consistency, then stir in the cooked meat and vegetables as soon as they came out of the oven. After selecting, scaling down, and preparing two of our existing stir-fry sauces, we quickly realized that we would need to make some adjustments—tasters described these microwaved sauces as muddied at best and off-flavored at worst.

Timing in the microwave proved to be key. Because we were working with a relatively small amount of sauce, it easily overreduced in the microwave, which resulted in bitter-tasting, salty sauce with a gloppy texture. After a variety of trials, we found that one minute was all our sauces needed to thicken to the

right consistency and become piping hot. In our Spicy Orange Sauce, the bright flavor of orange juice was dulled when cooked in the microwave; instead we relied on grated zest for orange flavor and stirred a little juice into the cooked sauce for freshness. In our Oyster Sauce, boldly flavored ingredients such as soy sauce, oyster sauce, a little chili paste, and sesame oil contributed complexity. Relying on these potent flavors allowed us to streamline our ingredient lists, keeping the sauces from tasting muddy and making less work for the cook.

Our components and process were finally set: Meat, vegetables, and aromatics were spread on a hot sheet pan and cooked in the oven; the accompanying sauce was cooked in the microwave; then everything was quickly combined while hot. With just a sheet pan and a large bowl, this incredibly quick and simple beef stir-fry was as easy to clean up as it was to make.

Sheet Pan Stir-Fried Beef with Snap Peas and Bell Pepper

SERVES 2

To make the beef easier to slice thin, freeze it for 15 minutes. This dish comes together quickly, so be ready to start cooking the sauce as soon as you put the meat and vegetables into the oven. Either the Oyster Sauce or Spicy Orange Sauce (recipes follow) works well with this stir-fry. Serve over Simple White Rice (see page 26).

8   ounces flank steak, trimmed and sliced thin across grain on bias (see note; see page 52)

6   ounces snap peas (about 3 cups), ends trimmed and strings removed (see page 72)

1   red bell pepper, stemmed, seeded, and sliced into ¼-inch-wide strips (see page 52)

2   tablespoons vegetable oil

2   garlic cloves, minced

½   teaspoon grated or minced fresh ginger
    Salt and pepper

1   recipe stir-fry sauce (recipes follow)

1   scallion, sliced thin on bias

1. Adjust oven rack to lowest position, place large rimmed baking sheet on rack, and heat oven to 500 degrees. Toss beef, snap peas, bell pepper, oil, garlic, and ginger together in large bowl and season lightly with salt and pepper.

2. Working quickly, spread beef and vegetables in even layer on hot baking sheet. Cook until beef is just cooked through and vegetables begin to brown, 8 to 10 minutes, stirring halfway through.

3. Transfer cooked beef and vegetables to bowl of warm stir-fry sauce and toss to combine. Sprinkle with scallion and serve.

Oyster Sauce

MAKES ENOUGH FOR 1 SHEET PAN STIR-FRY

Make sure not to overcook this sauce in the microwave or it will taste bitter and turn gloppy.

- 2 tablespoons water
- 2 tablespoons oyster sauce
- 5 teaspoons mirin
- 1 tablespoon brown sugar
- 1½ teaspoons soy sauce
- 1 teaspoon cornstarch
- ½ teaspoon toasted sesame oil
- ½ teaspoon sambal oelek chili paste

Whisk all ingredients together in large microwave-safe bowl. Microwave sauce (uncovered) until thickened, about 1 minute. Cover to keep warm until needed.

Spicy Orange Sauce

MAKES ENOUGH FOR 1 SHEET PAN STIR-FRY

Make sure not to overcook this sauce in the microwave or it will taste bitter and turn gloppy.

- 3 tablespoons water
- 1½ tablespoons soy sauce
- 1 tablespoon sugar
- 1 teaspoon cornstarch
- ⅛ teaspoon grated orange zest plus 1 tablespoon fresh orange juice
- ⅛ teaspoon red pepper flakes

Whisk water, soy sauce, sugar, cornstarch, orange zest, and pepper flakes together in large microwave-safe bowl. Microwave sauce (uncovered) until thickened, about 1 minute. Stir orange juice into sauce and cover to keep warm until needed.

NOTES FROM THE TEST KITCHEN

SLICING BEEF FOR STIR-FRY

1. Using a sharp chef's knife, slice the steak lengthwise into 2-inch-wide pieces.

2. Then cut each 2-inch-wide piece of steak across the grain into very thin slices.

CUTTING BELL PEPPERS INTO STRIPS

1. Slice off the top and bottom of the pepper and remove the seeds and stem. Slice down through the side of the pepper.

2. Lay the pepper flat on the cutting board and slice it into ¼-inch-wide strips.

PORK CHOPS WITH WARM POTATO SALAD

PORK CHOPS MAKE A GREAT MAIN COURSE ANY night of the week. And baking pork chops is among the most hands-off methods around. The downside is that the dry heat of the oven can result in dry meat. We wanted tender and juicy baked chops, and to up the ante we wanted to partner our chops with a flavorful side dish—using the same pan—for a simple yet satisfying oven-baked supper for two.

Today's lean pork chops are easy to overcook, rendering them chewy and desiccated. To mitigate the dryness, we typically brine the meat to keep it moist. Although this method is tried and true, it does require forethought and extra time, so we explored other options for keeping the pork moist during its stay in the oven. Our thoughts turned to other cuts of pork that stay naturally juicy. In addition to having more fat marbled into the meat, a pork rib or shoulder roast has a protective cap of fat that melts during cooking and essentially bastes the meat, adding flavor as well as ensuring juiciness. What if we mimicked this effect by wrapping the pork chops in bacon? We reasoned this could be the solution to two problems: In addition to protecting the pork and providing moisture during cooking, a crispy browned shell of bacon would serve, both visually and flavor-wise, as a kind of crust on the chops that wouldn't form otherwise given that we were cooking them in the oven.

We rubbed two pork chops with salt, pepper, and ground fennel seed (a classic pork seasoning), then layered two bacon slices lengthwise over each chop, overlapping them slightly and tucking the ends underneath. We set them on a baking sheet and roasted them in a 375-degree oven until they registered 140 degrees. When we pulled our chops out of the oven, the test appeared to be a total failure: The bacon was flabby and soggy, and the rendered fat and juice pooled around the chops. Tasting the meat, however, told a different story—the pork chops were incredibly moist and juicy throughout and had a slight smoky flavor imparted by the bacon.

Hoping to find the way to crisper bacon, we wondered if precooking it for a few minutes, before wrapping it around the meat, might help. We decided to enlist the help of the microwave. Sure enough, three minutes was enough time to allow some of the bacon fat to render, while still leaving the bacon pliable enough to wrap easily around the pork.

Giving the bacon a jump start in the microwave had helped; the bacon fat was now fully rendered, and less liquid pooled on the baking sheet. However, the bacon on the finished chops still wasn't as brown as we wanted. Cooking the pork at higher oven temperatures browned the bacon but dried out the pork. What if we cooked our chops at 375 degrees until they were almost done and then broiled them for the last few minutes to brown the bacon? This worked great; the meat remained juicy, and the bacon became beautifully crisp and brown under the heat of the broiler.

Inspired by the bacon, we decided that a warm, German-style roasted potato salad would be an appropriate side dish. Taking advantage of the large surface area of the baking sheet, we could simply roast the potatoes right alongside the pork, where they would absorb flavor from the juice and rendered bacon fat. We halved small red potatoes (our favorite for roasting because they hold their shape) and arranged them around the pork chops to maximize browning. While our pork was cooked to perfection and the bacon was crisp, the potatoes were only slightly browned and not quite tender. To solve this problem, we gave the potatoes a 20-minute head start in the oven, while we microwaved the bacon and prepared the pork. We then added the bacon-wrapped pork chops to the pan, and the potatoes finished cooking alongside the pork.

While the pork rested, we tossed the roasted potatoes with a simple Dijon vinaigrette that we had warmed in the microwave. We covered the salad and let it sit for a few minutes so the potatoes could absorb the dressing. Our pork chop dinner needed only one last touch; a generous handful of minced parsley, stirred into the salad, provided some color and fresh flavor.

Bacon-Wrapped Pork Chops with Warm Dijon Potato Salad

SERVES 2

We prefer to use extra-small red potatoes measuring less than 1 inch in diameter in this recipe, but you can substitute larger red potatoes, cut into ¾-inch chunks. The bacon should completely cover the top of your pork chops. If your bacon is narrow, you may need 3 slices per chop.

- 12 ounces extra-small red potatoes (about 12), halved (see note)
- 2 tablespoons olive oil
  Salt and pepper
- 4–6 slices bacon (4 to 6 ounces; see note)
- 2 (6- to 8-ounce) boneless center-cut pork chops, ¾ to 1 inch thick, trimmed, sides slit (see page 152)
- 1 teaspoon ground fennel seed
- 1 small shallot, minced
- 2 tablespoons low-sodium chicken broth
- 1½ teaspoons white wine vinegar
- ½ teaspoon Dijon mustard
  Pinch sugar
- 1 tablespoon minced fresh parsley

1. Adjust oven rack to upper-middle position and heat oven to 375 degrees. Line large rimmed baking sheet with aluminum foil. Toss potatoes with 1 tablespoon oil and season with salt and pepper. Lay potatoes, cut side down, on half of baking sheet. Roast until potatoes are just tender, about 20 minutes.

2. Meanwhile, lay bacon on large microwave-safe plate and weigh it down with second plate. Microwave bacon until slightly shriveled but still pliable, 1 to 3 minutes. Transfer bacon to paper towel–lined plate and let cool slightly.

3. Pat pork dry with paper towels, rub evenly with ground fennel, and season with salt and pepper. Following photos, shingle 2 or 3 slices bacon lengthwise over top of each pork chop so each chop is covered, tucking ends underneath to secure.

4. Remove potatoes from oven, arrange pork on empty half of baking sheet, and roast until pork registers 135 degrees on instant-read thermometer, 12 to 15 minutes.

5. Remove pork and potatoes from oven, position oven rack 6 inches from broiler element, and heat broiler. Broil pork and potatoes until bacon is crisp and browned and pork registers 140 to 145 degrees on instant-read thermometer, 2 to 4 minutes. Transfer pork to plate and let rest for 5 minutes.

6. Meanwhile, whisk remaining 1 tablespoon oil, shallot, broth, vinegar, mustard, and sugar together in large microwave-safe bowl. Microwave dressing (uncovered) until very hot, 1 to 2 minutes. Cover and keep warm until needed.

7. Whisk warm dressing to recombine, then stir in roasted potatoes and parsley. Season potato salad with salt and pepper to taste, cover, and let sit until potatoes have absorbed dressing, 5 to 10 minutes. Serve with pork.

NOTES FROM THE TEST KITCHEN

PREPARING BACON-WRAPPED PORK CHOPS

1. Shingle 2 or 3 bacon slices lengthwise over the top of the pork, overlapping them slightly and making sure the pork chop is covered by the bacon.

2. Then tuck the ends of the bacon slices underneath the chops to secure them.

THE BEST RIMMED BAKING SHEET

In the cooking-for-two kitchen, we don't use our baking sheets for cookies and sheet cakes only—we use them to cook dinners, too. Because our baking sheets are such essential go-to equipment, we wondered if there were any differences in the various models found at our local retail stores, or if just any baking sheet would do. We gathered eight sheets in a variety of materials and came to some interesting conclusions. We found that solid construction is more important than the choice of materials—a too-flimsy pan warps under high heat. Aluminum sheet pans will soften slightly beginning at temperatures of 400 to 500 degrees, and the metal will expand and contract. While steel won't soften significantly below 500 degrees, the different metals in aluminized steel can behave differently at high heat, leading to warping. A pan that is too lightweight also can transfer heat too intensely and burn baked goods. Size was important, too. We like pans that are 18 by 13 inches; any smaller, and parchment paper and standard cooling racks won't fit inside.

We found that the best rimmed baking sheet was the sturdy, reliable **Lincoln Foodservice Half-Size Heavy Duty Sheet Pan**, $15.99.

SPICY PORK TINGA

THE SPICY MEXICAN SHREDDED PORK KNOWN AS *tinga* boasts all the smoke and fork-tenderness of good barbecued pulled pork. But forget the hours of tending a grill—this dish never leaves the stove. In tinga, pork is spiced with chipotle chiles and bathed in a tomatoey sauce, for a conglomeration of smoky, spicy, and sweet flavors. Although it is traditionally served on tostadas, we wanted to swap out the tostadas (which must be fried) for rice for an easier take on this one-dish dinner. Our primary challenges would be to revamp the dish to include tender grains of rice while keeping all of the authentic flavors intact, and to bring the recipe down to a scale suitable for two.

In typical tinga recipes, cubes of boneless pork butt are simmered in salted water until they are very tender. Then the meat is drained, shredded, sautéed with chipotle chiles and oregano, and stewed in tomato sauce. When we first made our new pork and rice dish, we found that the amount of sauce in the original tinga recipe, while flavor-filled, was not nearly enough in which to cook a pot of rice. So we modified the sauce by adding some chicken broth and increasing the amount of aromatics, including onion, oregano, thyme, and chipotles. We found these aromatics to be fine additions, but we struggled with the tomato component.

We knew we wanted our sauce to have a rich tomato flavor, but we didn't want it to be overwhelmingly acidic. We liked using smooth tomato sauce, as it was thick but not so thick that it would prevent the rice from cooking. We added an 8-ounce can to the pan, which we bulked up with chicken broth to create enough liquid to cook the rice (we could determine correct amounts later), and hoped for the best. Unfortunately, the finished dish, when combined with the requisite bit of lime juice added before serving, was entirely too acidic. We found that dialing back on the amount of lime juice kept the acidity of the overall dish in check. Next we turned to the meat.

Choosing the right cut of pork to feed two was a challenge. Locating a pork butt small enough to serve two is practically impossible, so we needed to find an acceptable substitute. Country-style boneless pork ribs, cut from the fatty blade end of the loin, made a great replacement—they can be purchased individually, require little preparation, and have a composition similar to that of boneless pork butt.

While authentic tinga recipes avoid browning the pork so as not to compete with the tang and smokiness of the chipotle chiles, our dish would greatly benefit from the color and fond (the meaty browned bits on the bottom of the pot) developed during the browning process. After a few tests, we decided to cut the pork into 1-inch cubes instead of cooking the meat and shredding it later; tasters liked the way that substantial pieces of pork maintained their own identity in the rice, instead of disappearing into the pot the way the shreds did. After we browned and simmered our pork, the meat was very tender with a subtle, sweet taste. Our meat issues resolved, we tackled the rice.

After a few tests, we determined that we liked the flavor and texture of long-grain white rice in this dish more than any other kind of rice. We might have our rice chosen, but the cooking amounts were far from settled. It didn't take long for us to realize that, depending on the size of the pot and the amount of other ingredients included, small amounts of rice cook with variable predictability. One thing that helped was cooking the rice in the oven—the ambient heat creates a more even cooking environment than the stovetop. To determine the right amounts of rice and liquid to give us tender, slightly yielding grains, we began with ¾ cup of rice, ½ cup of chicken broth, and a single 8-ounce can of tomato sauce. Unfortunately, this batch left us with a dry pot with crispy bits of rice stuck to the bottom. Clearly we needed more cooking liquid. Our next attempt, made with 1 cup of broth, seemed to have the right amount of liquid—nothing stuck to the pot and the final dish had just the right amount of sauce. However, the grains of rice were still far too gummy for our taste.

Up until this point, we had not been rinsing the rice before cooking. Rinsing rice removes some of the surface starch that otherwise absorbs water during cooking and causes grains to stick and taste gummy. We found that this step helped tremendously. To further guarantee evenly cooked rice, we stirred the rice thoroughly yet gently a couple of times throughout cooking to keep the grains from becoming stuck in colder places in the pot. The next batch was perfect: substantial without being pasty, and fluffy enough to maintain its presence amid the rich pork and sauce.

True to its Mexican roots, tinga is always served with a wide range of garnishes. We wanted to keep this dish simple, so we looked more closely at which garnishes were essential. To cut the pork's richness, we liked adding fresh cilantro and lime juice. These provided brightness as well as unmistakable Mexican character. We also added sliced scallions to the mix for clean, subtle onion flavor. Tasters also liked queso fresco, diced avocado, and sour cream, but we leave the choice up to you. No matter what it's garnished with, sweet and spicy pork tinga is sure to be a hit.

Spicy Pork Tinga

SERVES 2

Be sure to stir the rice gently when cooking in steps 5 and 6; aggressive stirring will make the rice turn gluey. The saucepan should measure 8 to 10 inches in diameter; smaller or larger saucepans will yield inconsistently cooked rice. Serve with crumbled queso fresco, diced avocado, and sour cream.

12	ounces boneless country-style pork ribs, trimmed and cut into 1-inch pieces
	Salt and pepper
1	tablespoon olive oil
1	onion, minced
3	garlic cloves, minced
2	teaspoons minced chipotle chile in adobo sauce
1	teaspoon minced fresh oregano or ¼ teaspoon dried
½	teaspoon minced fresh thyme or ⅛ teaspoon dried
1	cup low-sodium chicken broth
1	(8-ounce) can tomato sauce
¾	cup long-grain white rice, rinsed (see page 118)
⅓	cup minced fresh cilantro
3	scallions, sliced thin
1½	teaspoons fresh lime juice

1. Adjust oven rack to lower-middle position and heat oven to 300 degrees. Pat pork dry with paper towels and season with salt and pepper. Heat oil in medium saucepan over medium-high heat until just smoking. Brown pork on all sides, 7 to 10 minutes; transfer to plate.

2. Add onion to fat left in pan and cook over medium heat until softened, about 5 minutes. Stir in garlic, chipotles, oregano, and thyme and cook until fragrant, about 30 seconds. Stir in broth and tomato sauce, scraping up any browned bits.

3. Return browned pork, with any accumulated juice, to pan and bring to simmer. Cover, transfer pot to oven, and cook until dinner fork slips easily in and out of pork, 75 to 90 minutes.

4. Remove pot from oven and increase oven temperature to 350 degrees. Let braising liquid settle for 5 minutes, then remove as much fat as possible from surface using large spoon.

5. Return pot to simmer over medium heat and stir in rice until evenly combined. Cover, return pot to oven, and continue to cook until rice is tender and liquid has been absorbed, 20 to 30 minutes, gently stirring rice from bottom of pot to top every 10 minutes.

6. Stir in cilantro, scallions, and lime juice. Season with salt and pepper to taste. Cover and let stand for 5 minutes before serving.

BRAZILIAN-STYLE BLACK BEAN AND PORK STEW

FEIJOADA, ONE OF BRAZIL'S MOST POPULAR DISHES, is a hearty stew featuring creamy black beans and smoky, tender pork. Conventional recipes for this dish serve eight or more, but we wanted to scale down the yield for two, while still preserving its bold, potent flavors. We thought a loose interpretation of this popular Brazilian dish had the makings of a hearty but not ho-hum stew for two.

Traditionally, feijoada is made with dried black beans and a variety of pork products. We wanted to streamline the hours-long process of making this stew, so we decided to turn to canned black beans. While we generally prefer dried beans to canned, we opted to go with the more convenient canned beans here since the stew would derive a good amount of flavor from the other components—namely, a hefty amount of aromatics and the ultimate flavor enhancer, pork. One 15-ounce can of black beans made a good base for a stew serving two.

Beans in hand, we considered the pork. Recipes for authentic feijoada use any number of pork products, including bacon, spareribs, pork loins, sausages, ham hocks, and salt pork. We wanted to choose a couple of the most flavorful pork products that nodded at the authentic dish, but that could be found easily and required little preparation before being added to the pot. We settled on sausage and ribs. For the sausage, we chose linguiça, which has a smoky flavor and is included in most traditional recipes. For the ribs, we selected bone-in country-style ribs. Unlike spareribs, which are sold in a whole rack weighing 3 pounds or more, country-style ribs can be purchased individually. For our scaled-down feijoada, 4 ounces of sausage and two 6-ounce ribs seemed like the right amount of meat. Cutting the sausage into ½-inch pieces ensured that it would be interspersed throughout the stew. We left the rib meat on the bones so that the bones could add flavor during simmering.

Our stew wouldn't have hours on the stovetop to simmer, so we looked for other ways to develop rich, deep flavor. Although not a traditional step in feijoada recipes, we started our stew by browning the ribs. In addition to giving the pork a nice, dark crust, this step produced flavorful browned bits, called fond, in the pan. When the garlic and onion mingled with the fond during their sauté, the flavor deepened exponentially. For more vegetal, spicy, and sweet notes, we added a bell pepper, jalapeño, and tomato to the pan.

After the aromatics and vegetables had softened, we stirred the beans, sausage, and cooking liquid into the pot. A combination of water and chicken broth provided the right mix of flavor—now the broth wasn't too chicken-y, nor was it too salty. Finally, we nestled the browned ribs in the broth and covered the pan so that the ribs would gently braise, ensuring moist, tender meat. After about 45 minutes of simmering, we cut the rib meat off the bones into bite-size pieces before tossing them back into the pan.

At this point, tasters were impressed by the flavor of the stew but thought it was too thin and didn't have that stick-to-your-bones consistency so typical of stews. Two steps helped thicken the broth and give it body. First, we added a bit of flour to the pot with the aromatics. Second, we mashed some of the beans against the side of the pan when we pulled the ribs out. Now we had a proper stew, with a thick, creamy, and flavorful broth.

Traditional feijoada recipes include one last touch that we agreed was necessary—a salsa, to dollop on individual portions of stew. The salsa adds a fresh, bright contrast to the rich stew. Because this salsa uses many of the same ingredients that we had used already—bell pepper, tomato, onion, and jalapeño—we simply prepared one set of ingredients and set some aside for the salsa before we started cooking. Tossed with cilantro, olive oil, and white wine vinegar, this distinct salsa had a fresh pungency that played perfectly against the deep, rich flavor of the beans and pork.

Brazilian-Style Black Bean and Pork Stew

SERVES 2

To make this dish spicier, add the chile seeds. Serve with Simple White Rice (page 26).

- 1 small green bell pepper, stemmed, seeded, and chopped fine
- 1 small ripe tomato (about 4 ounces), cored, seeded, and chopped fine
- 1 small onion, minced
- 1 jalapeño chile, stemmed, seeded, and minced (see note)
- 2 tablespoons olive oil
- 1 tablespoon white wine vinegar
- 1 tablespoon minced fresh cilantro
  Salt and pepper
- 2 (6-ounce) bone-in country-style pork ribs, trimmed
- 2 garlic cloves, minced
- 1 tablespoon all-purpose flour
- 1 (15-ounce) can black beans, drained and rinsed
- 4 ounces linguiça sausage, cut into ½-inch pieces
- ¾ cup water
- ½ cup low-sodium chicken broth
- 1 bay leaf

1. Combine 2 tablespoons bell pepper, 2 tablespoons tomato, 2 tablespoons onion, 1 tablespoon jalapeño, 1 teaspoon oil, vinegar, cilantro, ⅛ teaspoon salt, and pinch pepper in small bowl; set aside.

2. Pat pork dry with paper towels and season with salt and pepper. Heat 2 teaspoons more oil in medium saucepan over medium-high heat until just smoking. Brown pork on both sides, about 4 minutes per side; transfer to plate.

3. Add remaining 1 tablespoon oil to pan and heat over medium heat until shimmering. Add remaining bell pepper, remaining onion, and remaining jalapeño and cook until softened, about 5 minutes. Stir in garlic and remaining tomato and cook until fragrant, about 30 seconds. Stir in flour and cook for 30 seconds. Stir in beans, sausage, water, broth, and bay leaf, scraping up any browned bits.

4. Nestle ribs, with any accumulated juice, into pan and bring to simmer. Reduce heat to low, cover, and continue to simmer until ribs are tender, about 45 minutes.

5. Transfer pork to cutting board. Remove and discard bay leaf. Using back of wooden spoon, mash some of beans against side of pan. Slice pork off bones and cut into ¾-inch pieces, discarding bones. Stir pork into stew and return to brief simmer to reheat pork and thicken sauce if necessary, 1 to 3 minutes. Serve, passing salsa separately.

INDIVIDUAL CHICKEN POT PIES

FEW DISHES CAN WHET THE APPETITE LIKE CHICKEN pot pie. Those three little words conjure up images of flaky, buttery crust set atop moist chicken bathed in a rich, creamy sauce and surrounded by tender peas and carrots. But traditional pot pie recipes take a good chunk of time to prepare and serve 6, 8, or even 10 people. Since even the best crusts turn soggy by the next morning, these pies hardly make for great leftovers. We had our hearts set on a for-two pot pie that still offered the same tender, juicy chicken, flavorful vegetables, and rich sauce as the original crowd-pleaser, but was streamlined and wouldn't serve a small army.

Because we'd set our sights on a pot pie that served two, what if we made two (small) pot pies? We examined potential baking vessels, such as small gratin dishes, small pie plates, and various sizes of ramekins, and eventually selected two 12-ounce ramekins, which would provide enough depth to hold a good amount of filling and a generous surface area for plenty of crust on top. Most important, it seemed as if they would hold the right amount of pot pie for two hungry diners; the other vessels we'd considered looked as if they'd feed either two small children or two linebackers.

Next, we settled on strategy. Instead of fiddling with multiple pots on the stovetop, we knew that we wanted

to keep things simple and prepare our sauce, sauté our vegetables, and cook our chicken using just one pan. With our ramekins in hand, we got started.

Our choice of vegetables was easy: The classic combination of carrots and peas was what we wanted. Since frozen peas are processed at the height of ripeness and so offer as much sweetness and flavor as fresh peas, we opted to go with the more convenient of the two. Frozen peas need little cooking time, so we could stir them into the sauce, still frozen, just before baking our pot pies. Two carrots balanced out the peas. We sautéed them in butter with minced onion and celery to jump-start their cooking and provide a flavorful, aromatic base to our sauce. Tasters were pleased with the choice of vegetables, but we decided to consider a few other vegetables as well. Potatoes were simply too bulky for the ramekins and took up too much space. Cauliflower and broccoli became mushy when the pies were cooked, unless we took the extra step of browning them separately—a step we didn't want to add to our streamlined pot pies. Green bell peppers tasted too vegetal in the filling, but red bell peppers provided good texture and color. Because they took up a decent amount of space in the ramekins, we decided to save them for a variation.

Moving on to the sauce, we had a hunch that a traditional butter-and-flour roux, enhanced with chicken broth and enriched by heavy cream, would offer loads of flavor in a short amount of time. The problem was that we had little idea how much sauce we needed. Thinking that a dry pot pie would be far worse than a soupy one, we began our testing with a generous amount of sauce. Even though it looked creamy in the pot, once we added and cooked the chicken, its liquid turned our sauce into a runny mess that bubbled out of our ramekins. For the next test, we kept the liquid amounts intact but increased the amount of flour. We added the chicken and cooked the two pot pies and, not surprisingly, had the opposite problem on our hands— our pie fillings, instead of being coated in a silky sauce, were dry and surrounded by a chicken-flavored paste. Searching for a happy medium, we found that a sauce containing a moderate amount of flour (3 tablespoons) and reduced on the stove to 2 cups—a single cup per ramekin—gave us the right amount of sauce with a perfectly velvety texture.

Now that we had the beginnings of a tasty sauce, we moved on to the chicken, which we planned to poach

CLASSIC CHICKEN POT PIES

right in the sauce. We considered a variety of options but settled on boneless, skinless breasts since they cook quickly and need no preparation. The problem now was determining the right amount of meat. After making several pies with our standard two-person portion of 12 ounces of breast meat, we found that not only were our ramekins way too full, but they were also overwhelmed by the chicken. Cutting back to 8 ounces of meat remedied the problem while still providing a filling dinner for two when combined with the vegetables, topping, and rich sauce.

At this point, the flavor of the sauce was clean and nicely chicken-y, but without the benefit of the fond from browning the chicken (which we were simply poaching), it lacked savory depth. Some garlic, thyme, and parsley added flavor, but it was a bit of soy sauce, which the test kitchen often deploys to instill dishes with deep, meaty flavor, that gave our sauce complexity and made it taste as if it had been simmering all day.

For the topping, we knew that we wanted to stick with a traditional flaky, buttery pie crust. Anything else (some recipes call for biscuit or puff pastry topping)

NOTES FROM THE TEST KITCHEN

MAKING POT PIE DOUGH FOR TWO

1. After rolling out the dough to a 12-inch round on a sheet of parchment paper, use a ramekin as a guide to cut out two smaller rounds of dough that are ½ inch larger than the mouth of the ramekin.

2. Fold the outer ½-inch rim of dough of each round underneath and crimp the folded edge of dough to make an attractive fluted rim.

3. Using a paring knife, cut three oval-shaped vents, each about 1 inch long, in the center of each dough round. Slide the parchment paper onto a rimmed baking sheet, then parbake the dough for 10 to 12 minutes.

4. Gently lay each parbaked pie crust on top of the hot filling in each ramekin before baking the pot pies.

HAND MIXING PIE DOUGH

If you don't own a food processor, you can mix pie dough by hand. Freeze the butter in its stick form until very firm. Whisk together the flour and salt in a large bowl. Add the chilled shortening and press it into the flour using a fork. Grate the frozen butter on the large holes of a box grater into the flour mixture, then cut the mixture together, using two butter knives, until the mixture resembles coarse crumbs. Add the water as directed.

THE BEST STORE-BOUGHT PIE DOUGH

A flaky, buttery homemade pie crust is the ultimate crown for chicken pot pie, but it's also a fair amount of work. How much would we sacrifice by using a store-bought crust instead? To find out, we tried several types and brands, including both dry mixes (just add water) and ready-made crusts, either frozen or refrigerated. The dry mixes had flavor issues (they were either overly salty or overly sweet), and all required both mixing and rolling—not much work saved. The frozen crusts required zero prep work, but tasters found them pasty and bland, and they were impossible to pry from the flimsy foil "pie plate" in which they are sold. The one refrigerated contender, **Pillsbury Pie Crusts**, wasn't bad. Though the flavor was somewhat bland, the crust baked up to an impressive flakiness.

seemed to be missing the point. We scaled down our traditional pie dough recipe, which uses a combination of butter and shortening for both flavor and tenderness. After rolling out the dough, we trimmed it to fit our ramekins, fluted the edges, and cut a few decorative vents to let out the steam. We placed our crusts on top of the hot filling right before sticking the ramekins in the oven to cook. After 20 minutes, the pies smelled great and our hopes were high. However, much to our disappointment, the crusts had sunk into the baking dishes and turned soggy.

We played around with the cooking times and oven temperatures but eventually found that the most foolproof route to crispy pastry was to give the crusts a head start on their own. Parbaking the crusts on a baking sheet for about 10 minutes ensured that they stayed crisp on top of the filling, and a second spell in the oven on top of the pies melded the crust to the rest of the components. With this final adjustment, our pot pies emerged from the oven looking attractively golden with an aroma that was just as enticing.

For variety's sake, we also came up with two new takes on the classic pot pie. For a Southwestern twist, we added red bell pepper, corn, and a little chili powder to the rich, creamy filling. And to create an exotic, Indian-inspired supper, we added curry powder and cilantro to two more individual pot pies.

Classic Chicken Pot Pies

SERVES 2

We prefer the buttery flavor and flaky texture of homemade pie dough here; however, you can substitute store-bought pie dough if desired. If using store-bought pie dough, parbake the crusts for only 7 minutes in step 2. You will need two ovenproof 12-ounce ramekins or bowls for this recipe (see page 3).

- 1 recipe Savory Pie Dough (recipe follows; see note)
- 2 tablespoons unsalted butter
- 2 carrots, peeled and sliced ¼ inch thick
- 1 small onion, minced
- 1 small celery rib, sliced ¼ inch thick
  Salt and pepper
- 3 garlic cloves, minced
- 1 teaspoon minced fresh thyme or ¼ teaspoon dried

- ¼ teaspoon soy sauce
- 3 tablespoons unbleached all-purpose flour
- 1¾ cups low-sodium chicken broth
- ⅓ cup heavy cream
- 1 (8-ounce) boneless, skinless chicken breast, trimmed
- ¼ cup frozen peas
- 2 teaspoons minced fresh parsley
- ¼ teaspoon fresh lemon juice

1. Adjust oven rack to middle position and heat oven to 450 degrees.

2. Roll out dough on parchment paper to 12-inch round, about ¼ inch thick. Following photos on page 60, use ovenproof 12-ounce ramekin as guide to cut out two rounds of dough, about ½ inch larger than mouth of ramekin. Fold under and crimp outer ½ inch of dough, then cut 3 oval-shaped vents in center of each crust. Slide parchment paper with crusts onto rimmed baking sheet and bake until crusts just begin to brown and no longer look raw, 10 to 12 minutes; set aside.

3. Meanwhile, melt butter in medium saucepan over medium heat. Add carrots, onion, celery, and ½ teaspoon salt and cook until vegetables are softened and browned, 8 to 10 minutes. Stir in garlic, thyme, and soy sauce and cook until fragrant, about 30 seconds. Stir in flour and cook for 1 minute.

4. Slowly whisk in broth and cream, scraping up any browned bits. Nestle chicken into sauce and bring to simmer. Cover, reduce heat to medium-low, and cook until chicken registers 160 to 165 degrees on instant-read thermometer, 10 to 15 minutes. Transfer chicken to plate, let cool slightly, then shred into bite-size pieces following photo on page 71.

5. Meanwhile, return pan with sauce to medium heat and simmer until thickened and sauce measures 2 cups, about 5 minutes. Off heat, return shredded chicken, with any accumulated juice, to pan. Stir in peas, parsley, and lemon juice and season with salt and pepper to taste.

6. Divide filling between ramekins and place parbaked crusts on top of filling. Place pot pies on aluminum foil–lined baking sheet and bake until crusts are deep golden brown and filling is bubbling, 10 to 15 minutes. Let pot pies cool for 10 minutes before serving.

Chicken Pot Pies with Bell Pepper and Corn

Follow recipe for Classic Chicken Pot Pies, reducing number of carrots to 1. Substitute 1 red bell pepper, stemmed, seeded, and cut into ½-inch pieces, for celery. Add 1 teaspoon chili powder to pan with garlic. Substitute ¼ cup frozen corn for peas and 2 teaspoons chopped fresh basil for parsley.

Chicken Curry Pot Pies

Follow recipe for Classic Chicken Pot Pies, omitting thyme and peas. Add 1 teaspoon curry powder to pan with garlic. Substitute 2 teaspoons minced fresh cilantro for parsley.

Savory Pie Dough

MAKES ENOUGH FOR 2 INDIVIDUAL POT PIES

If you don't have a food processor, see the hand-mixing instructions on page 60.

- 1   cup (5 ounces) unbleached all-purpose flour
- ½   teaspoon salt
- 2   tablespoons vegetable shortening, cut into ½-inch pieces and chilled
- 4   tablespoons (½ stick) unsalted butter, cut into ¼-inch pieces and chilled
- 3–5 tablespoons ice water

1. Process flour and salt together in food processor until combined. Scatter shortening over top and process until mixture resembles coarse cornmeal, about 10 seconds. Scatter butter pieces over top and pulse until mixture resembles coarse crumbs, about 10 pulses. Transfer mixture to medium bowl.

2. Sprinkle 3 tablespoons water over mixture. Using stiff rubber spatula, stir and press dough until it sticks together. If dough does not come together, stir in remaining water, 1 tablespoon at a time, until it does.

3. Turn out dough onto counter. Shape into ball and flatten to 5-inch disk; wrap in plastic wrap and refrigerate for 1 hour. Before rolling out dough, let sit on counter to soften slightly, about 10 minutes. (Dough can be refrigerated for up to 2 days or frozen for up to 1 month. If frozen, let thaw completely on counter before rolling out.)

ROASTED CHICKEN BREASTS WITH VEGETABLES

ROASTED BONE-IN, SKIN-ON CHICKEN BREASTS CAN make for the ultimate elegant yet simple main course, especially when the meat is moist, tender, and well seasoned and the skin is crisp and golden brown. But the simplest dishes can also be the hardest to get right—dry, chalky meat and rubbery skin are all too often the norm. Most recipes try to cover up the bland, dry meat with too many herbs and spices. Others focus on getting the skin crisp, but at the expense of overdone meat below. Our goal was to create a recipe for simple roasted chicken breasts that would yield perfectly cooked meat and crispy skin, matched by a pile of hearty, well-seasoned root vegetables, for a stellar yet satisfying one-dish meal.

We started our testing by simply roasting two bone-in, skin-on chicken breasts (which are often conveniently packaged in pairs) in the oven at a range of heat levels, from 350 degrees all the way up to 500 degrees. We were dismayed to find that the meat emerged bone-dry every time. The skin, however, was noticeably different after each test. The skin roasted at 350 degrees was rubbery; at 500 degrees, it was burnt. A relatively high heat, 450 degrees, resulted in fairly crispy skin. Although we were almost there when it came to the skin, we still had our work cut out for us when it came to the meat.

Taking a lesson from the holiday bird, we elevated the chicken breasts while they cooked; placing them on a wire rack set over a rimmed baking sheet allowed hot air to circulate more freely around the meat. This step, combined with separating the skin from the breast meat, rendered more fat and therefore produced slightly crisper skin. Now the color of the skin was on track, but a super-crispy texture remained elusive.

Up to this point, we had been rubbing olive oil on the skin, which helped with browning and crisping. Now we tried rubbing some oil under the skin as well. The results were even better. For our next test, we used butter under the skin instead of oil—this was the best skin yet. As an added bonus, the butter basted the breast meat as it cooked, helping to keep it juicy. We tried swapping out the oil for butter on top of the skin as well, but the cold skin caused the butter to seize up, making spreading difficult. We stuck with oil alone on top.

With the chicken meat tender and juicy, and the skin crisp at last, it was time to consider the vegetables. We liked the combination of potatoes, parsnips, and carrots, which offered up both sweet and earthy flavors. Placing the vegetables on a strip of foil next to the chicken breasts worked well, and a mixture of olive oil, garlic, and rosemary brought out their flavors nicely. After half an hour in the oven, dinner was ready, and we were about to pat ourselves on the back when we noticed smoke emanating from the oven.

The high temperature was causing the rendered chicken fat, as well as the oil and butter, to drip into the baking sheet below, where it burned and smoked up the kitchen. We were dismayed to see not only smoke, but also rich, meaty flavor dripping and burning off. That's when a colleague suggested putting the root vegetables beneath the chicken, so that they could absorb any fat that dripped down. To better accommodate the vegetables, we switched from a rimmed baking sheet to a 13 by 9-inch baking dish. The vegetables had plenty of room in the dish, and now they were deliciously flavored with the drippings from our tender, juicy, crisp-skinned chicken breasts.

NOTES FROM THE TEST KITCHEN

TRIMMING SPLIT CHICKEN BREASTS

Using kitchen shears, trim off the rib sections from each breast, following the vertical line of fat from the tapered end of the breast up to the socket where the wing was attached. Trimming the rib sections helps ensure even cooking.

HOW TO ROAST CHICKEN AND VEGETABLES

Lay the chicken, skin side up, on a wire rack and carefully place the wire rack over the dish of vegetables (the rack may overhang the dish slightly).

Roasted Chicken Breasts with Root Vegetables
SERVES 2

If using kosher chicken, do not brine. If brining the chicken, do not season with salt in step 2. We prefer to use extra-small red potatoes measuring less than 1 inch in diameter in this recipe, but you can substitute larger red potatoes, cut into ¾-inch chunks. If your parsnips and carrots are very thick, slice them in half lengthwise first to ensure even cooking.

- 8 ounces extra-small red potatoes (about 8), halved (see note)
- 2 carrots, peeled and cut into 1-inch chunks (see note)
- 2 parsnips, peeled and cut into 1-inch chunks (see note)
- 1 shallot, peeled and quartered
- 4 garlic cloves, peeled
- 2 tablespoons olive oil
- 1 teaspoon minced fresh rosemary or ½ teaspoon dried
  Salt and pepper
- 2 (12-ounce) bone-in, skin-on split chicken breasts, trimmed (see photo), brined if desired (see note; see page 18)
- 2 tablespoons unsalted butter, cut into 2 pieces and softened
  Lemon wedges, for serving

1. Adjust oven rack to middle position and heat oven to 450 degrees. Toss potatoes, carrots, parsnips, shallot, garlic, 1 tablespoon oil, rosemary, ½ teaspoon salt, and ½ teaspoon pepper together in large bowl. Spread vegetables in 13 by 9-inch baking dish.

2. Pat chicken dry with paper towels and gently loosen center portion of skin covering each breast. Using spoon, place 1 piece of butter underneath skin of each breast, then gently press skin to spread out butter. Brush with remaining 1 tablespoon oil and season with salt and pepper.

3. Following photo, lay chicken, skin side up, on wire rack and carefully place over dish of vegetables (rack may overhang dish slightly). Roast until chicken registers 160 to 165 degrees on instant-read thermometer and vegetables are golden brown and tender, 25 to 35 minutes.

4. Transfer chicken to serving platter and let rest for 5 minutes. Season vegetables with salt and pepper to taste and transfer to platter. Serve with lemon wedges.

Roasted Chicken Breasts with Red Potatoes and Brussels Sprouts

When buying Brussels sprouts, choose those with small, tight heads, no more than 1½ inches in diameter. Be careful not to cut too much off the stem end when trimming the sprouts or the leaves will fall away from the core.

Follow recipe for Roasted Chicken Breasts with Root Vegetables, substituting 6 ounces small Brussels sprouts, stem ends trimmed, discolored leaves removed, and halved through stems, for carrots and parsnips. Substitute 1 teaspoon minced fresh thyme or ½ teaspoon dried for rosemary.

"UN-STUFFED" CHICKEN BREASTS WITH BROCCOLI

WHILE STUFFING CHICKEN BREASTS IS AN EASY WAY to gussy up the average weeknight dinner, we wanted a more streamlined approach so we could spend a few minutes preparing a simple side dish. Enter "un-stuffed" chicken breasts—instead of cutting the breasts open and stuffing them with filling, we would reverse the process and place the "stuffing" on top. To accomplish this we needed a crispy, appealing top coating (without the fuss of breading and frying) as well as a few super-flavorful ingredients to layer underneath. And since we hoped to turn our streamlined dish into a complete meal without using multiple pans, we needed to find a vegetable that would cook in about the same amount of time as the chicken.

We first turned our attention to the flavorful layers. Taking a cue from Italian cuisine, we decided to incorporate the defining ingredients of saltimbocca—prosciutto and sage, which combine to form a sharp, salty, slightly woodsy flavor profile. Although not traditional in saltimbocca, provolone, which is mild, tangy, and salty, seemed as if it would play well with these two ingredients.

To make our topping, we brushed our chicken breasts with mayonnaise (for a creamy layer that would also act as an adhesive), then added layers of cheese and prosciutto before sprinkling on some minced sage. We immediately liked the prosciutto and mayonnaise, but the cheese and sage required a few tweaks. At first, we tried using slices of provolone, but they tended to slide off the chicken; shredded cheese stayed in place. We had the same issue with the sage—the small pieces flew off the chicken quite easily. To get it to stay in place, we made it one of the layers and sprinkled it over the mayonnaise before placing the cheese and prosciutto.

Moving on to the crispy coating, we found crushed Ritz crackers to be perfect. Their buttery flavor and crunch added the taste (and visual appeal) of a breaded and fried stuffed chicken breast. We mounded the crushed cracker crumbs on top and pressed down to help them stick.

It was easiest to arrange the breasts on the sheet pan before topping them. We found that if we nestled the breasts side by side in the center of a baking sheet (alternating their orientation, thicker end to thinner end), we made the least mess, ensured that the toppings stayed put, and kept the chicken from overcooking. As an added bonus, this method also left plenty of space for our side dish.

We thought that broccoli would be a good match for our prosciutto-topped chicken breasts. Broccoli stands up well to roasting, and the high heat we were using

NOTES FROM THE TEST KITCHEN

PREPARING A BROCCOLI CROWN FOR ROASTING

1. After cutting off the stalk and setting it aside (do not discard), place the head upside down, then cut it in half through the central stalk.

2. Lay each half on its cut side. For each half, if it is 3 to 4 inches in diameter, cut it into 3 or 4 wedges, or into 6 wedges if 4 to 5 inches in diameter.

to cook the chicken was just right for caramelizing the natural sugars in the broccoli and concentrating its flavor. Contact with the hot pan is the key to browning, so we made sure to cut the broccoli in a way that would maximize its surface area. Starting with half a bunch of broccoli (just enough to serve two), we cut the head into uniform wedges that held the florets together. Turning our attention to the stalk, we sliced off the tough exterior, then we cut the stalk into long ½-inch-thick pieces to help promote even cooking. We tossed the broccoli with olive oil, salt, pepper, and a little sugar to encourage further browning before spreading it out in a single layer around the chicken.

By the time the chicken had reached 160 degrees and was ready to come out of the oven (about 20 minutes later), the broccoli looked nicely roasted; unfortunately, it had totally dried out. As it turns out, we had spread our small amount of broccoli far too thin on the baking sheet, so the broccoli rapidly lost its moisture and shriveled up. We knew that we didn't want to have to pull the broccoli out of the oven before the chicken was finished, but we sure didn't want to desiccate it. We decided, then, to start the chicken cooking by itself and add the broccoli partway through. Not only would this step reduce the roasting time for the broccoli, it would also preheat the pan, thereby jump-starting the roasting process, so the broccoli cooked through and browned before drying out.

After fiddling with the timing, we found that giving the chicken a six-minute head start before adding the broccoli gave us blistered, bubbled, and browned stalk pieces that were sweet and full-flavored, along with crispy-tipped crowns that tasted even better. We also found that spreading the broccoli evenly around the chicken breasts, and not just on one side of the pan, allowed more chicken (and its flavor) to intermingle with the broccoli for an overall better-tasting dish.

USE IT UP: BROCCOLI

Broccoli with Brown Butter, Parmesan, and Walnuts
SERVES 2

This simple side dish goes well with fish and poultry.

- 2 tablespoons unsalted butter
- 2 tablespoons walnuts, chopped coarse
- ½ bunch broccoli (about 12 ounces), florets cut into 1-inch pieces, stalks trimmed and sliced ¼ inch thick
  Salt and pepper
- 2 tablespoons grated Parmesan cheese

1. Microwave butter in microwave-safe bowl until melted, about 1 minute. Add nuts and continue to microwave until butter is well browned and walnuts are toasted, 2 to 3 minutes longer.

2. Meanwhile, bring 2 quarts water to boil in large saucepan. Add broccoli and 2 teaspoons salt and cook until just tender, about 2 minutes. Drain broccoli, pat dry with paper towels, and transfer to bowl. Toss broccoli with butter-nut mixture and Parmesan and season with salt and pepper to taste. Serve.

Prosciutto and Sage "Un-Stuffed" Chicken Breasts with Roasted Broccoli
SERVES 2

Nestle the chicken breasts close together on the baking sheet and place thicker end to thinner end so that they fit together nicely; this helps the toppings stay in place and prevents the chicken from overcooking. Be sure to season the chicken lightly before cooking; the cheese and prosciutto are already salty.

- 2 (6-ounce) boneless, skinless chicken breasts, trimmed
  Salt and pepper
- 1 tablespoon mayonnaise
- 1½ teaspoons minced fresh sage
- 4 thin slices prosciutto (about 3 ounces)
- 2 ounces sharp provolone cheese, shredded (about ½ cup)
- 7 Ritz crackers, crushed (about ⅓ cup)
- ½ bunch broccoli (about 12 ounces), crown and stalk separated, crown cut into large wedges (see page 64), stalk trimmed and sliced into ½-inch-thick planks about 3 inches long
- 2 tablespoons olive oil
- ¼ teaspoon sugar
  Lemon wedges, for serving

CHICKEN BOUILLABAISSE

1. Adjust oven rack to lower-middle position and heat oven to 475 degrees.

2. Pat chicken dry with paper towels and season with salt and pepper. Arrange chicken breasts side by side, thicker end to thinner end, in center of rimmed baking sheet. Spread mayonnaise on chicken, sprinkle sage on top, and top each breast with 2 slices prosciutto, tucking ends under chicken. Top each breast with ¼ cup cheese, sprinkle cracker crumbs over cheese, and press on crumbs to adhere. Bake chicken for 6 minutes.

3. Meanwhile, toss broccoli with oil and sugar and season with salt and pepper. Remove pan from oven and, working quickly, carefully lay broccoli, cut side down, in even layer on baking sheet around chicken.

4. Return pan to oven and bake until chicken registers 160 to 165 degrees on instant-read thermometer and broccoli is well browned and tender, 12 to 15 minutes. Let chicken and broccoli rest on baking sheet for 5 minutes. Serve with lemon wedges.

CHICKEN BOUILLABAISSE

THE LAND-LOVING TAKE ON A CLASSIC FRENCH seafood stew, chicken bouillabaisse, boasts a medley of Provençal flavors. The typical ingredient list includes various cuts of chicken, tomatoes, potatoes, leeks, fennel, onions, wine, garlic, saffron, and other aromatics. Bowls of the potently flavored stew are garnished with croutons and a rich rouille (a spicy, garlicky, bread-thickened mayonnaise) for textural contrast and a final bright burst of flavor. We liked all of these components and decided that chicken bouillabaisse shouldn't be written off the menu just because we were cooking for two. We decided to keep all the bold, rich flavors intact but to simplify the process by making a streamlined bouillabaisse.

Our stew base started with fennel, leeks, an onion, and a whole mess of garlic sautéed in olive oil. But since all of these aromatics turn sweet the longer they cook, the final stew was cloying. We knew to leave the fennel in place: It provided the anise backbone that is essential to bouillabaisse. When it came to cutting ingredients, garlic was a better candidate. The original recipe called for using a whole head of garlic in a recipe serving just four people, and even using half of a head seemed extreme for two servings. By cutting the amount down to a mere two cloves—sautéed briefly only after the other vegetables had softened—we were able to retain garlicky flavor while dialing back on sweetness. We also found that a single leek had enough of a presence on its own, and we were able to cut out the onion altogether.

With the aromatics settled, we tackled the sauce. Since we had already developed a strong aromatic background, we found that pantry-friendly store-bought chicken broth worked well as a stand-in for homemade chicken broth. To give the broth a little more body and a long-simmered taste, we added flour and tomato paste, along with the saffron, to our sautéed aromatics before adding the broth. For even greater depth and to keep in line with our Provençal flavor profile, we added a strip of orange zest to the sauce. A single ripe tomato added freshness, and small amounts of white wine and the French anise-flavored liqueur pastis served to echo the licorice essence of the fennel and add brightness.

While our sauce was well on its way to being full-flavored and balanced, we had a huge lingering problem: the chicken. Standard recipes called for 3 or more pounds of chicken pieces. To bring the chicken down to a manageable amount, we were faced with a choice between breast meat and thigh meat. After a few tests, we determined that the breasts were too bulky and took up too much room in our 10-inch skillet, plus they dried out quickly during the simmering time. Four thighs, on the other hand, yielded just the right amount of meat, fit well in our pan, and stayed moist and tender. To cook the thighs, we simply browned them in our pan, leaving behind flavorful browned bits upon which to build the sauce, then set them aside while we made the sauce. When the sauce was ready, we added the thighs back to the pan and simmered them until the meat was tender. We thought we were on the road to success until we noticed that the chicken skin that was submerged under the sauce was now unpleasantly flabby.

In an effort to keep the chicken skin crisp, we needed to find a way to bulk up the sauce to keep the skin afloat. We had yet to add the potatoes to the mix, so we took this opportunity to stir them in. After 15 minutes in the sauce, the potatoes were tender and flavorful, and they provided just enough heft to prop up our chicken so that the skin was positioned above the sauce. Yet even though our chicken cooked up with a nicely browned exterior, the skin was anything but crisp.

After taking a closer look, we realized that the steam rising from the simmering liquid was soaking the skin. Maybe the fix was as easy as switching from the stovetop to the oven, where the heat from above could keep moisture from condensing on the chicken. This was a giant step forward, but it wasn't forward enough. What if we placed the pan under the broiler just before serving? That did it: The intense blast of heat recrisped the skin in no time.

The crowning components of bouillabaisse are croutons topped with a decadent, savory rouille. To brighten the creamy base of the rouille, we added lemon juice and Dijon mustard; to maximize the flavor of the saffron while keeping the amount modest, we steeped the saffron in hot water. For the croutons, we simply drizzled a few slices of baguette with flavorful extra-virgin olive oil and sprinkled them with salt and pepper.

While not a daylong labor of love, our chicken bouillabaisse, with its crisp-skinned chicken, tender potatoes, and sweetly anise-y sauce, certainly tasted like it was.

NOTES FROM THE TEST KITCHEN

STORING LEFTOVER BAGUETTES

The rouille and croutons for our Chicken Bouillabaisse use several slices of baguette, but that leaves a good hunk of bread left over. We wanted to find the best way to store leftover sliced bakery bread and baguettes to keep the exterior crisp and the interior soft, so we grabbed a number of loaves and started cutting them in half. One loaf half was placed uncovered, cut side down, on the counter. A second loaf half was put in a paper bag and left on the counter, and a third was placed in a plastic bag and left on the counter. Finally, a fourth loaf half was wrapped in a plastic bag and refrigerated. It turns out that sometimes the easiest method works best—the loaf we kept uncovered, cut side down, on the counter had both the crispest crust and the softest interior after a day. The loaf wrapped in paper also kept its crisp crust but was slightly drier. The loaf stored in plastic on the countertop turned squishy, and the refrigerated loaf hardened and dried out. So if you're storing unused portions of crusty bread for just a day, store them cut side down on the countertop. If you need to store bread longer than that, store it in the freezer, wrapped in aluminum foil and sealed in a zipper-lock bag.

MAKING STRIPS OF ZEST

To remove long, wide strips of orange or lemon zest, we like to use a vegetable peeler. Try not to remove any of the white pith beneath the zest, as it is bitter.

Chicken Bouillabaisse

SERVES 2

Both the rouille and croutons can be made while the chicken bakes in the oven.

- 4 **(6-ounce) bone-in, skin-on chicken thighs, trimmed**
  Salt and pepper
- 1 **tablespoon olive oil**
- 1 **leek, white and light green parts only, halved lengthwise, sliced thin, and rinsed thoroughly (see page 186)**
- 1 **fennel bulb (about 12 ounces), trimmed of stalks, cored, and sliced thin (see page 92)**
- 2 **garlic cloves, minced**
- 1½ **teaspoons unbleached all-purpose flour**
- 1½ **teaspoons tomato paste**
- ⅛ **teaspoon saffron threads, crumbled**
- 1 **small Yukon Gold potato (about 6 ounces), cut into ¾-inch cubes**
- 1 **tomato, cored and chopped coarse**
- 1½ **cups low-sodium chicken broth**
- ¼ **cup dry white wine**
- 2 **tablespoons pastis or Pernod**
- 1 **(1½-inch) strip zest from 1 orange (see photo)**
- 1 **tablespoon minced fresh tarragon or parsley**
- 1 **recipe Croutons (recipe follows)**
- 1 **recipe Rouille (recipe follows)**

1. Adjust oven rack to middle position and heat oven to 375 degrees. Pat chicken dry with paper towels and season with salt and pepper. Heat oil in 10-inch oven-safe skillet over medium-high heat until just smoking. Brown chicken on both sides, about 5 minutes per side; transfer to plate.

2. Add leek and fennel to fat left in pan and cook over medium heat until softened, 5 to 7 minutes. Stir in garlic, flour, tomato paste, and saffron and cook until fragrant, about 30 seconds. Stir in potato, tomato, broth, wine, pastis, and orange zest and bring to simmer. Reduce heat to medium-low and simmer for 15 minutes.

3. Nestle chicken pieces, with any accumulated juice, skin side up, in pan, keeping skin above surface of liquid. Transfer skillet to oven and bake until thighs register 160 degrees on instant-read thermometer, 10 to 20 minutes.

4. Remove skillet from oven and heat broiler. Broil until chicken skin is crisp and thighs register 175 degrees on instant-read thermometer, 5 to 10 minutes.

5. Transfer chicken to plate and tent loosely with foil. Let braising liquid settle for 5 minutes, then remove as much fat as possible from surface using large spoon. Stir in tarragon and season with salt and pepper to taste. Divide bouillabaisse between two shallow bowls, place chicken on top, top with croutons and a dollop of rouille, and serve, passing extra rouille separately.

Croutons

MAKES 4 CROUTONS

The croutons can be toasted while the bouillabaisse is in the oven. For an attractive presentation, slice the bread on the bias. The croutons can be kept at room temperature for up to 4 hours before serving.

> 4 (¾-inch-thick) slices French baguette (see note)
> 1 tablespoon extra-virgin olive oil
> Salt and pepper

Adjust oven rack to lower-middle position and heat oven to 375 degrees. Arrange slices in single layer on rimmed baking sheet. Drizzle with olive oil and season with salt and pepper. Bake until light golden brown, 10 to 15 minutes.

Rouille

MAKES ABOUT ¾ CUP

The rouille can be made while the bouillabaisse is in the oven. Leftover rouille tastes great on sandwiches or as a sauce for fish or vegetables. The rouille can be refrigerated in an airtight container for up to 2 days.

> 2 tablespoons water
> ⅛ teaspoon saffron
> 3 (½-inch-thick) slices French baguette, crusts removed, torn into ½-inch pieces (about ¼ cup)
> 2 teaspoons fresh lemon juice
> 1 large egg yolk
> 1 small garlic clove, minced
> 1 teaspoon Dijon mustard
> ⅛ teaspoon cayenne pepper
> ¼ cup vegetable oil
> ¼ cup extra-virgin olive oil
> Salt and pepper

1. Microwave water and saffron in medium microwave-safe bowl until water is steaming, 10 to 20 seconds. Let sit for 5 minutes.

2. Stir in bread and lemon juice and let sit until liquid is absorbed, 3 to 5 minutes. Using whisk, mash bread mixture into uniform paste. Whisk in egg yolk, garlic, mustard, and cayenne until smooth.

3. Whisking constantly, slowly drizzle in vegetable oil until mixture has smooth mayonnaise-like consistency. Slowly whisk in olive oil. Season with salt and pepper to taste.

CHICKEN AND RICE DINNERS

CHICKEN AND RICE, IN ITS MANY FORMS, APPEARS on dinner tables the world over—and for good reason. When this classic one-pot preparation is done well, it is a comforting mélange of tender, juicy chicken and richly flavored, fluffy rice. And when vegetables are included, it quickly becomes a satisfying all-in-one meal. Unfortunately, this seemingly simple dish often suffers from poor execution with subpar rice and dried-out chicken. On top of these problems, the dish is usually prepared in vast, potluck-size amounts—hardly ideal when you want an easy dinner for two. Resolved to right the many wrongs perpetrated against this dish, we set about developing a scaled-down, foolproof method that would deliver juicy chicken, flavorful vegetables, and tender rice, every time.

First, we tackled the chicken. Chicken and rice typically falls into one of two camps. The first features a mix of bone-in chicken pieces (often cut from a whole bird) served on top of rice; in the other, homier, version, shreds of chicken are mixed into the rice. While we have had good versions of both, we opted to prepare the latter, as the shredded meat readily absorbs flavors and produces a more cohesive dish. We knew that dark meat, with its substantial connective tissue and fat, would provide more flavor than breast meat. We chose to use flavorful bone-in, skin-on thighs and thought four thighs provided a good amount of meat for two diners.

We browned the chicken thighs in the pan, then set them aside so we could sauté the aromatics in the rendered fat. We added the meat back to the pan to cook with the rice. Then, after cooking the meat through, we removed and discarded the skin and bones, shredded the meat, and stirred it back into the rice. The fat rendered from the skin and the gelatin eked from the bones lent the rice bold chicken flavor that tasters loved. We did, however, learn to be aggressive with our trimming to keep the final dish from becoming too greasy. We also drained off most of the fat from the pan after browning the chicken to prevent further greasiness from leaching into the dish. Having established the chicken cooking method, we moved on to the rice.

After a few tests, we found that long-grain white rice produced the most cleanly flavored and nicely textured grains for our dish, and that the oven produced more evenly cooked grains than the stovetop. Also, stirring the rice intermittently prevented the grains from sticking to the chicken and vegetables. We found that a medium-size saucepan was the right pan to use.

To determine the right amount of rice to liquid, we first tested 1 cup of rice to 1½ cups of chicken broth (our standard ratio). We stirred the rice (and chicken and vegetables) gently every 10 minutes. Unfortunately, we ended up with crunchy rice. We scaled our rice amount way down, landing at ½ cup, and scaled our liquid amount down to ⅔ cup. While we liked the final sauciness of this test, we couldn't get past the fact that the rice was now gummy.

We knew that our stirring method was contributing to the gumminess problem—the act of stirring loosens starches on the surface of the rice, allowing them to mix with available liquid and thicken into a paste. We couldn't take away this stirring step because the rice would not cook evenly, but perhaps we could remove the starch before it became a problem. A quick adjustment—rinsing the rice—fixed the gumminess.

Finally, we wanted a classic pair of vegetables to go with our chicken and rice, and that meant peas and carrots. After a few tests, we found that ½-inch pieces of carrot cooked at the same rate as the rice, making them an easy addition. Once the rice was cooked, we stirred in ½ cup of frozen peas, along with lemon juice, lemon zest, and parsley for a big hit of freshness. We were so pleased with our foolproof chicken and rice dish that we created two internationally inspired variations, one with tomato, chipotle chiles, and olives, and another Indian-style dish with cardamom, cumin, and raisins.

Classic Chicken and Rice with Carrots and Peas
SERVES 2

To keep the dish from becoming greasy, remove excess fat from the chicken thighs and trim the skin. Be sure to stir the rice gently when cooking in step 4; aggressive stirring will make the rice turn gluey. The saucepan should measure 8 to 10 inches in diameter; smaller or larger pans will yield inconsistently cooked rice.

    4   (6-ounce) bone-in, skin-on chicken thighs, trimmed
        (see note)
        Salt and pepper
    1   teaspoon olive oil
    1   small onion, minced
    1   garlic clove, minced
    ¼   teaspoon minced fresh thyme or pinch dried
    ⅔   cup low-sodium chicken broth
    ½   cup long-grain white rice, rinsed (see page 118)
    2   carrots, peeled and cut into ½-inch chunks
    ½   cup frozen peas
    2   tablespoons minced fresh parsley
    ¼   teaspoon grated lemon zest plus 1½ teaspoons
        fresh lemon juice

1. Adjust oven rack to middle position and heat oven to 350 degrees. Pat chicken dry with paper towels and season with salt and pepper.

2. Heat oil in medium saucepan over medium-high heat until just smoking. Brown chicken lightly on both sides, 3 to 4 minutes per side; transfer to plate.

3. Pour off all but 2 teaspoons fat left in pan, add onion, and cook over medium heat until softened and lightly browned, 5 to 7 minutes. Stir in garlic and thyme and cook until fragrant, about 30 seconds. Stir in broth, scraping up any browned bits. Return browned chicken, with any accumulated juice, to pan and bring to simmer. Cover, reduce heat to medium-low, and simmer gently for 20 minutes.

4. Stir in rice and carrots until evenly combined. Cover, transfer pan to oven, and cook until rice is tender and liquid has been absorbed, 20 to 30 minutes, gently stirring rice from bottom of pan to top every 10 minutes.

5. Transfer chicken to carving board and replace pan lid to keep rice warm. Let chicken cool slightly, then shred into large chunks following photo on page 71, discarding skin and bones.

6. Gently stir shredded chicken, peas, parsley, lemon zest, and lemon juice into rice. Cover and let sit until chicken and peas are warmed through, about 5 minutes. Season with salt and pepper to taste and serve.

VARIATIONS

Chicken and Rice with Tomato, Chipotles, and Olives

Follow recipe for Classic Chicken and Rice with Carrots and Peas, omitting thyme, carrots, peas, parsley, lemon zest, and lemon juice. Add ¾ teaspoon minced canned chipotle chile in adobo sauce to pan with garlic. Add 1 tomato, cored and chopped coarse, to pan with rice. Stir in ⅓ cup pitted green olives, chopped coarse, and 1 scallion, sliced thin, to pan with shredded chicken in step 6. Serve with lime wedges.

NOTES FROM THE TEST KITCHEN

SHREDDING CHICKEN OR PORK

Hold one fork in each hand, with the tines facing down. Insert the tines into the meat and gently pull the forks away from each other, breaking the meat into bite-size pieces or large chunks.

THE BEST LONG-GRAIN WHITE RICE

Higher-quality white rice offers a pleasing "al dente" texture and a natural, slightly buttery flavor. While most of this subtle variation comes from the varietal of rice, processing also affects flavor. All rice starts out brown; to become white, it is milled, a process that removes the husk, bran, and germ, which contain flavor compounds as well as nutrients. The longer the rice is milled, the whiter it becomes. Many brands of rice (except organic rice) are then enriched to replace lost nutrients. Unlike medium- or short-grain white rice, cooked long-grain white rice remains fluffy and separate because it contains less of a starch called amylopectin that makes rice stick together. We tasted six national brands of long-grain white rice, plain (steamed in our favorite rice cooker) and in a simple pilaf.

Lundberg Organic Long-Grain White Rice was our favorite; it stood out for its nutty, buttery flavor and distinct, smooth grains.

Biryani-Style Chicken and Rice with Caramelized Onion, Raisins, and Cardamom

Follow recipe for Classic Chicken and Rice with Carrots and Peas, omitting thyme, carrots, peas, and parsley. Substitute 1 large onion, halved and sliced thin, for minced small onion. In step 3, cook onion with ¼ teaspoon brown sugar and pinch salt over medium heat, stirring frequently, until golden and caramelized, 15 to 20 minutes, before adding garlic. Add ¾ teaspoon minced or grated fresh ginger, ⅛ teaspoon ground cardamom, ⅛ teaspoon ground cumin, and pinch crumbled saffron threads to pan with garlic. Add ⅓ cup raisins and 1 tablespoon minced fresh cilantro to pan with shredded chicken, lemon zest, and lemon juice in step 6.

CRISPY CHICKEN THIGHS WITH SNAP PEAS

WHEN IT COMES TO QUICK AND EASY WEEKNIGHT meals, chicken breasts are always first to come to mind. Thighs, by contrast, are typically associated with dishes that require at least some time simmering on the stove (think stews and braises). But roasted chicken thighs have moist, well-seasoned meat and crispy skin that is eminently appealing, and as a bonus, they are inexpensive and much less prone to drying out than lean breast meat. We thought chicken thighs would make a great centerpiece for a one-dish weeknight meal for two. Our goals were simple: We wanted crisp, golden skin; moist, tender meat; and a vegetable sidekick that would be done to perfection at the same time as the chicken.

We quickly discovered that the difficulties with roasting chicken thighs relate directly to the level of heat. If the oven is too hot, achieving crispy skin can be difficult because it doesn't have enough time to render its fat, but if the oven is too cool, the meat will cook through before the skin is browned and crisped. Roasting the thighs at 450 degrees yielded the best results: The meat was perfectly moist and tender after just 30 minutes and the skin was golden brown, although it wasn't quite crisp enough for our liking. To solve this problem, we tried finishing the chicken under the direct heat of the broiler. We were definitely pleased with the crispy texture, but the skin still seemed a bit too thick and fatty. Remembering a technique we have used to render fat when cooking duck, we tried slashing the skin a few times before placing the thighs in the oven. This trick worked like a charm; the skin rendered even more fat, leaving it thin and crisp.

Although the roasted thighs were great seasoned simply with salt and pepper, we wanted them to really shine. From our tests with roasted chicken breasts (see page 62), we knew that rubbing butter under the chicken skin was an easy way to increase moisture and promote even crisper skin. We simply rubbed the butter directly on the meat (under the skin) before slashing the skin.

Now it was time to complete our dish with the right vegetable. Green beans seemed like the perfect accompaniment to this weeknight meal. We tossed them with olive oil, spread them in the bottom of the broiler pan, and placed the chicken on the pan top. Since green beans can't withstand the entire cooking time, we added them toward the end of cooking just for the time the chicken went under the broiler. Unfortunately, this wasn't quite enough time for the beans. We wondered if snap peas, with their short cooking time and crisp texture, would yield better results. A first test was

promising. After five minutes under the broiler, the snap peas were perfectly cooked and crisp-tender, but they were mired in a greasy mess of oil and rendered chicken fat that caused them to get softer as time passed. Clearly, it was unnecessary to toss delicate snap peas in oil before the broiling step. In our next test we eliminated the oil and also drained the rendered fat from the pan before adding the snap peas. This was a big improvement, and the peas still got plenty of flavor from the fat that continued to render during the final minutes of broiling. By immediately transferring the peas to a serving bowl, we stopped them from overcooking and preserved their wonderful, crisp-tender texture. The freshness of the snap peas was a perfect complement to the crisp skin and rich meat of the chicken thighs.

Our chicken and vegetables were now cooked to perfection, but tasters felt the dish was shy on flavor. Reviewing our recipe, we found the easiest way to impart flavor was to add a few potent ingredients to the butter before rubbing it under the skin. We settled on an Asian-flavored butter with minced garlic, ginger, and five-spice powder—the flavored butter dripped down from the chicken as it cooked, giving the snap peas an extra boost of flavor. A final toss with a teaspoon of rice vinegar gave the snap peas a bright splash of acidity.

NOTES FROM THE TEST KITCHEN

TRIMMING SNAP AND SNOW PEAS

Use a paring knife and your thumb to snip off the tip of the pea and pull along the flat side of the pod to remove the string at the same time.

ENSURING CRISPY CHICKEN SKIN

To help render the fat, and guarantee crispy skin, make three diagonal slashes in the skin of each chicken thigh.

Crispy Chicken Thighs with Snap Peas
SERVES 2

If using kosher chicken, do not brine. If brining the chicken, do not season with salt in step 3. Be sure to transfer the cooked snap peas to a serving dish immediately to avoid overcooking. Five-spice powder can be found in the spice aisle of the supermarket.

1 tablespoon unsalted butter, softened
1 small garlic clove, minced
1 teaspoon minced or grated fresh ginger
¼ teaspoon five-spice powder (see note)
4 (6-ounce) bone-in, skin-on chicken thighs, trimmed, brined if desired (see note; see page 18)
2 teaspoons olive oil
   Salt and pepper
9 ounces snap peas (about 4½ cups), ends trimmed and strings removed (see photo)
1 teaspoon rice vinegar

1. Adjust oven rack to middle position and heat oven to 450 degrees. Line bottom of broiler pan with aluminum foil and cover with broiler-pan top.

2. Combine butter, garlic, ginger, and five-spice powder in small bowl. Pat chicken dry with paper towels. Gently loosen center portion of skin covering each thigh. Using spoon, place butter mixture underneath skin, then gently press skin to spread out butter. Lay chicken, skin side up, on broiler-pan top.

3. Following photo on page 72, make 3 diagonal slashes through skin of each thigh with sharp knife (do not cut into meat). Brush chicken with oil and season with salt and pepper. Roast until chicken registers 165 degrees on instant-read thermometer, 30 to 40 minutes.

4. Remove chicken from oven. Position oven rack 6 inches from broiler element and heat broiler. While broiler heats, carefully remove broiler-pan top with chicken from pan bottom; set aside. Drain fat from broiler-pan bottom, spread snap peas in pan, and season with salt and pepper. Place broiler-pan top, with chicken, over peas.

5. Broil chicken until skin is crisp and thighs register 175 degrees on instant-read thermometer, 5 to 10 minutes. Transfer chicken to platter and let rest for 5 minutes. Transfer snap peas to serving bowl, toss with vinegar, and serve with chicken.

SALMON WITH ASPARAGUS

SALMON IS RICH, BUTTERY, AND SATISFYING AND truly needs little in the way of adornment to make a terrific dinner. While there are many ways to prepare it, we wanted to use salmon as the basis for a simple skillet supper using a pan-searing method. In the test kitchen we've found that pan-searing is a great way to take advantage of salmon's high fat content and produce a flavorful caramelized crust that is hard to resist. Asparagus came to mind almost immediately as the perfect accompaniment. We hoped that a simple skillet method might deliver crisp, nicely browned spears to serve alongside our salmon with a wedge of lemon.

We decided to tackle the salmon first. We began by patting two salmon fillets dry with paper towels to ensure a good sear, then seasoned them liberally with salt and pepper. For cooking fish, we knew a nonstick skillet was a must to avoid the common issue of the fish sticking to the pan. The real question concerned the heat level. Knowing that we were after a good caramelized crust, we heated a generous tablespoon of oil over medium-high heat until it was just smoking. We placed the salmon in the skillet (skin side up) and let it cook. After just five minutes it had a nicely browned crust and was ready to be flipped to cook through on the second side. After some trial and error, we found it best to reduce the heat to medium and cook it a mere three minutes longer on the second side, just until it had turned from translucent to opaque. Any longer, and the salmon quickly went from velvety and moist to dry and chalky.

With our heat level and timing down, the salmon had an irresistibly supple texture that was right on, but the fish was overly greasy. Realizing that the salmon's high fat content was the cause, we cooked up another batch, this time using less oil. We found that a modest amount—just 2 teaspoons—was enough to brown two salmon fillets and achieve that caramelized crisp crust. When the salmon was cooked through, we transferred it to a platter to rest and turned our attention to the asparagus.

After wiping out our skillet (the fishy oil left in the pan would have ruined the more delicate flavor of the asparagus), we began testing different sizes of spears. The thinner spears were eliminated; they overcooked long before they could get a proper sear. Selecting thicker spears got us going in the right direction, but we were still a long way from getting them to brown properly. Over moderate heat, the spears took so long to develop a crisp, browned exterior that they overcooked. But cranking up the temperature was not the answer either—cooked this way, the spears skipped browning altogether and went straight to spotty and blackened while the interior didn't cook through.

After cooking several more rounds of asparagus, we hit on a winning method. We cooked the asparagus, covered, over medium heat using a combination of oil and butter. The butter, with a makeup that is 20 percent water, added enough moisture to start steaming the asparagus at the outset, and soon the asparagus began to release its own moisture. After five minutes, we uncovered the pan and cranked up the heat.

At this point the asparagus was bright green and just barely softened. Once the lid was removed, however, it was a race against the clock to try to get all the spears turned and browned all over before they overcooked and turned limp. But we made a fortunate discovery. Citing the pleasing contrast of textures, tasters actually

NOTES FROM THE TEST KITCHEN

THE BEST INEXPENSIVE NONSTICK SKILLET

We've always recommended buying inexpensive nonstick skillets, because with regular use the nonstick coating inevitably scratches, chips off, or becomes ineffective. Why spend big bucks on a pan that will last only a year or two? To find the best nonstick pan on the market, we tested seven contenders under $50 against our longtime favorite, the All-Clad Stainless 12-Inch Nonstick Frying Pan, $129.99, and the Best Buy from our previous testing, the Calphalon Simply Calphalon Nonstick Omelette Pan, $55. We tested the nonstick effectiveness of each pan by frying eggs and stir-frying beef and vegetables. To see which pans cooked food evenly and had good size and heft but were comfortable to maneuver, we made crêpes in each. We also ran them through a number of durability tests. We'd like to say our new favorite pan, the **T-Fal Professional Total Non-Stick Fry Pan**, aced every test, but a loose handle that resulted from the durability testing was a sign that it's not high-end cookware. Still, at $34.99 for the 12.5-inch pan ($29.95 for the 10.25-inch pan, and $25 for the 8-inch pan), it's a bargain, and it was the only pan in the lineup to give us the best of both worlds: an exceptionally slick, durable nonstick coating and top performance in cooking. As for the All-Clad, it is a solidly built pan and a terrific piece of cookware, but its coating became slightly worn by the end of our tests (meanwhile, the T-Fal remained perfectly slick). Because the All-Clad boasts a lifetime warranty, we still recommend it, but we'll be buying the T-Fal from now on for our own kitchens.

CHOOSING THE RIGHT SIZE SKILLET

When cooking for four or more, a large 12-inch skillet does the job, but using the same skillet to cook for two can result in disaster. Certain dishes, like our Spice-Rubbed Strip Steak (page 48) and Thai Red Curry with Shrimp (page 79), would scorch in a 12-inch skillet because there would be too much hot surface area (and heat) for too little food. Instead, we reach for a 10-inch skillet for these dishes. (Certain pasta dishes are the exceptions, as the large surface area is necessary to accommodate ample sauce and liquid to cook the pasta.) With a mix of skillet sizes on hand, you'll be able to make anything from Skillet-Glazed Pork Chops (page 14) to Chicken Paprikash (page 28). (See page 8 and above for information on our top-rated traditional and nonstick skillets.)

preferred the spears that were browned on one side only and remained bright green on the other—and we didn't give these half-browned spears the chance to overcook.

With all the components cooked and ready to go, it was time to assemble the meal. We were pleased with the distinct elements of the dish but found that the simple squeeze of lemon that we envisioned over the top was not enough to pull the meal together. Instead, we turned to a simple vinaigrette made with olive oil, lemon juice, Dijon mustard, and minced shallot and herbs. Drizzled over the salmon and asparagus, the vinaigrette added a final burst of freshness that brought the elements of our quick dinner together.

Salmon with Asparagus and Herb Vinaigrette
SERVES 2

To ensure even cooking, make sure to buy salmon fillets of equal size and thickness. This recipe works best with asparagus that is at least ½ inch thick near the base. Do not use pencil-thin asparagus because it cannot withstand the heat and will overcook.

2	(6-ounce) center-cut salmon fillets, about 1½ inches thick
	Salt and pepper
¼	cup olive oil
1	tablespoon unsalted butter
1	bunch thick asparagus (about 1 pound), tough ends trimmed (see note)
1	small shallot, minced
4	teaspoons fresh lemon juice
2	teaspoons minced fresh parsley, basil, or mint leaves
½	teaspoon Dijon mustard

1. Pat salmon dry with paper towels and season with salt and pepper. Heat 2 teaspoons oil in 10-inch non-stick skillet over medium-high heat until just smoking. Carefully lay salmon in skillet, skin side up, and cook until well browned on first side, about 5 minutes.

2. Flip salmon over, reduce heat to medium, and continue to cook until center of thickest part of fillets is still translucent when cut into with paring knife, and instant-read thermometer inserted in thickest part of fillets registers 125 degrees, about 3 minutes longer. Transfer salmon to platter, tent loosely with foil, and let rest while cooking asparagus.

SALMON WITH ASPARAGUS AND HERB VINAIGRETTE

3. Wipe out skillet with paper towels, add butter and 1 teaspoon more oil, and heat over medium heat until butter has melted. Add half of asparagus to skillet with tips pointed in one direction and add remaining spears with tips pointed in opposite direction. Sprinkle with ⅛ teaspoon salt and gently shake asparagus into even layer.

4. Cover and cook until spears are bright green and still crisp, about 5 minutes. Uncover, increase heat to high, and continue to cook until spears are tender and well browned on one side, 5 to 7 minutes, using tongs to move spears from center of pan to edge of pan to ensure all are browned.

5. Meanwhile, whisk remaining 3 tablespoons oil, shallot, lemon juice, parsley, and mustard together in small bowl and season with salt and pepper to taste. Transfer asparagus to platter with salmon, drizzle with vinaigrette, and serve.

SKILLET-BRAISED COD PROVENÇAL

IT'S EASY TO GET STUCK IN A RUT WHEN IT COMES to preparing cod since just about every cookbook (not to mention most restaurants) focuses either on traditional Boston baked cod (or one of its many variations) or breaded and fried cod. We were after a fresher approach, our sights set on a highly flavorful, but easy, braised cod recipe. Turning to the flavors of Provence for inspiration, we envisioned fish that was tender, moist, and flavorful, napped in an aromatic, garlicky tomato sauce that we could mop up with a good loaf of crusty bread.

The handful of recipes we tested produced tough, dry cod, dull and muddy flavors, and a sauce that was too thick or too thin, too sweet or too greasy. The biggest challenge would be cooking the cod to perfection, as it's meaty but lean and easily prone to drying out. We had our work cut out for us.

First, we focused on the sauce in which the cod would be braised. We started by sautéing a sliced shallot in extra-virgin olive oil, then added a generous four cloves of garlic and sautéed them briefly to bring out their flavor. Turning next to the tomatoes, the base of the braising liquid, we considered the most likely options: crushed, diced, or pureed canned tomatoes, or fresh tomatoes. Both crushed and pureed canned tomatoes produced a thick, sweet, overbearing sauce reminiscent of bad Italian restaurant food. Canned diced tomatoes, though more promising, presented the opposite problem: They contain a fair amount of liquid, and the resulting sauce was too thin. Fresh tomatoes were the clear winner. A single tomato, chopped, improved the texture and flavor dramatically. This sauce now coated the cod perfectly.

At this point, tasters were happy with the texture of the sauce, but the flavor was lacking. A few additions remedied the problem. A splash of white wine gave the sauce brightness and complexity. Our next thought was to add olives, a common ingredient in Provençal dishes and a good fit for fish. Sure enough, tasters approved. However, a modest amount (just ¼ cup) proved key— any more, and their intense briny flavor overwhelmed the sauce (and the fish). On a whim we added sliced fennel along with the shallot, and this was just what our sauce needed. The fennel added a clean, refreshing punch with its subtle anise flavor. With our sauce in good shape, we turned our attention to cooking the cod.

We found the keys to braising our fish were twofold: Low heat ensured that nothing burned, and a skillet with a tight-fitting lid trapped the heat so that the fish gently simmered. We nestled the cod into the simmering sauce and basted it quickly with the sauce to ensure that it was infused with flavor, then cooked it over medium-low heat, covered, for just 10 minutes. The fish emerged succulent and moist, and the sauce had good body.

As for seasonings, the combination of dried herbs referred to as herbes de Provence (a combination of lavender, marjoram, basil, fennel seed, rosemary, sage, summer savory, and thyme) seemed like a natural. But tasters said that these dried herbs were too strong, giving the sauce a flavor that bordered on medicinal. We realized that their powerful flavors needed a longer-cooking dish to mellow out. A simple combination of fresh thyme and parsley worked much better, and a final drizzle of fruity extra-virgin olive oil rounded out the flavors.

Skillet-Braised Cod Provençal

SERVES 2

Halibut, snapper, tilapia, bluefish, monkfish, or sea bass fillets are all good substitutions for the cod. If your fillets have skin on them, follow the instructions on page 39 to remove it. Serve with a loaf of crusty bread to soak up the extra sauce.

- 2 **(6-ounce) skinless cod fillets, 1 to 1½ inches thick (see note)**
- **Salt and pepper**
- 2 **tablespoons extra-virgin olive oil, plus extra for serving**
- 1 **fennel bulb (about 12 ounces), trimmed of stalks, cored, and sliced thin (see page 92)**
- 1 **shallot, halved and sliced thin**
- 4 **garlic cloves, minced**
- ½ **teaspoon minced fresh thyme or ⅛ teaspoon dried**
- 1 **large tomato, cored and chopped medium**
- ¼ **cup pitted kalamata olives, chopped coarse**
- ¼ **cup dry white wine or vermouth**
- 1 **tablespoon minced fresh parsley**

1. Pat cod dry with paper towels and season with salt and pepper.

2. Heat oil in 10-inch nonstick skillet over medium-high heat until shimmering. Add fennel, shallot, and ¼ teaspoon salt and cook until vegetables have softened, 5 to 7 minutes. Stir in garlic and thyme and cook until fragrant, about 30 seconds. Stir in tomato, olives, and wine and bring to simmer.

3. Nestle cod into skillet and spoon some of sauce over fish. Cover, reduce heat to medium-low, and cook cod fillets until centers are just opaque and register 135 degrees on instant-read thermometer, 8 to 10 minutes.

4. Transfer fish to individual plates. Stir parsley into sauce in pan and season with salt and pepper to taste. Spoon sauce around fish and serve, passing olive oil separately.

THAI RED CURRY WITH SHRIMP

LIKE MOST THAI FOOD, THAI CURRIES EMBRACE A delicate balance of tastes, textures, and colors that come together to create a harmonious whole. The two most common types of Thai curry are green and red, made from green curry paste and red curry paste. Both pastes are formed with aromatics like garlic, ginger, shallots, lemon grass, kaffir lime leaves, shrimp paste, and chiles, but green curry paste relies on fresh chiles, whereas red curry paste relies on potent dried red chiles. Preparing either one from scratch is an arduous process and a lengthy endeavor, which might make sense when cooking for a group. But when you're cooking for two, the process can be overwhelming and leave even the most enthusiastic cook clamoring for takeout. We set our sights on a streamlined Thai red curry for two; starting with the more pungent flavors of red curry from the outset would, we hoped, make for a curry scaled down in size, but not flavor. And while almost any protein can be found in Thai curry—chicken, beef, shrimp, and tofu—we chose shrimp for its convenience and quick-cooking nature.

Naturally, we turned to the curry first. Off the bat, we turned to jarred Thai curry paste. A few quick tests told us that just a small amount of this convenience product packed a punch when it came to both bright flavor and spice level. Satisfied with our selection, we moved on to the sauce itself.

Since we were making a Thai curry, we knew that coconut milk was a must. Yet while we like the flavor and texture of the full-fat variety, its richness benefits from some balance. We found that ¼ cup of chicken broth—to ¾ cup of coconut milk, for 1 cup of liquid total—was just the right amount to temper the coconut. Any less, and the coconut was overwhelming; any more, and the resulting sauce tasted brothy and thin. To further balance out the coconut milk, we added a few traditional but easy-to-find Thai staples: fish sauce, brown sugar, lime juice, and basil (either Thai basil or Italian basil work well).

Amid this testing, however, we discovered a problem. Even when using our favorite red curry paste, we were having difficulty maintaining a consistent flavor from batch to batch. Some trials tasted spicy and full of curry flavor, while others were overwhelmingly bland. We took a closer look at our curry paste and noticed that we had been using two different jars of the same red curry paste; one had simply been open longer than the other. Not surprisingly, the older paste lacked in spice and heat, and the curries made with it tasted bland. To draw forth the most flavor from our curry paste, regardless of how long the jar had been open, we sautéed, or bloomed, the paste in a little vegetable oil at the beginning of cooking to deepen its flavor. For added insurance, we also stirred in a little extra curry paste when the sauce was almost ready. Not only did this step guarantee deep flavor, but it also meant we could tailor the spice level to suit individual tastes. With the sauce finally balanced and brightly flavored, we addressed the remaining ingredients.

We tried a few combinations of vegetables. For our master recipe, tasters liked a combination of snap peas and sliced red bell pepper, both simmered until just crisp-tender; not only did these vegetables make for an even more colorful dish, but the contrast in texture

NOTES FROM THE TEST KITCHEN

SIZING SHRIMP

Shrimp are sold by size (small, medium, large, and so on) as well as by the number needed to make 1 pound, usually given in a range. Choosing shrimp by the numerical rating is more accurate than choosing by a size label, which varies from store to store. Here's how the two systems line up.

SMALL
51 to 60 per pound

MEDIUM
41 to 50 per pound

LARGE
31 to 40 per pound

EXTRA-LARGE
21 to 25 per pound

DEVEINING SHRIMP

1. Hold the shelled shrimp between your thumb and forefinger and cut down the length of its back, about ⅛ to ¼ inch deep, with a sharp paring knife.

2. If the shrimp has a vein, it will be exposed and can be pulled out easily. Once you have freed the vein with the tip of the knife, just touch the knife to a paper towel and the vein will stick to the towel.

CUTTING CARROTS INTO MATCHSTICKS

1. Slice the carrot on the bias into 2-inch-long, oval-shaped pieces.

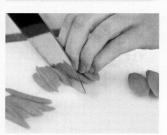

2. Lay the ovals flat on the cutting board, then slice them into 2-inch-long matchsticks, about ¼ inch thick.

and flavors (now we had added some sweetness to the mix) was unbeatable. For an equally colorful and flavorful variation, we swapped out the bell pepper and snap peas in favor of asparagus and carrots.

As for the shrimp, they were a snap. Once the vegetables were crisp-tender, we stirred in a half-pound of extra-large shrimp. In less than five minutes, the shrimp were done.

Served over a bowl of white rice, this shrimp curry exceeded our expectations: In less time than it took to get delivery, we had made a rich-tasting curry, with delicate shrimp and crisp-tender vegetables, and it boasted all the spicy, complex flavor of a from-scratch, took-hours-to-prepare curry sauce.

Thai Red Curry with Shrimp, Bell Pepper, and Snap Peas

SERVES 2

Depending on the freshness and spice level of your curry paste, you may need to add more or less to taste; season the sauce before you add the shrimp to make sure they do not overcook. If you can't find Thai basil leaves, regular basil will work fine. Serve with Simple White Rice (page 26).

- 2 teaspoons vegetable oil
- 2 teaspoons red curry paste, plus extra for seasoning (see note)
- ¾ cup coconut milk
- 1 tablespoon fish sauce
- 2 teaspoons brown sugar
- ¼ cup low-sodium chicken broth
- ½ teaspoon cornstarch
- 1 red bell pepper, stemmed, seeded, and sliced into ¼-inch-wide strips (see page 52)
- 4 ounces snap peas (about 2 cups), ends trimmed and strings removed (see page 72), sliced in half on bias
- 8 ounces extra-large shrimp (21 to 25 per pound), peeled, tails removed, and deveined (see page 78)
- ¼ cup loosely packed fresh Thai basil leaves (see note)
- 2 teaspoons fresh lime juice
  Salt

1. Heat oil in 10-inch nonstick skillet over medium-high heat until shimmering. Add curry paste and cook

until fragrant, about 30 seconds. Stir in coconut milk, fish sauce, and brown sugar. Whisk broth and cornstarch together in small bowl, then whisk mixture into skillet and bring to simmer.

2. Add bell pepper and snap peas and simmer until vegetables are crisp-tender and sauce has thickened slightly, 5 to 8 minutes. Season with curry paste to taste.

3. Stir in shrimp and continue to simmer until shrimp are fully cooked, 3 to 5 minutes. Off heat, stir in basil and lime juice. Season with salt to taste and serve.

VARIATION

Thai Red Curry with Shrimp, Asparagus, and Carrots
Follow recipe for Thai Red Curry with Shrimp, Bell Pepper, and Snap Peas, substituting ½ bunch asparagus (about 8 ounces), tough ends trimmed, sliced on bias into 2-inch pieces, for red bell pepper and 2 carrots, peeled and cut into 2-inch-long matchsticks (see page 78), for snap peas.

USE IT UP: COCONUT MILK

Piña Coladas
SERVES 2

We find it easiest to buy fresh pineapple that has already been peeled and cored. You can substitute 2 cups canned pineapple chunks, drained well, for the fresh pineapple.

- ¾ cup coconut milk
- ½ cup milk
- ⅓ cup dark rum
- 12 ounces peeled and cored fresh pineapple (see note), cut into 1-inch chunks (about 2 cups)
- 1 cup ice
- 2 teaspoons sugar, plus extra for seasoning
- 1 teaspoon fresh lime juice, plus extra for seasoning
  Pinch salt

Combine all ingredients in blender, with liquids on bottom. Blend on low speed until mixture is combined but still coarse in texture, about 10 seconds. Increase blender speed to high; puree until mixture is completely smooth, 20 to 40 seconds longer. Season with additional sugar and lime juice to taste and serve immediately.

PASTA WITH ROASTED CAULIFLOWER, GARLIC, AND WALNUTS

CHAPTER 3

PASTA FOR DINNER

SPAGHETTI WITH PECORINO ROMANO AND BLACK PEPPER

AT ONE TIME OR ANOTHER EVERYONE HAS TOSSED pasta with olive oil and Parmesan cheese for a quick pantry supper. Though it's far from haute cuisine, it's nonetheless satisfying. But the classic Roman dish *pasta alla cacio e pepe* (pasta with cheese and pepper) takes this same concept to new heights. Described as a popular "spaghetti party" dish often thrown together to cap off a night on the town, it combines long, thin pasta with Pecorino Romano and fresh-cracked black pepper. When done right, the strands of pasta are napped in a barely creamy sauce boasting intense cheese flavor and a peppery bite. We set out to create a recipe for this simple, speedy dinner, but instead of serving a gaggle of late-night revelers, ours would serve two.

An Internet search turned up dozens of approaches, including one from restaurateur and chef Mario Batali:

NOTES FROM THE TEST KITCHEN

THE BEST BOX GRATER
Our recipe for Spaghetti with Pecorino Romano and Black Pepper (page 84) calls for both finely grated and coarsely grated cheese, both of which can be attained using a box grater. To find the best box grater on the market, we tested eight models, grating Parmesan and mozzarella cheeses and raw potatoes on each of them. When it came to bells and whistles on the graters, nonskid bases and plastic measuring cup attachments were the main differentiating factors. Nonskid bases only slightly improved the graters' stability, but once the measuring cup attachments were in place, these rubber bases were irrelevant. Plastic measuring cup attachments were more appreciated, as these let the cook know when a certain quantity has been reached. The principal feature that significantly distinguished one grater from another was blade quality. Six graters featured traditionally deep punctures—fine for semisoft cheeses and softer vegetables, but no match for the shallower, razor-sharp edges on the two other models, which made grating Parmesan a snap. Of these two top performers, one pulled into the lead—the **OXO Good Grips Box Grater**, $17.95. With its slim body (ideal for easy storage), clearly marked container, and ultra-sharp grating surface, the OXO delivered on all fronts, and its low price tag—prices of tested graters went all the way up to $30—made it a smart choice as well.

Toss cooked pasta with a few tablespoons of olive oil and butter, add plenty of grated cheese and black pepper along with pasta water to keep it moist, toss, and serve. But when we tried his recipe, we couldn't get it to work. Instead of emulsifying into a creamy sauce after being tossed into the hot pasta, the Pecorino merely solidified into clumps and ended up stuck to the tongs. We tested a number of comparable recipes and had the same issue.

We decided to check in with our science editor, who revealed the likely problem. When cheese is heated, the fat that acts as a glue to keep the proteins stable begins to melt. When that happens, the cheese clumps. The solution he suggested was to add starch to replace the "glue" of the fat. We tried different forms of starch, first tossing cornstarch with the pasta to coat the cheese and prevent the proteins from sticking together. It worked, but by the time we used enough cornstarch to prevent clumping, it dulled the flavor of the cheese. Was there another way to get starch into the mix? Pasta releases starch into the cooking water as it boils, so maybe we could use this to our advantage. We reduced the amount of cooking water from our standard 4 quarts all the way down to 1 quart for 6 ounces of spaghetti (the right amount for two servings when paired with the creamy sauce). After cooking the spaghetti, we whisked some finely grated cheese into a half-cup of the starchy, semolina-infused water that remained. The results were the best yet, but some of the cheese was still clumping.

Researching the problem further, we discovered another factor that affects how proteins and fat interact: emulsifiers. Milk, cream, and fresh cheeses have special molecules that can associate with both fat and protein, acting as a sort of liaison between the two and keeping them from separating. But as cheese ages, which was the case with our Pecorino Romano, these molecules break down, losing their emulsifying power. We surmised that the addition of milk or cream would bridge the gap between the fat and protein; since we were already using butter, why not replace it with the same amount of cream? (At the same time, we reduced the amount of olive oil to satisfy a few tasters who found the dish greasy.)

This time, the cheese easily formed a light, perfectly smooth sauce when we tossed it with the spaghetti.

SPAGHETTI WITH PECORINO ROMANO AND BLACK PEPPER

Now for the real test: We placed a serving of pasta on the table and let it cool for a full five minutes. Even as it cooled, there wasn't a clump in sight. Garnished with even more grated Pecorino, our cheesy, peppery pasta was now worthy of a late-night spaghetti party—for two.

Spaghetti with Pecorino Romano and Black Pepper

SERVES 2

High-quality ingredients are essential in this dish; most important is imported Pecorino Romano—not the bland domestic cheese labeled "Romano." Use the small holes on a box grater to grate the cheese finely and the large holes to grate it coarsely. Though we usually recommend cooking pasta in lots of water, this recipe is an exception; the thick, starchy pasta cooking water is necessary for the consistency of the sauce. Be sure to measure the amount of water and stir the pasta often during cooking to prevent clumping. See page 85 for a tip on how to measure out long strands of pasta without using a scale.

- 3 ounces Pecorino Romano cheese, 2 ounces finely grated (about 1 cup) and 1 ounce coarsely grated (about ½ cup) (see note)
- 6 ounces spaghetti (see note)
- ½ teaspoon salt
- 1 tablespoon heavy cream
- 1 teaspoon extra-virgin olive oil
- ¾ teaspoon pepper

1. Place finely grated Pecorino in medium bowl.

2. Bring 1 quart water to boil in large pot. Add pasta and salt and cook, stirring often to prevent clumping, until al dente. Drain pasta in colander set over bowl, reserving cooking water, and return pasta to pot.

3. Slowly whisk ½ cup reserved pasta cooking water into finely grated Pecorino until smooth. Whisk in cream, oil, and pepper. Gradually pour cheese mixture over pasta, tossing to coat. Let pasta rest for 1 to 2 minutes, tossing frequently, adjusting sauce consistency with remaining reserved pasta cooking water as desired. Serve with coarsely grated Pecorino.

LINGUINE WITH ARUGULA-MINT PESTO

PESTO ISN'T JUST LIMITED TO THE FAMILIAR, garlicky blend of fresh basil, pine nuts, and Parmesan cheese—the word *pesto* actually refers to the paste the ingredients form, rather than to the specific ingredients. Looking for a new pasta dish we could add to our repertoire, we set out to create a new sauce to dress our linguine.

We began by choosing a potent ingredient to be the centerpiece of our pesto. Looking for something with a peppery bite, we considered watercress and arugula. Watercress was nixed quickly, as the stems didn't break down enough in the food processor. Arugula, with its leafy texture and small stems, worked much better.

While tasters liked the flavor of arugula in an early pesto test, they thought the sauce tasted a bit one-note and asked for more complexity. We considered a number of fresh herbs to supplement the arugula. An arugula-parsley combination worked OK, but tasters really liked the piquant punch of an arugula-mint pesto. The mint provided a cool, fresh note that balanced the spiciness of the arugula.

Considering two more ingredients found in traditional basil pesto—pine nuts and Parmesan cheese—we reached for walnuts and Manchego cheese, a Spanish sheep's milk cheese with a complex, buttery, nutty flavor profile and a texture similar to that of Parmesan. The earthy flavor of the walnuts helped balance the peppery arugula, especially after we toasted the nuts in a dry skillet to bring out their full flavor. The cheese, however, was a letdown; Manchego's nuances and complexity were lost amid the other flavors in the pesto. We decided to keep the traditional Parmesan in place; it worked well to provide the salty, nutty background notes in our dish.

Moving on to the garlic, we found that toasting it helped to mellow its harshness and bring out its sweet notes. After a few tests, we determined that a single clove prevented the pesto from being overly garlicky or harsh-tasting. For the extra-virgin olive oil, it was important to use high-quality oil for best flavor. A tablespoon of fresh lemon juice, a pinch of red pepper flakes, and ½ teaspoon of sugar rounded out the flavor of our pesto, balancing the acidity and adding just a touch of heat.

Although pesto is traditionally made using a mortar and pestle, we found a food processor to be quicker and more convenient. In just a minute, we had a finished sauce, saving us time and quite a bit of elbow grease.

When the pesto was combined with a pile of cooked linguine, the mingling aromas of mint and arugula were enough to make even the biggest basil devotees in the test kitchen hanker for a bite.

Linguine with Arugula-Mint Pesto
SERVES 2

Since the extra-virgin olive oil provides the base of the pesto, be sure to pick a flavorful, high-quality brand; our winning supermarket brand is Columela Extra Virgin Olive Oil. See the box at right for a tip on how to measure out long strands of pasta without using a scale. Toasting the garlic softens both its texture and raw bite.

- 1 garlic clove, unpeeled
- 4 ounces baby arugula (about 4 cups)
- ¾ cup tightly packed fresh mint leaves
- 2 tablespoons chopped walnuts, toasted (see page 240)
- 1 tablespoon fresh lemon juice
- ½ teaspoon sugar
- ⅛ teaspoon red pepper flakes
  Salt
- 3 tablespoons extra-virgin olive oil
- 6 ounces linguine (see note)
- ¼ cup grated Parmesan cheese, plus extra for serving

1. Toast garlic in small skillet over medium heat, shaking pan occasionally, until fragrant and color of clove deepens slightly, about 7 minutes. Let garlic cool slightly, then peel and chop.

2. Process garlic, arugula, mint, walnuts, lemon juice, sugar, red pepper flakes, and ½ teaspoon salt together in food processor until smooth, about 30 seconds. Scrape down sides of bowl with rubber spatula. With machine running, slowly drizzle in oil until incorporated, about 30 seconds.

3. Meanwhile, bring 4 quarts water to boil in large pot. Add pasta and 1 tablespoon salt and cook, stirring often, until al dente. Reserve ½ cup cooking water, then drain pasta and return it to pot.

4. Add pesto and Parmesan to pasta and toss to combine, adjusting sauce consistency with reserved pasta cooking water as desired. Season with salt to taste and serve with extra Parmesan.

NOTES FROM THE TEST KITCHEN

HOW TO COOK PASTA
If you ask 10 cooks how they cook pasta, you're likely to get 10 different answers. In an effort to standardize pasta cookery, we've come up with these guidelines that will guarantee perfect pasta every time.

USE PLENTY OF SALT: Many people dump oil into boiling pasta water, thinking it will keep the pasta from sticking together, but this is a myth. Adding oil does not prevent sticking; frequent stirring does. Skip the oil but make sure to add salt—roughly 1 tablespoon for 4 quarts of water—or the pasta will taste bland.

USE 4 QUARTS OF WATER IN A LARGE POT: This may sound like a lot of water for just two servings, but it will ensure that the pasta cooks evenly and doesn't clump.

TASTE PASTA OFTEN FOR DONENESS: Reading the instructions on the box is a good place to start, but for al dente pasta, you may need to shave a few minutes off the recommended time. When you start to get close to the recommended cooking time, begin tasting for doneness.

SAVE SOME COOKING WATER: Wait! Before you drain that pasta, measure about ½ cup of the cooking water from the pasta pot with a liquid measuring cup. Then drain the pasta and immediately toss it with the sauce. (Don't let the pasta sit in the colander too long; it will get very dry very quickly.) When you toss your sauce with the pasta, add some (or all) of the reserved pasta cooking water to thin the sauce as needed.

MEASURING PASTA SHAPES
The best method for measuring pasta is to weigh it using a scale. However, if you do not own a scale, we have provided the equivalent cup measurements for various shapes. Use dry measuring cups for the most accurate measurements, and pack them full.

PASTA TYPE	4 OUNCES	6 OUNCES
Farfalle	1¾ cups	2½ cups
Rigatoni, Rotini	1½ cups	2⅓ cups
Penne, Ziti	1¼ cups	2 cups
Campanelle	1⅓ cups	2 cups
Orecchiette	1 cup	1¾ cups

When 6 ounces of uncooked linguine, spaghetti, fettuccine, or vermicelli are bunched together into a tight circle, the diameter measures about 1⅛ inches.

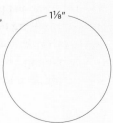
1⅛"

PASTA WITH ROASTED VEGETABLES

WHEN YOU'RE LOOKING FOR A STRAIGHTFORWARD, vegetable-rich pasta dish, pasta with roasted vegetables should fit the bill. But however simple the method might seem—cut vegetables, toss with oil, roast, and combine with pasta—rarely does the dish turn out as expected. The catch isn't so much the vegetables (which are sweet and complex if properly roasted) as the lack of a true sauce—most recipes attempt to unify the vegetables and pasta with olive oil and a little cheese. Although oil helps make the dish more cohesive, it also makes it greasy; using less oil solves that problem, of course, but is likely to leave you with a dry and boring dish. We wanted to create a simple sauce that would succeed in uniting vegetables, pasta, and cheese for a satisfying vegetable-inspired supper.

At the outset, we decided to develop a few different dishes, each focused on getting the best from a single vegetable. We settled on cauliflower (sweet and nutty when roasted), broccoli (which browns nicely and can be purchased in ready-to-cook bags of florets), and portobello mushrooms (for their intense, meaty taste). To roast the vegetables, we cut them into small pieces, which maximized the surface area available for browning; tossed them with oil, salt, pepper, and a little sugar to jump-start caramelization; and finally roasted them on a preheated baking sheet. (Preheating cuts the cooking time nearly in half and boosts browning dramatically.)

Now we were ready to face the central dilemma—the sauce. Our options included cream sauces, vegetable-based sauces, and vinaigrettes. First we tried an array of cream-based sauces, which added moisture to the pasta but muted the vegetable flavor. Vegetable-based sauces weren't much better: A puree of roasted red peppers overwhelmed the veggies, and a puree of roasted onions turned the pasta an unappetizing gray. Only a garlicky vinaigrette was a step in the right direction—we liked the way the garlic bumped up the overall flavor of the dish—but the vinegar was harsh. Cutting back on vinegar meant upping the oil, and then we were back where we started.

What we needed was an ingredient that could replace some of the oil, adding body and complementary flavor without overt richness. We found a solution without looking farther than our cutting board: garlic. When roasted, garlic turns sweet and buttery-soft, making it perfect for spreading on bread or adding depth to sauces. We wrapped a whole head of garlic in foil and roasted it at the same time that we were roasting the veggies. We gave the garlic some time to cool when it came out of the oven, then squeezed the roasted cloves from their skins and mashed them with extra-virgin olive oil and a little lemon juice. This creamy puree worked beautifully as a sauce, adding an earthy sweetness that complemented all three vegetables.

We were almost there, but we still wanted a bit more flavor and contrasting texture in each dish. The answer was to add herbs, nuts, and cheese—pantry ingredients and kitchen staples that took the pasta to a new level. We matched the cauliflower with parsley, walnuts, and sharp Parmesan; the broccoli with basil, almonds, and nutty Manchego; and the mushrooms with rosemary, pine nuts, and tangy Pecorino Romano.

USE IT UP: CAULIFLOWER

Marinated Cauliflower
MAKES 4 CUPS

The flavors in this dish intensify the longer the cauliflower marinates. Serve as an appetizer on crostini or as part of an antipasti platter.

- ¼ cup extra-virgin olive oil
- 2 tablespoons white wine vinegar
- 1 shallot, minced
- 1 garlic clove, minced
- 1 teaspoon Dijon mustard
- ¼ teaspoon sugar
-   Salt and pepper
- ½ head cauliflower (about 1 pound), trimmed, cored, and cut into 1-inch florets (about 4 cups; see page 87)

1. Whisk oil, vinegar, shallot, garlic, mustard, and sugar together in medium bowl. Season with salt and pepper to taste.

2. Bring 2 quarts water to boil in large saucepan. Add cauliflower and 1 tablespoon salt and cook, stirring often, until just tender, about 2 minutes. Drain cauliflower and briefly let dry on paper towel–lined plate.

3. Toss hot cauliflower with dressing, cover, and refrigerate for 24 hours or up to 3 days. Serve chilled or at room temperature.

Pasta with Roasted Cauliflower, Garlic, and Walnuts

SERVES 2

Other pasta shapes can be substituted for the campanelle; however, their cup measurements may vary (see page 85). For efficiency's sake, consider preparing the cauliflower after you put the garlic in the oven. See page 86 for a recipe to use up the leftover cauliflower.

- 1 head garlic, papery skin removed, top quarter of head cut off and discarded (see photo)
- 3 tablespoons plus ½ teaspoon extra-virgin olive oil
- ½ head cauliflower (about 1 pound), trimmed, cored, and cut into 1-inch florets (about 4 cups; see photos) (see note)

  Salt and pepper
- ⅛ teaspoon sugar
- 1 tablespoon fresh lemon juice, plus extra for seasoning
- ⅛ teaspoon red pepper flakes
- 6 ounces campanelle (about 2 cups; see note)
- 1 ounce Parmesan cheese, grated (about ½ cup)
- 2 teaspoons minced fresh parsley
- 2 tablespoons chopped walnuts, toasted (see page 240)

1. Adjust oven racks to middle and lower-middle positions and heat oven to 500 degrees.

2. Cut one 12-inch sheet of foil and spread flat on counter. Place garlic head, cut side up, in center of foil. Drizzle ½ teaspoon oil over garlic and seal packet. Place packet on lower-middle rack and empty baking sheet on middle rack. Roast garlic for 20 minutes.

3. Meanwhile, toss cauliflower, 1 tablespoon more oil, ½ teaspoon salt, ⅛ teaspoon pepper, and sugar together in large bowl. Working quickly, spread cauliflower in even layer on hot baking sheet. Roast cauliflower on middle rack until well browned and tender and garlic is very tender, 10 to 15 minutes, stirring cauliflower halfway through.

4. Open garlic packet and set aside to cool. Transfer cauliflower to cutting board, let cool slightly, then chop into rough ½-inch pieces; set aside. Squeeze cooled roasted garlic cloves from skins into small bowl. Using fork, mash garlic to smooth paste, then stir in lemon juice and red pepper flakes. Slowly whisk in remaining 2 tablespoons oil.

5. Meanwhile, bring 4 quarts water to boil in large pot. Add pasta and 1 tablespoon salt and cook, stirring

PREPARING CAULIFLOWER

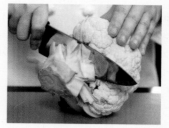

1. After pulling off the outer leaves, trim off the stem near the base of the head.

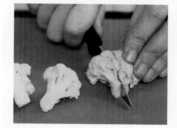

2. Turn the cauliflower upside down so that the stem is facing up. Using a sharp knife, cut around the core to remove it.

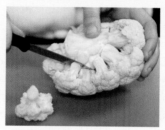

3. Using the tip of a knife, separate the florets from the inner stem.

4. Cut the florets in half, or in quarters if necessary, so that individual pieces measure about 1 inch.

PREPARING GARLIC FOR ROASTING

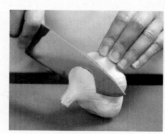

Rinse the garlic head and remove the outer papery skin. Cut the top quarter off the head of garlic and discard.

often, until al dente. Reserve ½ cup cooking water, then drain pasta and return it to pot.

6. Add chopped cauliflower, garlic sauce, 2 tablespoons reserved pasta cooking water, ¼ cup Parmesan, and parsley to pasta and toss to combine, adjusting sauce consistency with additional reserved pasta cooking water as desired. Season with salt, pepper, and additional lemon juice to taste. Sprinkle individual portions with remaining ¼ cup Parmesan and walnuts and serve.

VARIATIONS

Pasta with Roasted Broccoli, Garlic, and Almonds
Follow recipe for Pasta with Roasted Cauliflower, Garlic, and Walnuts, substituting 4 cups broccoli florets for cauliflower and reducing roasting time for broccoli in step 3 to 8 to 10 minutes. Substitute 1 ounce Manchego cheese, grated (about ½ cup), for Parmesan, 2 tablespoons chopped fresh basil for parsley, and 2 tablespoons slivered almonds, toasted (see page 240), for walnuts.

Pasta with Roasted Mushrooms, Garlic, and Pine Nuts
Follow recipe for Pasta with Roasted Cauliflower, Garlic, and Walnuts, substituting 4 portobello mushroom caps (about 1½ pounds), cut into ¾-inch slices, for cauliflower and reducing amount of salt to ⅛ teaspoon; roast as directed in step 3, flipping mushrooms over halfway through. Substitute 1 ounce Pecorino Romano cheese, grated (about ½ cup), for Parmesan, 1 teaspoon minced fresh rosemary for parsley, and 2 tablespoons pine nuts, toasted (see page 240), for walnuts.

PASTA AND SQUASH

WHEN SUMMER SQUASH AND ZUCCHINI ARE AT THE height of ripeness, our thoughts turn to pasta paired with squash. While this duo sounds like the perfect marriage, most of the time it ends in disappointment. The pasta and the squash are bland, and the squash is often so watery that it quickly turns to mush. We wanted to make the most of summer's bounty and develop a recipe that would keep our squash tender and fresh-tasting as well as highlight its natural sweetness.

The first step was tackling the problem of mushy squash. Peeling the squash proved futile, producing the mushy dish that we were hoping to avoid. Similarly, blanching or boiling the squash resulted in flavorless dishes rife with sodden squash. Sautéing, too, produced squishy squash. Even when the pan was not crowded (a crowded pan causes foods to steam rather than sauté), the squash cooked in its own juice and became mushy.

The problem was clear enough: There was too much moisture in the pan. Both zucchini and summer squash are 95 percent water—more watery than any other vegetable except leafy greens. For tender, non-mushy squash that had any flavor at all we'd have to find a way to ditch some of the liquid. We'd already found that leaving the skin on helped to keep the pieces intact and prevented them from breaking down. Also, it was clear that any water-based cooking methods (such as boiling or steaming) were out of the question; adding moisture to this dish just made matters worse.

In the past, we've had luck salting eggplant and tomatoes when we needed to rid them of excess liquid. Could the same approach be successfully employed with our squash? We salted a pound of sliced squash and let it sit in a colander nestled in a bowl. Thirty minutes later, the squash had released almost 3 tablespoons of liquid—a promising sign. We blotted the squash dry with paper towels and, not wanting to employ any method that would add back the water, decided to sauté this batch. Bingo: Browned squash came out of the pan. We found that cutting the squash in slices ½ inch thick gave us just the right size and texture to toss with pasta.

Looking to other elements to contribute flavor to our dish, we thought of extra-virgin olive oil, as well as garlic. The oil helped coat the pasta and the garlic added a pungent bite. Tasters also gave a thumbs-up to halved grape tomatoes, added to the pan just until they softened, for their sweetness and color. Fresh chopped herbs, in the form of parsley or mint, added still more color as well as their clean and pungent flavors. Tasters also approved of a handful of crumbled cheese; goat cheese with the parsley for one pasta dish, feta cheese with the mint for a second.

But something was still lacking. We then tried a batch with a few tablespoons of salty, briny capers and olives. These ingredients transformed our pasta and squash dishes into something extraordinary. We experimented with some acidic ingredients and found that lemon juice and zest and a bit of red wine vinegar added an extra punch of brightness that played off the sweetness of the squash.

As for the pasta, a bite-size shaped pasta, such as farfalle, suited the squash best. At last, we had paired squash and pasta—and the match was anything but boring.

Pasta and Squash with Tomatoes, Capers, and Goat Cheese

SERVES 2

Other bite-size pasta shapes can be substituted for the farfalle; however, their cup measurements may vary (see page 85).

    2 zucchini or summer squash (about 1 pound),
       ends trimmed, halved lengthwise and
       cut into ½-inch pieces
       Salt and pepper
    6 ounces farfalle (about 2½ cups; see note)
    2 tablespoons extra-virgin olive oil
    2 large shallots, minced
    6 ounces grape tomatoes (about 1 cup), halved
    2 tablespoons capers, rinsed and chopped coarse
    1 teaspoon grated lemon zest plus 1 tablespoon
       fresh lemon juice
    2 tablespoons minced fresh parsley
    2 ounces goat cheese, crumbled (about ½ cup)

1. Toss zucchini with ½ teaspoon salt, place in large colander, and let drain for 30 minutes. Spread zucchini evenly on double layer of paper towels and pat dry with additional paper towels, wiping off any residual salt.

2. Meanwhile, bring 4 quarts water to boil in large pot. Add pasta and 1 tablespoon salt and cook, stirring often, until al dente. Reserve ½ cup cooking water, then drain pasta and return it to pot.

3. While pasta is cooking, heat 1 tablespoon oil in 12-inch nonstick skillet over high heat until just smoking. Add zucchini and cook, stirring occasionally, until golden brown and slightly charred, 5 to 7 minutes; transfer to large plate.

4. Add 2 teaspoons more oil to skillet and heat over medium heat until shimmering. Add shallots and cook, stirring frequently, until softened and browned, 2 to 3 minutes. Stir in tomatoes and cook until slightly softened, about 1 minute. Add browned zucchini, capers, lemon zest, and ¼ teaspoon pepper and cook, stirring constantly, until combined and heated through, about 30 seconds.

5. Add zucchini mixture, remaining 1 teaspoon oil, lemon juice, and parsley to pasta and toss to combine, adjusting sauce consistency with reserved pasta cooking water as desired. Season with salt and pepper to taste. Sprinkle individual portions with goat cheese and serve.

VARIATION

Pasta and Squash with Tomatoes, Olives, and Feta

SERVES 2

Other bite-size pasta shapes can be substituted for the farfalle; however, their cup measurements may vary (see page 85). See page 163 for a recipe to use up the leftover feta.

    2 zucchini or summer squash (about 1 pound),
       ends trimmed, halved lengthwise and
       cut into ½-inch pieces
       Salt and pepper
    6 ounces farfalle (about 2½ cups; see note)
    2 tablespoons extra-virgin olive oil
    1 small red onion, minced
    2 garlic cloves, minced
    6 ounces grape tomatoes (about 1 cup), halved
    2 tablespoons pitted, quartered kalamata olives
    ½ teaspoon grated lemon zest plus 1 teaspoon
       fresh lemon juice
    2 tablespoons minced fresh mint
    1 teaspoon red wine vinegar
    2 ounces feta cheese, crumbled (about ½ cup)

1. Toss zucchini with ½ teaspoon salt, place in large colander, and let drain for 30 minutes. Spread zucchini evenly on double layer of paper towels and pat dry with additional paper towels, wiping off any residual salt.

WHOLE-WHEAT SPAGHETTI WITH FENNEL AND ITALIAN SAUSAGE

2. Meanwhile, bring 4 quarts water to boil in large pot. Add pasta and 1 tablespoon salt and cook, stirring often, until al dente. Reserve ½ cup cooking water, then drain pasta and return it to pot.

3. While pasta is cooking, heat 1 tablespoon oil in 12-inch nonstick skillet over high heat until just smoking. Add zucchini and cook, stirring occasionally, until golden brown and slightly charred, 5 to 7 minutes; transfer to large plate.

4. Add 2 teaspoons more oil to skillet and heat over medium heat until shimmering. Add onion and cook, stirring frequently, until softened and browned, 2 to 3 minutes. Stir in garlic and cook until fragrant, about 30 seconds. Stir in tomatoes and cook until slightly softened, about 1 minute. Add browned zucchini, olives, lemon zest, and ¼ teaspoon pepper and cook, stirring constantly, until combined and heated through, about 30 seconds.

5. Add zucchini mixture, remaining 1 teaspoon oil, lemon juice, mint, and vinegar to pasta and toss to combine, adjusting sauce consistency with reserved pasta cooking water as desired. Season with salt and pepper to taste. Sprinkle individual portions with feta and serve.

WHOLE-WHEAT SPAGHETTI WITH SIMPLE SAUCES

WHOLE GRAINS SEEM TO BE EVERYWHERE WE LOOK nowadays—especially when it comes to pasta. But while whole-wheat pasta has a robust, hearty flavor that can be distinctive, rustic, and nutty, it lacks the versatile, blank-slate quality that makes traditional white pasta so easy to sauce. Still, while this whole-grain product may not take well to just any sauce (particularly acidic, tomato-based sauces), its particular flavor profile becomes a real advantage when combined with the right ingredients. We set out to design a couple of sauces that would provide just the right complement to the hearty flavor and firm texture of whole-wheat pasta; we chose spaghetti for the shape to give our dish a traditional feel.

Since tomato sauce is almost never the right choice for capitalizing on this pasta's robust flavors, we tried pestos and rich cream-based sauces—pairing them with whole-wheat spaghetti—but after testing both options, we were no closer to finding a solution to the sauce problem. There were just too many flavors and textures in these sauces to compete with the complexity of the pasta. Our answer, it seemed, was to simplify our approach. We turned to *aglio e olio*, Italy's bold garlic-and-red-pepper-flake-flavored olive oil sauce. With this simple go-to sauce as a base, we could sauté lots of chunky vegetables that would both soak up the oil's flavor and provide a counterpoint to the pasta's hearty texture.

We settled on two vegetables—asparagus and fennel—that required no parcooking and neither competed with nor faded in the presence of the earthy spaghetti. We sautéed each in extra-virgin olive oil over medium-high heat until they turned crisp-tender and sweet, then cleared the center of the pan to make way for a generous hit of minced garlic (three cloves) and ¼ teaspoon of red pepper flakes for a spicy but not incendiary sauce. The aromatics bloomed quickly in the sizzling oil, at which point we stirred them into the vegetables for even distribution. Next, we reserved some of the spaghetti cooking water and added it to the cooked vegetable mixture. The starch from the pasta water did its usual job, thickening the liquid exuded by the vegetables and helping the sauce cling to the spaghetti when the two were combined.

For more textural contrast and more emphasis on the nutty taste of the spaghetti, we worked in meaty ingredients that would enhance the taste of other components in the mix. Salty pancetta was a natural partner for the asparagus, and anise-accented Italian sausage paired perfectly with the fennel. We finished each version with a handful of freshly grated Pecorino Romano. The cheese provided a rich, salty tang that tasters preferred over Parmesan.

Our two whole-wheat spaghetti dinners were satisfying and flavorful, but with a palmful of chopped pine nuts for texture and chopped basil for a fresh touch, they were perfect.

PREPARING FENNEL

1. Cut off the stems and feathery fronds. (The fronds can be minced and used as a garnish, if desired.)

2. Trim a very thin slice from the base and remove any tough or blemished outer layers from the bulb.

3. Cut the bulb in half through the base. Use a small, sharp knife to remove the pyramid-shaped core.

4. Slice each fennel half into thin strips. For chopped fennel, cut the strips crosswise into small pieces.

THE BEST WHOLE-WHEAT PASTA

We recently bought 18 nationally distributed brands of whole-wheat and multigrain spaghettis and sampled them plain with olive oil, rating them on flavor and texture. Then we tasted the top 10 with marinara and pesto. Most of the 100 percent whole-wheat and 100 percent whole-grain pastas scored low, garnering descriptions like "doughy," "sour," and "fishy." But there was one dark horse that came in on top: Italian-made **Bionaturae Organic 100% Whole Wheat Spaghetti,** made entirely of whole wheat but with an appealingly chewy and firm texture. Its secrets? Custom milling and low-and-slow drying, which guarantee complex, wheaty flavor.

Whole-Wheat Spaghetti with Fennel and Italian Sausage

SERVES 2

Since the extra-virgin olive oil provides the base of the sauce, be sure to pick a flavorful, high-quality brand; our winning supermarket brand is Columela Extra Virgin Olive Oil. See page 85 for a tip on how to measure out long strands of pasta without using a scale.

- 2 tablespoons extra-virgin olive oil (see note)
- 3 garlic cloves, minced
- ¼ teaspoon red pepper flakes
  Salt
- 4 ounces sweet Italian sausage, casings removed
- 1 small fennel bulb (about 8 ounces), trimmed of stalks, cored, and sliced thin (see photos)
- ¼ cup pine nuts, toasted (see page 240) and chopped coarse
- ¼ cup chopped fresh basil
- 1 tablespoon fresh lemon juice
- 6 ounces whole-wheat spaghetti (see note)
- ¼ cup grated Pecorino Romano cheese

1. Combine oil, garlic, red pepper flakes, and ¼ teaspoon salt in small bowl; set aside.

2. Cook sausage in 12-inch nonstick skillet over medium-high heat, breaking up meat with wooden spoon, until browned and crisp, 5 to 7 minutes. Using slotted spoon, transfer sausage to paper towel–lined plate.

3. Add fennel and ⅛ teaspoon salt to fat left in pan and cook over medium-high heat, stirring often, until softened, 5 to 7 minutes. Clear center of skillet, add oil-garlic mixture, and cook, mashing mixture into pan, until fragrant, about 20 seconds. Off heat, stir in sausage, nuts, basil, and lemon juice.

4. Meanwhile, bring 4 quarts water to boil in large pot. Add pasta and 1 tablespoon salt to boiling water and cook, stirring often, until al dente. Reserve ½ cup cooking water, then drain pasta and return it to pot.

5. Add sauce and ⅓ cup reserved pasta cooking water to pasta and toss to combine, adjusting sauce consistency with remaining reserved pasta cooking water as desired. Season with salt to taste, sprinkle with cheese, and serve.

Whole-Wheat Spaghetti with Asparagus and Pancetta

SERVES 2

Since the extra-virgin olive oil provides the base of the sauce, be sure to pick a flavorful, high-quality brand; our winning supermarket brand is Columela Extra Virgin Olive Oil. See page 85 for a tip on how to measure out long strands of pasta without using a scale.

- **2 tablespoons plus 2 teaspoons extra-virgin olive oil (see note)**
- **3 garlic cloves, minced**
- **1 tablespoon capers, rinsed and coarsely chopped**
- **¼ teaspoon red pepper flakes**
   Salt
- **2 ounces pancetta, cut into ¼-inch pieces**
- **½ bunch asparagus (about ½ pound), tough ends trimmed, sliced on bias into 1-inch pieces**
- **1 large shallot, thinly sliced**
- **¼ cup pine nuts, toasted (see page 240) and chopped coarse**
- **¼ cup chopped fresh basil**
- **1 tablespoon fresh lemon juice**
- **6 ounces whole-wheat spaghetti (see note)**
- **¼ cup grated Pecorino Romano cheese**

1. Combine 2 tablespoons oil, garlic, capers, red pepper flakes, and ¼ teaspoon salt in small bowl; set aside.

2. Heat remaining 2 teaspoons oil in 12-inch nonstick skillet over medium-high heat until shimmering. Add pancetta and cook until crisp, 3 to 5 minutes. Using slotted spoon, transfer pancetta to paper towel–lined plate.

3. Add asparagus and shallot to fat left in pan and cook until softened, 2 to 4 minutes. Clear center of skillet, add oil-garlic mixture, and cook, mashing mixture into pan, until fragrant, about 20 seconds. Off heat, stir in pancetta, nuts, basil, and lemon juice.

4. Meanwhile, bring 4 quarts water to boil in large pot. Add pasta and 1 tablespoon salt to boiling water and cook, stirring often, until al dente. Reserve ½ cup cooking water, then drain pasta and return it to pot.

5. Add sauce and ⅓ cup reserved pasta cooking water to pasta and toss to combine, adjusting sauce consistency with remaining reserved pasta cooking water as desired. Season with salt to taste, sprinkle with cheese, and serve.

ORECCHIETTE WITH BROCCOLI RABE

THE ITALIAN REGION OF PUGLIA, LOCATED ON THE "boot" of the country, is known for its simple, rustic cuisine. Orecchiette, the distinctive little ear-shaped pasta, hails from this area and so appears in many recipes. One especially popular dish pairs orecchiette with bitter broccoli rabe and sweet, rich Italian sausage. We hoped to bring this trio to our side of the pond for a straightforward yet utterly satisfying entrée for two.

We started with the broccoli rabe, a spicy and bitter green. The differing textures and thicknesses of this vegetable (thick stalks, tender leaves, and small florets) can make it difficult to cook it evenly. We had to devise a method that would soften the stalks but keep the florets and leaves from becoming mushy. We tested steaming and boiling. Steaming cooked this tough green unevenly. By the time the thick stalks had softened, the tender florets were mushy. Boiling did a better job of cooking the various parts of this plant at the same rate; because boiling broccoli rabe takes but a few minutes, there is less time for the florets to become mushy.

To prepare the broccoli rabe, we trimmed the tough ends and cut the rest of the stalks into 1½-inch pieces. We then tossed them into the boiling water and cooked them for about two minutes—just long enough for the broccoli rabe to become intensely green and slightly tender. To drain off the excess liquid, which would dilute our dish, we set the greens on a layer of paper towels, which absorbed the water. Then, instead of dumping out the richly flavored water we'd used to cook the broccoli rabe, we used it to cook the orecchiette. With the pasta and broccoli rabe ready to go, we turned to the other ingredients.

Next up, the sausage. We browned it in a large skillet until the fat rendered and the sausage was browned, breaking up any big pieces as we were cooking it. Rather than drain off the rendered fat, we kept it in the pan, hoping that it would provide enough of a base for a silky, richly flavored sauce.

With the sausage browned, we could add our aromatics to the pan. We stirred in some garlic and red pepper flakes. For added complexity and depth of flavor, we relied on a secret weapon frequently deployed in the test kitchen: anchovy. A single minced fillet deepened the overall flavors of the dish immensely. Once the aromatics became fragrant, we tossed in the blanched broccoli rabe and added the contents of the pan to the drained orecchiette. But when we tossed the pasta with the sausage–broccoli rabe mixture and sprinkled some Pecorino Romano over the top, we found that no amount of reserved pasta cooking water could make the sauce thick and silky. In fact, adding too much extra cooking water just diluted the flavors of our dish. Tasters thought the individual ingredients tasted great on their own, but they weren't coming together in a unified dish.

Looking for other ways to both bring the elements of our pasta dinner together and give the sauce that silky, thick consistency, we hit on a one-two punch that worked well. First, we added some chicken broth to the pan; the broth boosted the other flavors without overwhelming them and provided a rich backbone of flavor. Second, we stirred in some flour when we sautéed the aromatics. Just a teaspoon gave our sauce the right consistency.

Now we had a richly flavored pasta dish, boasting big bites of sweet, meaty sausage, spicy broccoli rabe, and tender pasta, all draped in a luscious, silky sauce.

Orecchiette with Broccoli Rabe and Italian Sausage

SERVES 2

Other pasta shapes can be substituted for the orecchiette; however, their cup measurements may vary (see page 25). Don't confuse broccoli rabe with broccoli or broccolini; broccoli rabe is a member of the turnip family and has a peppery bite. Chicory or turnip greens can be substituted for the broccoli rabe.

- ½ **bunch broccoli rabe (about ½ pound), tough ends trimmed, cut into 1½-inch lengths (see note)**
- **Salt**
- 2 **tablespoons extra-virgin olive oil**
- 8 **ounces sweet Italian sausage, casings removed**
- 3 **garlic cloves, minced**
- 1 **anchovy fillet, rinsed and minced**
- 1 **teaspoon unbleached all-purpose flour**
- ¼ **teaspoon red pepper flakes**
- ¾ **cup low-sodium chicken broth**
- 6 **ounces orecchiette (about 1¾ cups; see note)**
- ¼ **cup grated Pecorino Romano cheese, plus extra for serving**

1. Bring 4 quarts water to boil in large pot. Add broccoli rabe and 1 tablespoon salt and cook, stirring often, until broccoli rabe turns bright green, about 2 minutes. Using slotted spoon, transfer broccoli rabe to paper towel–lined plate; set aside.

2. Heat oil in 12-inch nonstick skillet over medium-high heat until shimmering. Add sausage, breaking up meat with wooden spoon, and cook until browned and crisp, 5 to 7 minutes. Stir in garlic, anchovy, flour, and red pepper flakes and cook until fragrant, about 30 seconds. Stir in broth and bring to simmer. Cook, stirring occasionally, until sauce has thickened slightly, about 1 minute. Stir in broccoli rabe and toss until coated; set aside.

USE IT UP: BROCCOLI RABE

Sautéed Broccoli Rabe with Garlic and Lemon
SERVES 2

For a spicy dish, add a pinch of red pepper flakes with the garlic in step 2. This side dish pairs well with chicken and pork.

- ½ **bunch broccoli rabe (about ½ pound), tough ends trimmed, cut into 1½-inch lengths**
- **Salt and pepper**
- 2 **tablespoons extra-virgin olive oil**
- 2 **garlic cloves, sliced thin**
- ½ **teaspoon grated lemon zest**

1. Bring 2 quarts water to boil in large saucepan. Add broccoli rabe and 2 teaspoons salt and cook, stirring often, until broccoli rabe turns bright green and tender, 2 to 4 minutes. Drain broccoli rabe and transfer to paper towel–lined plate.

2. Heat oil in 10-inch nonstick skillet over medium heat until shimmering. Add garlic and cook until fragrant and golden, about 1 minute. Stir in broccoli rabe and cook until heated through, 3 to 5 minutes. Off heat, stir in lemon zest, season with salt and pepper to taste, and serve.

3. Meanwhile, return water to boil, add pasta, and cook, stirring often, until al dente. Reserve ½ cup cooking water, then drain pasta and return it to pot.

4. Add sausage mixture and Pecorino to pasta and toss to combine, adjusting sauce consistency with reserved pasta cooking water as desired. Season with salt to taste and serve with extra Pecorino.

VARIATION

Orecchiette with Broccoli Rabe and White Beans
Follow recipe for Orecchiette with Broccoli Rabe and Italian Sausage, omitting sausage and anchovy. Increase amount of garlic to 4 cloves and substitute ¾ cup vegetable broth for chicken broth. Add ¾ cup drained and rinsed canned cannellini beans to skillet with broth in step 2. Add 2 tablespoons pine nuts, toasted (see page 240), to pasta with sauce in step 4. Season with 1½ teaspoons red wine vinegar, or to taste, before serving.

USE IT UP: CANNELLINI BEANS AND CHICKPEAS

Hummus
MAKES ABOUT 1 CUP

The hummus can be refrigerated in an airtight container for up to 3 days.

- ¾ cup drained and rinsed canned cannellini beans or canned chickpeas
- 2 tablespoons tahini
- 2 tablespoons extra-virgin olive oil, plus extra for drizzling
- 2 tablespoons water
- 4 teaspoons fresh lemon juice, plus extra to taste
- 1 small garlic clove, minced
  Salt
- ⅛ teaspoon ground cumin
  Pinch cayenne pepper
- 1 teaspoon minced fresh cilantro (optional)

Process beans, tahini, olive oil, water, lemon juice, garlic, ¼ teaspoon salt, cumin, and cayenne together in food processor until smooth, about 30 seconds. Season with salt and lemon juice, adding extra to taste. Transfer hummus to serving bowl and chill until flavors have blended, about 30 minutes. Drizzle with olive oil, sprinkle with cilantro (if using), and serve.

WEEKNIGHT BOLOGNESE WITH LINGUINE

BOLOGNESE IS OFTEN CONSIDERED THE KING OF Italian meat sauces. Yet given the amount of time and energy it takes to prepare, home-cooked Bolognese often leaves us feeling more like a lowly servant than royalty. The effort involved in making Bolognese hardly seems worthwhile unless you're feeding the entire Roman Legion. We set about developing a recipe for authentic-tasting Bolognese that could be cooked on a weeknight and would be appropriate for just two—not a whole army.

The test kitchen's standard Bolognese recipe starts with softening onion and carrot in butter in a large Dutch oven before searing equal parts ground beef, pork, and veal to develop rich meatiness. Next, milk, white wine, and a 28-ounce can of whole tomatoes (processed until almost smooth) are added successively and gently reduced over two hours until the pot is almost dry. Our challenge would be cutting back on the simmering time while finding ways to develop the complexity of flavor usually achieved through hours of cooking. First, though, we would need to rescale this recipe to make it work for two.

We whittled the amount of ground meat down to 6 ounces and realized that purchasing 2 ounces each of ground beef, pork, and veal would be difficult in most supermarkets. To simplify the recipe, we settled on meatloaf mix, which is a combination of these meats. (If you can't find meatloaf mix, 80 percent lean ground beef works well, too.) To create the sauce, we reduced the amount of liquid to ¾ cup of whole milk and ¼ cup of white wine (for 1 cup total of liquid) and substituted a 14.5-ounce can of diced tomatoes that we processed until smooth.

With our recipe amounts now adjusted for two people, we needed to cut the simmering time. It turns out that simmering Bolognese gently over a long period of time accomplishes two things: It concentrates the flavor of the meat and aromatics, and it tenderizes the browned meat. We wondered if the simmering time could be reduced if we didn't brown the meat (which develops flavor but also toughens the meat). For our next batch we added the ground meat and cooked it for only a minute (enough time to break it into smaller pieces) before adding the milk. After reducing the milk, wine, and tomatoes, we found the meat supremely tender after just 40 minutes of simmering. By not browning the meat, however, we lost some of the meaty flavor. To boost the savory richness of the dish, we browned a blend of pancetta (which seemed a more authentic choice than bacon), some dried porcini, and half a minced anchovy (the latter two are test kitchen favorites for upping meaty flavor) before adding the onion and carrot to the pot; the flavor combination worked like a charm.

To simplify prep we put our food processor to work on all of our aromatic ingredients. First, we pulsed big chunks of onion and carrot along with the porcini, pancetta, and anchovy; after about 10 pulses, we had a finely minced mixture. We set that mixture aside and then quickly processed the tomatoes. The only manual prep left was mincing a clove of garlic (which often managed to escape the blades of the food processor). Finally, we had a great-tasting, quick, and easy Bolognese sauce. All that was left was the pasta.

As we reached for a pot to cook the pasta, we wondered if there was enough moisture in the pan to cook the pasta through—this would save us time both up front (we wouldn't have to wait for the water to boil) and at the end (it would cut back on the dreaded dishwashing). To cook the pasta with our sauce, we would have to add at least some water to allow the pasta to soften. To figure out the amount we'd need, we added 6 ounces of pasta and varying amounts of water to dilute finished batches of our Bolognese. We then covered the pot and vigorously simmered the pasta until al dente. Two cups of water proved just the right amount, producing nicely cooked pasta and a thickened, but not gluey, sauce. To save time we added the linguine with the processed tomatoes, which easily recouped a quarter of an hour but kept the tomatoes from reducing. To add back concentrated tomato flavor, we stirred in 1 tablespoon of tomato paste.

Last we addressed one lingering flavor issue. Bolognese should offer sweet resonance to balance the richness of the meat and the acidity of the wine and tomatoes. The sauce was light on sweetness at this point, so we added ½ teaspoon of sugar with the garlic.

Rich, meaty, complex, and slightly sweet, our Bolognese sauce now delivered on all of the promises of a traditional slow-cooked version—but it's made with just one pan and is on the table in less than an hour.

NOTES FROM THE TEST KITCHEN

THE BEST TOMATO PASTE

Tomato paste is basically tomato puree with most of the moisture cooked out. It adds body, color, and intensity to many dishes, including pastas, stews, and soups. To find out which brand is best, we gathered 10 brands for a tasting: nine in small cans and one in a toothpaste-like tube. We had tasters sample the paste straight from the container, cooked by itself, and cooked in marinara sauce.

When the brands were sampled uncooked, tasters were split between those that tasted bright and acidic, like fresh tomatoes, and those with deep "cooked" tomato flavor. Many downgraded brands for "dried herb" notes, including oregano. Because tomato paste is usually cooked, we sautéed each brand in a skillet and tasted again. Some pastes became dull; others sprang to life. In the marinara sauce, tasters leaned toward those pastes that provided long-simmered flavor and depth. But ultimately, we found that while better tomato pastes improved the taste of the marinara, no brand ruined the dish. Overall scores were relatively close, but one paste came in slightly ahead of the pack. **Goya** tomato paste was praised for its "bright, robust tomato flavor." Tasters liked its sweetness (this brand had one of the highest levels of natural sugars in the lineup), yet found it well balanced.

Weeknight Bolognese with Linguine
SERVES 2

If you can't find meatloaf mix, which is made up of equal parts ground beef, veal, and pork, you can substitute 80 percent lean ground beef. See page 85 for a tip on how to measure out long strands of pasta without using a scale. When adding the pasta in step 5, stir gently to avoid breaking the noodles; after a minute or two they will soften enough to be stirred more easily. If necessary, add hot water, 1 tablespoon at a time, to adjust the consistency of the sauce before serving.

- 1 small onion, cut into 1-inch pieces
- 1 carrot, peeled and cut into 1-inch pieces
- 1½ ounces pancetta, cut into 1-inch pieces
- ¼ ounce dried porcini mushrooms, rinsed
- ½ anchovy fillet, rinsed
- 1 (14.5-ounce) can diced tomatoes
- 1 tablespoon unsalted butter
- 1 garlic clove, minced

½ teaspoon sugar

6 ounces meatloaf mix (see note)

¾ cup whole milk

1 tablespoon tomato paste

¼ cup dry white wine

2 cups water

6 ounces linguine (see note)

Salt and pepper

Grated Parmesan cheese, for serving

1. Pulse onion, carrot, pancetta, porcini, and anchovy in food processor until finely chopped, 10 to 15 pulses; transfer to bowl. Pulse tomatoes with their juice until mostly smooth, about 8 pulses.

2. Melt butter in 12-inch nonstick skillet over medium heat. Add processed onion mixture and cook until softened and lightly browned, 5 to 7 minutes. Stir in garlic and sugar and cook until fragrant, about 30 seconds.

3. Stir in meatloaf mix, breaking up meat with wooden spoon, and cook for 1 minute. Stir in milk, scraping up any browned bits, bring to simmer, and cook until almost completely evaporated, 8 to 10 minutes.

4. Stir in tomato paste and cook for 1 minute. Stir in wine, bring to simmer, and cook until almost completely evaporated, 3 to 5 minutes.

5. Add processed tomatoes, water, and pasta and bring to rapid simmer. Cover and simmer vigorously, stirring often, until pasta is tender and sauce is thickened, 12 to 16 minutes. Off heat, season with salt and pepper to taste and serve with Parmesan.

TORTELLINI WITH VEGETABLES

IT'S A COMMON WEEKNIGHT DINNER SCENARIO: Boil up store-bought tortellini, toss with jarred sauce, and cover it all up with a healthy mound of grated Parmesan. This kind of dinner may be easy and quick, but it's far from being flavorful or exciting. While we do appreciate the convenience of store-bought tortellini, we're inevitably frustrated by lackluster weeknight tortellini recipes. Whether drowned in a bland cream sauce, overcooked and blown out, or sharing the bowl with sad-looking vegetables, store-bought tortellini

often seems to earn its poor reputation. Recognizing the potential of these prepackaged pasta purses for a weeknight dinner for two, we committed ourselves to developing a recipe featuring properly cooked tortellini, fresh vegetables, and a luxurious, flavor-packed sauce. First up, we tackled the tortellini.

While some specialty markets sell freshly made tortellini, it's difficult to track down and always expensive. We wanted an accessible recipe featuring one of the three styles found in supermarkets: fresh, frozen, and dried. We experimented with a package of each, cooking the tortellini according to the directions on the package. The dried tortellini proved the clear loser of the group, taking the longest time to cook and suffering from a rubbery texture. The race between fresh and frozen was closer, but in the end fresh won for its silkier texture and brighter flavor. After testing a range of fresh tortellini fillings, we settled on the simplest: cheese, since it would give us the most freedom in creating a sauce and choosing vegetables.

Riding high on the success of our Weeknight Bolognese with Linguine (page 96), in which we cooked the pasta in the meaty sauce, we decided to use just one pan to both cook the pasta and build the sauce. We melted butter in a 12-inch skillet (the right size for a 9-ounce package of tortellini) and softened onion and garlic to establish an aromatic foundation. Next, we stirred in 4 cups of chicken broth (which provided more flavor than water) and the tortellini. Once the pan came to a simmer, we cooked it vigorously until the liquid had reduced to a lightly thickened sauce, which took about 15 minutes. To our dismay, this tortellini had turned from delicately shaped crescents to bloated, mushy spheres. While dried pasta requires a substantial amount of liquid to soften, tortellini, with its higher moisture content, absorbs less liquid as it cooks and requires less simmering to become tender. We then tested a few more batches of tortellini with 4 cups, 3 cups, and 2 cups of chicken broth, respectively; 2 cups was the magic number. This batch of tortellini cooked up tender in about seven minutes, at which point the broth had reduced to a nice sauce. Having ironed out our method, we addressed the vegetables and flavorings.

As our goal was a fresh-tasting, vibrant dish, we decided to focus on spring vegetables like artichokes, asparagus, fennel, peas, and spinach. Tasters liked the aniselike sweetness of fennel and the delicate elegance of peas and spinach. While artichokes and asparagus both provided welcome texture, tasters preferred this dish without their assertive flavors. Since peas and spinach are at their best when barely cooked through, we stirred them in at the last minute. Fennel, on the other hand, really shines when lightly caramelized. We tried swapping ½-inch pieces of fennel for the onion in our recipe, allowing it to slowly soften and brown in the butter before adding the broth and pasta. This method eked sweet, rich flavor from the fennel that tasters loved.

NOTES FROM THE TEST KITCHEN

PREGRATING YOUR OWN PARMESAN

While some shortcuts are acceptable in the cooking-for-two kitchen (think prepackaged broccoli florets and store-bought pie dough), the tasteless powdered Parmesan that comes in a green can is not one of them. In tests, we've also found that the higher-grade pregrated cheese in the refrigerator section of the supermarket is uneven in quality. But what about pregrating your own Parmesan to always have it at the ready? Do you sacrifice any flavor for convenience? To find out, we divided a block of Parmigiano-Reggiano in two, reducing one half to a powder in a food processor and leaving the other whole. We stored both in the refrigerator for two weeks, then compared them side by side on their own, mixed into polenta, and added to breading for chicken. After two weeks of storage, tasters were hard-pressed to detect a difference between the cheeses, even in the side-by-side tasting. But after a full month of storage, tasters found a noticeable drop-off in flavor. So to save time and make dinner prep easier, we think pregrating is fine, as long as you don't store the cheese longer than two to three weeks.

To make quick work of grinding Parmesan, process 1-inch chunks in a food processor (no more than 1 pound at a time) until ground into coarse particles, about 20 seconds. Refrigerate in an airtight container until ready to use.

BUYING TORTELLINI

When shopping for tortellini, you'll likely find three options available at your local supermarket: dried, frozen, and fresh. We tasted them all side by side and here's what we found. The dried tortellini, usually found in the spaghetti aisle, is unimpressive, with a stale flavor and rubbery texture. We don't recommend it. The frozen variety is a bit better; once cooked, this tortellini is more moist than the dried. But fresh tortellini, available in the deli section in plastic 9-ounce packages (perfect for two), is head and shoulders better than either of the other two. It has a clean flavor and fine texture that are about as close as you can get to homemade pasta.

To meld the flavors of our vegetables with a touch of richness and complementary sweetness, we stirred in a small amount of cream with the peas and spinach. This addition gave our broth-based sauce body while balancing the flavors of the dish nicely. A good dose of grated Parmesan also helped boost sauciness and flavor, and a splash of lemon juice added brightness. Tasters were really coming around to our reinvention of store-bought tortellini but felt this sauce was too sweet. To counter the sweetness from the cream, fennel, and peas, we crisped a few slices of prosciutto for a garnish.

Miles away from the average quick-fix tortellini dinner, our dish was a satisfying mélange of tender pasta, fresh vegetables, an ethereal sauce, and crispy prosciutto.

Tortellini with Crispy Prosciutto and Spring Vegetables

SERVES 2

If necessary, add hot water, 1 tablespoon at a time, to adjust the consistency of the sauce before serving. You can find the tortellini in the deli section of the supermarket.

- **4 thin slices prosciutto (about 1 ounce), cut into ¼-inch pieces**
- **1 tablespoon unsalted butter**
- **1 small fennel bulb (about 8 ounces), trimmed of stalks, cored, and cut into ½-inch pieces (see page 92)**
- **2 garlic cloves, minced**
- **2 cups low-sodium chicken broth**
- **1 (9-ounce) package fresh cheese tortellini (see note)**
- **3 ounces baby spinach (about 3 cups)**
- **½ cup frozen peas**
- **¼ cup heavy cream**
- **¼ cup grated Parmesan cheese, plus extra for serving**
- **2 teaspoons fresh lemon juice**
- **Salt and pepper**

1. Cook prosciutto in 12-inch nonstick skillet over medium heat until browned and crisp, 5 to 7 minutes. Using slotted spoon, transfer prosciutto to paper towel–lined plate and reserve for serving.

2. Melt butter in skillet over medium heat. Stir in fennel and cook until browned, 6 to 9 minutes. Stir in garlic and cook until fragrant, about 30 seconds.

TORTELLINI WITH CRISPY PROSCIUTTO AND SPRING VEGETABLES

3. Stir in broth and tortellini and bring to rapid simmer. Simmer vigorously, stirring often, until tortellini is tender and sauce is thickened, 6 to 9 minutes.

4. Stir in spinach, peas, and cream and cook over low heat, stirring gently but constantly, until spinach is wilted and tortellini is coated with sauce, 2 to 3 minutes.

5. Off heat, stir in Parmesan and lemon juice and season with salt and pepper to taste. Sprinkle individual portions with crisped prosciutto and serve with extra Parmesan.

SKILLET CARBONARA

PASTA CARBONARA, A POPULAR ROMAN DISH, features a creamy egg sauce that cooks into a velvety consistency from the heat of just-drained pasta. Crisp bites of bacon punctuate the dish and hot garlic gives it a kick. This is no diet food, but the indulgent nature of carbonara is one reason it is offered on every trattoria menu. Although recipes for this cheesy, bacon-laced favorite abound and the ingredient list is minimal, it remains a dish that inspires both awe and fear in would-be cooks. It's a simple dish, but the final minutes can be cruel. If the mixture is too hot, the eggs curdle. If it's not hot enough, the cheese won't melt. And don't even think of letting this dish sit around while you set the table—in the blink of an eye, velvety carbonara turns into a heavy, clumpy tangle. We wanted to transform carbonara into a more forgiving, but still flavorful, supper and set out to cook the entire recipe—from bacon to pasta—in the same skillet.

Most recipes start with boiling pasta in a big pot of water. Meanwhile, white wine is reduced on the stovetop with garlic and black pepper. The pasta is drained and tossed with the white wine mixture, along with bacon, eggs, a little cream, and lots of Pecorino Romano. It's these ingredients that form the rich, creamy sauce, cooked from the heat of the noodles. With the basic outline of our recipe in mind, we gathered the ingredients and headed into the test kitchen.

To start, we crisped and rendered bacon and set it aside, then cooked two cloves of garlic, pepper, and white wine until reduced. We wanted to cook our pasta in the same skillet, and for 6 ounces of pasta, we found that we needed just over 2 cups of water. While spaghetti or linguine is traditional in this dish, we opted for penne, which provided big, hearty bites of pasta that would stand up to the creamy sauce.

When the pasta was just about done, we got ready to add the eggs and cheese, but we faced the usual conundrum: The eggs couldn't cook for long or they'd curdle, but the cheese needed time to melt. The first step was to use just one egg to simplify the issue. At the same time, we whisked some heavy cream into the egg (the cream diluted the egg, preventing it from coagulating as quickly). Despite these efforts, the egg still curdled before the cheese melted. Stirring in additional heavy cream made the carbonara too rich. We tried milk, but it separated in the last few moments of cooking. The solution? Evaporated milk. Because evaporated milk is stabilized, it worked beautifully and never separated. We found one downside: The sauce was a bit too thick. Cutting the sauce with a little chicken broth was an easy fix—and the broth also boosted the flavor of this subtle sauce.

Our skillet carbonara was almost perfect, but when we sprinkled the bacon over the top, tasters complained that it seemed too sparse and disconnected from the dish. Going up on the amount of bacon just made for an overly bacon-y topping. That's when we had the idea to combine the bacon with some bread crumbs to create a more even, cohesive layer on top of the penne. Broiled until golden brown, the bacon-enhanced bread-crumb topping provided the perfect crisp foil for the tender, creamy pasta below.

Skillet Carbonara Casserole

SERVES 2

Other pasta shapes can be substituted for the penne; however, their cup measurements may vary (see page 85).

- 4 ounces bacon (about 4 slices), chopped fine
- 1 slice high-quality white sandwich bread, torn into pieces
- 2½ ounces Pecorino Romano cheese, grated (about 1¼ cups)
- Salt and pepper
- 1 large egg
- ½ cup evaporated milk
- ½ cup low-sodium chicken broth
- 2 garlic cloves, minced

½ cup white wine

2¼ cups water

6 ounces penne (about 1¾ cups; see note)

1. Adjust oven rack to upper-middle position and heat broiler. Cook bacon in 12-inch nonstick skillet over medium heat until browned and crisp, about 8 minutes. Transfer bacon to paper towel–lined plate. Pour off fat left in pan and reserve 1 tablespoon.

2. Pulse 1 tablespoon cooked bacon, 2 teaspoons reserved fat, bread, 2 tablespoons cheese, and ¼ teaspoon pepper in food processor until coarsely ground, about 6 pulses; set aside. In medium bowl, whisk remaining cheese, egg, milk, and broth together.

3. Add remaining 1 teaspoon reserved fat to skillet and return to medium heat until shimmering. Add garlic and cook until fragrant, about 30 seconds. Stir in wine and cook until reduced to 2 tablespoons, about 3 minutes. Add water, pasta, ½ teaspoon salt, and ¼ teaspoon pepper and bring to rapid simmer. Cover and simmer vigorously, stirring often, until pasta is al dente and most of liquid is absorbed, 10 to 15 minutes.

4. Off heat, add egg mixture and remaining cooked bacon to pasta and toss to combine. Top with bacon-bread mixture, transfer to oven, and broil until golden brown, about 2 minutes. Let pasta cool for 5 minutes before serving.

BAKED ZITI

BAKED ZITI IS AN ITALIAN-AMERICAN CLASSIC THAT almost always makes an appearance at church suppers and potluck dinners. With its bubbling, gooey cheese and rich tomato sauce enrobing tender pasta, it's easy to see why this dish is so popular. But since almost all recipes make enough food to satisfy the entire congregation or neighborhood, this dish rarely shows up on the dinner table for two. We wanted a baked ziti that was rich and cheesy, but we didn't want tons of leftovers to clog up the fridge.

For our baked ziti for two, we started with the pasta. Following our established method for cooking pasta, we brought 4 quarts of water to a boil in a large pot before adding 6 ounces of ziti and a single tablespoon of salt. From our years of experience cooking baked

pasta, we knew that the cooked ziti would continue to absorb liquid while it baked in the oven (baking the dish serves to melt the cheese and meld the flavors of the dish), so we were careful to cook the pasta just shy of al dente to avoid overblown pasta in the final dish. While the pasta cooked, we prepped the ingredients for the sauce. Once the pasta was ready, we drained it and set it aside while we built the sauce in the same pot.

The sauce for baked ziti should be somewhat smooth and thick, but not completely uniform; it should have some chunks of tomato scattered throughout. We began our testing with a combination of tomato sauce and diced tomatoes, which we mashed so they'd blend in but still provide some texture. Cooked with olive oil, garlic, and red pepper flakes, this sauce had good flavor, but tasters thought that it was too thin for baked ziti. In our next test, we tried canned crushed tomatoes, which are a mix of tomato chunks and puree; this time, tasters found the sauce too thick. Finally, we tried whole canned tomatoes, which we processed briefly in the food processor. The processed whole tomatoes offered the freshest tomato flavor and were just the right consistency. Simmering our sauce for 15 minutes rid the tomatoes of their raw flavor and concentrated their sweetness.

Looking for ways to bulk up the sauce, we considered a few additions. Ground beef seemed out of place, but sausage, a common ingredient in meaty zitis, sounded appealing. Before building the sauce, we added some sweet Italian sausage to the pot and browned it. This time around, we ditched the olive oil and used the rendered fat to sauté our garlic and red pepper flakes. We had amped up the meatiness of our sauce, but we thought it could benefit from another vegetable. Green bell pepper tasted too bitter, but red bell pepper added a nice, sweet vegetal note. The resulting sauce was the best-tasting one yet—it was rich and meaty, sweet and savory.

With our sauce finished, it was time to assemble the dish. We tossed the pasta into the sauce and divided the mixture between two small gratin dishes (the low sides of these dishes allowed for more browning). We then topped each dish with some shredded mozzarella and baked our mini baked zitis in a 475-degree oven. After 10 minutes, the cheese was melted and bubbly—things were looking good. The results of this test, however, were a letdown.

Though the sauce had bright, fresh tomato flavor and meaty depth, it was a bit thin and lacked the usual creaminess found in baked ziti. In many recipes, mozzarella cheese is used to bind the pasta together and add creamy richness, but after just one test, tasters admitted they preferred the mozzarella as its own cheesy layer on top of the pasta. We tried ricotta, which is often used in baked ziti, but tasters thought the finished dish was too pedestrian. Scanning the refrigerator for other ways to enrich the sauce, we spied a container of heavy cream. This was the answer to our prayers. Just ⅓ cup of heavy cream gave our sauce the right consistency and richness without weighing it down.

One final problem was plaguing our tasters: The portions were rather rich and large. Our 6 ounces of ziti absorbed moisture from the sauce while baking and had become an intimidating, mozzarella-capped mountain of pasta. We decided to scale back the amount of pasta to a more appropriate 4 ounces.

Our mini baked zitis with sausage were now flavorful, saucy, and satisfying—and just the right amount for two perfect servings.

Baked Ziti with Sausage

SERVES 2

Other pasta shapes can be substituted for the ziti; however, their cup measurements may vary (see page 85). You will need two shallow 2-cup gratin dishes (measuring approximately 9 by 6 inches; see page 3), or you can substitute one 8-inch square baking dish.

- 1 (28-ounce) can whole tomatoes
- 4 ounces ziti (about 1¼ cups; see note)
  Salt
- 6 ounces sweet Italian sausage, casings removed
- ½ red bell pepper, stemmed, seeded, and cut into ½-inch pieces
- 4 garlic cloves, minced
- ⅛ teaspoon red pepper flakes
- ⅓ cup heavy cream
- 2 tablespoons chopped fresh basil
- 4 ounces mozzarella cheese, shredded (about 1 cup)

1. Adjust oven rack to middle position and heat oven to 475 degrees. Pulse tomatoes with their juice in food processor until coarsely chopped and no large pieces remain, 6 to 8 pulses.

2. Bring 4 quarts water to boil in large pot. Add pasta and 1 tablespoon salt and cook, stirring often, until al dente. Reserve ½ cup cooking water, then drain pasta and transfer it to large bowl.

3. Add sausage to pot and cook over medium-high heat, breaking up meat with wooden spoon, until fat begins to render, about 2 minutes. Stir in bell pepper and cook until tender and sausage is lightly browned, about 5 minutes. Stir in garlic and red pepper flakes and cook until fragrant, about 30 seconds. Stir in processed tomatoes and simmer gently until tomatoes no longer taste raw and sauce has thickened, about 15 minutes.

4. Off heat, stir in cream and basil and season with salt to taste. Add sauce to pasta and toss to combine, adjusting sauce consistency with reserved pasta cooking water as desired. Divide pasta evenly between two shallow 2-cup gratin dishes. Sprinkle ½ cup mozzarella over top of each dish.

5. Bake until cheese has melted and browned and pasta has heated through, 10 to 15 minutes. Let pasta cool for 5 minutes before serving.

NOTES FROM THE TEST KITCHEN

WAITING TO PREP GARLIC

Before beginning any recipe, we always make sure to have each ingredient prepared and measured into its own bowl. This is especially important when cooking for two; because you're using smaller amounts and fewer ingredients, cooking times are shorter and recipes as a whole move more quickly. But not all ingredients can be prepped ahead of time. Case in point: garlic. Pressing garlic breaks down the clove's cell structure, exposing it to oxygen. The longer the garlic is exposed to the air, the more quickly it loses its flavor. In addition, oxygen can cause the sulfur compounds in the garlic to turn green or blue. The solution to this problem? Wait until you're ready to use the garlic to press or slice it. This will guarantee that it provides its full, garlicky flavor to any dish (and doesn't turn a funny color).

WHITE SPINACH LASAGNA

IN NORTHERN ITALY, WHERE SPINACH LASAGNA HAS its roots, cooks keep things simple, combining layers of homemade pasta, fresh spinach, béchamel (white sauce), and cheese. The delicate, savory white sauce balances the robust flavor of the cooked spinach, and the melted cheese provides a golden crown and gooey bites within the casserole. Sadly, when translated for the American dinner table, white spinach lasagna loses its elegance and morphs into a heavy, bland dish with layers of dull, flavorless spinach sandwiched between overcooked noodles. We wanted a recipe that kept the refinement of the traditional dish, with a rich (but not heavy) sauce, a flavorful spinach filling, and tender noodles—but scaled down for two.

Right away, we addressed the baking vessel, considering everything from gratin dishes to loaf pans. Gratin dishes didn't provide enough height for us to properly layer our lasagna, so they were out. A regular-size loaf pan, measuring approximately 9 by 5 inches, gave us a good amount of lasagna for two diners, but the lasagna seemed a bit casual when compared to the elegant, petite lasagnas produced by two mini loaf pans. Because we wanted to echo the refinement of authentic Italian white spinach lasagna, we settled on the mini loaf pans.

In prior testing, we'd found we preferred no-boil lasagna noodles to regular dried. No-boil noodles are simply more convenient and don't become waterlogged; they taste much better, too. We'd also found that the secret of no-boil noodles is to leave the sauce a little on the thin side. The noodles can then absorb liquid without drying out the dish overall. Since the mini loaf pans were too small to accommodate the lasagna noodles, we needed to break them into smaller pieces that would fit the pan and sit in a single layer.

Moving on to the spinach filling, we had two options: fresh and frozen spinach. First we tested fresh spinach, but it released so much liquid that the finished lasagnas were waterlogged and flavorless. The fresh spinach would clearly need to be blanched briefly, then squeezed dry, before we could layer it between the lasagna noodles. We took this path and, sure enough, our lasagnas tasted great and weren't watery in the least. However, this extra step required the use of another pot and added about 20 minutes to our cooking time. We decided to see how frozen spinach would do. The frozen spinach was definitely a time-saver—no precooking required (it just had to be thawed and squeezed dry)—but we wondered how its flavor would compare to that of the blanched fresh spinach. We had tasters sample mini lasagnas prepared with each and were shocked to find that they thought both tasted good. Not surprisingly, the convenience of frozen spinach won out.

Next we moved on to the béchamel sauce, which is a classic milk sauce thickened with a roux, a mixture of flour and butter. To boost the flavor of the sauce, we sautéed a shallot and some garlic in the butter before adding the flour and milk. After a few tests, we determined that 2 cups of milk and just 2 tablespoons of flour thickened to the proper consistency—rich and clingy, but not gluey or gloppy. Freshly grated nutmeg, a spice commonly paired with spinach, lent depth and sweetness, and sprinklings of salt and pepper enhanced the overall flavor of the béchamel. To simplify the layering process, we stirred the spinach directly into the sauce instead of keeping it as its own layer.

We had the final element to consider: the cheese. Traditional spinach lasagnas rely on both mozzarella and ricotta for a combination of milky, salty flavor and creamy richness. While we saw no reason to depart from tradition, we thought some grated Parmesan added a nice kick to the mild, milky ricotta. An egg helped to thicken and bind the ricotta and Parmesan mixture, and chopped basil added flavor and freshness.

After carefully layering the noodles, spinach-enhanced béchamel, ricotta mixture, and mozzarella into two mini loaf pans, we baked our lasagnas. We tested a range of times but found that half an hour worked best, allowing plenty of time for the noodles to cook through and the cheese to melt into a rich layer on top. Covering the lasagnas with foil for the first 20 minutes of baking prevented them from drying out and helped the noodles soften properly. For the last 10 minutes of baking, we removed the foil to facilitate browning.

When we pulled the loaf pans from the oven, they were greeted with oohs and aahs. One forkful told us our two mini lasagnas weren't just cute—they were also the best spinach lasagnas we'd ever tasted.

PREPARING NOODLES FOR INDIVIDUAL LASAGNAS

Carefully break the lasagna noodles into pieces that will fit easily into the mini loaf pans. When assembling the lasagnas, continue to break the noodles as needed to create a single layer without overlapping.

OUR FAVORITE NO-BOIL LASAGNA NOODLES

Over the past few years, no-boil (also called oven-ready) lasagna noodles have become a permanent fixture on supermarket shelves. Much like "instant rice," no-boil noodles are precooked at the factory. The extruded noodles are run through a water bath and then dehydrated mechanically. During baking, the moisture from the sauce softens, or rehydrates, the noodles, especially when the pan is covered as the lasagna bakes. We prefer **Barilla** no-boil noodles for their delicate texture, which resembles that of fresh pasta.

FREEZING LEFTOVER RICOTTA

When we're cooking for two, we generally don't use up a full 8-ounce container of ricotta. But if you're not using the leftovers to make another recipe, can you freeze the extras? Ricotta is a fresh cheese that contains a lot of water, so our suspicion was that freezing would cause the extra water to leach out when thawed, giving the cheese a gritty texture and chalky taste. To find out, we froze a few previously opened containers of ricotta for two months, then defrosted them to make two batches each of manicotti, ricotta cheesecake, and a simple pasta dish, one with the previously frozen ricotta and one with fresh ricotta. We also tasted both ricottas plain. When the ricotta was sampled plain, most tasters preferred the never-frozen version for its smooth, clean taste. The frozen ricotta was more granular and slightly watery. Few tasters could detect any differences in the manicotti and cheesecake. But the frozen ricotta, uncooked and tossed with pasta, was noticeably granular. So go ahead and freeze extra ricotta—just make sure to use it in a cooked application.

White Spinach Lasagna

SERVES 2

Do not substitute fat-free ricotta here. You will need two 5½ by 3-inch loaf pans or pans of similar size for this recipe (see page 3). The number of noodles you will need depends on the size of both the noodles and the baking pan; the lasagna has a total of three noodle layers. See page 138 for a recipe to use up the leftover ricotta cheese.

- 4 ounces whole-milk or part-skim ricotta cheese (about ½ cup) (see note)
- 1½ ounces Parmesan cheese, grated (about ¾ cup)
- 3 tablespoons chopped fresh basil
- 1 large egg, lightly beaten
- Salt and pepper
- 2 tablespoons unsalted butter
- 1 shallot, minced
- 2 garlic cloves, minced
- 2 tablespoons unbleached all-purpose flour
- 2 cups whole milk
- Pinch ground nutmeg
- 10 ounces frozen spinach, thawed, squeezed dry, and chopped coarse
- 3–6 no-boil lasagna noodles, broken into pieces to fit into pans (see note; see photo)
- 4 ounces whole-milk mozzarella cheese, shredded (about 1 cup)

1. Adjust oven rack to middle position and heat oven to 400 degrees. Stir ricotta, ½ cup Parmesan, basil, egg, ⅛ teaspoon salt, and ⅛ teaspoon pepper together in bowl.

2. Melt butter in medium saucepan over medium heat. Add shallot and cook until softened, about 2 minutes. Stir in garlic and cook until fragrant, about 30 seconds. Stir in flour and cook for 1 minute. Slowly whisk in milk. Bring to simmer and cook, stirring occasionally, until sauce has thickened slightly, about 10 minutes.

3. Off heat, whisk in nutmeg. Stir in spinach, breaking up any clumps, until well combined. Season with salt and pepper to taste.

4. Spray two 5½ by 3-inch loaf pans with vegetable oil spray. Layer ¼ cup spinach mixture, 1 layer of noodles, ¼ cup ricotta mixture, and 2 tablespoons mozzarella into each pan. Repeat layering process.

WHITE SPINACH LASAGNA

5. Layer ¼ cup more spinach mixture into each pan, top with 1 more layer of noodles, and cover with remaining spinach mixture. Sprinkle evenly with remaining mozzarella and Parmesan.

6. Cover pans tightly with foil that has been sprayed with vegetable oil spray (or use nonstick foil). Bake until sauce bubbles lightly around edges, 20 to 25 minutes. Remove foil; continue to bake until hot throughout and cheese is browned in spots, about 10 minutes longer. Let cool for 10 minutes, carefully remove from pans, and serve.

MUSSELS MARINARA

THERE'S A LOT TO LIKE ABOUT MUSSELS. THEY'RE inexpensive (under $5 per pound), quick-cooking, and flavorful. They're also easy to purchase by the pound—and one pound is just the right amount for two servings. And since most mussels at the market nowadays are rope-cultured and virtually free of sand and grit, they require minimal prep. All of these characteristics make this bivalve the perfect foundation for a weeknight supper. We decided to focus on developing a recipe for one of our favorite preparations: mussels marinara, where mussels are draped in a spicy tomato sauce and served with crusty bread or pasta. Before choosing the pasta and determining the best way to cook the mussels, we set about developing our sauce.

While the term *marinara* generally conjures images of a thick, smooth tomato sauce, most of the recipes we tested for mussels marinara produced brothy and chunky sauces. The few versions that did feature a smooth sauce were generally panned by tasters, who felt this style lacked contrast and texture. After tasting a half-dozen variations on the mussels marinara theme, we found that our ideal sauce was indeed brothy with tender chunks of tomato, relatively spicy, and rich with seafood brininess. While testing canned tomato products for our baked ziti (see page 101), we determined that processed whole tomatoes produced a fresh-tasting sauce with some texture, so we decided to start there (we'd keep the sauce on the thinner side with the addition of some water later on). For flavor, we sautéed a few cloves of garlic, some red pepper flakes (for a little heat), and a single anchovy, minced. The anchovy brought some depth and added a backbone of rich flavor. After a few minutes, we stirred in the processed tomatoes to cook off their raw taste. Using this sauce as the base of our working recipe, we turned our attention to the pasta.

Using the pasta-cooking technique established in our Weeknight Bolognese with Linguine (page 96), we decided to cook our pasta in the sauce. We added 6 ounces of myriad pasta shapes and sizes (with enough water for them to properly cook and the sauce to be slightly thinned) to batches of our sauce and simmered them vigorously until the pasta was tender and the sauce was thickened. Tasters immediately showed a preference for long noodles, which seemed to grab more of the sauce when twirled onto a fork. After testing linguine, spaghetti, vermicelli, cappellini, and bucatini, we settled on humble spaghetti, which offered substantial texture without stealing the spotlight from our sauce. With our pasta of choice and a working tomato sauce recipe, we tackled the true star of this dish: the mussels.

Our standard technique for cooking mussels and clams involves steaming them in a pot until they pop open, using a little water or wine. This method allows the bivalves' liquor to be strained of grit before it makes it into the final dish, an important step for clams. But

---

NOTES FROM THE TEST KITCHEN

DEBEARDING MUSSELS

Mussels contain a small weedy beard that can be difficult to tug out of place. The easiest way to perform this task is to trap the beard between the side of a small paring knife and your thumb and pull to remove it.

SELECTING AND STORING MUSSELS
When selecting mussels, look for ones that are tightly closed or snap shut when tapped; gaping, open, or cracked mussels may be dying or dead and should not be eaten. Mussels should be stored in a bowl in the refrigerator and used within a day or two. Do not store them in a sealed container, as this will cause them to die. Before cooking, they may need to be scrubbed as well as debearded.

since mussels contain very little sand, we wondered if we could use a different, simpler approach. Sticking with our one-pan technique, we tried adding the mussels directly to the skillet as the pasta finished simmering. After a few tests we found that it took just a couple of minutes for the shells to open and release their briny juice into the pot. This technique left us with perfectly cooked mussels and pasta, and no additional cooking steps. With our goal of a weeknight dinner for two of mussels marinara in sight, we took a final look at the flavors of our sauce.

While tasters liked the texture of our sauce, many found the anchovy to be overpowering. To ensure that the mussels remained in the foreground, we cut the minced anchovy to just half a fillet. This sauce offered better balance but lacked a certain ocean brininess that tasters expected. Looking to a close relative of mussels, we tried substituting a bottle of clam juice for some of the cooking water. This swap did the trick, bolstering brininess while reinforcing the subtle complexity of the mussels. A handful of minced parsley added a final punch of freshness to our mussels and spaghetti. And while we loved this sauce with spaghetti alone, we felt that garlicky toasted bread served alongside was the perfect vehicle for sopping up the rich sauce.

Mussels Marinara with Spaghetti
SERVES 2

See page 85 for a tip on how to measure out long strands of pasta without using a scale. When adding the pasta in step 3, stir gently to avoid breaking the noodles; after a minute or two they will soften enough to be stirred more easily. If necessary, add hot water, 1 tablespoon at a time, to adjust the consistency of the sauce before serving. Drizzle with extra-virgin olive oil and serve with Garlic Toasts (recipe follows).

 1 (28-ounce) can whole tomatoes
 4 teaspoons extra-virgin olive oil
 1 small onion, minced
 3 garlic cloves, minced
 ½ anchovy fillet, rinsed and minced
 ¼ teaspoon red pepper flakes
 1½ cups water
 ½ cup bottled clam juice

 6 ounces spaghetti (see note)
 1 pound mussels, scrubbed and debearded (see page 106)
 2 tablespoons minced fresh parsley
    Salt and pepper

1. Pulse tomatoes with their juice in food processor until coarsely chopped and no large pieces remain, 6 to 8 pulses.

2. Heat 1 tablespoon oil in 12-inch nonstick skillet over medium heat until shimmering. Stir in onion and cook until softened, about 5 minutes. Stir in garlic, anchovy, and red pepper flakes and cook until fragrant, about 30 seconds. Stir in processed tomatoes and simmer gently, stirring occasionally, until tomatoes no longer taste raw, about 10 minutes.

3. Add water, clam juice, and pasta and bring to rapid simmer. Cover and simmer vigorously, stirring often, for 12 minutes. Stir in mussels, cover, and continue to simmer vigorously until pasta is tender and mussels have opened, about 2 minutes longer.

4. Uncover, reduce heat to low, and stir in remaining 1 teaspoon oil and parsley. Cook, tossing pasta gently until well coated with sauce, 1 to 2 minutes. Discard any mussels that have not opened, season with salt and pepper to taste, and serve.

Garlic Toasts
MAKES 4 TOASTS

Be sure to use a high-quality, crusty bread, such as a baguette; do not use sliced sandwich bread. The garlic toasts can be kept at room temperature for up to 4 hours before serving.

 4 (1-inch-thick) slices rustic bread (see note)
 1 garlic clove, peeled
 4 teaspoons extra-virgin olive oil
    Salt and pepper

Position oven rack 6 inches from broiler element and heat broiler. Arrange bread in single layer on baking sheet and broil until lightly toasted on both sides, 2 to 4 minutes, flipping slices halfway through. Rub garlic clove over one side of each slice. Drizzle toasts with oil, season with salt and pepper to taste, and serve.

SOPA SECA

THE NAME OF THIS MEXICAN DISH, LITERALLY translated, is "dry soup." Don't let the name fool you, however; *sopa seca* is neither dry nor a soup. Although it starts off looking like a soup, when completed it is a distinctive pasta dish flavored with tomatoes, onions, and sometimes chiles. We wanted to bring this unique casserole of sorts to the dinner table for two as a new, exciting offering for pasta night.

We began by doing a little research. Of the dozen sopa seca recipes we found, the one aspect they all shared was the use of *fideos* as a base. Fideos are coils of vermicelli that have been toasted until golden brown; they contribute a wonderful nuttiness to sopa seca. The fideos are placed in a baking dish, topped with a separately made sauce (the soup part), and baked until all the liquid is absorbed and the pasta is tender (the dry part). But the similarities among the sopa seca recipes stopped there. It was clear we had our work cut out for us.

Our first step was addressing the pasta. While traditional pretoasted coiled vermicelli offered great flavor, it was hard to find; we didn't want to have to order an ingredient online for a pasta supper, so we looked for a substitute. We found that regular dried vermicelli, broken in half and toasted in a skillet until golden brown, closely approximated the texture and depth of flavor of pretoasted vermicelli. For two servings, we only needed about a third of a pound, which could be toasted in a single batch. Next, we focused on the "soup" of this dish.

The use of tomatoes among the recipes varied greatly. Some recipes called for fresh tomatoes, others canned, and still others listed jarred salsa as the tomato ingredient. We tried all three variations and found that canned diced tomatoes worked the best and yielded the most consistent results. The fresh tomatoes, while preferred slightly over canned for their flavor, led to inconsistent results due to the varied moisture content in fresh tomatoes. Jarred salsa was the worst—it gave the finished dish an artificial flavor. In addition to the tomato base, sopa seca recipes usually include a liquid component, normally chicken broth or water. In our tests, chicken broth was favored slightly over water because of its greater richness.

The use of chiles also varied from recipe to recipe. We tried four options. In our first test we used no chiles at all. It was soon obvious, however, that if we wanted multiple dimensions to our sopa seca, chiles were a must. Next up were fresh jalapeños. Although they definitely added a spark, some tasters felt they gave the dish too much raw chile flavor. The third trial included dried ancho chiles. Many testers liked the smokiness of these chiles, but they required a lengthy soaking period that complicated the cooking process and added too much time for a simple dinner for two. Our final alternative was to use canned chipotle chiles; these turned out to be the best option. They provided a smoky background, like the anchos, without the long preparation time, and they added spiciness, like the jalapeños, without the raw taste.

In addition to the chiles, we liked chorizo (an easy-to-find sausage commonly used in Mexican cuisine) and a clove of garlic, minced, for extra flavor. Onions were found in most recipes; we found that a single small onion provided sufficient aromatic background. To bring additional heft to the dish, we added canned black beans.

Up to this point, we had been toasting the vermicelli and sautéing the aromatics, chiles, and chorizo in a skillet, before combining the ingredients, with the tomatoes and beans, in a small baking dish, following the cooking method we encountered time and again in our research. But halfway through testing, we realized we could skip the baking dish and cook our sopa seca right in the pan on the stovetop. After toasting the vermicelli and sautéing the additional ingredients, we added the chicken broth, beans, and tomatoes and simmered the mixture, covered, until most of the liquid was absorbed and the pasta was tender, which took just 10 minutes.

NOTES FROM THE TEST KITCHEN

BREAKING VERMICELLI IN HALF

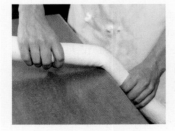

To keep the pasta from flying everywhere, roll it up in a kitchen towel, center the bundle over the counter's edge, and push down to break the pasta in the middle of the bundle.

After sprinkling some cheese over the noodles—tasters preferred Monterey Jack—we let the pan sit, covered, until the cheese melted and formed a gooey layer. To finish the dish and add freshness, we topped it with minced cilantro.

Though we were far from Mexico, we were right on the money when it came to our one-pan sopa seca, which boasted all the authentic flavors and textures of this south-of-the-border favorite.

Sopa Seca with Chorizo and Black Beans
SERVES 2

See page 85 for a tip on how to measure out long strands of pasta without using a scale. To make the dish spicier, increase the amount of chipotle chiles by 1 or 2 teaspoons. If necessary, add hot water, 1 tablespoon at a time, to adjust the consistency of the sauce before adding the cheese. Serve with diced avocado and thinly sliced scallions. See page 119 for a recipe to use up the leftover black beans.

- **6 ounces vermicelli, broken in half (see note; see page 108)**
- **1 tablespoon vegetable oil**
- **1 small onion, minced**
- **2 ounces chorizo sausage, halved lengthwise and sliced ¼ inch thick**
- **1 garlic clove, minced**
- **1 teaspoon minced canned chipotle chile in adobo sauce (see note)**
- **2 cups low-sodium chicken broth**
- **¾ cup drained and rinsed canned black beans**
- **¾ cup canned diced tomatoes, drained, juice reserved**
  Salt and pepper
- **1 ounce Monterey Jack cheese, shredded (about ¼ cup)**
- **2 tablespoons minced fresh cilantro**

1. Toast vermicelli in 1 teaspoon oil in 12-inch non-stick skillet over medium-high heat, tossing frequently with tongs, until golden, 3 to 4 minutes. Transfer to paper towel–lined plate.

2. Add remaining 2 teaspoons oil and onion to skillet and cook over medium heat until softened, about 5 minutes. Stir in chorizo, garlic, and chipotles and cook until fragrant, about 30 seconds.

3. Stir in broth, beans, tomatoes, reserved juice, and toasted vermicelli and bring to rapid simmer. Cover and simmer vigorously, stirring often, until vermicelli is tender, about 10 minutes.

4. Off heat, season with salt and pepper to taste. Sprinkle cheese over top, cover, and let stand until cheese melts, 2 to 4 minutes. Sprinkle with cilantro and serve.

PORK LO MEIN

PORK LO MEIN IS LIKE FRIED RICE: ORDER IT FROM your typical takeout joint, and the dish invariably disappoints with greasy flavors and sodden vegetables. Unwilling to go without this addictive dish, which is full of ingredients we love—springy noodles, smoky barbecued pork, and pungent vegetables—we decided to bring an authentic version home. Using just one pan to keep things simple and scaled for two, we set about developing a recipe that featured noodles tossed in a salty-sweet sauce, accented with bits of smoky *char siu* (barbecued pork) and still-crisp cabbage.

First we had to find a suitable replacement for the char siu. This Chinese specialty takes the better part of a day to prepare, and while enterprising cooks might attempt it themselves, it's better left to restaurants. Initially we considered pork tenderloin, which provides a good amount of meat for two. The only problem is that tenderloin, while tender, can be a little bland—worlds apart from the richly flavored, well-marbled pork shoulder traditional to char siu. Pork shoulder itself was out—it requires hours of cooking to become fall-apart tender. Pork belly is popular in Chinese cooking, but this fat-streaked meat from the underside of the pig is almost impossible to find at the supermarket. The most sensible option was country-style pork ribs. Though fatty, these meaty ribs from the upper side of the rib cage have the same rich flavor as pork shoulder; plus, they're naturally tender and often packaged in smaller quantities than other cuts of pork—a real bonus when you're cooking for two.

Following the protocol for char siu, we wanted to marinate the pork before cooking. To avoid a dish that was overly greasy, we first trimmed the ribs of excess fat and cut them into thin strips that would allow the marinade to penetrate more efficiently. We then soaked the meat in a classic Chinese mixture of hoisin sauce, oyster sauce, soy sauce, and toasted sesame oil. After 15 minutes, we removed the pork from the liquid and seared it quickly over high heat in a nonstick skillet. After one bite it was clear we were on the right track. The meat cooked up tender and juicy on the inside, with a crisp, browned exterior.

Pork issues settled, we were ready to tackle the noodles. Lo mein literally translates to "tossed noodles," referring to the way the strands, made from wheat and egg and resembling thick spaghetti, are tossed in sauce. Traditionally the dish calls for fresh noodles, which, unfortunately, cannot be cooked in less than a few quarts of boiling water lest they become extremely gummy. Since we planned on cooking our pasta in

the pan, these were ruled out. We scanned the shelves of our pantry for alternatives and landed on a box of dried linguine. Despite their flat shape, these long Italian strands are similar in width to Chinese noodles. We added 6 ounces of linguine to the pan with 2½ cups of water and simmered it vigorously until tender. These noodles had much the same texture and flavor as their Chinese counterpart. All that was left was to figure out the vegetables and the sauce.

We opted for traditional choices—napa cabbage, scallions, and shiitake mushrooms—stir-frying them in a little vegetable oil with garlic and fresh ginger after cooking the meat. For the sauce, tasters decided the same mixture we had been using for the marinade, with some Asian chili-garlic sauce mixed in, was ideal for seasoning the vegetables and noodles. With chewy noodles coated in a flavorful sauce, tender, browned pork, and crisp, fresh-tasting vegetables, our pork lo mein really delivers.

USE IT UP: NAPA CABBAGE

Garlicky Braised Napa Cabbage
SERVES 2

The key to this dish is reducing the sauce until it becomes syrupy enough to cling to the cabbage.

- 1 tablespoon vegetable oil
- ½ small head napa cabbage (about ½ pound), halved
- 3 garlic cloves, minced
- ⅛ teaspoon red pepper flakes
- ½ cup low-sodium chicken broth
- 2 tablespoons hoisin sauce

1. Heat oil in 12-inch nonstick skillet over medium heat until shimmering. Add cabbage, cut side down, and cook until golden brown on both cut sides, 5 to 7 minutes. Stir garlic and red pepper flakes into skillet and cook until fragrant, about 30 seconds.

2. Add broth and hoisin sauce and bring to simmer. Reduce heat to low, cover, and simmer until cabbage is tender and paring knife inserted into root end meets little resistance, about 10 minutes.

3. Using tongs, gently transfer cabbage to plate. Continue to simmer sauce over medium heat until syrupy, about 2 minutes. Return cabbage to skillet, discarding any accumulated cabbage liquid, and coat well with sauce, about 1 minute. Serve.

Pork Lo Mein
SERVES 2

See page 85 for a tip on how to measure out long strands of pasta without using a scale. When adding the linguine in step 5, stir gently to avoid breaking the noodles; after a minute or two they will soften enough to be stirred more easily. This dish is moderately spicy; to make it less spicy, use less Asian chili-garlic sauce.

- 5 teaspoons soy sauce, plus extra for serving
- 1 tablespoon oyster sauce
- 1 tablespoon hoisin sauce
- 1 teaspoon toasted sesame oil
- 8 ounces boneless country-style pork ribs, trimmed of excess fat and sliced thin crosswise
- 5 teaspoons vegetable oil
- 2 tablespoons Chinese rice cooking wine or dry sherry
- 4 ounces shiitake mushrooms, stemmed, halved if large
- 4 scallions, white and green parts separated, whites sliced thin and greens cut into 1-inch lengths
- 1 garlic clove, minced
- 1 teaspoon grated or minced fresh ginger
- 2½ cups water
- 6 ounces linguine (see note)
- ½ small head napa cabbage (about ½ pound), cored and sliced thin (about 2½ cups; see page 112)
- 1 teaspoon Asian chili-garlic sauce (see note)

PORK LO MEIN

1. Whisk soy sauce, oyster sauce, hoisin sauce, and sesame oil together in medium bowl. In separate bowl, toss pork with 1 tablespoon soy sauce mixture and refrigerate at least 15 minutes or up to 1 hour.

2. Heat 2 teaspoons vegetable oil in 12-inch nonstick skillet over high heat until just smoking. Add pork, breaking up any clumps, and cook without stirring until beginning to brown, about 1 minute. Stir pork and continue to cook until just cooked through, 1 to 2 minutes longer.

3. Add wine and cook until almost completely evaporated, about 1 minute. Transfer pork to clean medium bowl.

4. Add remaining 1 tablespoon vegetable oil to skillet and return to high heat until just smoking. Add mushrooms and cook until light golden brown, about 5 minutes. Stir in scallion whites, garlic, and ginger and cook until fragrant, about 30 seconds.

5. Stir in water and pasta and bring to rapid simmer. Simmer vigorously, stirring often, until linguine is tender, 12 to 16 minutes. Stir in cabbage and continue to cook until cabbage is wilted and sauce is thickened, about 2 minutes longer.

6. Reduce heat to low and stir in remaining soy sauce mixture, browned pork, chili-garlic sauce, and scallion greens. Cook, tossing pasta gently until well coated with sauce, about 2 minutes. Season with soy sauce to taste and serve.

NOTES FROM THE TEST KITCHEN

SHREDDING NAPA CABBAGE

1. Cut the cabbage into quarters, then trim and discard the hard core.

2. Then flatten and cut each stack of cabbage leaves into thin strips.

RICE NOODLES WITH SHRIMP

SOUTHEAST ASIAN NOODLE DISHES, ESPECIALLY those that hail from Vietnam, are the perfect remedy for a dulled palate. Hot, sweet, bright, and pungent, these preparations wake the senses and can provide welcome variety on the dinner table. While we have had memorable takeout versions, we've also been disappointed on more than one occasion by lackluster noodles. Even more frustrating are the numerous "authentic" recipes we've labored over, only to toss the inedible concoction into the trash. The problems we encounter time and again are gummy noodles, overcooked seafood or meat, and unbalanced sauces. Our goal was to learn from others' mistakes and produce a consistently superlative Vietnamese-style rice noodle dish that could be prepared for just two people using one pan; we wanted the ease of takeout without the mess or the leftovers.

First, we'd need to find the right noodle; flat rice noodles, or rice sticks, the type of noodles used in Southeast Asian cuisine, come in a variety of sizes. Wide noodles (½ inch and up), thin noodles (about ⅛ inch thick), and vermicelli-style noodles all have specific recommended uses and cooking times. We decided to use thin noodles for this dish as they cook more quickly than wide noodles but have more resilience and texture than vermicelli-style noodles. We found three different methods for preparing them: soaking them in room-temperature water, soaking them in hot tap water, and boiling them. We quickly rejected both boiling and soaking in room-temperature water; boiling yielded gummy, sticky noodles, and room-temperature water was insufficient to soften the noodles. We finally tried soaking the noodles in water that had been brought to a boil. These noodles softened and turned limp and pliant but were not fully tender. Drained, they were loose and separate and cooked through easily with stir-frying. The result? Noodles that were at once pleasantly tender and chewy.

Although the cooking time for noodle dishes is short, the ingredient lists generally aren't. Sweet, salty, sour, and spicy are the flavor characteristics of Vietnamese cooking, and they should be equally balanced. Fish sauce and soy sauce supply a salty pungency; sugar gives sweetness; heat comes from chiles (usually in sauce or paste form); lime juice provides acidity; and cilantro, mint, or other more exotic herbs provide citrusy brightness.

Garlic and shallots anchor the cuisine, providing heady, robust flavors.

With our basic ingredients in hand, we set off to find out which ones—and what amounts—were key to success. For 6 ounces of rice noodles we needed 2 tablespoons of fish sauce and almost half that amount of soy sauce (4 teaspoons) to give our dish a rich, savory foundation. For balanced sweetness and heat, we added a tablespoon of sugar and just a teaspoon of sriracha sauce. To finish the dish, we found that hefty amounts of fresh lime juice (5 teaspoons) and cilantro leaves (¼ cup) were needed for bright, tangy flavor and freshness. Now we had a balanced expression of the flavors of Southeast Asia.

As for the aromatics, two garlic cloves were sufficient for a strong backbone. Shallots had a surprising impact on flavor—just two thinly sliced small shallots produced a round, full sweetness and depth of flavor. To coax the right character out of these two aromatics, we found that cooking them just briefly was critical; now they tasted sharp and sweet.

Among the long list of other ingredients that often turn up in this style of noodle dish, tasters preferred shrimp, shiitake mushrooms, and snow peas. We used large shrimp to keep balance in the dish (no one element should be the focus). For the vegetables, tasters liked the shiitakes thinly sliced and the snow peas halved. Having assembled our key ingredients, we set about finding the best way to combine them in our skillet.

Our first instinct was to sear the shrimp to develop their flavor, but repeated tests showed it was too easy to overcook them (even when seared on just one side). Instead, we decided to marinate them with some of the sauce ingredients and cook them briefly at the last minute. To recoup the loss of seared shrimp flavor, we sautéed the shiitakes until golden brown to develop their flavor before stirring in the shallots and garlic. To this flavorful mélange we then added the drained noodles, shrimp, snow peas, a little chicken broth, and the remaining sauce. After 2 to 3 minutes of stirring, the shrimp were cooked through and we added the lime juice and cilantro. While tasters loved the flavors and contrasting textures of this dish, everyone found the noodles gummy. To ensure that they retained their pleasantly firm texture, we added them after the shrimp and snow peas were just cooked through.

Sweet, spicy, tart, and unctuous, our Vietnamese-inspired rice noodles were an instant hit in the test kitchen, where everyone wanted to take them home.

Rice Noodles with Shrimp, Shiitakes, and Snow Peas

SERVES 2

To make this dish less spicy, reduce the amount of sriracha sauce to ½ teaspoon.

- 2 **tablespoons fish sauce**
- 4 **teaspoons soy sauce**
- 4 **teaspoons vegetable oil**
- 1 **tablespoon sugar**
- 1 **teaspoon sriracha sauce (see note)**
- 8 **ounces large shrimp (31 to 40 per pound), peeled, tails removed, and deveined (see page 78)**
- 5 **cups boiling water**
- 6 **ounces (⅛-inch-wide) dried flat rice noodles**
- 4 **ounces shiitake mushrooms, stemmed and sliced thin**
- 2 **small shallots, sliced into thin rings**
- 2 **garlic cloves, minced**
- 3 **ounces snow peas (about 1½ cups), ends trimmed and strings removed (see page 72), sliced in half**
- ½ **cup low-sodium chicken broth**
- 5 **teaspoons fresh lime juice**
- ¼ **cup loosely packed fresh cilantro leaves**

1. Whisk fish sauce, soy sauce, 2 teaspoons oil, sugar, and sriracha together in small bowl. In separate bowl, toss shrimp with 2 tablespoons sauce mixture and refrigerate for at least 15 minutes or up to 1 hour.

2. Combine water and noodles in large bowl and let stand, stirring occasionally, until noodles are softened, pliable, and just tender, about 10 minutes. Drain.

3. Heat remaining 2 teaspoons oil in 12-inch nonstick skillet over high heat until just smoking. Add mushrooms and cook until golden brown, about 5 minutes. Stir in shallots and garlic and cook until fragrant, about 30 seconds.

4. Stir in remaining sauce mixture, shrimp, snow peas, and broth and cook until shrimp are just cooked through, about 3 minutes. Stir in drained noodles and lime juice and cook, tossing noodles gently, until well coated with sauce, about 1 minute. Sprinkle with cilantro and serve.

TOFU SALAD WITH VEGETABLES

FARRO RISOTTO

THERE'S SOMETHING INTRINSICALLY APPEALING about a simple, creamy, velvety risotto. But sometimes we crave a heartier, more rustic grain than Arborio rice. In search of a grain that also offered its own unique flavor, we came across farro. A whole-grain relative of wheat, farro emigrated from central Italy to the United States about a decade ago, though only in the past few years has it gained widespread popularity, appearing on more and more restaurant menus as well as in supermarkets. Italians, who have enjoyed farro for centuries, prepare the grain much as they cook Arborio rice for risotto, by cooking the farro slowly into a creamy dish called *farrotto*. The apparent difference between the two, and thus farro's appeal, lies in the hearty, nutty flavor and more satisfying chew of the farro. We set out to come up with an easy-to-make, accessible farrotto recipe of our own, one that produced a satisfying dish for two that was creamy and rich, while highlighting farro's unique flavor and texture.

We began by researching cooking methods, hoping to avoid the traditional, fussy risotto-style cooking method, in which small increments of warm liquid are added to the farro, then the grain and liquid are stirred constantly until the liquid has been absorbed and the farro is completely cooked and tender (or one's arm falls off). Right away, we came across a much simpler method; there were only two additions of warmed liquid and a few stirs during cooking. But this recipe called for far too much liquid—about 4 cups to under a cup of farro. The resulting dish was all liquid and no creamy sauce, and the fact that this recipe used the lid (relying on residual heat to finish the cooking) only worsened the problem because the excess liquid couldn't evaporate. If we cut back on the liquid even a little, the grains cooked unevenly. This method wasn't going to work, but we did learn a few valuable lessons. First, the farro clearly required less liquid than Arborio rice, which usually relies on a 4-to-1 or 3-to-1 ratio of liquid versus rice; and second, because of this lesser amount of liquid, stirring was a must to ensure even cooking.

For our next test, we tried a different method, which called for less liquid, no lid, and more (though not non-stop) stirring. We started by sautéing an onion until soft, then added the farro and toasted the grains briefly. We ladled about half the warmed liquid (1¼ cups) into the pot, let it simmer for a full 12 minutes, and gave it just a few stirs. Then in the last few minutes we finished

NOTES FROM THE TEST KITCHEN

ALL ABOUT FARRO

Farro is a whole-grain form of wheat that has been enjoyed for centuries in Tuscany and central Italy. Italians traditionally cook farro in the same manner as Arborio rice to create a creamy dish called farrotto. Thanks to praise for farro from scores of culinary magazines and top chefs, it is gaining favor with home cooks and is more widely available than it once was (farro can be found in the grains aisle at the supermarket or at gourmet markets). We love it for its slightly sweet, big, nutty flavor and chewy texture, not to mention its health benefits (it is high in fiber and protein). We found that the best way to cook farro is to leave it uncovered and stir it often. Uncovered, the liquid is able to evaporate slowly as the farro cooks. Frequent stirring helps release the starches in the farro, creating a rich and creamy consistency.

STORING LEMONS

It seems that in the test kitchen, our lemons shrivel up in the blink of an eye. To find the best way to store them so they'd keep, we tested three different methods, both at room temperature and in the refrigerator: in an uncovered container, in a sealed zipper-lock bag, and in a sealed zipper-lock bag with a small amount of water added (thinking it would help the lemon retain moisture). We recorded the fruits' weights at the start of the experiment and then every few days to measure moisture loss.

All the lemons stored at room temperature hardened after a week. The refrigerated samples fared much better: The uncovered lemons (which we kept in the crisper drawer) began to lose a small amount of moisture after the first week; the lemons stored in zipper-lock bags, both with and without water, didn't begin to dehydrate until four weeks had passed. As it turned out, the water wasn't offering any preservation benefits, but the zipper-lock bag did seal in some moisture. For the juiciest, longest-lasting lemons, then, the best approach is to seal them in a zipper-lock bag and refrigerate.

with incremental broth additions and constant stirring. This method was the best yet, producing tender, evenly cooked grains with a subtle chew, swimming in a creamy, but not gummy, sauce. After a few rounds of tests, we found that a roughly 2-to-1 ratio of liquid to grain was just right for farrotto. We found that the acidic wine conflicted with the farro's flavor, so we dropped it and stuck with just water and vegetable broth for savory flavor. Our tasters were impressed that the transformation took just 25 minutes. But we had to wonder: Could we make the process any easier?

We reviewed our progress and what we'd learned. Stirring was a must for even cooking; a 2-to-1 ratio of liquid to farro and cooking without a lid allowed for the right consistency (not to mention the fact that no lid made sense because we had to stir fairly often). Could we simplify adding the liquid? We wondered if we could pour it in all at once, and furthermore, did it even need to be warmed? For our next run-through we added all the liquid (unheated) at once to the grains in the pot, we stirred the mixture often, and we cooked it without a lid. This batch took exactly the same amount of time as in the previous successful test, the results looked identical, and tasters couldn't tell the difference. Given how much easier it was to add the broth all at once, and that we didn't have to heat it up separately first, we had a clear winner.

With our simplified method in place, we turned our attention to flavorings. While an onion was certainly a good start, a few more aromatics, in the form of garlic and thyme, gave the dish more depth. For a fresh, vegetal touch and some sweetness, we stirred in some baby arugula and cherry tomatoes toward the end of cooking; this way, they cooked slightly but still retained some freshness.

Up to this point, we had been tasting the finished farro plain, but now we wondered if we could make things a little richer with butter and Parmesan. Following classic risotto technique, we stirred in ¼ cup of grated Parmesan and a tablespoon of butter off the heat. Tasters loved this version but wanted some brightness to match. A bit of lemon zest and a squeeze of fresh lemon juice did the trick; we had finally arrived at a satisfying, accessible new dish that paid proper homage to this antique grain.

Farro Risotto with Arugula, Cherry Tomatoes, and Lemon

SERVES 2

For a creamy texture, be sure to stir the farro often in step 2. Serve with a simple green salad.

    1   tablespoon olive oil
    1   small onion, minced
        Salt and pepper
    1   garlic clove, minced
    ½   teaspoon minced fresh thyme or ⅛ teaspoon dried
    ¾   cup farro
    1½ cups vegetable broth
    1   cup water
    6   ounces cherry tomatoes (about 1 cup), quartered
    2   ounces baby arugula (about 2 cups)
    ¼   cup grated Parmesan cheese
    1   tablespoon unsalted butter
    ¼   teaspoon grated lemon zest plus 1 teaspoon fresh lemon juice

1. Heat oil in medium saucepan over medium heat until shimmering. Add onion and pinch salt and cook until softened, about 5 minutes. Stir in garlic and thyme and cook until fragrant, about 30 seconds.

2. Stir in farro and cook until lightly toasted, about 2 minutes. Stir in broth and water and bring to simmer. Reduce heat to medium-low and continue to simmer, stirring often, until farro is tender, 20 to 25 minutes.

3. Stir in tomatoes and arugula and continue to cook until vegetables are softened, about 1 minute. Off heat, stir in Parmesan, butter, lemon zest, and lemon juice. Season with salt and pepper to taste and serve.

VARIATION

Farro Risotto with Fennel, Radicchio, and Balsamic Vinegar

Follow recipe for Farro Risotto with Arugula, Cherry Tomatoes, and Lemon, substituting ½ fennel bulb (about 4 ounces), trimmed of stalks, cored, and chopped fine (see page 92), for onion. Substitute ½ small head radicchio (about 3 ounces), cored and sliced thin, for tomatoes and arugula, and 2 teaspoons balsamic vinegar for lemon zest and lemon juice. Drizzle with additional balsamic vinegar to taste before serving.

SKILLET BROWN RICE AND BEANS

RICE AND BEANS ARE A DUO APPRECIATED IN MANY cultures, but many renditions are vegetarian, generally because of the expense or lack of availability of meat; in these dishes, spices and vegetables add flavor and interest. But when prepared for the American dinner table, recipes for rice and beans usually deliver just that: a plain bowl of rice plus a scoop of boring beans. We wanted a more coherent dish, one in which the grain

---

NOTES FROM THE TEST KITCHEN

RINSING RICE

To remove excess starch from white or brown rice, rinse it under cold water until the water runs clear. With less starch, the grains of rice will cook up fluffier and more separate.

THE BEST LONG-GRAIN BROWN RICE

With so many brands of brown rice on the market, we wanted to find out which offered the best flavor and texture. We started by taking a look at brown rice itself, which is essentially a less-processed version of white rice. Each individual grain of rice is made up of an endosperm, germ, bran, and a hull or husk. The husk is the protective outermost layer and must be removed. White rice is stripped of all but the endosperm, whereas brown rice retains the germ and bran, which give brown rice a firmer texture and a nuttier, earthier flavor than that of white rice.

For our tasting, we sampled five brands of long-grain brown rice prepared two ways: steamed in a rice cooker and baked in the oven. While most were fairly neutral in flavor, one brand boasted distinct nutty and toasty flavors. In both taste tests, **Goya Brown Rice Natural Long Grain Rice** came out on top—though by a slim margin. What separated it from the rest of the group was a bolder, more distinct flavor.

---

and beans mingled, one that offered more excitement than the typical starving student fare. We hoped to be inspired by Caribbean and South American recipes, so that we could enliven this classic and bring it to the dinner table for two.

While most traditional recipes call for long-grain white rice, we knew we wanted something with more texture and chew. To nail down the grain, we cooked pots of brown rice (both medium- and long-grain), wild rice, and barley before stirring in some beans in a simplified take on rice and beans. The barley and wild rice were certainly heartier than white rice, but tasters thought they felt out of place in our Latin-inspired dish. Brown rice, on the other hand, provided a great balance of texture and flavor. Tasters preferred the texture of long-grain brown rice to that of medium-grain, which tended to cook up stickier. Having settled on the perfect rice, we started to put the dish together. Following the lead of traditional rice and beans recipes, we cooked an onion in oil before stirring in ½ cup of long-grain brown rice. Once the grains became fragrant, we stirred in half a can of beans—for such a simple, straightforward dish, dried beans took more time and preplanning than we liked—and a cup of vegetable broth for flavor. We covered the pan and let everything simmer away until the rice was tender. Unfortunately, it never reached that point.

After about 25 minutes, the broth had been completely absorbed by the rice and beans, and the bottom of the pan had started to burn. It was clear that the addition of the beans was throwing off our standard rice-to-water ratio of 1 to 2. It took doubling the amount of liquid—we went all the way up to 2 cups of broth—for the rice to become tender. The beans, on the other hand, didn't fare so well; after 45 minutes of simmering, they were blown out and mushy. To solve the problem, we stirred them in halfway through. We now had tender rice and intact beans; it was time to add some excitement to our meatless main dish.

To complement the black beans, we toasted some corn kernels before stirring in the rice; when we added the beans to the pan, we also stirred in some grape tomatoes, which we'd quartered. Tasters loved the textural contrast and sweetness provided by the corn, but they were disappointed with the soggy, lifeless tomatoes. We wondered if the tomatoes would be better added fresh at the end of cooking. To give them more flavor, we had the idea to make a quick "salsa"—we combined them with sliced scallions, citrusy cilantro, and tart lime juice and mounded this salsa on top of the finished dish. This mix of bright flavors and textures provided the ideal counterpoint to the hearty richness of the rice and beans. Adding two cloves of garlic, cumin, and cayenne pepper to the skillet with the rice was the final adjustment needed to create a potent backbone of flavor in our dish.

Our new skillet rice and beans supper was so easy, we decided to use it as a palette for two exotic variations. For an Indian-inspired take on rice and beans, we combined chickpeas, garam masala, and coconut milk; for a Spanish-style entrée, we included saffron and parsley, both of which provided bursts of color and flavor.

USE IT UP: BLACK BEANS

Smoky Black Bean Salsa
MAKES ABOUT 2 CUPS

Do not substitute frozen corn for the fresh corn here; if you don't have fresh corn, ¾ cup minced bell pepper can be substituted. For a spicier salsa, add more chipotles. Serve with tortilla chips or as a topping for grilled meats or fish. The salsa can be refrigerated in an airtight container for up to 2 days; season with additional lime juice, salt, and pepper before serving.

¾–1¼   **cups drained and rinsed canned black beans**
   1   **ear fresh corn, husk and silk removed, kernels cut from cob (about ¾ cup; see page 50) (see note)**
   1   **plum tomato, cored and chopped medium**
   2   **tablespoons minced fresh cilantro**
   2   **tablespoons olive oil**
   2   **tablespoons fresh lime juice**
   1   **small shallot or scallion, minced**
   1   **teaspoon minced canned chipotle chile in adobo sauce (see note)**
      Salt and pepper

Toss all ingredients together in medium bowl and season with salt and pepper to taste. Let sit for 15 minutes before serving.

Skillet Brown Rice and Beans with Corn and Tomatoes
SERVES 2

We prefer the flavor of fresh corn in this recipe; however, ¾ cup frozen corn, thawed and patted dry, can be substituted.

   4   **teaspoons extra-virgin olive oil**
   1   **small onion, minced**
   1   **ear fresh corn, husk and silk removed, kernels cut from cob (about ¾ cup; see page 50) (see note)**
  ½   **cup long-grain brown rice, rinsed (see page 118)**
   2   **garlic cloves, minced**
  ½   **teaspoon ground cumin**
      Pinch cayenne pepper
   2   **cups vegetable broth**
  ¾   **cup drained and rinsed canned black beans**
      Salt and pepper
   6   **ounces grape tomatoes (about 1 cup), quartered**
   2   **scallions, sliced thin**
   2   **tablespoons minced fresh cilantro**
   2   **teaspoons fresh lime juice**

1. Heat 2 teaspoons oil in 10-inch nonstick skillet over medium heat until shimmering. Add onion and cook until softened and lightly browned, 5 to 7 minutes. Stir in corn and cook until lightly browned, about 4 minutes. Stir in rice, garlic, cumin, and cayenne and cook until fragrant, about 30 seconds.

2. Stir in broth and bring to simmer. Cover and simmer gently over medium-low heat, stirring occasionally, for 25 minutes.

3. Stir in beans, cover, and continue to simmer until liquid has been absorbed and rice is tender, 20 to 25 minutes longer. Season with salt and pepper to taste.

4. Meanwhile, combine remaining 2 teaspoons oil, tomatoes, scallions, cilantro, and lime juice in small bowl and season with salt and pepper to taste. Sprinkle tomato mixture over rice and beans before serving.

VARIATIONS

Skillet Brown Rice and Chickpeas with Coconut Milk
See page 95 for a recipe to use up the leftover chickpeas, and page 79 for a recipe to use up the leftover coconut milk.

Follow recipe for Skillet Brown Rice and Beans with Corn and Tomatoes, substituting 1 yellow bell pepper, stemmed, seeded, and chopped fine, for corn and ½ teaspoon garam masala for cumin. Reduce amount of vegetable broth to 1¼ cups and add ¾ cup coconut milk to skillet with broth. Substitute ¾ cup drained and rinsed canned chickpeas for black beans.

Spanish-Style Skillet Brown Rice and Chickpeas
See page 95 for a recipe to use up the leftover chickpeas.

Follow recipe for Skillet Brown Rice and Beans with Corn and Tomatoes, substituting 1 red bell pepper, stemmed, seeded, and chopped fine, for corn and pinch saffron threads, crumbled, for cumin. Substitute ¾ cup drained and rinsed canned chickpeas for black beans. Substitute 2 tablespoons minced fresh parsley for cilantro and 2 teaspoons fresh lemon juice for lime juice.

STUFFED ACORN SQUASH

EVEN AT THE BEST RESTAURANTS, VEGETARIAN dinners are usually limited to either ho-hum pasta dishes or scaled-up veggie-laden side dishes or salads. We wanted a veggie-driven entrée, but it had to feel like a full, satisfying meal that even an ardent carnivore would enjoy. When we began considering the options, stuffed vegetables seemed like a good place to start. A quick search turned up countless recipes for the usual suspects: stuffed tomatoes, stuffed zucchini, and stuffed eggplant. These all felt like side dishes, so we kept looking for the right vegetable for the job. Then we came across a handful of recipes for stuffed winter squash. If we could come up with both the right filling and the right cooking method to marry the squash and filling without a lot of fuss, hearty and rich-tasting winter squash sounded like the foundation for a winning vegetarian supper for two.

After considering all the varieties of winter squash, we quickly settled on acorn squash. Not only does it boast plenty of visual appeal on the plate, but one squash, split in half and stuffed, seemed just right for two servings. We knew from test kitchen experience that the best way to develop flavor in winter squash is to roast it, but many recipes for stuffed squash have the cook fill the squash prior to roasting. After a few tests, it was clear that this cooking method led to two separate entities—the roasted squash and the mound of filling—and neither was cooked just right. We wanted an integrated dish, in which the filling didn't seem like an afterthought; also, the squash had to be tender and the filling had to stay moist. Our plan was simple: Precook the squash, prepare the filling, and then marry the two by cooking the combined dish briefly in the oven.

So with our strategy in place, the first questions were: At what temperature and for how long should we roast the squash? After a few tests, we confirmed that roasting the halved and seeded acorn squash in a 400-degree oven for about 45 minutes did the trick. Lower temperatures simply took too long, and higher temperatures burned the edges of the squash before it had a chance to cook through. We found that roasting the squash cut side down on a foil-lined baking sheet in the lower part of the oven helped to caramelize the flesh of the squash, concentrating its sweet, nutty flavor. Now that the squash was cooked, it was ready to be filled.

After testing several filling bases, we found that bread cubes were a quick and convenient option, but their mushy texture after being cooked in the hollowed-out squash made them a poor choice. Cooked grains proved a much more reliable base. We tested couscous and brown rice, and in the search for something heartier, we grabbed some barley off the shelf. Couscous, while a good choice for vegetables like zucchini, was too delicate to stand up to the meaty squash. Brown rice was better, but barley was the clear winner. It made a rustic, hearty filling base to which tasters gave a unanimous thumbs-up. There are a few varieties of barley sold, and for the best texture and a reasonable cooking time, we opted to use pearl barley rather than hulled or instant. (See page 122 for more information about barley.)

When preparing barley as a side dish, in the past the test kitchen has had success cooking it like risotto, adding liquid incrementally to create a velvety sauce that envelops the grain during cooking. While this is appealing on its own, it seemed a little rich and out of place in this context. Furthermore, the risotto method is time-consuming, and we were already preroasting the squash. We wanted to keep things simple, so we settled on boiling the barley in water like pasta and simply

STUFFED ACORN SQUASH WITH BARLEY

draining it. This took just 20 minutes or so, and we could get it cooking while the squash was in the oven.

While the barley cooked, we began to explore flavorings for the filling. We started by sautéing some aromatics for depth, settling on fennel to complement the earthy barley, along with a shallot and a generous amount of garlic. As for spices and herbs, ground coriander lent warmth and thyme added fresh floral flavor. Next we stirred the cooked and drained barley into the pan. For textural contrast, tasters approved of toasted pine nuts. Then all we had to do was fill the precooked squash with our filling and pop it into the oven for 10 minutes to meld the two components.

Our barley-stuffed squash was getting there, but the filling was too crumbly, and the dish didn't feel unified. Maybe making the filling more cohesive would help. Cheese seemed like a logical choice; grated Parmesan lent an appealing nutty richness and also helped bind the grains together. But still, it wasn't enough. As we were scooping out a bite of the moist squash to pair with a spoonful of barley from our latest test batch, we had an idea. What better way to bind the barley and marry it with the squash than to mix the two together? For our next test, after roasting the squash, we scooped out the cooked flesh, leaving a thin border, and stirred

it into the barley. Then we mounded the mixture into the squash shells. This was the cohesive, hearty, and appealing meal we were after.

All our stuffed squash halves needed were a few finishing touches. We took some of the Parmesan cheese (just ¼ cup) out of the filling and used it as a topping instead, which lent visual appeal once browned in the oven and a nutty, salty punch. Finally, a splash of balsamic vinegar drizzled over the stuffed squash just before serving brightened the flavors and elevated this unique dish to where it belonged—center stage at dinnertime.

Stuffed Acorn Squash with Barley
SERVES 2

Make sure to use pearl barley, not hulled barley, in this recipe—hulled barley takes much longer to cook. See page 123 for a recipe to use up the leftover fennel.

1 small acorn squash (about 1½ pounds), halved and seeded
2 tablespoons olive oil
Salt and pepper
¼ cup pearl barley (see note)
½ fennel bulb (about 6 ounces), trimmed of stalks, cored, and chopped fine (see page 92)
1 shallot, minced
3 garlic cloves, minced
½ teaspoon ground coriander
¼ teaspoon minced fresh thyme or pinch dried
1½ ounces Parmesan cheese, grated (about ¾ cup)
2 tablespoons minced fresh parsley
2 tablespoons pine nuts, toasted (see page 240)
1 tablespoon unsalted butter
Balsamic vinegar, for serving

1. Adjust oven racks to upper-middle and lower-middle positions and heat oven to 400 degrees. Line rimmed baking sheet with aluminum foil and spray with vegetable oil spray.

2. Brush cut sides of squash with 1 tablespoon oil, season with salt and pepper, and lay cut side down on prepared baking sheet. Roast on lower-middle rack until tender (tip of paring knife can be slipped into flesh with no resistance), 45 to 55 minutes. Remove squash from oven and increase oven temperature to 450 degrees.

NOTES FROM THE TEST KITCHEN

ALL ABOUT BARLEY
Our recipe for Stuffed Acorn Squash with Barley gets a hearty, nutty-flavored filling that also happens to be vegetarian with the help of barley. While barley might be most familiar as a key ingredient in beer, this cereal grain is nutritious; it's high in both fiber and protein, and it has a nutty flavor that is similar to that of brown rice. It is great in soups and in salads, as risotto, and as a simple side dish. Barley is available in multiple forms. Hulled barley, which is sold with the hull removed and the fiber-rich bran intact, is considered a whole grain and is higher in nutrients than pearl (or pearled) barley, which is hulled barley that has been polished to remove the bran. Then there is quick-cooking barley, which is available as kernels or flakes. Hulled barley, which is hard to find in most supermarkets, takes a long time to cook and should be soaked prior to cooking. Pearl barley cooks much more quickly, making it a more versatile choice.

3. Meanwhile, bring 2 cups water to boil in small saucepan. Stir in barley and ¼ teaspoon salt and cook until barley is tender, 20 to 25 minutes. Drain and set aside.

4. Wipe saucepan dry, add remaining 1 tablespoon oil, and heat over medium heat until shimmering. Stir in fennel and shallot and cook until softened and lightly browned, 5 to 7 minutes. Stir in garlic, coriander, and thyme and cook until fragrant, about 30 seconds.

5. Off heat, stir in cooked barley, ½ cup Parmesan, parsley, pine nuts, and butter. Season with salt and pepper to taste.

6. Flip roasted squash over and scoop out flesh, leaving ⅛-inch thickness of flesh in each shell. Gently fold cooked squash into barley mixture, then mound mixture evenly in squash shells. (Stuffed squash can be covered loosely with plastic wrap and refrigerated for up to 4 hours. Finish and bake as directed, increasing baking time to 25 to 30 minutes.)

7. Sprinkle squash with remaining ¼ cup Parmesan. Bake on upper-middle rack until cheese is melted, 5 to 10 minutes. Drizzle with balsamic vinegar to taste and serve.

USE IT UP: FENNEL

Fennel, Apple, and Shallot Salad
SERVES 2

This salad makes a bright—and speedy—accompaniment to simply prepared pork and chicken dishes.

½   **fennel bulb (about 6 ounces), trimmed of stalks, cored, and sliced thin (see page 92)**

1   **small Granny Smith apple, cored, quartered, and sliced thin crosswise**

1   **shallot, sliced thin**

1   **tablespoon minced fresh tarragon, parsley, or dill**

1   **tablespoon extra-virgin olive oil**

2   **teaspoons cider vinegar**

    Salt and pepper

Toss all ingredients together in medium bowl, season with salt and pepper to taste, and serve.

NORTH AFRICAN VEGETABLE AND BEAN STEW

LOOKING FOR A RICH-TASTING, SATISFYING VEG-etable stew, we hit upon the cuisine of North Africa. Cooks in this region rely on heady, potent spices and meaty, filling vegetables to provide depth, complexity, and richness to meatless soups and stews, resulting in a supper that rarely leaves diners hungry. We set out to re-create the flavors of a Moroccan and Tunisian stew, one that featured a spicy, tomatoey base studded with a balanced selection of leafy and hearty vegetables, meaty beans, and bites of pasta. Stew is often made in quantities fit for a crowd, but scaling this hearty recipe down to size would give us a unique new dinner-for-two alternative.

We started by testing a number of North African vegetable stew recipes to determine what we liked best. While they varied widely, almost all delivered on their promise of rich, deep flavors and satisfying textures. Unfortunately, along with great flavor came the difficulty of finding certain ingredients, such as *harissa* (a paste made from ground chiles, cumin, coriander, garlic, and olive oil) and *ras el hanout* (an exotic blend of spices). In addition, many stews required soaking a variety of dried beans or making fresh pasta; these were nonstarters for a stew for two—they were time-consuming and we'd have so many other flavorful elements in our pot. We decided to follow basic stew-making protocol—sauté aromatics and spices; add broth, vegetables, beans, and pasta; and finish with flavorful garnishes—and streamline the process along the way. Starting with the foundation of our stew, we considered the spices first.

Meaning "head of the shop," ras el hanout is a proprietary blend of a spice seller's top spices. Although ras el hanout can vary considerably from store to store, it often includes cinnamon, paprika, nutmeg, cardamom, cumin, and coriander. It's somewhat difficult to find stateside, but it's a combination of spices most cooks already have on hand, so we decided to make our own. To test a few different blends, we cobbled together a working recipe for our stew. First, we softened a small onion in olive oil, then added a test batch of ras el hanout and a clove of garlic. Next, we stirred in a little flour to add body and thickness. Once the spices became fragrant and the flour had lost its raw flavor, we stirred in vegetable broth and simmered the mixture for 20 minutes. Using this method, we tested and tasted a dozen different combinations of spices. Tasters overwhelmingly preferred mixes that contained a modest list of spices, as these produced a cleaner-tasting broth. In the end, cumin, paprika, coriander, and cinnamon proved the winners, offering a warm, complex array of flavors. Next, we tackled the "meat" of our stew.

The recipes we tested contained a large mix of vegetables, beans, and pastas. Our favorites included dried chickpeas and dried butter beans (lima beans), fresh pasta, and a laundry list of vegetables. As with our ras el hanout, we set about paring this list down. First, we addressed the vegetables. Since our stew would also feature beans and pasta, we limited the number of vegetables in the pot. Tomatoes were a given, and for a hearty green, we settled on Swiss chard (half of a bunch proved right for two bowls of stew). We also liked the sweetness contributed by a carrot. We chose to sauté the chopped chard stems with the onion and add the greens toward the end of cooking in order to obtain the best flavor and texture from both. The carrot we liked cut into ½-inch pieces, as it retained some bite and didn't disintegrate into the stew. While tasters appreciated the textures of the carrot and chard, they didn't care for chunks of tomato in the final stew. Wishing to keep the tomato flavor but ditch the chunks, we switched to tomato paste, which gave us a rich, deep flavor. Next, we set about determining the best way to incorporate the beans and pasta.

Beans play an important role in North African vegetable stews, as they provide much of the protein and hearty texture associated with meat. The most traditional stews we tasted featured both chickpeas and butter beans, which offered a balance of bite, earthiness, and creaminess. With convenience in mind, we settled on canned chickpeas and canned butter beans, now available in many supermarkets (if you cannot find canned butter beans, you can substitute frozen baby lima beans).

As for the pasta, most of the traditional stews featured thin, short noodles, but tasters found them difficult to scoop up with a spoon. Instead, they liked smaller, shorter shapes, especially ditalini. With a hearty vegetable and bean stew on the stove, we focused on one last ingredient.

Harissa, like ras el hanout, is a ubiquitous North African ingredient. Since harissa is made from ingredients most cooks already stock in their pantry, and we needed only a few tablespoons, buying a whole jar seemed wasteful, so we decided to make our own. We combined our spices, garlic, and olive oil in a small bowl, then microwaved them briefly to bring out their flavors. We spooned our harissa into the stew until tasters were satisfied with both heat and spice levels, reserving the rest for diners to add to their bowls. A final shower of parsley provided a dose of freshness to our boldly flavored North African stew—which was a definite (and delicious) break from the norm.

North African Vegetable and Bean Stew
SERVES 2

You can substitute store-bought harissa if you wish, but be aware that spiciness can vary greatly by brand. You can substitute ½ cup frozen baby lima beans for the butter beans. See page 95 for a recipe to use up the leftover chickpeas.

STEW
- 1 tablespoon extra-virgin olive oil
- 1 small onion, minced
- ½ bunch Swiss chard (about 6 ounces), stems and leaves separated, stems chopped fine and leaves sliced ½ inch thick (see page 125)
- 1 garlic clove, minced
- ¼ teaspoon ground cumin
- ⅛ teaspoon paprika
- ⅛ teaspoon ground coriander
- ⅛ teaspoon ground cinnamon
- 2 teaspoons unbleached all-purpose flour
- 1½ teaspoons tomato paste
- 3 cups vegetable broth
- 1 carrot, peeled and cut into ½-inch pieces
- ½ cup drained and rinsed canned chickpeas
- ½ cup drained and rinsed canned butter beans (see note)
- ¼ cup ditalini
- 2 tablespoons minced fresh parsley
  Salt and pepper

HARISSA
- 1½ tablespoons extra-virgin olive oil
- 2 teaspoons paprika
- 1 small garlic clove, minced
- 1 teaspoon ground coriander
- ¼ teaspoon ground cumin
- ⅛ teaspoon cayenne pepper
- ⅛ teaspoon salt

1. FOR THE STEW: Heat oil in large saucepan over medium heat until shimmering. Stir in onion and chard stems and cook until softened, about 5 minutes. Stir in garlic, cumin, paprika, coriander, and cinnamon and cook until fragrant, about 30 seconds. Stir in flour and tomato paste and cook for 1 minute.

2. Stir in broth and carrot and bring to boil. Reduce heat to medium-low and simmer gently for 10 minutes. Stir in chard leaves, chickpeas, butter beans, and pasta and continue to simmer until vegetables and pasta are tender, 10 to 15 minutes longer.

3. FOR THE HARISSA: Meanwhile, combine all harissa ingredients in small microwave-safe bowl and microwave until bubbling and fragrant, 15 to 30 seconds; let cool briefly.

4. Off heat, stir parsley and 1 tablespoon harissa into stew. Season with salt and pepper to taste and serve, passing remaining harissa separately.

NOTES FROM THE TEST KITCHEN

PREPARING SWISS CHARD AND HEARTY GREENS

1. The leaves and stems of Swiss chard and other hearty greens cook at different rates and must be separated prior to cooking. To do this, cut away the leafy green portion from the stem using a chef's knife.

2. Then stack several leaves on top of one another and slice the leaves crosswise in the desired thickness.

3. Finally, gather together the stems and trim and chop them.

BLACK BEAN CHILI

BLACK BEAN CHILI IS THE VEGETARIAN'S ANSWER TO hearty, satisfying meat chili, but so often it can turn out dull and unremarkable. Most versions we've come across over the years either taste like warmed black beans straight from the can, or they follow a kitchen-sink philosophy and include a hodgepodge of vegetables. We wanted a chili that was primarily about the beans, which should be creamy, tender, and well seasoned. It should have enough complexity and depth to hold your interest for a whole bowl; although not meaty, it needed to taste rich and be satisfying. If this wasn't already a tall order, we also set about making just enough chili to feed two. We started with the beans.

The first question was what type of beans to use: canned or dried. While we typically use canned beans in chilis, a test pitting them against dried beans made it clear that, in this case, dried beans were the only way to go. It's easy to add richness to canned beans using ingredients like bacon, salt pork, and sausage (all flavorings in various types of chili), but those weren't options in our vegetarian chili. Therefore, a long cooking time was going to be necessary to develop depth and complexity in our chili, and for this we needed dried beans. As for quantity, we found that ⅔ cup of dried beans proved ample for two generous servings.

Usually we prefer to soak beans in a saltwater solution (or brine them) prior to cooking, as this step softens the tough bean skins and helps them cook faster, but in this case we were after a thick, creamy chili and a portion of burst beans would only contribute to our desired texture.

To ensure gentle, even heat (and for more hands-off cooking time), we decided to simmer our chili in the oven. After testing a range of temperatures from 250 to 400 degrees, we determined that 325 degrees worked best. Higher temperatures caused too vigorous a simmer and burst every single bean, and lower temperatures meant too long a cooking time.

Because we were cooking unsoaked and unseasoned beans, we had to use a combination of vegetable broth and water to give the chili a flavorful backbone; a single cup of each provided enough liquid to cook the beans and gave us a thick, creamy chili. We also wanted to include tomatoes, a traditional ingredient that lends brightness and acidity to chili. After testing fresh chopped tomatoes, canned diced tomatoes, canned crushed tomatoes, tomato puree, and tomato sauce, tasters preferred the smooth texture and rich flavor of the tomato sauce. One 8-ounce can provided a solid tomato base without treading into marinara territory. Since acidic ingredients can toughen beans by preventing their cells from absorbing water, we added the tomato sauce to the pot halfway through cooking. A pinch of baking soda, stirred in at the beginning of cooking, helped to keep the acidity of our chili under control and ensured that our beans stayed dark and didn't turn gray or drab.

Confident that we had hashed out the cooking method, we looked for ways to boost the meaty flavor of the chili. Looking for something that would complement but not overwhelm the black beans, we hit on mushrooms, which can amplify the savory flavor of dishes. We made three batches of beans, adding a different sliced mushroom to each; we tried white, cremini, and portobello mushrooms. While tasters found that the portobellos' bold, earthy flavor dominated the chili, they praised the cremini and white mushrooms for complementing the beans with their meaty texture and rich flavor. Since it was a tie between the two, we opted to go with the more readily available white mushrooms.

To further ensure that the mushrooms played a supporting role to the beans, we chopped them fine, then sautéed them with some onion to drive off moisture and create a flavorful fond on the bottom of the pan. The chopped pieces of mushroom were now hard to identify as mushrooms given the rich, dark color of the chili, but they still provided plenty of flavor, texture, and body. An additional test determined that pulsing the mushrooms in the food processor produced the same results as chopping by hand but took a fraction of the time.

As for aromatics and spices, in addition to onion, we stirred in garlic, chili powder, and a bay leaf. Whole cumin seeds and minced chipotles added depth and smokiness. So far, so good; but something was missing. Looking for another way to deepen the flavor of the chili, we reviewed existing recipes for black bean chili again, hoping for inspiration. We noticed that a few called for mustard seeds. It seemed a bit odd for chili, but we were curious and gave it a shot, adding a sprinkling with the other aromatics. We found that the chili now had an appealing pungency and an additional level of complexity that tasters immediately noticed but

couldn't identify. We eventually settled on ¾ teaspoon of mustard seeds (more than this, and the chili took on a bitter taste) rounded out by some brown sugar. To enhance the flavor of the mustard seeds we toasted them, along with the cumin seeds, before incorporating them into the chili. Finally, for some textural contrast and a bit more sweetness, we added half of a red bell pepper, cut into ½-inch pieces; stirring it in with the tomato sauce preserved its color and texture.

With a spritz of lime juice and a sprinkling of minced cilantro, this rich, hearty chili was so satisfying, no one missed the meat.

Black Bean Chili

SERVES 2

We strongly prefer the texture and flavor of mustard seeds and cumin seeds in this chili; however, ground cumin and dry mustard can be substituted—add ⅛ teaspoon ground cumin and/or ⅛ teaspoon dry mustard to the pot with the chili powder in step 3. Serve with sour cream, shredded cheddar or Monterey Jack cheese, chopped tomatoes, and/or minced onion.

- 4 ounces white mushrooms, broken into large pieces
- 1 tablespoon vegetable oil
- 1 small onion, chopped medium
- 2 garlic cloves, minced
- ¾ teaspoon minced canned chipotle chile in adobo sauce
- ¾ teaspoon mustard seeds (see note), toasted (see page 240)
- ½ teaspoon cumin seeds (see note), toasted (see page 240)
- 2 teaspoons chili powder
- 1 cup vegetable broth
- 1 cup water
- 4 ounces dried black beans (about ⅔ cup), picked over and rinsed
- ¾ teaspoon light brown sugar
  Pinch baking soda
- 1 bay leaf
- 1 (8-ounce) can tomato sauce
- ½ red bell pepper, stemmed, seeded, and cut into ½-inch pieces
- 2 tablespoons minced fresh cilantro
  Salt and pepper
  Lime wedges, for serving

1. Adjust oven rack to lower-middle position and heat oven to 325 degrees. Pulse mushrooms in food processor until uniformly coarsely chopped, about 8 pulses.

2. Heat oil in large ovensafe saucepan over medium-high heat until shimmering. Add onion and processed mushrooms, cover, and cook until vegetables are very wet, about 3 minutes. Uncover and continue to cook until vegetables are dry and browned, 5 to 7 minutes longer.

3. Stir in garlic, chipotles, mustard seeds, and cumin seeds and cook until fragrant, about 30 seconds. Stir in chili powder and cook, stirring constantly, until fragrant, about 1 minute (do not let it burn). Stir in broth, water, beans, sugar, baking soda, and bay leaf and bring to simmer. Cover, transfer pot to oven, and cook for 1 hour.

4. Stir in tomato sauce and bell pepper, cover, and continue to cook in oven until beans are fully tender, 1 to 1½ hours longer.

5. Being careful of hot pot handle, remove pot from oven. Remove and discard bay leaf. Bring chili to simmer over medium heat and cook, uncovered, until thickened, 5 to 10 minutes. Stir in cilantro, season with salt and pepper to taste, and serve with lime wedges.

BLACK BEAN BURGERS

IT'S HARD TO DENY THE APPEAL OF A JUICY, MEATY, craggy burger. But what if you're trying to consume less beef? Is there a worthy substitute so that burger night isn't a thing of the past? Recently, we've seen black bean burgers popping up on more restaurant menus. For these vegetarian burgers, black beans are mashed and combined with herbs, seasonings, and a binder, then formed into patties and pan-seared. With the meaty, satisfying flavor of black beans, we could certainly see the draw. We set out to make a fast, flavorful recipe that yielded two impressive black bean burgers.

We started by testing a few existing recipes, and the common problems were clear. Most black bean burgers are a labor of love, requiring mashing, chopping, and measuring before mixing everything together—much more involved than their beefy brethren. And many of these recipes were just not worth this effort—countless patties came out of the pan dry, pasty, or falling apart, not to mention bland in flavor. Our burgers would need to possess appealing texture, robust flavor, and the ability to go from pan to plate without falling into pieces.

We looked first at the black beans. Most of the recipes for burgers we had sampled called for canned black beans. Not only were canned beans a time-saver compared to soaking and simmering dried beans, but a single can conveniently provided the right amount to make two burgers.

Our test recipes had revealed two main preparation styles for the beans: mashing some and leaving some whole, or mashing all of them. Not surprisingly, burgers made with all mashed beans had an unappealing pasty consistency. The burgers made with a combination of half mashed and half whole beans fared much better, offering good textural contrast. But these burgers had another problem; we could rarely make a patty that didn't fall apart before it was cooked through. We wondered if adding an egg would help hold our burgers together (eggs are great binders for dishes like meatloaf and meatballs). Opening up a couple more cans of beans, we experimented with batches of burgers made with one egg and two eggs. The batch with two eggs was too moist, making a mixture more like a batter than a burger. The batch with one egg, however, had the proper amount of moisture and held together perfectly. Success!

It was time to look at additional ingredients. A few recipes we had come across included chopped vegetables, herbs, and spices. This idea seemed promising since it could result in more flavor and texture. We tested common choices for vegetables first: onion, garlic, shallot, celery, mushrooms, and bell pepper. Tasters felt that the onion and garlic were overpowering, but milder shallot provided a nice pungency. Celery and mushrooms both added a meaty texture and rich flavor, but they required precooking to avoid tasting raw—too much work for our two burgers. But finely chopped raw bell pepper added the flavor and texture we were looking for. As for herbs and spices, tasters liked Southwestern flavors best—cilantro, cumin, and cayenne. As a final addition, a little olive oil brought our burgers' richness to just the right level.

Now our burgers had excellent flavor and texture, but with more ingredients in the mix, an old problem cropped up again: The burgers were struggling to hold together. Having maxed out on the amount of egg we could use, and recognizing that the mashed beans played a part in binding, we tried increasing the ratio of mashed beans to whole, finally settling on a roughly 3-to-1 ratio. At this ratio, our burgers held together well, and with the whole beans and bell pepper lending texture, they weren't too mushy. To further ensure stability, we also incorporated panko to help absorb any excess moisture from the vegetables.

Served on buns with all the fixings, our black bean patties meant that burger night was back—and better than ever.

Black Bean Burgers

SERVES 2

Avoid overmixing the bean mixture in step 1 or the texture of the burgers will be mealy. Serve with your favorite burger toppings, or omit the buns and serve over mixed greens.

- 1 large egg
- 2 tablespoons olive oil
- ½ teaspoon ground cumin
- ¼ teaspoon salt
- ⅛ teaspoon cayenne pepper
- 1 (15-ounce) can black beans, drained and rinsed
- 1 cup panko bread crumbs
- ½ red bell pepper, stemmed, seeded, and chopped fine
- 2 tablespoons minced fresh cilantro
- 1 small shallot, minced
- 2 buns, toasted

1. Whisk egg, 1 tablespoon oil, cumin, salt, and cayenne together in small bowl. In separate large bowl, mash 1¼ cups beans with potato masher until mostly smooth. Stir in egg mixture, remaining ½ cup beans, panko, bell pepper, cilantro, and shallot until just combined.

2. Divide bean mixture into 2 equal portions and lightly pack into 1-inch-thick patties.

3. Heat remaining 1 tablespoon oil in 10-inch nonstick skillet over medium heat until shimmering. Carefully lay patties in skillet and cook until well browned on both sides, 4 to 5 minutes per side. Serve on buns.

VARIATION

Black Bean Burgers with Corn and Chipotle Chiles
Follow recipe for Black Bean Burgers, substituting 1½ teaspoons minced canned chipotle chile in adobo sauce for cayenne. Stir in ⅓ cup frozen corn, thawed and patted dry, with bell pepper in step 1.

NOTES FROM THE TEST KITCHEN

THE BEST CANNED BLACK BEANS

Most canned black beans have three main ingredients: beans, water, and salt. So how different could they taste? Plenty different, we found out when we sampled six national brands in a blind test. The three brands that scored the highest all have more than 400 milligrams of sodium per ½-cup serving; simply adding salt to the low-scoring brands that had far less salt didn't help. Tasters also disliked mushy beans. The difference between firm and mushy beans hinges on a balance between chemistry (in the form of salt and other additives) and how hot and how long the beans are cooked during canning. The beans need salt for good flavor, but too much can make them mushy. This is why two of our salty, highly ranked brands include calcium chloride, which counteracts the softening power of sodium. But **Bush's Best**, our winning brand, does not. How they achieve firm beans with lots of salt and no calcium chloride is proprietary manufacturing information, we're told, but odds are that to preserve more of their firm texture, Bush's quickly processes their beans with less heat than the other brands.

VEGETABLE AND BEAN TOSTADAS

SOUTH OF THE BORDER, TOSTADAS (TOASTED OR fried corn tortillas) play host to an endless array of toppings, from silky shreds of slow-cooked pork to thick spreads of meaty refried beans and guacamole. Piled high with shredded cabbage, charred slices of pepper, and sweet onions, and garnished with fresh cheese and *créma* (a smooth, tangy cultured cream), tostadas make an exciting meal out of simple ingredients. While most traditional tostada recipes are anything but vegetarian, we felt that since they're topped with such a range of ingredients, we could surely ditch the meat yet still have a filling and boldly flavored supper on our hands.

Because they are the foundation of the dish, the tostadas seemed the right place to start. Traditionally, tostadas are made from 6-inch corn tortillas that are fried in either lard or vegetable oil until golden brown and crisp. While this method certainly delivers a delicious crunch, it also demands a pot of frying oil and some cleanup. Wishing for the same crunch without the greasy mess, we decided to try baking our own tostadas,

VEGETABLE AND BEAN TOSTADAS

and after a slew of tests we figured out the best method. We sprayed six tortillas (three per person seemed a good serving) with vegetable oil spray, spread them on a baking sheet, and baked them in a 450-degree oven. After about 10 minutes, we pulled out perfectly golden, ultra-crispy tostadas. With no fryer oil to dispose of, and no stovetop to clean, we moved on to the toppings.

Mashed beans are commonly used in tostadas—vegetarian or otherwise—not just for flavor and texture but also to serve as the "cement" that holds other components to the crisped tortilla. To keep this recipe from being too time-consuming, we decided to work with canned beans (since these beans were going to be mashed, the superior texture of the dried beans was not much of an issue). We narrowed the field to pinto beans, black beans, and kidney beans. We rinsed the beans, mashed them, then cooked them with a little oil and water until they thickened to a consistency similar to that of refried beans. Tasters unanimously chose pinto beans for their mild flavor and creamy texture. But they agreed they wanted the consistency to be even creamier and the flavor more complex. We tried whirling the beans in the blender before cooking, but they turned gummy and pasty. Adding vegetable broth instead of water helped the flavor, but then someone suggested using the canning liquid. This took care of both problems at once, as cooking the beans in their own starchy juice upped the level of creaminess noticeably and amplified the beans' flavor.

With the texture just right, it was time to adjust the seasoning of the beans. Many recipes call for cumin or coriander, and most add heat in the form of fresh or pickled jalapeños or cayenne. Tasters thought both the cumin and the coriander were too potent. For the heat, everyone favored the briny flavor of the pickled jalapeños over that of both cayenne and fresh jalapeños. They liked it so much they wanted even more, and the addition of 1 tablespoon of the jalapeño brine did the trick. These beans were ready for our tostadas.

It was time to move on to the vegetables. To keep our recipe easy and quick, we decided to simply sauté the vegetables for our tostadas, forgoing the more time-consuming methods of grilling and roasting. We made four batches of tostadas, spreading each with our mashed beans, then topping them with a different sautéed vegetable—onion, sliced portobello mushrooms, yellow squash, and bell peppers—to find our favorites. The squash was immediately dismissed for its mushy texture. We thought portobello mushrooms would be nice because of their meaty texture, but tasters thought the beans muted their flavor too much. Ultimately, we liked a mix of sliced onion and bell pepper, a combination that brought a hint of sweetness that complemented the slight spiciness of the beans. To brighten them up and add a hit of freshness, we tossed the vegetables with a bit of lime juice after they were cooked.

Many versions of tostadas we had come across were topped off with a spicy cabbage slaw. We thought it could provide a nice crunchy contrast to the beans and vegetables, so we decided to follow suit. Instead of making a dressing, we opted to simply toss the cabbage with more of the jalapeño brine. We tested slaws made from green cabbage, red cabbage, and bagged coleslaw mix. The red cabbage leached reddish liquid everywhere, turning our tostadas an unappealing pink color. While the green cabbage was better, the ease of using bagged coleslaw mix pushed it into the winner's circle.

For the usual toppings, crumbled queso fresco, a mild, briny fresh cheese, was a must, as was fresh cilantro, which provided a citrusy punch. Sour cream, a stand-in for traditional but hard-to-find créma, seemed to dull the dish's other elements. Combining the sour cream with a little lime juice approximated the looser consistency and sharper flavor of the créma, providing just the right balance of creaminess and acidity.

Vegetable and Bean Tostadas

SERVES 2

If you prefer, you can substitute ready-made tostadas (see page 131). Queso fresco is a fresh, soft Mexican cheese available in many markets; however, feta works well, too. Don't drain the canned pinto beans, as the canning liquid is part of the recipe. See page 131 for a recipe to use up the leftover coleslaw mix, page 163 for a recipe to use up the leftover feta cheese, and page 178 for a recipe to use up the leftover sour cream.

  6 **(6-inch) corn tortillas (see note)**
      Vegetable oil spray
  1 **tablespoon vegetable oil**
1½ **green bell peppers, stemmed, seeded,**
      and sliced thin
  1 **onion, halved and sliced thin**
  2 **garlic cloves, minced**
4½ **teaspoons fresh lime juice**
      Salt and pepper

1 (15-ounce) can pinto beans, liquid reserved (see note)

1½ teaspoons finely chopped jarred pickled jalapeños, plus 2 tablespoons jalapeño brine

½ (10-ounce) bag coleslaw mix (about 2⅓ cups)

2 ounces queso fresco or feta cheese, crumbled (about ½ cup) (see note)

¼ cup sour cream

1 tablespoon minced fresh cilantro

1. Adjust oven rack to middle position and heat oven to 450 degrees. Spray tortillas with vegetable oil spray and spread on rimmed baking sheet. Bake until lightly browned and crisp, 8 to 10 minutes.

2. Meanwhile, heat 1½ teaspoons oil in 10-inch skillet over medium heat until shimmering. Add peppers and onion and cook until softened and lightly browned, 5 to 7 minutes. Stir in garlic and cook until fragrant, about 30 seconds. Off heat, stir in 1½ teaspoons lime juice and season with salt and pepper to taste. Transfer vegetables to medium bowl and cover to keep warm.

3. Add remaining 1½ teaspoons oil to skillet and heat over medium heat until shimmering. Add beans and their liquid, pickled jalapeños, and 1½ teaspoons jalapeño brine. Cook, mashing beans with potato masher, until mixture is thickened, about 5 minutes. Season with salt and pepper to taste. Transfer beans to bowl and cover to keep warm.

4. In separate bowl, toss coleslaw mix with remaining 4½ teaspoons jalapeño brine and season with salt and pepper to taste.

5. Spread bean mixture evenly over crisp tortillas, then top with cheese, vegetables, and slaw. Whisk sour cream and remaining 1 tablespoon lime juice together, then drizzle over top. Sprinkle with cilantro and serve.

NOTES FROM THE TEST KITCHEN

THE BEST CORN TOSTADAS
Homemade tostadas are easy to make, but if you don't have the time, there's an alternative. We compared our own baked tostadas to five packaged brands, both plain and with refried beans. To our surprise, one brand gave our homemade tostadas a run for their money. **Mission Tostadas Estilo Casero** boasted a nutty corn flavor and a pleasingly rustic texture.

BAKED POLENTA DINNERS

WHILE POLENTA IS OFTEN AN AFTERTHOUGHT IN this country, meant to round out a meaty main course into a complete meal, in Italy, it frequently takes center stage, garnished by a modest pile of sautéed vegetables or a light sauce. We set our sights on a simple polenta dish that would make a sophisticated dinner for two, featuring a layer of soft polenta draped with a satisfying mix of toppings. And we hoped to use one pan to pull off our refined dinner, thereby keeping our meal streamlined and the dirty dishes to a minimum.

Since we wanted our dinner to cook in one skillet, we knew that if we wanted to precook any of the topping ingredients, we would have to do it before making the polenta. We wanted our recipe to feel rustic yet bright and fresh, so we chose summer squash and tomatoes as the accent pieces. We started by sautéing the squash separately in a 10-inch skillet in order to rid it of excess moisture and encourage browning. After transferring the squash to a bowl, we sautéed some onion, garlic, and fresh thyme (for its sweet, woodsy notes) in the empty skillet to establish a flavor base. Next we had to make a decision about the tomatoes. Canned options didn't offer the freshness we were looking for, and plum tomatoes broke down too quickly in the hot skillet. In the end, we found that halved cherry tomatoes softened just enough to make our topping saucy, while still providing textural interest. With our topping sorted out, we moved on to the polenta.

Since there were other ingredients in our dish to help define its flavor profile, we wanted to employ a simple cooking method; we were hoping to skip the more involved and time-consuming procedures traditionally used by Italian cooks to turn out rich-tasting plates of pure polenta. Starting out, we knew the polenta had to be added slowly to boiling salted water to prevent clumping. Whisking constantly also helped. To give the flavor of the polenta a boost, we tried cooking it in boiling milk in our empty skillet. The milk complemented the flavor of the polenta nicely, but it also added an unwelcome slimy texture. Using a combination of roughly 1 part milk to 3 parts water, we were able to add some richness to the polenta without ruining its creamy texture. After about 12 minutes of gentle simmering, our polenta had reached a silky consistency. To ensure that this texture would remain once we added the topping and baked it, we finished it with a little butter. A bit more minced garlic, added raw, further improved flavor.

When the polenta was fully cooked, we smoothed it into an even layer in the skillet, spread the squash-tomato mixture over the top, and sprinkled on a combination of Parmesan and mozzarella cheeses. We found that either cheese on its own didn't provide the creaminess, richness, and flavor we were after. We tried mixing the cheeses directly into the polenta but found that they caused the polenta to stiffen, a problem that would be compounded by the time in the oven. Instead, we sprinkled the cheeses on top, and after about 20 minutes in a 450-degree oven, they had melted and formed a golden crown.

After a sprinkling of chopped fresh basil, which complemented the summery notes of our topping, we served up heaping spoonfuls of our new vegetarian baked polenta. Tasters—fervent meat eaters included—were so excited about the dish's satisfying balance of creamy polenta and fresh flavors that we decided to come up with a couple of variations. For a heartier winter supper, we paired radicchio with braised winter squash, and for a nod to classic Italian cuisine, we combined mushrooms, spinach, and tomatoes.

Baked Polenta with Tomatoes, Summer Squash, and Fresh Mozzarella

SERVES 2

Zucchini can be substituted for the yellow squash. Be sure to use traditional dried polenta here, not instant polenta or precooked logs of polenta; dried polenta can be found alongside cornmeal or pasta in the supermarket (it looks like large-ground cornmeal). When stirring the polenta, make sure to reach the sides and bottom of the skillet to ensure even cooking. Be sure to use a nonstick-safe whisk here. It is important to cook the polenta over low heat; if your stovetop runs hot, and you do not have a flame tamer, see page 133 to make one.

TOPPING

- **5 teaspoons olive oil**
- **1 yellow squash (about 8 ounces), halved lengthwise and sliced ¼ inch thick (see note)**
- **Salt and pepper**
- **1 small onion, minced**
- **3 garlic cloves, minced**
- **½ teaspoon minced fresh thyme or ⅛ teaspoon dried**
- **6 ounces cherry tomatoes (about 1 cup), halved**

POLENTA

- **1⅔ cups water**
- **½ cup whole milk**
- **Salt and pepper**
- **½ cup polenta (see note)**
- **2 tablespoons unsalted butter**
- **1 garlic clove, minced**
- **2 ounces fresh mozzarella cheese, cut into ¼-inch pieces (about ½ cup)**
- **¼ cup grated Parmesan cheese**
- **2 tablespoons chopped fresh basil**

1. FOR THE TOPPING: Adjust oven rack to middle position and heat oven to 450 degrees. Heat 1 tablespoon oil in 10-inch ovensafe nonstick skillet over medium-high heat until shimmering. Stir in squash and ⅛ teaspoon salt and cook until spotty brown and tender, about 8 minutes; transfer to large bowl.

2. Heat remaining 2 teaspoons oil in skillet over medium heat until shimmering. Add onion and cook until softened, about 5 minutes. Stir in garlic and thyme and cook until fragrant, about 30 seconds. Stir in tomatoes and cook until just softened, about 2 minutes.

Transfer to bowl with squash. Season vegetables with salt and pepper to taste.

3. FOR THE POLENTA: Wipe out skillet with paper towels. Add water, milk, and ½ teaspoon salt to skillet and bring to boil over medium-high heat. Slowly add polenta while whisking constantly in circular motion to prevent clumping.

4. Bring polenta to simmer, stirring constantly. Reduce heat to low, cover, and cook, stirring often and vigorously, until polenta becomes soft and smooth, 10 to 15 minutes. Off heat, stir in butter and garlic and season with salt and pepper to taste.

5. Smooth polenta into even layer in skillet. Spoon topping evenly over polenta, then sprinkle with mozzarella and Parmesan. Bake until cheese is melted and golden, 15 to 20 minutes. Let cool for 10 minutes, sprinkle with basil, and serve.

NOTES FROM THE TEST KITCHEN

TAMING THE FLAME
A flame tamer (or heat diffuser) is a metal disk that can be fitted over an electric or gas burner to reduce the heat to a bare simmer, a necessity for well-made polenta. If you don't have a flame tamer (it costs less than $10 at most kitchen supply stores), you can easily make one.

Take a long sheet of heavy-duty foil and shape it into a 1-inch-thick ring that will fit on your burner. Make sure that the ring is of an even thickness so that the pan will rest flat on it.

BUYING PREPPED BUTTERNUT SQUASH
When you're cooking for two, you may not need a whole butternut squash to prepare one recipe. Fortunately, supermarkets have made things easier by cutting and peeling whole squash for you. But how do the flavor and texture of this time-saver squash stand up to those of a whole squash you cut up yourself? The test kitchen has found that whole squash that you peel and cube yourself can't be beat in terms of flavor and texture, but when you are trying to make the most of every minute or are preparing a smaller amount of squash, the peeled, halved squash is perfectly acceptable. However, we recommend avoiding the precut chunks; test kitchen tasters agree they are dry and stringy, with barely any squash flavor.

VARIATIONS

Baked Polenta with Braised Radicchio and Winter Squash

SERVES 2

Be sure to use traditional dried polenta here, not instant polenta or precooked logs of polenta; dried polenta can be found alongside cornmeal or pasta in the supermarket (it looks like large-ground cornmeal). When stirring the polenta, make sure to reach the sides and bottom of the skillet to ensure even cooking. Be sure to use a nonstick-safe whisk here. If using prepeeled and seeded squash from the supermarket, you will need 8 ounces for this recipe.

TOPPING

- 5 teaspoons olive oil
- ⅓ medium butternut squash, peeled, seeded, and cut into ½-inch cubes (about 1½ cups) (see note)
  Salt and pepper
- 1 small onion, halved and sliced thin
- 3 garlic cloves, minced
- ½ teaspoon minced fresh thyme or ⅛ teaspoon dried
- ⅔ cup vegetable broth
- 1 small head radicchio (about 6 ounces), halved, cored, and cut into ½-inch pieces

POLENTA

- 1⅔ cups water
- ½ cup whole milk
  Salt and pepper
- ½ cup polenta (see note)
- 2 tablespoons unsalted butter
- 1 garlic clove, minced
- 2 ounces fresh mozzarella cheese, cut into ¼-inch pieces (about ½ cup)
- ¼ cup grated Parmesan cheese
- 2 tablespoons walnuts, toasted (see page 240) and chopped coarse
- 2 tablespoons minced fresh parsley
  Balsamic vinegar, for serving

1. FOR THE TOPPING: Adjust oven rack to middle position and heat oven to 450 degrees. Heat 1 tablespoon oil in 10-inch ovensafe nonstick skillet over medium-high heat until shimmering. Stir in squash and ⅛ teaspoon salt and cook until spotty brown, 15 to 20 minutes; transfer to large bowl.

2. Heat remaining 2 teaspoons oil in skillet over medium heat until shimmering. Add onion and cook until softened, about 5 minutes. Stir in garlic and thyme and cook until fragrant, about 30 seconds. Stir in browned squash and broth and simmer until squash is just tender, 5 to 7 minutes. Slowly stir in radicchio and cook until wilted and tender, about 2 minutes. Transfer vegetables to large bowl and season with salt and pepper to taste.

3. FOR THE POLENTA: Wipe out skillet with paper towels. Add water, milk, and ½ teaspoon salt to skillet and bring to boil over medium-high heat. Slowly add polenta while whisking constantly in circular motion to prevent clumping.

4. Bring polenta to simmer, stirring constantly. Reduce heat to low, cover, and cook, stirring often and vigorously, until polenta becomes soft and smooth, 10 to 15 minutes. Off heat, stir in butter and garlic and season with salt and pepper to taste.

5. Smooth polenta into even layer in skillet. Spoon topping evenly over polenta, then sprinkle with mozzarella and Parmesan. Bake until cheese is melted and golden, 15 to 20 minutes. Let cool for 10 minutes. Sprinkle with walnuts and parsley and drizzle lightly with balsamic vinegar before serving.

Baked Polenta with Mushrooms, Spinach, and Tomatoes

SERVES 2

Be sure to use traditional dried polenta here, not instant polenta or precooked logs of polenta; dried polenta can be found alongside cornmeal or pasta in the supermarket (it looks like large-ground cornmeal). When stirring the polenta, make sure to reach the sides and bottom of the skillet to ensure even cooking. Be sure to use a nonstick-safe whisk here.

TOPPING

- 5 teaspoons olive oil
- 1 pound white mushrooms, quartered
- ⅛ ounce dried porcini mushrooms (about 2 tablespoons), rinsed and minced
- Salt and pepper
- 1 small onion, halved and sliced thin
- 3 garlic cloves, minced
- ½ teaspoon minced fresh rosemary or ⅛ teaspoon dried
- 6 ounces baby spinach (about 6 cups)
- 6 ounces cherry tomatoes (about 1 cup), halved

POLENTA

- 1⅔ cups water
- ½ cup whole milk
- Salt and pepper
- ½ cup polenta (see note)
- 2 tablespoons unsalted butter
- 1 garlic clove, minced
- 2 ounces fresh mozzarella cheese, cut into ¼-inch pieces (about ½ cup)
- ¼ cup grated Parmesan cheese
- 2 tablespoons chopped fresh basil

1. FOR THE TOPPING: Adjust oven rack to middle position and heat oven to 450 degrees. Heat 1 tablespoon oil in 10-inch ovensafe nonstick skillet over medium-high heat until shimmering. Stir in white mushrooms, porcini mushrooms, and ⅛ teaspoon salt, cover, and cook until mushrooms are very wet, about 3 minutes. Uncover and continue to cook until mushrooms are browned, 3 to 6 minutes; transfer to large bowl.

2. Heat remaining 2 teaspoons oil in skillet over medium heat until shimmering. Add onion and cook until softened, about 5 minutes. Stir in garlic and rosemary and cook until fragrant, about 30 seconds. Stir in spinach and tomatoes and continue to cook until vegetables are softened, about 1 minute. Transfer to bowl with mushrooms. Season vegetables with salt and pepper to taste.

3. FOR THE POLENTA: Wipe out skillet with paper towels. Add water, milk, and ½ teaspoon salt to skillet and bring to boil over medium-high heat. Slowly add polenta while whisking constantly in circular motion to prevent clumping.

4. Bring polenta to simmer, stirring constantly. Reduce heat to low, cover, and cook, stirring often and vigorously, until polenta becomes soft and smooth, 10 to 15 minutes. Off heat, stir in butter and garlic and season with salt and pepper to taste.

5. Smooth polenta into even layer in skillet. Spoon topping evenly over polenta, then sprinkle with mozzarella and Parmesan. Bake until cheese is melted and golden, 15 to 20 minutes. Let cool for 10 minutes, sprinkle with basil, and serve.

EGGPLANT CASSEROLE

EGGPLANT PARMESAN HAS A LOT OF APPEAL BECAUSE it has the same Italian, tomato-sauced, comfort-food profile as manicotti or lasagna but offers a break from the noodles and meat. But while the dish is essentially just eggplant, tomato sauce, and cheese, traditional recipes for eggplant Parmesan casserole are notoriously tedious and messy. Typically, sliced eggplant is salted, breaded, and then deep-fried in multiple batches before being layered, topped with sauce and cheese, and baked. Add to this the fact that most versions turn out disappointingly greasy and soggy after all that work. We understood why most people would rather not bother. Could we breathe some life into this classic combination and develop a streamlined technique for a modern, more balanced take on eggplant parmesan that wouldn't fill our fridge with a week's worth of leftovers?

We decided we needed to break from tradition and interpret eggplant Parmesan more loosely to meet our goals. Right off the bat we eliminated the breading process. It was simply too fussy, and all the oil the coating absorbed made the dish too greasy. Of course, we would still need to cook the eggplant before putting it in the casserole, so the question was how.

Sautéing or frying eggplant, breaded or unbreaded, is problematic because eggplant is essentially a sponge, ready to absorb anything, and it's packed with water. This one-two punch transforms raw eggplant into oil-soaked mush before it has a chance to caramelize. For this reason, eggplant is often salted before cooking to draw out liquid. While we weren't limiting ourselves to 30 minutes for our casserole for two, salting the eggplant wasn't that appealing because we'd still have to devote some time to cooking it. For a quicker, more hands-off route, we wondered if the high heat of the oven, combined with a small amount of oil, could both evaporate the juice and concentrate the vegetable's flavor.

After determining that a single eggplant would provide two ample servings, we sliced our eggplant, tossed it with olive oil and salt, then spread it out on a baking sheet and cooked it in the oven until browned (a good indicator that the bulk of the moisture was gone). This initial test was promising—excess moisture had evaporated and the eggplant had browned evenly—so we focused on fine-tuning details. For the best appearance, taste, and texture, we settled on unpeeled ¾-inch-thick rounds. These slices seemed a little on the thick side when raw, but once roasted they shrank to a manageable size that retained presence and meatiness when layered with other ingredients.

After some experimentation we found that roasting our eggplant required 2 tablespoons of oil: 1 tablespoon to coat all of the eggplant rounds and 1 tablespoon to coat the baking sheet and prevent sticking. Flipping the slices partway through ensured even cooking, and at 450 degrees, the slices became fully tender and dark golden brown in about 40 minutes.

With the eggplant roasting in the oven, we had time to grate some cheese and whip up a quick tomato sauce. For the cheese, Parmesan was a given, but mozzarella is standard in many eggplant Parmesan recipes as well, serving as the binder for the casserole. We agreed to use both.

USE IT UP: CRUSHED TOMATOES

Quick Creamy Tomato Soup
SERVES 2

Serve with the classic accompaniment: a grilled cheese sandwich.

- 1 tablespoon unsalted butter
- 1 shallot, minced
- 2 garlic cloves, minced
- ½ teaspoon sugar
- 2 tablespoons dry red or white wine
- 1¾ cups canned crushed tomatoes
- 1 cup water
- ¼ cup heavy cream or half-and-half
- Salt and pepper

1. Melt butter in small saucepan over medium heat. Add shallot and cook until softened, 2 to 3 minutes. Stir in garlic and sugar and cook until fragrant, about 30 seconds. Stir in wine and cook for 1 minute. Stir in tomatoes and water, bring to simmer over medium-high heat, and cook until thickened, about 3 minutes.

2. Puree soup in blender until smooth, about 30 seconds; return to saucepan. Stir in cream and reheat gently over low heat, about 1 minute. Season with salt and pepper to taste and serve.

EGGPLANT CASSEROLE WITH TOMATO SAUCE AND MOZZARELLA

A couple of cloves of minced garlic, sautéed in olive oil, started off our quick sauce, followed by 1¼ cups of crushed tomatoes. Five minutes of simmering cooked out the raw tomato flavor. After seasoning with salt and pepper, we finished the sauce with some chopped fresh basil and moved on to putting the casserole together.

While a 13 by 9-inch baking dish is our go-to dish for full-size casseroles, we needed something more appropriately sized for two. After rummaging through our collection of casseroles and baking dishes, we found the perfect candidate: an 8½ by 5½-inch baking dish. In our dish, we layered sauce, roasted and cooled eggplant, more sauce, then cheese, and repeated the process. The casserole went into a 375-degree oven, covered with foil to keep it from drying out. When the eggplant was hot throughout, we took the foil off so that the top of the casserole could brown.

The result? Very close—but no cigar. Tasters were impressed by the flavor of this dish but felt it wasn't hearty enough to stand alone as a main course. Thinking that perhaps our efforts to lighten the dish had gone too far, we considered some options for bulking it back up. We first tried a layer of ricotta, which adds depth and interest to many vegetarian Italian dishes without making them overbearing or greasy. We mixed some ricotta with Parmesan, salt, pepper, and an egg yolk for stability before spreading the mixture into two thin but distinct layers in our casserole.

To our surprise, understated ricotta was the solution, in this case imparting richness and body to the casserole while still allowing the eggplant to be the front-runner.

For a final touch, we decided the casserole would benefit from a crispy topping as a nod toward the traditional breaded and fried version of this dish. After the casserole was in the oven, we tossed together some panko bread crumbs, olive oil, Parmesan, and a clove of garlic, then when the foil came off the baking dish, we sprinkled on the panko topping so that it could get crisp and brown in the oven.

Our streamlined take on eggplant Parmesan was just as satisfying as the old-fashioned comfort-food version, but easier to prepare and sized just right for two diners—traits that we have to admit are comforting all on their own.

Eggplant Casserole with Tomato Sauce and Mozzarella

SERVES 2

You will need a shallow 8½ by 5½-inch baking dish with straight sides that are no more than 2 inches high for this recipe (see page 3). See page 135 for a recipe to use up the leftover crushed tomatoes and page 138 for a recipe to use up the leftover ricotta cheese.

- 3 tablespoons olive oil
- 1 medium eggplant (about 1 pound), sliced into ¾-inch-thick rounds
  Salt and pepper
- 3 garlic cloves, minced
- 1¼ cups canned crushed tomatoes
- 1 tablespoon chopped fresh basil
- 4 ounces whole-milk or part-skim ricotta cheese (about ½ cup)
- 1 ounce Parmesan cheese, grated (about ½ cup)
- 1 large egg yolk
- 4 ounces whole-milk mozzarella cheese, shredded (about 1 cup)
- ¼ cup panko bread crumbs

1. Adjust oven rack to middle position and heat oven to 450 degrees. Line rimmed baking sheet with parchment paper and brush with 1 tablespoon oil. Toss eggplant with 1 tablespoon more oil and ½ teaspoon salt and arrange in single layer on prepared baking sheet. Roast eggplant until golden brown, 35 to 45 minutes, flipping halfway through. Let eggplant cool until needed. Reduce oven temperature to 375 degrees.

2. Meanwhile, heat 2 teaspoons more oil and 2 teaspoons minced garlic in small saucepan over medium heat until fragrant but not brown, 1 to 2 minutes. Stir in tomatoes, bring to simmer, and cook until sauce is thickened and measures about 1 cup, 3 to 5 minutes. Off heat, stir in basil and season with salt and pepper to taste. Cover to keep warm.

3. In medium bowl, mix together ricotta, 6 tablespoons Parmesan, egg yolk, ⅛ teaspoon salt, and ⅛ teaspoon pepper.

4. Evenly layer ¼ cup tomato sauce, half of roasted eggplant, ¼ cup more tomato sauce, half of ricotta mixture, and ½ cup mozzarella into 8½ by 5½-inch baking dish, in that order. Repeat layering process. (Casserole can be covered with plastic wrap and refrigerated for up to 1 day; remove plastic wrap and proceed as directed, increasing covered baking time to 35 minutes.)

5. Cover dish tightly with aluminum foil that has been sprayed with vegetable oil spray (or use nonstick foil). Bake until filling is bubbling, about 25 minutes.

6. Meanwhile, mix remaining 1 teaspoon oil, remaining 1 teaspoon minced garlic, remaining 2 tablespoons Parmesan, and panko together in medium bowl; season with salt and pepper to taste. Remove foil from casserole, sprinkle with panko mixture, and continue to bake until topping is spotty brown and crisp, 20 to 25 minutes. Let casserole cool for 10 minutes before serving.

USE IT UP: RICOTTA

Orecchiette with Ricotta and Mint
SERVES 2

This light pasta dish pairs well with simply prepared fish and chicken. You can use any amount between ½ cup and ¾ cup ricotta in this recipe, which is handy because small containers of ricotta can vary slightly in size. Other pasta shapes can be substituted for the orecchiette; however, their cup measurements may vary (see page 85).

6 ounces orecchiette (about 1¾ cups; see note)
  Salt and pepper
4–6 ounces whole-milk or part-skim ricotta cheese
  (½–¾ cup; see note)
2 tablespoons extra-virgin olive oil
2 tablespoons minced fresh mint
1 tablespoon fresh lemon juice
½ small garlic clove, minced

1. Bring 2 quarts water to boil in medium saucepan. Add pasta and 2 teaspoons salt and cook, stirring often, until al dente. Reserve ½ cup cooking water, then drain pasta and return it to pot.

2. Add ricotta, oil, mint, lemon juice, and garlic to pasta and toss to combine, adjusting sauce consistency with reserved pasta cooking water as desired. Season with salt and pepper to taste and serve.

ZUCCHINI, TOMATO, AND RICOTTA TARTS

AMONG ALL THE SAVORY TARTS AND PIES WE'VE enjoyed, one of our favorites is the vegetable tart, a simple dish with a tender crust filled with a layer of mild cheese and a true emphasis on fresh vegetables. When done well, it's the perfect way to showcase summer's bounty. Unfortunately, most recipes require far too much work for the dense crust and watery filling they deliver. We wanted a stellar example of this seasonal treat, so we set about developing a recipe that would yield two individual tarts. We started with the crust.

We love the flavor of an all-butter crust, but getting an all-butter dough into a single tart shell in one piece is stressful enough—often requiring going in and out of the refrigerator to keep the dough from getting too soft. We figured two small all-butter crusts would be double the headache, so we turned to testing pat-in-the-pan-style crusts.

We tried several recipes, which included everything from shortening to eggs and even cream cheese, but they all produced crusts that were too cookielike and crumbly—and, more important, the intense butter flavor we wanted in this tart was lost. We returned to a basic crust recipe that relied on butter for the dairy ingredient. We began our tests by cutting the butter into the flour but quickly turned to the food processor to speed things up. This worked like a charm—the dough was firm enough to press into the pans and baked as evenly as a traditional rolled tart dough. Better yet, the butter was evenly distributed throughout the dough (thanks to our food processor), so we got big bites of crispy, buttery crust with each forkful. Parbaking ensured that our crust wouldn't slump, shrink, or get soggy. Next we turned to the filling, starting with the cheese.

Since we wanted the vegetables to be the star, we didn't need much, just a thin, creamy layer to hold on to the vegetables and add an appealing contrasting texture. We made two tarts, one with shredded mozzarella and olive oil, and one with ricotta and olive oil. The mozzarella-only version yielded an unappealing, rubbery layer of cheese that congealed when cooled. All ricotta was better, but too watery. What if we used a combination? To test this, we mixed ricotta, mozzarella, olive oil, and a little salt and pepper together and spread it into an even layer in the bottom of a tart shell. This combination was a hit. The ricotta provided just the right creamy texture, and the mozzarella helped hold the filling together and prevented it from oozing too much when the tart was sliced.

Moving on to the vegetables, first we had to determine which ones to use. Since our parbaked crust required little additional cooking, we needed to pick vegetables that would cook quickly. After some experimentation, we decided to go with two of summer's brightest stars, zucchini and tomato. Both offered freshness to balance our buttery crust and turned perfectly tender in a relatively short time. While sliced rounds of plum tomatoes and zucchini work well in a 9-inch tart, they were way too big for our scaled-down version. Getting creative, we decided to try thinly sliced cherry tomatoes and thin half-moons of zucchini. We alternated tomato and zucchini slices in a fan around the perimeter of the tart and filled the center with a quartered cherry tomato. Our tarts looked great, but once in the oven, the vegetables exuded moisture during cooking, and the resulting tarts were a waterlogged mess. To fix the problem, we salted the vegetables after slicing them and allowed them to drain on paper towels, then blotted them dry and layered them in the shells over the cheese. These tarts came out of the oven with just a glossy sheen of moisture, still slightly juicy but far from waterlogged.

For a final flavor boost, we drizzled a touch of olive oil mixed with minced garlic over the tarts before baking. When we pulled the tarts out of the oven, we let them cool for a few minutes and sprinkled them with some chopped fresh basil. Fresh yet rich, crispy, and creamy, our tarts were both lovely to look at and satisfying to savor.

Zucchini, Tomato, and Ricotta Tarts
SERVES 2

Yellow squash can be substituted for the zucchini. See page 138 for a recipe to use up the leftover ricotta.

- **9 cherry tomatoes**
  Salt and pepper
- ½ **small zucchini (about 3 ounces), halved lengthwise, sliced ⅛ inch thick**
- 2 **tablespoons extra-virgin olive oil**
- 1 **small garlic clove, minced**

- 2 **ounces whole-milk or part-skim ricotta cheese (about ¼ cup)**
- 2 **tablespoons shredded whole-milk mozzarella cheese**
- 1 **recipe All-Butter Tart Shells (recipe follows), baked and cooled**
- 1 **tablespoon chopped fresh basil**

1. Adjust oven rack to middle position and heat oven to 425 degrees. Slice 7 tomatoes into ⅛-inch-thick rounds (you should get about 5 slices from each tomato); quarter remaining 2 tomatoes.

2. Toss tomatoes with ¼ teaspoon salt and spread out on paper towels. Toss zucchini with ¼ teaspoon salt and spread out on paper towels. Let vegetables drain for 30 minutes; gently blot vegetables dry before using.

3. Meanwhile, combine 1 tablespoon oil and garlic in small bowl. In separate bowl, combine remaining 1 tablespoon oil, ricotta, and mozzarella and season with salt and pepper to taste.

4. Spread ricotta mixture evenly in tart shells. Following photo on page 140, shingle alternating slices of tomato and zucchini around outside edge of tarts. Place quartered tomatoes in center of tarts. Drizzle garlic-oil mixture over vegetables.

5. Bake tarts on rimmed baking sheet until cheese is bubbling and vegetables are slightly wilted, 20 to 25 minutes. Let tarts cool on baking sheet for 20 minutes.

6. To serve, remove outer metal ring of each tart pan, slide thin metal spatula between tart and tart pan bottom, and carefully slide tart onto plate. Sprinkle with basil and serve warm or at room temperature.

All-Butter Tart Shells
MAKES TWO 4-INCH TART SHELLS

You will need two 4-inch fluted tart pans with removable bottoms for this recipe (see page 3). The baked and cooled tart shells can be stored at room temperature for up to 1 day.

- ½ **cup plus 2 tablespoons (3⅛ ounces) unbleached all-purpose flour**
- 1½ **teaspoons sugar**
- ¼ **teaspoon salt**
- 4 **tablespoons (½ stick) unsalted butter, cut into ½-inch pieces and chilled**
- 2 **tablespoons ice water**

MAKING A TART SHELL

1. Tear each piece of dough into walnut-size clumps and spread them evenly in one of the prepared tart pans.

2. Working outward from the center, press the dough into an even layer, then press it up the sides and into the fluted edges of each tart pan.

3. Use your thumb to level off the top edge. Use this excess dough to patch any holes.

4. Lay plastic wrap over the dough and smooth out any bumps using your fingertips before freezing the tart shells until firm.

LAYERING TOMATO AND ZUCCHINI TARTS

Shingle alternating slices of tomato and zucchini around the outside edge of the tart. Then place the quartered tomatoes in the center of each tart.

1. Spray two 4-inch tart pans with removable bottoms with vegetable oil spray. Pulse flour, sugar, and salt together in food processor until combined, about 4 pulses. Scatter butter pieces over flour mixture and pulse until mixture resembles coarse sand, about 15 pulses. Add 1 tablespoon ice water and process until large clumps of dough form and no powdery bits remain, about 5 seconds. (If dough doesn't clump, add remaining 1 tablespoon water and pulse to incorporate, about 4 pulses.)

2. Divide dough into 2 equal pieces. Following photos, tear each piece of dough into walnut-size clumps, then pat dough into prepared tart pans. Lay plastic wrap over dough and smooth out any bumps or shallow areas using your fingertips. Place tart shells on large plate and freeze until firm, about 30 minutes, or up to 1 day.

3. Adjust oven rack to middle position and heat oven to 350 degrees. Remove plastic wrap and place frozen tart shells on baking sheet. Gently press piece of heavy-duty aluminum foil that has been sprayed with vegetable oil spray against dough and over edges of each tart pan. Fill shells with pie weights and bake until top edges of dough just start to color and surface of dough under foil no longer looks wet, 35 to 45 minutes.

4. Carefully remove foil and weights from tart shells and continue to bake until just golden, 5 to 10 minutes longer. Let tart shells cool on wire rack.

TOFU SALAD

ALL TOO OFTEN TOFU IS A SUPPORTING PLAYER AND not the star of the show, most notably in curries and stir-fries, where lots of other potent flavors provide distraction. We wanted to develop a recipe that was all about the tofu and in which its most admirable qualities would really stand out. After all, it is filling (and a great source of protein for vegetarians), boasts a creamy texture, and marries well with lots of different flavors. Could we develop a satisfying salad that put the tofu front and center?

We began our testing with the tofu. We cut extra-firm, firm, and soft tofu into ¾-inch pieces and dressed them with a basic working dressing. Tasters all agreed that the extra-firm and firm tofus were too firm, almost rubbery, in this context. They unanimously chose soft tofu for its creamy, custardlike texture. To rid the tofu of excess moisture, which would water down our salad, we patted it dry before cutting it into cubes.

While tofu would be the star, we needed other vegetables to fill out our salad. We wanted the vegetables to be crisp and bright, a nice counterpoint to the creamy texture of the tofu, so we knew they would remain raw. Without any cooking involved, we found that vegetables like broccoli and green beans lent an unappealing toughness, and mild vegetables like zucchini and squash did not offer enough flavor. Tasters liked carrots, snow peas, and bell pepper for both their crisp textures and bright colors, so all three made the cut. Bean sprouts, which are often used in Asian cooking, added a nice crunch and clean flavor.

It was time to move on to the dressing. We limited our scope to creating a boldly flavored Asian-inspired dressing and started by testing peanut butter and soy sauce as the base. The soy sauce made for a dressing that didn't coat the tofu well, but the peanut butter flavor held its own with the tofu and vegetables, adding just the right sweetness and nutty flavor. To balance out the dressing, we supplemented the peanut butter with hoisin sauce, lime juice, sesame oil, and garlic, a combination that created the right balance of salty, acidic, and savory. A little chili-garlic sauce added a touch of heat. To achieve the consistency we wanted, we found that some hot water thinned the dressing out perfectly for coating the tofu and vegetables. This bold dressing tasted great, but once it was tossed with the tofu and vegetables, the tofu seemed washed out.

In the test kitchen, we have developed ways to boost the flavor of tofu, including glazing, marinating, and broiling. After a few tests, we quickly settled on broiling, which was the easiest and quickest solution; glazing required the use of a skillet and time devoted to monitoring the stovetop, and marinating required at least half an hour. Before broiling our tofu, we brushed it with some of the dressing, then popped it into the oven until it turned spotty brown. A few minutes later, the tofu emerged lightly charred and flavorful.

Our tofu now had great flavor and gave the salad more of an identity. After broiling the tofu, we gently tossed it with our crisp and colorful vegetables and the remaining dressing. Thinly sliced scallion, minced cilantro, and toasted sesame seeds gave our salad just the right finishing touches.

Tofu Salad with Vegetables

SERVES 2

We prefer the texture of soft tofu in this recipe; however, firm tofu may be substituted.

DRESSING

4½ teaspoons creamy peanut butter
4½ teaspoons hot water
2 tablespoons hoisin sauce
1 tablespoon vegetable oil
2 teaspoons fresh lime juice
1 teaspoon toasted sesame oil
1 small garlic clove, minced
¾ teaspoon Asian chili-garlic sauce
¼ teaspoon salt

SALAD

1 (14-ounce) block soft tofu, patted dry and cut into ¾-inch pieces (see note)
4 ounces snow peas (about 2 cups), ends trimmed and strings removed (see page 72), cut into ½-inch pieces
½ red or yellow bell pepper, stemmed, seeded, and cut into ½-inch pieces
1 cup bean sprouts
1 carrot, peeled and shredded
1 scallion, sliced thin on bias
2 tablespoons minced fresh cilantro
2 teaspoons sesame seeds, toasted (see page 240)
Salt and pepper

1. FOR THE DRESSING: Whisk peanut butter and water together until smooth, then whisk in remaining dressing ingredients until combined. (Dressing can be refrigerated in airtight container for up to 4 days; whisk to recombine; season with salt to taste before using.)

2. FOR THE SALAD: Position oven rack 6 to 7 inches from broiler element and heat broiler. Line rimmed baking sheet with aluminum foil. Toss tofu with half of dressing and spread out on prepared baking sheet. Broil tofu until spotty brown, 5 to 8 minutes.

3. Meanwhile, toss snow peas, bell pepper, bean sprouts, carrot, and scallion with remaining dressing in large bowl until well combined. Gently fold in broiled tofu, cilantro, and sesame seeds. Season with salt and pepper to taste and let sit until flavors meld, about 15 minutes. Serve.

GRILLED PIZZA WITH CHARRED ROMAINE AND RED ONION SALAD

GRILLED ARGENTINE STEAKS WITH PLANTAINS

OF ALL THE COOKING TRADITIONS INVOLVING live fire and a piece of meat, none is more sacred than preparing the perfect grilled steak. In Argentina especially, where cattle farming is a major industry and the per-capita beef consumption is the highest in the world (roughly 150 pounds annually), grilling steaks over burning embers is not just a means of getting dinner on the table, but a nationwide ritual. In contrast to the American method of slapping meat over a blazing fire to sear hard and fast, Argentine steaks are grilled low and slow over hardwood logs, not charcoal, which imbues them with a smokiness that is subtler and more complex than the typical "barbecue" flavor one comes to expect of meat grilled stateside. *Churrasco* (which refers to both the technique and the grilled meat itself) tastes the way a roaring fireplace smells: warm (not hot) and woody (not smoky). We set out to see if we could re-create this Argentine classic in an American backyard for two diners.

The first order of business was sorting out which cut of meat to use. Many of the churrasco cuts popular in Argentina aren't available in this country, so we started by determining the ideal size of our steak. Traditional churrasco steaks are about 1½ inches thick, which allows for the exterior to develop significant charring before the interior cooks through. But when we shopped for steaks, we found that steaks this thick weighed no less than a pound. While it seemed like a lot of meat for two, we knew that the right thickness was essential to getting the authentic texture and flavor in our meat, so we decided (not very reluctantly) we'd have to deal with a few extra slices of steak.

To start our testing, we selected four flavorful steaks from our supermarket butcher case: strip steak, shell steak, tri-tip, and bottom round. We built a moderately hot fire by spreading a full chimney's worth of charcoal around the bottom of the grill (tactics for pumping up wood-grilled flavor would come later), salted each of the steaks generously, cooked them to medium-rare, let them rest briefly, and then sliced them across the grain. Tri-tip and bottom round were out. Though each offered decent flavor, tasters found them a tad tough and dry.

Meanwhile, well-marbled strip steak boasted big beefy flavor, not to mention an interior that was both moist and pleasantly chewy. Shell steak, a flavorful sirloin cut, lost a few votes for its stringier texture, but we found that it works fine if you can't find strip steak.

Our steak selected, we turned to the issue of building up the essential wood-smoke flavor. Cooking over actual logs was out of the question—this was a grilled dinner for two, not an Outward Bound excursion. Instead, we tried various wood chunk and chip alternatives (soaked and unsoaked, foil-wrapped and unwrapped). Unsoaked chunks proved best. Four pieces nestled around the perimeter of the fire lasted long enough to tinge the steak with a subtle essence of burning wood. Placing the lid on the grill for the first few minutes of cooking helped to quickly trap smoke flavor.

NOTES FROM THE TEST KITCHEN

PREPARING PLANTAINS FOR THE GRILL

1. Plantains are not as easy to peel as bananas. After trimming the ends, cut the plantain in half and make a slit in the peel of each piece with a paring knife, from one end to the other end. Then peel away the skin with your fingers.

2. After removing the peel, cut each piece of plantain in half lengthwise.

HOW HOT IS YOUR FIRE?
To determine the heat level of the cooking grate itself, heat up the grill and hold your hand 5 inches above the grate, counting how long you can comfortably keep it there. Note that this works with both charcoal and gas grills.

Hot fire	2 seconds
Medium-hot fire	3 to 4 seconds
Medium fire	5 to 6 seconds
Medium-low fire	7 seconds

Unfortunately, we still hadn't nailed the requisite deep brown char without overcooking the interior. Without resorting to dry-aging the steak for days, we needed to figure out a way to drive off the exterior moisture so that a deep crust could form. In the past we've found that the dry environment of the freezer can rob food of its moisture; here that would be exactly what we wanted. We salted the steak and then left it uncovered in the freezer until firm, about an hour. Sure enough, the meat emerged from the freezer practically bone-dry, and it browned within moments of hitting the grill. Even better, the partially frozen steak could stand about five more minutes of fire, adding up to more char and more flavor.

Our crust was closer but missing something: The mahogany-hued char of an Argentine steak snaps with each bite, almost as if the meat were sheathed in an invisible layer of breading. To re-create this distinctive crunch, we tried adding a small amount of cornstarch to the salt rub—a trick we've used in the past to crisp up everything from turkey skin to potatoes. This twist had two results: We were able to cut the freezing time to 30 minutes, since cornstarch is another moisture-eating powerhouse, and we got a steak with all the color and snap we were looking for, because the starches in cornstarch enhance browning.

The final touch was the requisite *chimichurri*, a sauce with sharp, grassy flavors meant to offset the rich, unctuous qualities of the meat. Our tasters leaned toward one of the most traditional forms: fresh parsley, cilantro, oregano, garlic, red wine vinegar, red pepper flakes, and salt whisked together with fruity extra-virgin olive oil.

When it came to the side dish, however, we side-stepped tradition. Although plantains are not a typical side dish for churrasco, we thought their sweetness would complement the rich steak and pungent chimichurri. Plantains, a Latin American staple, take well to the smokiness of the grill and require little more than a quick sear for browning.

We started with two ripe, nearly black plantains, which are sweeter and easier to peel than the starchier green ones that are often fried. After conducting some experiments grilling whole, unpeeled plantains, we found it best to peel and quarter them first. After brushing the plantains with oil to prevent sticking, we tossed them onto the grill while the steak rested. Five minutes later, the plantains were moderately charred on the outside and the interiors cooked through and tender.

After a few bites of the crisp-crusted, wood-smoked steak, flanked by the sweet, charred plantains (both splashed with bright chimichurri), we patted ourselves on the back, thrilled with our updated take on an age-old Argentine tradition.

Grilled Argentine Steaks with Plantains and Chimichurri Sauce

SERVES 2

If you don't have kosher salt, ¼ teaspoon table salt can be substituted in step 1 and ¾ teaspoon in step 2. Our preferred steak for this recipe is strip steak; a less expensive alternative is a boneless shell sirloin steak (or top sirloin steak). We prefer oak wood chunks, but other types can be used. To perforate the pie plate (if using a gas grill), use a paring knife to cut 6 to 8 slits in the bottom; this will allow smoke to escape. We prefer the steak cooked to medium-rare, but if you prefer it more or less done, see the guidelines in "Testing Meat for Doneness" on page 149.

SAUCE

- 1 teaspoon hot water
- ¼ teaspoon dried oregano
- 3 tablespoons minced fresh parsley
- 2 tablespoons minced fresh cilantro
- 2 tablespoons extra-virgin olive oil
- 1 small garlic clove, minced
- 1 tablespoon red wine vinegar
- ½ teaspoon kosher salt (see note)
- Pinch red pepper flakes
- Pinch sugar

STEAK AND PLANTAINS

- 1 teaspoon cornstarch
- Kosher salt (see note) and pepper
- 1 (1-pound) boneless strip steak, about 1½ inches thick (see note)
- 2 large ripe plantains (10 to 12 ounces each), halved crosswise, peeled, and sliced lengthwise (see page 144)
- 1 tablespoon vegetable oil
- 4 (2-inch) unsoaked wood chunks (see note)
- 1 (9-inch) perforated disposable aluminum pie plate (if using gas) (see note)

1. FOR THE SAUCE: Combine hot water and oregano in small bowl and let sit for 5 minutes. Whisk in remaining sauce ingredients and let sit at room temperature for 1 hour. (Sauce can be refrigerated in airtight container for up to 2 days; return to room temperature before serving.)

2. FOR THE STEAK AND PLANTAINS: Combine cornstarch and 1½ teaspoons kosher salt in small bowl. Pat steak dry with paper towels and rub entire surface evenly with cornstarch mixture. Place on wire rack set inside rimmed baking sheet and freeze steak, uncovered, until firm, about 30 minutes (but no more than 1 hour). Before grilling, season steak with pepper. Brush plantains with oil and season with salt and pepper.

3A. FOR A CHARCOAL GRILL: Open bottom grill vents completely. Light large chimney starter filled with charcoal briquettes (100 briquettes; 6 quarts). When coals are hot, pour them in even layer over grill. Using tongs, place wood chunks directly on top of coals, spacing them evenly around perimeter of grill. Set cooking grate in place, cover, and open lid vents completely. Heat grill until hot, about 5 minutes.

3B. FOR A GAS GRILL: Turn all burners to high, cover, and heat grill until hot, about 15 minutes. Place wood chunks in pie plate and set on one side of grill. Close lid and heat until wood chunks begin to smoke, about 5 minutes. (Adjust burners as needed to maintain hot fire; see page 144.)

4. Clean and oil cooking grate. Place steak on grill (next to, but not over, wood chunks if using gas), cover grill, and cook until steak begins to char on first side, 2 to 3 minutes. Flip steak and continue to cook, covered, until second side begins to char, 2 to 3 minutes longer.

5. Flip steak again and cook until first side is well charred, 2 to 3 minutes. Flip steak again and cook until second side is well charred and steak registers 120 to 125 degrees on instant-read thermometer (for medium-rare), about 4 minutes. Transfer steak to carving board, tent loosely with foil, and let rest.

6. While steak rests, grill plantains (covered if using gas) until spottily charred on both sides, 5 to 7 minutes, flipping plantains halfway through. Transfer plantains to serving platter. Cut steak into ½-inch-thick slices and serve with plantains and sauce.

GRILLED BEEF TENDERLOIN WITH GREEN BEANS

THOUGH IT IS MILD IN FLAVOR, NOTHING BEATS THE extravagantly buttery texture of beef tenderloin. But this tender cut of meat has an extravagant price tag to match, which means that preparing a whole roast for a crowd is an expensive proposition. However, a small tenderloin roast (a center cut of the larger beef tenderloin) is just the right size for two people. Since the grill is just the place to instill mild meat with some smoky flavor, we decided to take the fancy tablecloth outside for a scaled-down, special-occasion meal off the grill. We planned on a boldly flavored sauce to further enhance the flavor of the meat, as well as a steakhouse-worthy accompaniment to complete the meal.

First, we focused on finding a reliable grilling method for the tenderloin. Although more affordable than a full-size tenderloin, our roast was still not cheap by any standards, and overcooking was not an option. We started with the simplest method: We rubbed the roast with oil, salt, and pepper, then cooked it over a single-level fire, meaning a full chimney of charcoal spread evenly across the bottom of the grill. When the interior of the roast was medium-rare (120 to 125 degrees), the exterior still looked gray and washed out. Eventually the roast developed some decent browning, but by then it was completely overcooked.

We had better luck when we piled all the coals on one side of the grill to make a half-grill fire with two different cooking zones. Now we could sear the meat over the hot coals until it developed a moderately browned exterior, before transferring it to the cooler side and covering the grill so that the roast could finish cooking through over the indirect heat. Even on the cooler side, we knew that our small roast could overcook fast, so we made sure to pull it off the grill once it reached 120 degrees (for medium-rare). In addition to a nicely browned crust and a rosy, medium-rare interior, this method increased the tenderloin's total time on the grill to nearly 30 minutes—plenty of time for our beef to pick up rich, smoky flavor from the grill.

While our roast rested, we had time to find a partner for our elegant beef tenderloin. Green beans came to mind—they'd provide some balance to our dish and a light, fresh counterpoint to the rich, buttery meat. While thin, just-picked green beans are best gently steamed to preserve their delicate texture, the green beans available

GRILLED BEEF TENDERLOIN WITH GREEN BEANS AND BLUE CHEESE DRESSING

at grocery stores year-round are often thicker and tougher. In the past, we have found that the high heat of roasting transforms these over-the-hill green beans, and we thought grilling (though unconventional) might be another way to breathe new life into this vegetable.

We tossed ½ pound of trimmed green beans with oil, salt, and pepper before carefully placing them perpendicular to the grill grate so that they wouldn't fall through. Without being turned, the green beans were crisp-tender and spotty brown after six minutes. Tasters were instantly won over by these full-flavored and sweet caramelized beans.

For a lively finish to the beans, we felt an homage to classic steakhouse dinners would be in order and made a simple blue cheese dressing. While rich and creamy dressings often include mayonnaise, sour cream, and buttermilk, we didn't want to call for a smidgen of each, because we needed just a small amount of sauce. After some experimentation, we settled on a base of 2 tablespoons of sour cream, enhanced with the same amount of milk (more of a household staple than buttermilk); the former gave the dressing body and tang without being too heavy, and the latter thinned it to the proper consistency without diluting the flavor. In addition to ¼ cup of blue cheese, a minced shallot and a splash of lemon juice cut the richness and sharpened the cheese flavor. A little sugar balanced out the flavors of our steakhouse-style dressing, which elevated our simple green beans to special-occasion status.

Grilled Beef Tenderloin with Green Beans and Blue Cheese Dressing

SERVES 2

We prefer this roast cooked to medium-rare, but if you prefer it more or less done, see our guidelines in "Testing Meat for Doneness" on page 149. See page 178 for a recipe to use up the leftover sour cream.

BLUE CHEESE DRESSING

- 1 ounce Gorgonzola cheese, crumbled (about ¼ cup)
- 2 tablespoons milk
- 2 tablespoons sour cream
- 1 small shallot, minced
- 1 teaspoon fresh lemon juice
- ¼ teaspoon sugar
  Salt and pepper

TENDERLOIN AND BEANS

- 1 (1-pound) center-cut beef tenderloin roast, trimmed
- 2 tablespoons vegetable oil
  Salt and pepper
- 8 ounces green beans, trimmed

1. FOR THE DRESSING: In medium bowl, mash cheese and milk together with fork until no large clumps remain. Whisk in sour cream, shallot, lemon juice, and sugar. Season with salt and pepper to taste and refrigerate until needed.

2. FOR THE TENDERLOIN AND BEANS: Pat tenderloin dry with paper towels, rub with 1 tablespoon oil, and season with salt and pepper. Toss green beans with remaining 1 tablespoon oil and season with salt and pepper.

3A. FOR A CHARCOAL GRILL: Open bottom grill vents completely. Light large chimney starter filled with charcoal briquettes (100 briquettes; 6 quarts). When coals are hot, pour them in even layer over half of grill, leaving other half empty. Set cooking grate in place, cover, and open lid vents completely. Heat grill until hot, about 5 minutes.

3B. FOR A GAS GRILL: Turn all burners to high, cover, and heat grill until hot, about 15 minutes. Leave primary burner on high and turn off other burner(s). (Adjust primary burner as needed to maintain grill temperature around 350 degrees.)

4. Clean and oil cooking grate. Place tenderloin on hotter part of grill and cook (covered if using gas) until lightly browned on all sides, 8 to 10 minutes, turning as needed.

5. Slide tenderloin to cooler part of grill, cover, and cook until meat registers 120 to 125 degrees on instant-read thermometer (for medium-rare), 15 to 20 minutes. Transfer tenderloin to carving board, tent loosely with foil, and let rest for 15 minutes.

6. While tenderloin rests, carefully place green beans on hotter part of grill, perpendicular to bars on cooking grate, and cook until spotty brown and tender, 6 to 8 minutes. Transfer beans to serving platter and tent loosely with foil to keep warm.

7. Cut tenderloin into ½-inch-thick slices. Drizzle beans with 2 tablespoons blue cheese dressing and serve with beef, passing remaining dressing separately.

NOTES FROM THE TEST KITCHEN

TESTING MEAT FOR DONENESS

An instant-read thermometer is the most reliable method for checking the doneness of poultry and meat. To use an instant-read thermometer, simply insert it through the side of a chicken breast, steak, or pork chop. The chart below lists temperatures at which the meat should be removed from the heat, as the temperature of the meat will continue to climb between 5 and 10 degrees as it rests. (Thin cutlets cook too quickly for an actual doneness test and you will have to rely more on visual cues and cooking times.)

WHEN IS IT DONE?

MEAT	COOK UNTIL IT REGISTERS	SERVING TEMPERATURE
Chicken and Turkey Breasts	160 to 165 degrees	160 to 165 degrees
Chicken Thighs	175 degrees	175 degrees
Pork	140 to 145 degrees	150 degrees
Beef and Lamb		
Rare	115 to 120 degrees	125 degrees
Medium-rare	120 to 125 degrees	130 degrees
Medium	130 to 135 degrees	140 degrees
Medium-well	140 to 145 degrees	150 degrees
Well-done	150 to 155 degrees	160 degrees

PIMENTO CHEESEBURGERS AND POTATO WEDGES

GO TO ANY COOKOUT AND YOU'RE MORE THAN likely guaranteed to see burgers on the menu. That's because they're affordable, easy to prepare, cook quickly, and need little adornment—all qualities that hold true when cooking for two. But sometimes we want our everyday burgers jazzed up a bit, so we set our sights on a popular, ultra-cheesy burger from the South: the pimento cheeseburger. Many Americans are vaguely aware of pimento cheese as the orange stuff Southerners smear on crackers or celery sticks and wash down with sweet tea. The neon spread—made with orange cheddar, chopped pimentos, mayonnaise, and, depending on whom you ask, onion, Worcestershire, olives, or hot sauce—tastes as bright as it looks. After we did a little research on burgers made with this spread, it was clear that these aren't ordinary cheeseburgers, where a mediocre slice of cheese plays second fiddle to the burger. With these burgers, the emphasis would be firmly on the cheese. So we started there.

After tasting a few brands of pimento cheese purchased at the supermarket, we decided that this was one convenience product that's not worth the convenience and headed to the test kitchen to concoct our own. We started with the key ingredients: grated extra-sharp cheddar (sharp and mild varieties lacked zip), chopped pimentos (which are jarred sweet red peppers), and mayonnaise (which gives the cheese its soft consistency). Then we tested the most common add-ins, including Velveeta cheese, hot sauce, Worcestershire sauce, cayenne, paprika, dry mustard, jalapeños, garlic, and dill pickles. Our tasters ended up going minimalist. They gave the nod to cayenne pepper and dry mustard, both of which added bite, and they deemed everything else superfluous.

Next we got our burgers ready for the grill. As we've found in the past, tasters preferred the flavor and fat of 85 percent lean ground beef. We settled on 6-ounce patties, which would give us a good amount of surface area for the cheese. For seasoning, salt and pepper were givens, but we wanted the burger to have some additional flavor so that it could stand up to the pimento cheese. Worcestershire sauce, which we'd rejected in the cheese, imparted richness and tang to the beef. We formed two patties and tossed them onto a hot grill; when they were almost done, we slathered on the spread. Unfortunately, the mayonnaise that made the pimento cheese easy to spread also caused it to slide off the sizzling burgers and scorch on the hot coals. Without the moistening power of the mayonnaise, however, the cheddar hardened into greasy orange slabs on the burgers. We remembered that a few pimento cheese recipes had included cream cheese as well as mayonnaise, so we tried adding cream cheese to our original cheese blend. This mixture was spreadable, melted gently, and stayed put atop the patty.

These burgers were well on their way, but our tasters demanded more of the creamy orange stuff. Could we stuff the burgers with cheese? We carefully formed patties around a blob of the soft spread, but during cooking the cheese oozed out of several and burned. We tried chilling the spread before stuffing the burgers to buy more time before it melted on the grill. This improved the odds of keeping the cheese inside, but it was still hit or miss. Next we tried freezing the cheese in small, 2-tablespoon dollops. The cheese stayed solid while we shaped the patties, which allowed us to take more care when composing them. After several construction experiments, we found that the cheese stayed put during grilling if we divided the meat for each patty in half and wrapped the cheese twice. That way, we could be sure the cheese was firmly centered in, and fully contained by, the meat. Finally, cooking the burgers over a medium fire, instead of a hot fire, proved best; the gentle heat cooked the burger more evenly, keeping our construction intact.

The burgers looked great as they rested on a platter, but the first bite triggered a burst of orange lava that burned the chin of more than one taster. The fix was twofold: Omit the mayonnaise from the portion of pimento cheese reserved for inside the burgers, and let the cooked burgers rest for a full five minutes before tucking in. Satisfied with our pimento cheese formula, not to mention our novel construction technique, we turned our attention to the empty space on the grill, intending to fill it with a tasty side dish.

Inspired by the time-honored pairing of fries and burgers, we decided to create a grilled rendition of the combo. Steak fries, which wouldn't slip through the grate and were easy to prep, seemed perfect. We decided to incorporate some garlic into our grilled potato recipe to offset the richness of the pimento cheese.

Russets are the potato of choice when it comes to steak fries, so we sliced two russets into wedges, tossed them with olive oil, salt, and pepper, and set them on the grill. By the time the inside was cooked through, the potatoes were dry, with a leathery exterior. Parcooking the potatoes in the microwave helped, but they were still mealy and leathery. Abandoning the russets, we turned to Yukon Gold potatoes, which have less starch and more water, and found that they were better suited to the grill. After about 10 minutes of grilling, the exteriors were crisp and the interiors were tender and creamy.

It was time to incorporate the garlic. We tried the easiest path—tossing the parcooked potatoes with minced garlic—but the raw garlic burned on the grill. Adding the garlic to the potatoes after grilling them left a harsh aftertaste. What if we infused the olive oil with the garlic? We combined a handful of minced garlic and the olive oil in a small bowl and heated it in the microwave to allow the garlic to perfume the oil. We then strained the garlic solids out of the oil and tossed the strained oil with the potatoes before parcooking them. This was a resounding success: The garlic infused the oil, and the oil infused the potatoes with good garlicky bite.

That left one issue: What should we do with the garlic we'd strained out of the oil? Tossing it on the grilled wedges didn't work; the garlic burned and tasted bitter. Instead, we made a quick dipping sauce for our spuds, combining the garlic with mayonnaise and lemon juice.

At long last, we had an exciting new burger-and-fry combo that would leave smiles on the faces of Northerners and Southerners alike.

Grilled Pimento Cheeseburgers and Potato Wedges with Garlic Mayonnaise
SERVES 2

Do not use meat leaner than 85 percent or the burgers will be dry. Try to use potatoes of a similar size and cut them into even wedges so that all of the pieces cook at the same rate. Be sure to let the burgers rest for a full 5 minutes (tented with foil) before eating them or the hot, cheesy center will spurt out. The buns can be toasted on the grill while the burgers rest in step 8.

PIMENTO CHEESE
- **3 ounces extra-sharp cheddar cheese, shredded (about ¾ cup)**
- **3 tablespoons jarred pimentos, drained and minced**
- **2 tablespoons cream cheese, softened (about 1 ounce)**
- **¼ teaspoon dry mustard**
- **Pinch cayenne pepper**
- **2 teaspoons mayonnaise**

BURGERS
- **12 ounces 85 percent lean ground beef (see note)**
- **1½ teaspoons Worcestershire sauce**
- **¼ teaspoon salt**
- **¼ teaspoon pepper**
- **2 buns, toasted (see note)**

POTATOES
- **4 garlic cloves, minced**
- **3 tablespoons olive oil**
- **¼ cup mayonnaise**
- **1 teaspoon fresh lemon juice**
- **Salt and pepper**
- **2 Yukon Gold potatoes (about 8 ounces each), each cut into 8 wedges (see note)**

1. FOR THE PIMENTO CHEESE: Mix cheddar, pimentos, cream cheese, mustard, and cayenne together in small bowl. Drop two 2-tablespoon portions of cheese mixture onto small plate and flatten gently into ¾-inch-thick disks using your palm. Cover tightly with plastic wrap and freeze until firm, at least 2 hours. Stir mayonnaise into remaining pimento cheese; refrigerate until needed.

2. FOR THE BURGERS: Combine ground beef, Worcestershire sauce, salt, and pepper in bowl and gently knead until well incorporated. Divide meat into 4 equal portions and flatten into patties. Following photos, seal 2 patties securely around each frozen cheese disk.

3. FOR THE POTATOES: Combine garlic and oil in small microwave-safe bowl and microwave until garlic is fragrant, about 1 minute. Strain garlic oil through fine-mesh strainer into large microwave-safe bowl. Mix strained garlic solids with mayonnaise and lemon juice in medium bowl and season with salt and pepper to taste; refrigerate until serving time.

4. Add potatoes to bowl with strained garlic oil, season with salt and pepper, and toss to coat. Cover and microwave until potatoes begin to soften but still hold their shape, 3 to 6 minutes, shaking bowl to redistribute potatoes halfway through.

5A. FOR A CHARCOAL GRILL: Open bottom grill vents completely. Light large chimney starter filled three-quarters with charcoal briquettes (75 briquettes;

4½ quarts). When coals are hot, spread two-thirds of them evenly over half of grill and remaining coals evenly over other half of grill. Set cooking grate in place, cover, and open lid vents completely. Heat grill until hot, about 5 minutes.

5B. FOR A GAS GRILL: Turn all burners to high, cover, and heat grill until hot, about 15 minutes. Leave primary burner on high and turn other burner(s) to medium. (Adjust burners as needed to maintain hot fire and medium fire on separate sides; see page 144.)

6. Clean and oil cooking grate. Place burgers on cooler part of grill, cover, and cook until well browned on both sides and cooked through, 12 to 16 minutes, flipping burgers halfway through. Meanwhile, lay potatoes, cut side down, on hotter part of grill and cook until browned on all sides, 6 to 8 minutes, turning as needed.

7. Slide potatoes to cooler part of grill (or turn all burners to medium if using gas) and continue to cook until potatoes are tender, 2 to 4 minutes longer. Meanwhile, spread cheese-mayonnaise mixture over burgers, cover, and continue to cook until mixture is slightly melted, about 1 minute.

8. Transfer burgers to serving platter, tent loosely with foil, and let rest for 5 minutes. Transfer potatoes to separate platter. Place burgers on buns and serve with potatoes and garlic mayonnaise.

NOTES FROM THE TEST KITCHEN

BUILDING PIMENTO CHEESEBURGERS

1. Divide each portion of meat in two and wrap half around one disk of frozen cheese, taking care to completely and snugly enclose the cheese.

2. Mold the remaining half portion of meat around the mini patty and tightly seal the edges. Gently and uniformly flatten each to form 1-inch-thick patties that will cook evenly and contain the hot cheese.

GRILLED THIN-CUT PORK CHOPS WITH ASPARAGUS

JUICY, TENDER GRILLED PORK CHOPS WITH AN irresistible golden brown crust are not so difficult to achieve when the chops are 1 inch or more thick, but what if you're working with thinner chops? After all, these chops are easier to come by at the supermarket, cook in the blink of an eye, and are inexpensive. Unfortunately, because they are so thin, by the time they pick up any crusty char and distinctive grill flavor, they've become tough and dry. We wanted to find a way to grill these quick-cooking chops to achieve the same golden brown crust and juicy, flavorful meat as chops twice their size. And with only two chops on the grill, we wanted to round out the meal with a worthy side dish.

Since we knew a hot fire would be essential to achieving browning on the surface of our chops, we needed some insurance against the meat drying out over the heat. Brining, or soaking the chops in a saltwater solution, helps meat retain moisture, so we began by brining two bone-in, ½-inch-thick rib chops (center-cut chops work well, too) and then set them on the hot grill. After a couple of minutes per side, they were cooked to a safe 145 degrees. We let the chops rest briefly before reaching for our forks, but while the chops were juicy, they hadn't spent enough time over the fire to get a distinct char. We needed a way to accelerate the formation of a good crust.

Thinking back to our Grilled Argentine Steaks (page 145), we wondered if we could take advantage of the drying power of our freezer again. We thought that partially freezing the chops might actually be a solution here, since the dry environment of a freezer could cause rapid evaporation on the surface of the meat. We also figured that partially frozen chops could stay on the grill longer. But we didn't want to both brine (which takes about 30 minutes) and freeze (another 30 minutes) our chops, so we opted to simply sprinkle them with salt before freezing them. We hoped salting the meat would ensure well-seasoned, juicy chops. After these chops had been over the coals for four minutes per side (about twice as long as chops from the refrigerator), they were juicy. Still, despite the extra time on the grill, they were only starting to caramelize when it was time to take them off.

To encourage caramelization, which yields a flavorful crust, we sprinkled the chops with sugar, which has the ability to promote browning. While this worked well, brown sugar worked even better, adding good caramel flavor. But the char level of our chops still needed some work. We tried rubbing vegetable oil on the chops, but it just dripped off the firm, frozen meat. Melted butter did the same. As a last-ditch effort, we turned to softened butter, which we hoped would stay on the chops longer. We mixed a tablespoonful with the brown sugar (and a sprinkle of black pepper) and brushed the mixture on both sides of each chop. We grilled the first side and held our breath as we flipped the chops over. The difference was remarkable—the chops were golden brown with a crusty char that tasted as good as it looked. Because butter contains small amounts of protein and lactose (milk sugar), it enhances the browning of anything it touches, creating hundreds of rich, nutty new flavor compounds.

Finishing the cooked chops with more butter gave our lean chops more richness and offered us the chance to introduce additional flavors. We made an easy compound butter by mixing another tablespoon of softened butter with chives, lemon zest, and Dijon mustard. After grilling the pork, we placed a pat of the butter on each hot chop, where it melted into a piquant, buttery sauce that played nicely off the mild meat.

For a side dish, we were after something simple and as quick-cooking as the chops. Asparagus fit the bill. We followed our standard protocol for grilling asparagus: We snapped off the woody ends, tossed the spears with olive oil, and cooked them over a hot fire. Minutes later, the slender spears came off the grill sweet and juicy. Though this method was incredibly easy, and the flavor of our asparagus was decent, we wondered if brushing the spears with butter instead of oil would enhance their flavor and texture as it did with our chops. We brushed a second batch of asparagus with melted butter before seasoning the spears with salt and pepper and throwing them on the grill. Sure enough, tasters found the asparagus brushed with melted butter to be more flavorful than the asparagus brushed with oil. After a brief chat with our science editor, we learned that the moisture content of the butter was responsible. Butter is 16 percent water, and this moisture subjects the asparagus to a brief period of steaming before it burns off from the intense heat

of the grill—just long enough to break down the cell structure of the spears' outer skin and allow more of the sugars inside to be coaxed out and caramelized. To amp up the flavor of our asparagus ever so slightly, we mixed some minced garlic with the melted butter. Now the asparagus was well browned and enlivened with a hit of garlic.

As for the fire, we determined that the hot fire over which we cooked the chops was too intense; the asparagus burned before it was completely tender. A medium-hot fire worked best. Since we wanted to cook the asparagus and pork at the same time, we set up our grill to allow for a hot fire on one side and a medium-hot fire on the opposite side.

Our grilled thin-cut pork chops were so juicy and flavorful, we decided we couldn't leave well enough alone. For another equally delicious and easy recipe, we swapped out the mustard, chives, and lemon zest in favor of Asian chili-garlic sauce, cilantro, and lime zest for a whole new flavor profile.

Grilled Thin-Cut Pork Chops with Asparagus
SERVES 2

If you don't have kosher salt, ¼ teaspoon table salt can be substituted in step 1. Use asparagus that is at least ½ inch thick near the base. Do not use pencil-thin asparagus because it cannot withstand the heat and will overcook.

PORK

- 2 (8-ounce) bone-in rib or center-cut pork chops, about ½ inch thick, trimmed, sides slit (see page 152)
- ½ teaspoon kosher salt (see note)
- 2 tablespoons unsalted butter, softened
- 1 teaspoon minced fresh chives
- ¼ teaspoon Dijon mustard
- ¼ teaspoon grated lemon zest
- ½ teaspoon brown sugar
- ¼ teaspoon pepper

ASPARAGUS

- 2 garlic cloves, minced
- 2 tablespoons unsalted butter, melted
- 1 bunch thick asparagus (about 1 pound), tough ends trimmed (see note)
- Salt and pepper

1. FOR THE PORK: Pat pork dry with paper towels and rub chops evenly with salt. Place on wire rack set inside rimmed baking sheet and freeze pork chops, uncovered, until firm, about 30 minutes (but no more than 1 hour).

2. Mix 1 tablespoon butter, chives, mustard, and lemon zest together in small bowl and refrigerate until serving time. In separate bowl, mix remaining 1 tablespoon butter, sugar, and pepper; set aside at room temperature. Before grilling, pat chops dry with paper towels and spread room-temperature butter mixture evenly over all sides.

3. FOR THE ASPARAGUS: Combine garlic and melted butter in bowl, then brush over asparagus. Season with salt and pepper.

4A. FOR A CHARCOAL GRILL: Open bottom grill vents completely. Light large chimney starter filled with charcoal briquettes (100 briquettes; 6 quarts). When coals are hot, spread two-thirds of them evenly over half of grill and remaining coals evenly over other half of grill. Set cooking grate in place, cover, and open lid vents completely. Heat grill until hot, about 5 minutes.

4B. FOR A GAS GRILL: Turn all burners to high, cover, and heat grill until hot, about 15 minutes. Leave primary burner on high and turn other burner(s) to medium-high. (Adjust burners as needed to maintain hot fire and medium-hot fire on separate sides; see page 144.)

5. Place chops on hotter part of grill, cover, and cook until chops are well browned on both sides and register 140 to 145 degrees on instant-read thermometer, 6 to 8 minutes, flipping chops halfway through. Meanwhile, place asparagus on cooler part of grill and cook until spotty brown and tender, 5 to 7 minutes, turning as needed.

6. Transfer asparagus and pork to serving platter. Spoon chilled butter mixture over pork. Tent loosely with foil and let rest for 5 minutes before serving.

VARIATION

Spicy Thai Grilled Thin-Cut Pork Chops with Asparagus

Follow recipe for Grilled Thin-Cut Pork Chops with Asparagus, omitting chives, mustard, and lemon zest. Mix 1 teaspoon minced fresh cilantro, ½ teaspoon Asian chili-garlic sauce, and ¼ teaspoon grated lime zest with 1 tablespoon butter in step 2 and refrigerate until serving time.

GRILLED PORK TENDERLOIN WITH CARROTS

BECAUSE OF ITS COMPACT SIZE AND SHAPE, PORK tenderloin is a good candidate for both the grill (it leaves ample space for a sidekick) and dinner for two. But the leanness of pork tenderloin can make it a challenge to cook: Little fat translates to little flavor and meat that easily dries out. It's no wonder, then, that our research yielded few recipes for grilled pork tenderloin that didn't involve a spice crust, which promises to add texture and flavor to this lean, mild cut. But though it might deliver flavor, the typical coating does nothing for the texture. After surveying a sample of existing recipes, we found that in even the best versions, ground spices left the pork with a sandy exterior that was more spice dusted than crusted. We vowed that our version would have a flavorful crunch and would be matched with a simple and delicious side dish that could be grilled at the same time.

Before we started testing the crust, we established our cooking method. We planned to create a fire with two cooking zones by piling a full chimney of coals evenly on half of the grill. We'd start the pork directly over the coals to brown the exterior, then slide it to the cooler area so that the interior could gently finish cooking through. After a few tests, we found this method worked well. With the cooking method worked out, we could move on to the larger issue: building a substantial spice crust.

Since ground spices didn't cut it in the recipes we tested, we decided to try whole spices. We brushed a pork tenderloin with olive oil before sprinkling it with a mixture of black peppercorns, coriander seeds, and mustard seeds (a flavor combination we liked in ground form). Once the meat hit the grill, most of the spices tumbled off. The few odd seeds that managed to stay put, however, were crunchy and flavorful.

Clearly, unlike ground spices, which stick to the meat's surface moisture, the whole spices needed some assistance. Thinking "sticky," we tried brushing the pork with honey, maple syrup, and even corn syrup before sprinkling on the spices. Each helped the spices stick but also caused the pork to stick to the grate. Next we tried mayonnaise, then mustard, to anchor the spices. The meat didn't stick to the grill, but the spices didn't stick to the meat. Stumped, we went back to basics and tried a basic breading method. We dredged the tenderloin in flour, dipped it in a beaten

egg, and then coated it with the spices instead of the usual bread crumbs. This gave us the best crust so far, but the egg coating was spongy and tough. Losing the egg yolk solved that problem. Finally, we pitted flour against cornstarch as a dredge for the meat. Tasters preferred the lightness and cling of cornstarch to the slightly gummy flour. A spritz of vegetable oil spray right before grilling ensured adhesion.

Now our pork was definitely crusty—to a fault. The egg white coating glued the spices so successfully that each bite tasted like potpourri. If we used fewer spices than the scant 2 tablespoons we'd been using, the pork was sparsely coated. To stretch the crust, we cracked the whole spices, which retained plenty of crunch and better covered the meat. We also tried augmenting the spices with bread crumbs, flour, and cornmeal. In the end, 2 teaspoons of cornmeal gave the crust more coverage, more texture, and a subtle toasty flavor. Finally, we needed salt to season the meat and sugar to tame the spices. Three-quarters of a teaspoon each of coarse sugar and kosher salt added balance and further crunch.

For a side dish, we liked the idea of carrots; we thought their natural sweetness would make the perfect complement to our spice-crusted pork. First we prepped the carrots for the grill. Starting with peeled carrots, we tried grilling them whole, halved lengthwise, and quartered lengthwise. The whole carrots rolled around the grill as we chased them with tongs; they also failed to brown. The quartered carrots were so thin, they tended to burn and stick to the grate, making it difficult to flip them. The halved carrots were the clear winner: They cooked evenly, and the cut side provided a flat surface, allowing for sufficient browning and stability (no more carrots rolling off the grill).

To jump-start the cooking process and ensure tender interiors by the time the outsides were nicely charred, we found it best to parcook the carrots before grilling them. Some recipes we found began with steaming or blanching the carrots, but we wanted a more streamlined approach. We decided to try the microwave. We brushed the halved carrots with olive oil, seasoned them with salt and pepper, and microwaved them until they just began to soften, about five minutes. Once the pork was moved to the cooler side of the grill to finish cooking, we placed the carrots on the hotter side. Several minutes later, the carrots were handsomely charred on the outside and tender and creamy on the inside.

As for flavors, we decided we wanted a sauce that could do double duty and be served with both carrots and pork. (Even with our flavorful crunchy crust, the lean interior of the tenderloin needed a flavor boost.) Since we had mustard seeds in our spice crust, a simple mustard-honey vinaigrette seemed just right. Coarse, whole-grain mustard echoed the potent flavors of the cracked-spice crust on our pork tenderloin. Minced shallot and a little red wine vinegar rounded out the vinaigrette with some piquancy and acidity, and a handful of minced parsley added a fresh touch.

Spice-Crusted Grilled Pork Tenderloin with Carrots and Mustard-Honey Vinaigrette

SERVES 2

Try to use carrots of a similar size so that they cook at the same rate; very large carrots can be quartered. If the pork is "enhanced" (see page 14 for more information), do not brine. If brining the pork, omit the salt in step 3. If you don't have kosher salt, ½ teaspoon table salt can be substituted in step 3. We prefer Demerara and turbinado sugar for their crunch, and the larger grains are easier to rub on the meat, but plain brown sugar works, too. To crack the spices, place them in two zipper-lock bags, one inside the other, and press or gently pound with a skillet, rolling pin, or meat mallet.

CARROTS AND VINAIGRETTE

 4 carrots, peeled and halved lengthwise (see note)
 ¼ cup olive oil
    Salt and pepper
 1 small shallot, minced
 2 tablespoons minced fresh parsley
 1 tablespoon whole-grain mustard
 2 teaspoons honey
 1 teaspoon red wine vinegar

PORK

 2 tablespoons cornstarch
 1 large egg white
 1 tablespoon mustard seeds, cracked (see note)
 2 teaspoons coriander seeds, cracked (see note)
 2 teaspoons cornmeal
 ¾ teaspoon black peppercorns, cracked (see note)
 ¾ teaspoon kosher salt (see note)
 ¾ teaspoon Demerara or turbinado sugar
    (see note)

 1 (12-ounce) pork tenderloin, trimmed, brined
    if desired (see note; see page 18)
    Vegetable oil spray

1. FOR THE CARROTS AND VINAIGRETTE: Place carrots in single layer on large microwave-safe plate, brush with 1 tablespoon oil, and season with salt and pepper. Cover and microwave until carrots just begin to soften but still hold their shape, 4 to 6 minutes, flipping carrots halfway through.

2. Whisk remaining 3 tablespoons oil, shallot, parsley, mustard, honey, and vinegar together in small bowl. Season with salt and pepper to taste; set aside for serving.

3. FOR THE PORK: Place cornstarch in shallow bowl or pie plate. Beat egg white in second shallow bowl or pie plate until foamy. Combine mustard seeds, coriander seeds, cornmeal, peppercorns, salt, and sugar in third bowl or plate. Pat pork dry with paper towels. Following photos, dredge pork lightly with cornstarch, shaking off excess, then coat with egg white, allowing excess to drip

---

NOTES FROM THE TEST KITCHEN

MAKING THE SPICE CRUST FOR PORK TENDERLOIN

1. After placing the cornstarch, beaten egg white, and spices in shallow plates, dredge the pork in the cornstarch. This will help the egg white adhere.

2. Then coat the pork with the egg white, allowing the excess to drip off.

3. Finally, roll the pork tenderloin in the spice mixture to coat the pork evenly, pressing on the spices to help them adhere.

back into bowl, and coat evenly with spice mixture, pressing on spices to adhere. Before grilling, spray coated pork lightly with vegetable oil spray.

4A. FOR A CHARCOAL GRILL: Open bottom grill vents completely. Light large chimney starter filled with charcoal briquettes (100 briquettes; 6 quarts). When coals are hot, pour them in even layer over half of grill, leaving other half empty. Set cooking grate in place, cover, and open lid vents completely. Heat grill until hot, about 5 minutes.

4B. FOR A GAS GRILL: Turn all burners to high, cover, and heat grill until hot, about 15 minutes. Leave primary burner on high and turn off other burner(s). (Adjust primary burner as needed to maintain grill temperature around 350 degrees.)

5. Clean and oil cooking grate. Place pork on hotter part of grill and cook (covered if using gas) until browned on all sides, 6 to 8 minutes, turning as needed.

6. Slide pork to cooler part of grill, cover, and continue to cook until pork registers 140 to 145 degrees on instant-read thermometer, 6 to 12 minutes longer. Meanwhile, place carrots on hotter part of grill and cook until tender and spottily charred, 6 to 10 minutes, turning as needed.

7. Transfer pork to carving board, tent loosely with foil, and let rest for 5 minutes. Transfer carrots to serving platter and drizzle with 2 tablespoons reserved vinaigrette. Cut pork into ¼-inch-thick slices and serve with carrots, passing remaining vinaigrette separately.

GRILLED TURKEY BURGERS WITH WARM POTATO SALAD

A LEAN, FULLY COOKED TURKEY BURGER, SEASONED with salt and pepper, is typically a weak stand-in for an all-beef burger. Simply put, it is often dry, tasteless, and colorless. We wanted a turkey burger with beef burger qualities—dark and crusty on the outside and full-flavored and juicy in every bite.

To start, we took a close look at the ground turkey sold at various markets and found three general types: ground white meat, ground dark meat, and meat labeled 93 percent lean ground turkey. After we shaped the three types into burgers (6 ounces each) and grilled

them side by side, tasters preferred the ground dark meat for its deeper flavor and juicier texture, followed by the 93 percent lean meat (the ground white meat was dry and had little flavor). But ground dark meat can be hard to find, so we opted for the 93 percent lean turkey meat, which is widely available, and forged ahead in search of a fix for its drier texture.

To add some moisture to the burger, we tried a whole host of ingredients (a mashed bread and milk mixture, mashed beans, and rehydrated mushrooms among them) with little success. All of these ingredients either contributed a strong flavor that overshadowed the turkey or failed to add any moisture to the patties. Then we tried ricotta cheese. Rich and moist, it was exactly what we were looking for, giving our burgers the boost they needed without dominating the meat's flavor.

Turkey burgers often lack the rich, meaty bite of a beef burger, so to amplify their flavor we turned to Worcestershire sauce and Dijon mustard. These sharp, tangy flavors were just what our burgers needed.

As for doneness level, turkey burgers should be cooked all the way through for safety reasons, but finding the right heat level is tricky: Too high, and they burn before they're done; too low, and they emerge pale and steamed. A two-level fire proved to be the right solution. The burgers could be seared over high heat and then cooked through, covered, at a cooler heat level.

Now that our burgers were perfected, we needed to round out our meal. Keeping in line with our light (yet meaty) turkey burgers, we decided to make a bright, fresh-tasting grilled potato salad. We planned to toss the potatoes with tender baby greens (spicy arugula would add some punch) and dress the whole thing with a citrusy vinaigrette for a summery, clean-flavored dish that would straddle the line between potato salad and green salad.

We halved and skewered three small red potatoes, which would hold their shape over the high heat of the grill, before parcooking them in the microwave and grilling them. Besides yielding perfectly cooked potatoes—with well-browned exteriors, smooth and creamy interiors, and plenty of smoky flavor—the skewers held the whole lot of them together, allowing for hassle-free transfer from kitchen to grill to serving platter.

GRILLED TURKEY BURGERS WITH WARM POTATO AND ARUGULA SALAD

For a simple yet brightly flavored vinaigrette, we whisked together olive oil, lemon juice (for acidity and clean lemon flavor), and lemon zest (for intense, aromatic lemon flavor). In addition to salt and pepper, a small clove of minced garlic added depth and some sugar balanced the tartness.

We wanted to serve the potatoes warm, so we waited until the burgers were almost done before we put the skewers on the grill. When the potatoes were fully browned, we slid them to the cooler side for a few minutes to become fully tender, then slid them off the skewers and right into the bowl with the vinaigrette. After we added the arugula, however, there was still something missing. A few chopped kalamata olives remedied the problem; they contributed a briny bite that brought all the flavors of our warm potato salad into focus.

NOTES FROM THE TEST KITCHEN

SKEWERING POTATOES FOR THE GRILL

Place a potato half cut side down on the counter and pierce it through the center with a skewer. Repeat, holding the already-skewered potatoes for better leverage.

STORING CUT TOMATOES

Sliced tomato is a classic burger topping, but when you're serving up two burgers, what do you do with the extra tomato? We cut a dozen ripe tomatoes in two, stored half of each in the fridge, and kept the other half at room temperature (both wrapped tightly in plastic). After a few days, the halves at room temperature had begun to soften, but the refrigerated halves were still as firm as the day they were cut. Upon tasting, however, we found that the refrigerated halves were bland and mealy compared with the never-refrigerated halves. Our advice? Keep cut tomatoes tightly wrapped at room temperature and eat them within a few days. The shelf life gained by refrigeration doesn't make up for the loss in flavor and texture.

Grilled Turkey Burgers with Warm Potato and Arugula Salad

SERVES 2

Do not use ground turkey breast here (also labeled 99 percent fat-free) or the burgers will be very dry. We prefer the richer flavor and softer texture of whole-milk ricotta here, but part-skim or fat-free will also work. You will need two 12-inch wooden skewers for this recipe. Serve the burgers with traditional fixings, such as sliced tomato and red onion, if desired. The buns can be toasted on the grill while the burgers rest in step 6. See page 138 for a recipe to use up the leftover ricotta cheese.

BURGERS

- 12 ounces 93 percent lean ground turkey (see note)
- 2 ounces whole-milk ricotta cheese (about ¼ cup) (see note)
- 1 teaspoon Worcestershire sauce
- 1 teaspoon Dijon mustard
- ¼ teaspoon salt
- ¼ teaspoon pepper

SALAD

- 8 ounces small red potatoes (about 3), halved and skewered (see photo)
- ¼ cup olive oil
  Salt and pepper
- ½ teaspoon grated lemon zest plus 1 tablespoon fresh lemon juice
- 1 small garlic clove, minced
- 1 teaspoon sugar
- 2 ounces baby arugula (about 2 cups)
- 2 tablespoons pitted kalamata olives, chopped
- 2 buns, toasted (see note)

1. FOR THE BURGERS: Break ground turkey into small pieces in bowl. Add ricotta, Worcestershire sauce, mustard, salt, and pepper and gently knead until well incorporated. Divide meat into 2 equal portions, then form gently into 1-inch-thick patties. Place patties on plate, cover with plastic wrap, and refrigerate until needed.

2. FOR THE SALAD: Place skewered potatoes on large microwave-safe plate and poke each potato several times with skewer or fork. Brush with 1 tablespoon oil and season with salt and pepper. Microwave until potatoes begin to soften but still hold their shape, 6 to 8 minutes, flipping potatoes halfway through. Whisk remaining 3 tablespoons oil, lemon zest and juice, garlic, sugar, ⅛ teaspoon salt, and ⅛ teaspoon pepper together in large bowl; set aside for serving.

3A. FOR A CHARCOAL GRILL: Open bottom grill vents completely. Light large chimney starter filled with charcoal briquettes (100 briquettes; 6 quarts). When coals are hot, spread two-thirds of them evenly over half of grill and remaining coals evenly over other half of grill. Set cooking grate in place, cover, and open lid vents completely. Heat grill until hot, about 5 minutes.

3B. FOR A GAS GRILL: Turn all burners to high, cover, and heat grill until hot, about 15 minutes. Leave primary burner on high and turn other burner(s) to medium. (Adjust burners as needed to maintain hot fire and medium fire on separate sides; see page 144.)

4. Clean and oil cooking grate. Place burgers on hotter part of grill and cook (covered if using gas) until well browned on both sides, 5 to 7 minutes, flipping burgers halfway through.

5. Slide burgers to cooler part of grill, cover, and continue to cook until they register 160 to 165 degrees on instant-read thermometer, 5 to 7 minutes longer, flipping burgers halfway through. Meanwhile, place potatoes, cut side down, on hotter part of grill and cook until browned on both sides, 5 to 7 minutes, flipping potatoes halfway through.

6. Transfer burgers to serving platter, tent loosely with foil, and let rest for 5 minutes. Slide potatoes to cooler part of grill and continue to cook, covered, until tender, 2 to 4 minutes longer.

7. Remove potato skewers from grill and carefully slide potatoes off skewers into bowl of reserved dressing. Add arugula and olives, season with salt and pepper to taste, and toss gently. Place burgers on buns and serve with salad.

VARIATION

Grilled Smoky Southwestern Turkey Burgers with Warm Potato and Arugula Salad

Follow recipe for Grilled Turkey Burgers with Warm Potato and Arugula Salad, omitting Worcestershire sauce. Add 1 minced garlic clove, 1 teaspoon minced canned chipotle chile in adobo sauce, and ½ teaspoon cumin to turkey mixture in step 1.

GRILLED CORNELL CHICKEN WITH BELGIAN ENDIVE

LOOKING FOR A NEW TAKE ON GRILLED CHICKEN, we discovered a much-loved regional favorite, Cornell chicken. This uniquely tangy, crisp-skinned chicken was invented in the 1940s by the late Dr. Robert Baker, a Cornell University professor, and it has been a star attraction at the New York State Fair ever since. Even today, his recipe remains unchanged at the Baker's Chicken Coop stand at the fair: Half chickens are basted with a tangy vinegar-based sauce while they cook over a custom-made grill that elevates the birds exactly 26 inches above the coals. The combination of low heat and continual basting with the special sauce produces one-of-a-kind results.

Unfortunately, recipes that try to adapt Baker's chicken to the backyard grill, where the fire is much closer to the cooking grate, are problematic. The oily basting sauce inevitably drips off the chicken and into the fire, where it causes flare-ups that blacken the outside of the chicken before the inside has cooked through. We set out to figure out how to achieve the crisp skin and deeply seasoned meat of the hallmark dish, in a portion scaled for two.

We started with the chicken. The original recipe begins with whole chickens, which are split in half to lie flat on the grill. But even the smallest chicken yields too much meat for two. We tried Cornish game hens, but they didn't keep with the spirit of the original recipe. Chicken quarters (drumstick and leg, still attached) felt more appropriate, as they were rustic and more casual and seemed like a natural offering at a state fair.

Next we addressed the sauce, which is used to continually baste the chickens while cooking. The recipes we found were pretty standard: 2 parts vinegar to 1 part vegetable oil, along with poultry seasoning (a dried herb and spice mix of thyme, sage, and marjoram, among other ingredients), salt, and a beaten egg, which acts as a thickener. Since we were scaling the sauce down, we didn't want to call for half an egg, so we tried omitting it; but this thin mixture ran off the chicken as fast as we could brush it on.

Because the sauce is essentially a vinaigrette, we tried using mustard as the thickener (we often use it to help emulsify vinaigrettes). The sauce now clung to our chicken, and it had decent flavor, but it wasn't as bold as it should be.

Switching from vegetable oil to olive oil helped add flavor, and bumping up the amount of vinegar (to equal parts vinegar and oil) finally produced the bright pungency we were after. Fresh rosemary and dried sage provided woodsy, earthy notes that countered the vinegar. We had to apply this sauce only three times during cooking to match the amount of flavor achieved with continual basting with a thinner sauce. Less basting not only meant less work, but it also made for crisper skin.

While our leg quarters now had a flavorful crust, the meat underneath tasted bland. Soaking the chicken in a saltwater brine before cooking helped to season the meat, and adding vinegar to the brine brought the tangy pucker all the way down to the bone. For even more flavor, we reached for the poultry seasoning, which combined a number of dried herbal flavors in one convenient package, and rubbed it into the skin before grilling.

For grilling our chicken, we needed to minimize flare-ups from the rendering fat and sauce dripping on the coals. After some experimentation, we found it best to build a half-grill fire. In this grill setup, all the coals are placed on one side of the grill, effectively creating a hot zone and a cool zone. Food placed on the cool side can cook gently with the cover on, with no risk of flare-ups. We started the chicken skin side up to slowly render the fat, then flipped it skin side down to brown, briefly sliding it directly over the coals for the final few minutes of cooking to fully crisp the skin.

To round out the meal, we looked for a simple but lively side dish that would pair well with the tangy chicken. Endive is typically served raw in salads, but grilling it made an elegant partner for our rustic grilled chicken. When grilled, endive softens slightly but still holds its shape, and the intense heat mellows its bitterness.

After determining that we needed three heads of endive for two servings, we tried grilling them whole, but they charred too much on the outside before the interior could cook through. We had far better results when we sliced each head in half lengthwise. As long as a piece of the core was attached, the layers of leaves stayed together. We brushed the halves with olive oil and tossed them onto the grill.

After about five minutes, the endive was slightly wilted and browned, needing just a drizzle of the vinaigrette and a sprinkling of Parmesan shavings.

Grilled Cornell Chicken with Belgian Endive
SERVES 2

Because this chicken soaks in a flavored brine, do not use kosher chicken or it will taste too salty. Do not brine the chicken longer than 1 hour or the vinegar will make the meat mushy. Poultry seasoning is a mix of herbs and spices that can be found in the spice aisle at the supermarket. When trimming the endive, it's important not to trim too much off the stem or the leaves will fall apart during grilling. Use a vegetable peeler to shave the Parmesan.

CHICKEN

- 2 cups cider vinegar
- ⅓ cup salt
- 2 (12-ounce) chicken leg quarters (see note), trimmed
- 1 teaspoon poultry seasoning (see note)
- ¼ teaspoon pepper

TANGY MUSTARD SAUCE AND ENDIVE

- 3 tablespoons cider vinegar
- 1 tablespoon Dijon mustard
- 1 teaspoon minced fresh rosemary
- ¼ teaspoon dried sage
  - Salt and pepper
- ¼ cup olive oil
- 3 heads endive, stem ends trimmed, halved lengthwise through core (see photos)
- 1 tablespoon thinly shaved Parmesan cheese (see note)

NOTES FROM THE TEST KITCHEN

PREPARING ENDIVE FOR GRILLING

1. With a knife, shave off the discolored end of the endive. Cut the thinnest slice possible—you want the layers of leaves to remain intact as the endive cooks.

2. Cut the endive in half lengthwise through the core end.

1. FOR THE CHICKEN: In large bowl, whisk vinegar, salt, and 1 quart water together until salt dissolves. Submerge chicken in brine, cover, and refrigerate for at least 30 minutes or up to 1 hour. Remove chicken from brine, rinse, and pat dry with paper towels. Combine poultry seasoning and pepper in bowl, then rub evenly over chicken.

2. FOR THE MUSTARD SAUCE AND ENDIVE: Whisk vinegar, mustard, rosemary, sage, ¼ teaspoon salt, and ¼ teaspoon pepper together in medium bowl. Slowly whisk in 3 tablespoons oil until incorporated. Measure out and reserve 3 tablespoons sauce for serving. Brush endive with remaining 1 tablespoon oil and season with salt and pepper.

3A. FOR A CHARCOAL GRILL: Open bottom grill vents completely. Light large chimney starter filled with charcoal briquettes (100 briquettes; 6 quarts). When coals are hot, pour them in even layer over half of grill, leaving other half empty. Set cooking grate in place, cover, and open lid vents completely. Heat grill until hot, about 5 minutes.

3B. FOR A GAS GRILL: Turn all burners to high, cover, and heat grill until hot, about 15 minutes. Leave primary burner on high and turn off other burner(s). (Adjust primary burner as needed to maintain temperature of 350 degrees.)

4. Clean and oil cooking grate. Place chicken, skin side up, on cooler part of grill and brush with 1½ tablespoons sauce reserved for cooking. Cover grill and cook until chicken is well browned on bottom and registers 150 degrees on instant-read thermometer, 20 to 30 minutes, brushing with 1½ tablespoons more sauce.

5. Using two spatulas, gently flip chicken skin side down and move to hotter part of grill. Brush with remaining sauce reserved for cooking and continue to cook (covered if using gas) until skin is golden brown and crisp and chicken registers 175 degrees on instant-read thermometer, 6 to 10 minutes longer. Meanwhile, place endive, cut side down, on hotter part of grill and cook until slightly wilted and browned on all sides, about 5 minutes, turning as needed.

6. Transfer endive and chicken to serving platter and let chicken rest for 5 minutes. Drizzle 1 tablespoon sauce reserved for serving over endive and sprinkle with Parmesan. Serve, passing remaining reserved sauce separately.

BARBECUED CHICKEN WITH MEXICAN GRILLED CORN

CHICKEN ON THE GRILL USUALLY MEANS ONE THING: sweet, spicy barbecued chicken. While a slathering of thick barbecue sauce added to chicken toward the end of the cooking time can give the meat an attractive, tasty glaze, it never flavors more than the surface of the meat and can make the skin flabby. Our goal was clear: We wanted classic barbecue flavor in our chicken through and through—not just on top. In addition, we wanted to pair our chicken with a great grilled side.

For our chicken, we chose convenient bone-in chicken breasts. While exploring options to flavor our chicken, we landed on dry spice rubs. Dry spice rubs are rubbed into the chicken before cooking, thereby penetrating and flavoring the meat straight down to the bone, and they don't cause the skin to become soggy. Plus, rubs are fuss-free—simply stir together spices, no cooking required. The only thing missing from a rub is the lacquered glaze of a barbecue sauce. To that end, we sought to develop a dry rub that would do double duty, both flavoring and glazing the chicken.

We knew that sugar would be a key ingredient in our rub to duplicate the sweetness of barbecue sauce and help form a glaze (when sugar meets heat, it melts), so this was where we started our tests. We tested white sugar (too sweet in the quantity necessary), light brown sugar (not bad), and more complexly flavored dark brown sugar (the hands-down winner). Dark brown sugar has almost 20 percent more moisture than white sugar, which helps it melt reliably.

For the spices, we were after the classic barbecue flavors; paprika and chili powder provided the right color and flavor. Onion powder mimicked the fresh onion in homemade sauces, and dry mustard lent brightness. Salt, pepper, and cayenne rounded out the rub.

To ensure that the flavors of the rub penetrated the meat, we carefully separated the skin from the meat and applied the rub over and under the skin. Letting the chicken rest for at least 30 minutes gave the rub time to season the meat and make it juicier. During this rest, the salt and sugar acted as a shallow brine and pulled some of the moisture in the chicken to the surface; we hoped this would jump-start the glazing process.

We were now ready to cook our chicken. Our established test kitchen technique for grilling bone-in breasts calls for a half-grill fire, which is made by placing a full chimney of coals on one half of the grill, thereby producing two zones of heat. A short stint over the hot coals—at the beginning and/or end of cooking—allows the skin to crisp quickly, and the cooler zone allows the chicken to cook through gently without the rendering fat from the skin dripping on the coals and causing an inferno. Unfortunately, we found that our technique was too much for our sugary glaze, as it quickly turned into a charred mess. After some experimentation, we learned that we didn't need to cook the chicken on the hotter part at all—the sugar in the rub ensured a caramelized exterior. However, even though it was on the cooler side for the duration of the cooking time, the chicken was getting too dark and charred in places. Reducing the amount of coals to three-quarters of a chimney (or reducing the heat to medium-low on a gas grill) proved to be the solution.

Although the rub was no longer burning, we now had another problem. A single coating of the rub started out promising but resulted in a skimpy, blotchy glaze by the time the chicken was completely cooked. After some experimentation, and after logging hours at the grill, we hit upon the technique of dredging the chicken breasts in the dry rub a second time halfway through cooking, once the sugar began to melt. The second coating adhered to the sticky, partially melted base coat, and together they melted into a very nice lacquer. True, it's a bit of a messy process, but tongs prevent burnt fingers and keep hands clean. The lower heat of our grill let the skin slowly render, and the melting fat blended with the dry rub and enriched the glaze. As we let the cooked chicken rest, covered with foil, the residual heat melted any intact grains of sugar that had survived the grill.

For a side dish, we decided to pair our American grilled classic with one from Mexico—street corn. In this dish, corn on the cob is grilled until it's intensely sweet, smoky, and charred, then is slathered with a cheesy, creamy sauce spiked with lime juice and chili powder. Our challenge would be to deliver authentic flavor without relying on hard-to-find ingredients.

Starting with two ears of corn, we removed all but the innermost layer of husk, which would serve to protect the corn from the hot coals, trapping moisture and allowing the corn to steam. We waited until our chicken was nearly cooked through before tossing the two ears onto the grill. While this method delivered juicy, smoky corn, it didn't give us enough charring to replicate the smoky flavor of Mexican street corn.

In our next test, we opted to ditch the husk completely and grilled the corn directly on top of the cooking grate, brushing the ears with oil first to prevent them from sticking. We also covered the corn with an aluminum roasting pan before covering the grill. This trapped a layer of heat next to the corn, creating a sort of oven within an oven; the intensified heat produced perfectly cooked corn with great charred flavor in just 10 minutes.

For the sauce, we opted for a base of mayonnaise, which made a suitable stand-in for the traditional *créma* (soured Mexican cream) called for in authentic recipes. Looking for a more accessible substitute for the Mexican cheeses used for street corn, we hit upon feta, which provided just the right crumbly texture and salty flavor. As for other seasonings, tasters appreciated the usual additions of cilantro, lime juice, garlic, and chili powder. While we waited for the grill to heat up, we mixed our sauce in a large bowl, so that we could toss the corn immediately into the sauce as it came off the grill.

With a few unconventional techniques, we had brought classic American barbecued chicken to the dinner table for two. Our chicken breasts were juicy and moist, coated with a sweet and spicy glaze, and a south-of-the-border dish made the perfect bright, zesty counterpoint.

Barbecued Dry-Rubbed Chicken with Mexican Grilled Corn

SERVES 2

Four bone-in, skin-on chicken thighs or drumsticks can be substituted for the breasts; you will need to cook them in step 6 until they register 175 degrees on an instant-read thermometer. We prefer the flavor of dark brown sugar in this recipe; however, light brown sugar can be substituted. Apply the second coating of spices with a light hand or they won't melt into a glaze. See page 163 for a recipe to use up the leftover feta cheese.

CHICKEN

- **1 tablespoon dark brown sugar (see note)**
- **1 teaspoon paprika**
- **¾ teaspoon chili powder**

¾ teaspoon pepper

½ teaspoon dry mustard

½ teaspoon onion powder

¼ teaspoon salt

    Pinch cayenne pepper

2 (12-ounce) bone-in, skin-on split chicken breasts (see note), trimmed (see page 63)

CORN

¼ cup mayonnaise

2 tablespoons minced fresh cilantro

1 teaspoon fresh lime juice

1 small garlic clove, minced

½ teaspoon chili powder

1 ounce feta cheese, crumbled (about ¼ cup)

2 ears fresh corn, husks and silk removed

2 teaspoons olive oil

    Salt and pepper

1 (13 by 9-inch) disposable aluminum roasting pan

    Lime wedges, for serving

1. FOR THE CHICKEN: Combine sugar, paprika, chili powder, pepper, mustard, onion powder, salt, and cayenne in small bowl. Transfer 1½ tablespoons spice mixture to pie plate; set aside for cooking.

2. Pat chicken dry with paper towels and gently loosen center portion of skin covering each breast by sliding your fingers between skin and meat. Rub remaining spice mixture over and underneath skin of each breast. Transfer chicken to large plate, cover with plastic wrap, and refrigerate for at least 30 minutes or up to 1 hour.

3. FOR THE CORN: Mix mayonnaise, cilantro, lime juice, garlic, and chili powder together in medium bowl. Fold in feta; refrigerate until needed. Brush corn with oil and season with salt and pepper.

4A. FOR A CHARCOAL GRILL: Open bottom grill vents completely. Light large chimney starter filled three-quarters with charcoal briquettes (75 briquettes; 4½ quarts). When coals are hot, pour them in even layer over half of grill, leaving other half empty. Set cooking grate in place, cover, and open lid vents completely. Heat grill until hot, about 5 minutes.

4B. FOR A GAS GRILL: Turn all burners to high, cover, and heat grill until hot, about 15 minutes. Leave primary burner on high and turn other burner(s) off.

(Adjust primary burner as needed to maintain temperature of 325 degrees.)

5. Clean and oil cooking grate. Place chicken, skin side down, on cooler part of grill, with thicker sides of breasts facing hotter part of grill. Cover grill and cook until skin is well browned and crisp, 20 to 25 minutes.

6. Using tongs, lightly dredge skin sides of breasts in reserved spice rub. Return chicken, skin side up, to cooler part of grill and continue to cook, covered, until rub has melted into glaze and chicken registers 160 to 165 degrees on instant-read thermometer, 15 to 20 minutes longer. Meanwhile, place corn on hotter part of grill, cover with aluminum roasting pan, and cook until lightly charred on all sides, 7 to 12 minutes, turning as needed.

7. Transfer corn to bowl with mayonnaise mixture and toss to coat. Transfer chicken to serving platter, tent loosely with foil, and let rest for 5 minutes. Serve chicken with corn and lime wedges.

USE IT UP: FETA CHEESE

Spicy Whipped Feta

MAKES ABOUT 1 CUP

It is important to rinse the feta before using it in this recipe or the dip will be too salty. Serve with pita chips, wedges of warm pita bread, or slices of baguette. Sprinkle with sliced scallions and minced fresh parsley, cilantro, and/or mint before serving, if desired.

6 ounces feta cheese, crumbled (about 1½ cups), rinsed (see note)

3 tablespoons extra-virgin olive oil, plus extra for serving

1 tablespoon water

1 teaspoon fresh lemon juice

½ teaspoon paprika

¼ teaspoon cayenne pepper

⅛ teaspoon pepper

Process all ingredients together in food processor until smooth, about 20 seconds. Transfer mixture to serving bowl, cover with plastic wrap, and refrigerate until firm, about 2 hours or up to 2 days. Drizzle with additional extra-virgin olive oil before serving.

GRILLED TUNA STEAKS AND BOK CHOY SLAW

GREAT GRILLED TUNA DELIVERS A WORLD OF contrasts: a thin layer of hot, grilled meat with an intense smoky char wrapped around a cool, delicately flavored, tender, and moist center. Grilling tuna just right might be old hat for a seasoned chef or restaurant line cooks, but a few preliminary tests turned out steak after steak with either a rare center and no char, or a great sear enveloping a dry, mealy interior. And in every case, a strong fishy odor dominated what we'd always regarded as a very mild fish.

The problem is that tuna is extremely lean, making it especially prone to drying out. An overcooked steak or salmon fillet, while not ideal, has enough interior fat to keep it relatively moist and palatable; overcook your tuna, however, and dinner is done. In order to preserve its texture, it simply must be served rare or medium-rare. That's where the grill method becomes tricky. How do you char the outside of a tuna steak while leaving the interior untouched?

We began by selecting fresh, 1-inch-thick tuna steaks—any thinner, and we'd never be able to keep them on the grill long enough to achieve a decent crust without overcooking their insides. We knew that using direct heat with a hot fire, and getting the tuna on and off the grill as quickly as possible, would be the best approach. Half the grill was more than enough space for our two steaks, so when our coals were lit we piled the full chimney's worth evenly on one side of the grill to make a super-hot cooking zone.

To keep the fish from sticking on the grill, we covered the grate with aluminum foil and preheated it over the coals, which allowed us to easily brush away any built-up debris. We then applied several layers of oil with paper towels to build up a nonstick surface before adding the steaks. The fish gave a promising sizzle when it hit the superheated grates, but the finished product was far from ideal: The exteriors were dry and stringy with a fishy aroma, and though the fish bore distinct grill marks, most of it emerged unappetizingly gray with pallid flavor to match.

Dried herbs and spices brown much faster than meat, and while a good coating of them gave the fish charred flavor, their intense flavors overwhelmed the tuna. We decided to step away from spices and herbs and move on to another ingredient that can enhance browning: oil.

Oil doesn't brown on its own, but it does help to distribute heat evenly over the surface of the fish, and it adds a little fat, keeping the exterior of the fish from tasting too dry and stringy. But when we pulled our olive oil–rubbed steaks off the fire, the tuna (though slightly moister) still lacked grill flavor.

After talking with our science editor, we realized that in order to moisten the tuna's flesh, the oil must be able to penetrate and coat the muscle fibers on a microscopic level. But tuna is full of water, and, as the saying goes, oil and water don't mix. For the oil to coat the muscle fibers, it had to be in a state where it wouldn't repel water. We immediately thought of an emulsified vinaigrette, in which the oil is dispersed in tiny droplets in the vinegar (often with the aid of an egg yolk, mustard, or mayonnaise), where it would be unaffected by water from the fish. As long as the flavor of the vinaigrette did not overpower the taste of the tuna itself, coating the fish in such an emulsion might be just the ticket.

Tuna pairs well with many flavors, but we settled on the bright flavors of an Asian-inspired dressing. We whisked together a mixture of olive oil, soy sauce, rice wine vinegar, minced ginger, and Dijon mustard. When we brushed this mixture on the fish before grilling it, the effect was immediate. The dressing (and its oil) clung to the fish, moistening its outer layer and solving the problem of dry, stringy flesh. The acid in the vinaigrette also neutralized the fishy odor we had noticed earlier. Now only one hurdle remained: improving browning.

In the past, we've successfully used sugar to enhance browning on meat; would the same work for fish? Adding some sugar to the vinaigrette did achieve the browning we wanted, but only after eight minutes on the grill, by which time the delicate fish was overdone. We knew that before granulated sugar could brown, it has to first break down into simpler sugars, which takes time. Since honey is made primarily of simple sugars, it is already primed for browning, and we reasoned it would deliver the same results faster.

Indeed, the effect of a small amount of honey (1½ teaspoons) on browning was dramatic, and its sweetness improved the flavor of the vinaigrette. While we were at it, we decided to further boost the flavor of the dressing with sliced scallions, red pepper flakes, and toasted sesame oil. We made sure to make a little extra, so that we would have a sauce for serving with the tuna.

GRILLED TUNA STEAKS WITH SOY-GINGER VINAIGRETTE AND BOK CHOY SLAW

To round out our meal, we hit on the idea of adding some vinaigrette to grilled Chinese cabbage, giving us the makings of a warm, Asian-inspired slaw. We halved a small head of bok choy through the stem end, leaving the core intact (which holds the leaves together on the grill). Once the tuna was off the grill, we threw the bok choy (after brushing it with oil and sprinkling it with salt and pepper) over the still-hot coals. Just a few minutes later, we removed the slightly wilted, browned cabbage from the grill and sliced it into thin strips before tossing it with some of our reserved dressing. The stalks of the bok choy retained a crunch, which contrasted nicely with the wilted, smoky leaves. A grated carrot added bright color and gave the dish a true slaw identity.

Our fish came off the grill with everything we'd hoped for: attractive grill marks, a nicely charred, pleasantly smoky crust, and a rosy, melt-in-your-mouth center. And the bonus: We now had a warm bed of lively bok choy slaw for the fish to land on.

Grilled Tuna Steaks with Soy-Ginger Vinaigrette and Bok Choy Slaw

SERVES 2

We prefer our tuna served rare (opaque at the perimeter and translucent red at the center when checked with the tip of a paring knife) or medium-rare (opaque at the perimeter and reddish pink at the center). If you like your fish cooked medium, observe the timing for medium-rare, then tent the steaks loosely with foil for 5 minutes before serving. To achieve a nicely grilled exterior and a rare center, it is important to use fish steaks that are at least 1 inch thick. Do not remove the core from the bok choy; it will help keep the leaves together on the grill.

- 2 **tablespoons rice wine vinegar**
- 2 **tablespoons soy sauce**
- 4 **teaspoons Dijon mustard**
- 1½ **teaspoons toasted sesame oil**
- 1½ **teaspoons honey**
- 2 **scallions, sliced thin**
- 1½ **teaspoons minced or grated fresh ginger**
- ¼ **teaspoon red pepper flakes**
- ½ **cup olive oil**
- 1 **small head bok choy (about 1 pound), halved lengthwise through core (see note)**

- **Salt and pepper**
- 2 **(8-ounce) tuna steaks, about 1 inch thick (see note)**
- **Vegetable oil, as needed for seasoning grill**
- 1 **carrot, peeled and shredded**

1. Whisk vinegar, soy sauce, mustard, sesame oil, honey, scallions, ginger, and red pepper flakes together in medium bowl. Slowly whisk in 7 tablespoons oil until incorporated. Measure out and reserve ½ cup dressing for serving.

2. Brush bok choy with remaining 1 tablespoon oil and season with salt and pepper. Season tuna with salt and pepper and brush both sides with remaining dressing.

3A. FOR A CHARCOAL GRILL: Open bottom grill vents completely. Light large chimney starter filled with charcoal briquettes (100 briquettes; 6 quarts). When coals are hot, pour them in even layer over half of grill, leaving other half empty. Loosely cover cooking grate with large piece of heavy-duty aluminum foil, position grate over coals, cover grill, and open lid vents completely. Heat grill until hot, about 5 minutes.

3B. FOR A GAS GRILL: Turn all burners to high, loosely cover cooking grate with large piece of heavy-duty aluminum foil, cover, and heat grill until hot, about 15 minutes. (Adjust burners as needed to maintain hot fire; see page 144.)

4. Remove foil with tongs and discard, then clean cooking grate. Using tongs, dip wad of paper towels in vegetable oil and thoroughly oil cooking grate. Repeatedly brush cooking grate with additional oil until it is black and glossy, 5 to 10 more times. (Let any flames die down before grilling.)

5. Gently place tuna on grill (on hotter part of grill if using charcoal) and cook (covered if using gas) until grill marks form and bottom of fish is opaque, about 1½ minutes. Gently flip fish with two spatulas and continue to cook until grill marks form on second side, about 1½ minutes (for rare) or 3 minutes (for medium-rare) longer. Transfer fish to large plate and let rest.

6. While fish rests, place bok choy on grill (on hotter part of grill if using charcoal), cut side down, and cook until slightly wilted and well browned on all sides, about 5 minutes, turning as needed.

7. Transfer bok choy to cutting board and slice into thin strips, discarding core. Toss bok choy with carrot and ⅓ cup reserved dressing in bowl. Serve fish and bok choy, passing remaining dressing separately.

GRILLED PIZZA WITH ROMAINE SALAD

WITH A LIGHTLY CHARRED, CRACKLY-CRISP, SMOKY crust decorated with perfectly balanced, flavorful toppings, grilled pizza has become a staple not only of restaurants but also of home grills. Pizza, as it turns out, is a natural fit for the grill: The super-hot fire mimics a super-hot pizza oven, giving the crust great char and crispness. It also has the distinct advantage of letting you enjoy homemade pizza in the summer without having to blast your oven. But grilling pizza can be a production for the cook, who must navigate several rounds of dough on the hot grates, then flip them without injury. We thought making pizza for two would be easier, streamlining the process and making it less intimidating for the home cook. We aimed to cook enough pizza for two in one batch, perhaps even squeezing in a side dish, before it was time to sit down to eat (cook included).

Grilled pizza is nothing without a great-tasting crust, so this was where we started. We wanted a scaled-down dough recipe that yielded about 8 ounces, enough for two 9-inch pizzas, which we reasoned would be easier to flip on the grill than one large pizza. Dough for grilled pizza has to be slack enough to be stretched thin—thinner than baked pizza, so that it can cook through quickly on the grill—yet strong enough not to rip. High-protein bread flour generally makes a stronger dough than all-purpose flour (by encouraging gluten development), and a head-to-head test proved it. As for the ratio of water to flour, the wetter the dough, the easier it was to stretch and the crisper the crust, but at a cost: The dough was intractably sticky. We backed off on the water a little at a time until the dough, though still pretty wet, could be worked without clinging too firmly to our hands or the counter.

Olive oil adds flavor and richness to a lean dough. In this case, 1½ teaspoons was noticeable, but twice that was better yet. The dough seemed smoother, more supple, and less sticky. We also noticed that the higher amount of oil prevented the dough from sticking to the grill. Within 30 seconds over the fire, the crust easily released. In other recipes the dough is slicked with oil before grilling for the same effect, but we found this method caused flare-ups as oil dripped onto the hot coals.

Most recipes we found shared a similar cooking method. The crust is cooked on one side over a medium-hot, two-level fire until crisp, then flipped, topped, and finished on the cool side of the fire. This method worked if we cooked one pizza at a time; trying to fit both crusts on one half of the grill invariably led to burnt edges and singed fingers. But we wanted our pizzas done at the same time so the cook wasn't playing catch-up at the dinner table.

To get more space on the grill, we tried a single-level hot fire but soon realized that this was too risky an approach, since there was no easy retreat for the dough if it started burning. Lowering the temperature of the fire made the technique safer, but the crust was dense and anemic in color and flavor. After trying several different arrangements of coals, we found that a single-level, medium-hot fire spread over three-quarters of the grill bottom (like a pie with a wedge missing) gave us enough heat and real estate to cook both pizzas at once and a safety zone onto which we could slide any crust that was at risk of burning—a rare but real threat.

To top the pizza, we needed a sauce that wouldn't soak through the thin crust. A few chopped plum tomatoes made an easy and fresh substitute for sauce, but they were still too watery. To draw off excess juice, we tossed the tomatoes with salt and drained them on paper towels for 15 minutes. Tasters liked classic seasonings: a pinch of red pepper flakes, a clove of minced garlic, a tablespoon of olive oil, and a scattering of chopped fresh basil. For cheese, we liked traditional shredded mozzarella along with a bit of freshly grated Parmesan for a salty bite. We found it was preferable to top the pizzas on a baking sheet (after cooking one side) rather than directly on the grill. Covering the topped pizzas with the grill lid for a few minutes trapped enough heat to finish cooking the crust, melt the cheese, and heat the tomatoes. In a matter of minutes, we now had two hot pizzas ready to eat.

For an accompaniment, we decided to put a sophisticated spin on the basic pizza parlor salad. We ditched the iceberg lettuce and instead selected a head of romaine lettuce, which we halved through the core and grilled until it was smoky, beautifully browned, and spottily charred on the edges. Red onion, cut into rounds and grilled on a skewer to keep the pieces from falling through the grate, provided a crunchy and pungent sweetness. The romaine halves and onion rounds looked so attractive coming off the grill that we opted to serve them whole. With a drizzle of balsamic vinaigrette and a sprinkle of shaved Parmesan cheese, our deconstructed salad was ready.

When our pizzas were done (so that they could be served piping hot, we grilled the salad first), we had two picture-perfect pies that tasted so good, they disappeared before anyone could get out a camera.

NOTES FROM THE TEST KITCHEN

STORE-BOUGHT PIZZA DOUGH
The dough is probably the trickiest part of making pizza at home. While pizza dough is nothing more than bread dough with oil added for softness and suppleness, we have found that minor changes can yield dramatically different results. We think homemade dough is worth the modest effort, but we have to admit prepared dough can be a great time-saving option for pizza night. Many supermarkets and pizzerias sell their dough for just a few dollars a pound, and the dough can be easily frozen. We found that store-bought dough, dough from a local pizzeria, and refrigerated pop-up canisters of pizza dough (such as Pillsbury) all worked well and tasted fine, but we recommend buying dough from a pizzeria, where it is more likely to be freshly made. Note that while most supermarket dough is sold in 1-pound bags, you will need only 8 ounces of dough for our pizza recipe.

MAKING GRILLED PIZZA

1. To easily and safely transfer the dough to the grill, use tongs to slide the dough from an inverted baking sheet onto the grill. Repeat with the second dough round.

2. When the dough is covered with bubbles and the bottom is spotty brown, return the pizza crusts to the inverted baking sheet, browned sides up. Then add the toppings and slide the rounds back onto the grill.

Grilled Pizza with Charred Romaine and Red Onion Salad
MAKES 2 INDIVIDUAL PIZZAS

We like to use our Basic Pizza Dough (page 169) here; however, you can substitute premade pizza dough from the supermarket. You will need one 12-inch metal skewer for this recipe. Do not remove the core from the lettuce; it will help keep the leaves together on the grill. Use a vegetable peeler to shave the Parmesan.

PIZZA

- 12 ounces plum tomatoes (about 3 medium), cored, seeded, and cut into ½-inch pieces
  Salt and pepper
- 2 tablespoons chopped fresh basil
- 2 tablespoons extra-virgin olive oil
- 1 small garlic clove, minced
- ⅛ teaspoon red pepper flakes
- 3 ounces mozzarella cheese, shredded (about ¾ cup)
- ¼ cup grated Parmesan cheese
- 8 ounces pizza dough (see note)

SALAD

- 3 tablespoons extra-virgin olive oil
- 2 teaspoons balsamic vinegar
- 1 teaspoon honey
- ½ teaspoon Dijon mustard
- 1 small garlic clove, minced
  Salt and pepper
- 1 red onion, sliced into ¾-inch-thick rounds
- 1 large heart romaine lettuce, halved lengthwise through core (see note)
- 2 tablespoons shaved Parmesan cheese (see note)

1. FOR THE PIZZA: Toss tomatoes with ¼ teaspoon salt, spread on paper towel–lined plate, and let drain for 15 minutes. Combine drained tomatoes, basil, 1 tablespoon oil, garlic, and red pepper flakes in bowl and season with salt and pepper to taste. In separate bowl, combine mozzarella and Parmesan.

2. Turn dough out onto lightly floured counter and divide into 2 equal pieces. Working with 1 piece at a time, press into small circle, then roll and stretch dough to form 9-inch circle. (If dough shrinks when rolled out, cover with plastic wrap and let rest for 5 minutes.) Lay dough rounds on separate pieces of parchment paper dusted with flour; they can be stacked on top of one another. Cover with plastic wrap.

3. FOR THE SALAD: Whisk 2 tablespoons oil, vinegar, honey, mustard, and garlic together in small bowl. Season with salt and pepper to taste; set aside for serving. Thread onion rounds, from side to side, onto 12-inch metal skewer. Brush skewered onion and romaine with remaining 1 tablespoon oil and season with salt and pepper.

4A. FOR A CHARCOAL GRILL: Open bottom grill vents completely. Light large chimney starter filled with charcoal briquettes (100 briquettes; 6 quarts). When coals are hot, spread in even layer over three-quarters of grill, leaving one quadrant free of coals. Set cooking grate in place, cover, and open lid vents completely. Heat grill until hot, about 5 minutes.

4B. FOR A GAS GRILL: Turn all burners to high, cover, and heat grill until hot, about 15 minutes. Leave primary burner on high and turn off other burner(s). (Adjust primary burner as needed to maintain hot fire on one side; see page 144.)

5. Clean and oil cooking grate. Place skewered onion on hotter part of grill; cook (covered if using gas) until spottily charred on both sides, 8 to 10 minutes, flipping onion halfway through. Meanwhile, cook romaine on hotter part of grill next to onion until spottily charred on all sides, about 2 minutes, turning as needed. Transfer onion and romaine to serving platter, remove onion from skewer, and tent loosely with foil to keep warm.

6. Lightly flour rimless (or inverted) baking sheet. Invert 1 dough round onto prepared baking sheet, peel off parchment, and reshape as needed. Working quickly, carefully slide round onto hotter part of grill. Repeat with second dough round. Cook (covered if using gas) until top of dough is covered with bubbles and bottom is spotty brown, about 1 minute, poking large bubbles with tongs as needed. (Check bottom of crust continually and slide to cooler part of grill if browning too quickly.)

7. Using tongs, return crusts to inverted baking sheet, browned sides up. Brush with remaining 1 tablespoon oil, sprinkle with cheese mixture, then top with tomato mixture. Return pizzas to hotter part of grill, cover grill, and cook until bottoms are well browned and cheese is melted, 2 to 4 minutes, checking bottoms frequently to prevent burning. Transfer pizzas to cutting board.

8. Drizzle onion and romaine with reserved dressing and sprinkle with Parmesan. Slice pizzas and serve with salad.

Basic Pizza Dough

MAKES 8 OUNCES DOUGH

All-purpose flour can be substituted for the bread flour, but the resulting crust will be a little less chewy. If desired, you can slow down the dough's rising time by letting it rise in the refrigerator for 8 to 16 hours in step 2; let the refrigerated dough soften at room temperature for 30 minutes before using.

- 1 **cup bread flour (5½ ounces), plus extra as needed (see note)**
- 1 **teaspoon sugar**
- ¾ **teaspoon instant or rapid-rise yeast**
- ½ **teaspoon salt**
- 1 **tablespoon extra-virgin olive oil, plus extra for bowl**
- ½ **cup warm water**

1. Pulse flour, sugar, yeast, and salt together in food processor (fitted with dough blade if possible) to combine. With processor running, slowly pour oil, then water, through feed tube and process until dough forms sticky ball that clears side of bowl, 1½ to 2 minutes. (If, after 1 minute, dough is sticky and clings to blade, add extra flour, 1 tablespoon at a time, as needed until it clears side of bowl.)

2. Turn out dough onto lightly floured counter and form into smooth, round ball. Place dough in lightly oiled bowl and cover tightly with greased plastic wrap. Let rise in warm place until doubled in size, 1 to 1½ hours. (Once risen, dough can be sealed in zipper-lock bag and frozen for up to 1 month; let thaw on counter for 2 to 3 hours, or overnight in refrigerator, before using.)

FETTUCCINE ALFREDO

FETTUCCINE ALFREDO

TRADITIONAL FETTUCCINE ALFREDO IS MADE WITH aged Parmesan, butter, heavy cream, and fresh egg fettuccine. Boasting almost 600 calories and over 40 grams of fat per serving, this dish is something we indulge in only once, maybe twice, a year. With such a nice combination of ingredients, we wondered if it was time to apply a lighter touch to this Italian classic. Given its simplicity and the fact that it relies on just a handful of ingredients—making it an ideal weeknight pasta supper for two—we decided to give it a try.

Classic Alfredo sauce is made by simmering and reducing heavy cream until it thickens to a sauce-like consistency, before being finished with butter and cheese. Setting the issue of the butter and Parmesan aside for the time being, we began looking for a way to replace at least some of the heavy cream; if we could find an acceptable substitute for this keystone ingredient, one that still remained rich, saucy, and flavorful, the odds were good that we could make a decent light Alfredo sauce.

We began modestly, by simply cutting back on the amount of heavy cream and attempting to find a way to thicken it. Using just ½ cup of heavy cream, to form a sauce that would coat 6 ounces of dried fettuccine (a more accessible option than fresh pasta), we tried two thickening options—a roux (a mixture of flour and butter) and cornstarch (which we often use to thicken gravies and sauces). Giving both of these a go in a basic Alfredo sauce, we found that the roux, although it performed nicely, produced a thicker, slightly pasty sauce with a floury flavor. The cornstarch worked much better, producing a clean, silky sauce that allowed the Parmesan flavor to shine. Because we weren't cooking the sauce for long, the raw taste of the flour in the roux didn't have time to cook off. Our choice was obvious—using cornstarch both trimmed a significant amount of fat and helped to produce a silky sauce. Although we still had a long way to go, we now believed we were on the right track.

Encouraged by our lightened yet silky sauce, we wondered if we could replace the small amount of heavy cream with a lower-fat alternative, such as half-and-half, milk, or evaporated milk. The milk-based sauce was disastrous—it curdled and turned a drab shade of gray. The evaporated milk made a nice creamy sauce, but tasters found that its sweet, milky flavor overwhelmed the Parmesan, and in the end, the sauce didn't taste like a traditional Alfredo. The half-and-half, on the other hand, produced a stellar sauce with good creamy body and a simple but rich flavor—tasters unanimously approved.

The next ingredient we put to the test was the Parmesan, the key flavor in an Alfredo sauce. Parmesan amounts ranged from ½ cup to 2 cups in other recipes once we scaled down the amounts for two servings, so for our recipe we started out at the high end of the range (with 2 cups of cheese) and made batches of Alfredo with incrementally less cheese. At ¼ cup of cheese, tasters cried uncle. We found that going back up to ½ cup cheese produced a sauce with a rich, nutty, cheesy flavor; any less, and the Parmesan flavor was absent.

As for the butter, we whisked various amounts of it into the finished sauce to see if we could cut the fat further. Some recipes call for up to 6 tablespoons; we made sauce after sauce with less and less butter until we had eliminated it altogether. Tasters actually preferred the flavor of this Alfredo without any butter—they thought the butter muted the Parmesan flavor and felt the sauce was plenty rich on its own.

We noticed that without the butter, though, the sauce began drying out when it was tossed with the cooked pasta. To fix this problem, we simply replaced the butter with pasta cooking water (which is lightly starchy and seasoned) to help keep the sauce fluid. Also, we found that whisking the cooking water into the sauce, before adding the cooked pasta, and tossing the pasta and sauce together over low heat just before serving helped the pasta absorb additional flavor and ensured that the sauce stayed creamy. Serving the finished pasta in warmed bowls provided further insurance against the sauce drying out.

Seasoned simply with salt, pepper, and a pinch of nutmeg for a savory yet sweet undertone, our fettuccine Alfredo might have fewer calories and less fat, but it still boasts all the rich, cheesy flavor of a full-fat plate of this Italian classic—so now we have no problem polishing it off.

Fettuccine Alfredo

SERVES 2

See page 85 for a tip on how to measure out long strands of pasta without using a scale. For the best flavor, we recommend using Parmigiano-Reggiano cheese in this recipe. The texture of the sauce changes dramatically as the dish stands for even a few minutes; serving in warmed bowls helps to ensure that the dish retains its creamy texture while it's being eaten.

½ cup half-and-half
Salt and pepper
Pinch freshly grated nutmeg
½ teaspoon cornstarch
6 ounces fettuccine (see note)
1 ounce Parmesan cheese, grated fine (about ½ cup) (see note)

1. Bring 4½ quarts water to boil in large pot. Using ladle or heatproof measuring cup, fill 2 individual serving bowls with about ½ cup boiling water each; set bowls aside to warm.

2. Meanwhile, bring ¼ cup half-and-half, ⅛ teaspoon salt, and nutmeg to simmer in medium saucepan. Whisk cornstarch and remaining ¼ cup half-and-half together, then whisk into simmering mixture. Continue to simmer sauce, whisking constantly, until it has thickened, about 1 minute. Cover and set aside to keep warm.

3. Add pasta and 1 tablespoon salt to boiling water and cook, stirring often, until al dente. Reserve ½ cup cooking water, then drain pasta.

4. Return half-and-half mixture to medium-low heat and whisk in ¼ cup reserved pasta cooking water. Slowly whisk in Parmesan. Add pasta and cook, coating pasta evenly with sauce, until sauce has thickened slightly, about 1 minute. Season with pepper to taste. Working quickly, empty serving bowls of water, divide pasta between bowls, and serve. (If pasta sauce becomes too thick, adjust sauce consistency with remaining ¼ cup pasta cooking water as desired.)

PER SERVING: Cal 440; Fat 12g; Sat fat 7g; Chol 30mg; Carb 67g; Protein 18g; Fiber 3g; Sodium 660mg

SPAGHETTI AND TURKEY MEATBALLS

IN TRADITIONAL RECIPES FOR SPAGHETTI AND meatballs, the meatballs are fried in about a cup of oil to get a crisp crust, then they're simmered in a tomato sauce that is also heavy on olive oil. With 40-plus grams of fat per serving, it's a dinner that's far from healthy—not to mention labor-intensive, since making a flavorful tomato sauce can take all day. We set out to create meatballs that were healthier than their old-fashioned counterparts but that still had all the same comforting flavor. We also wanted a quick tomato sauce that only tasted as if it had simmered for hours, scaled down to yield two perfect portions, not enough to feed a big Italian family.

We started with the meat. Ground turkey seemed like a healthier option than beef, so we gathered the options: white meat ground turkey, dark meat ground turkey, and a combination of the two. Meatballs made with all dark meat were nearly as high in fat as ground beef meatballs, so we crossed that contender off the list. Meatballs made with all white meat were tough and grainy. Tasters unanimously preferred meatballs made with a combination of white and dark meat (labeled 93 percent lean). They had a meaty flavor and cooked up to a soft, moist texture, and by switching from beef to turkey, we quickly cut almost 15 grams of fat per serving. Using just 8 ounces of ground turkey yielded eight meatballs—perfect for two people.

Next, we moved on to the binding ingredients, which keep the meatballs tender and prevent them from falling apart during cooking. We started with eggs. Our favorite classic meatball recipe relies on just a yolk (a whole egg makes the mixture too sticky), but we thought for this light version it was worth trying an egg white instead. These meatballs didn't hold together, and they tasted too lean, so we went back to the yolk. We weren't surprised that these meatballs were a breeze to handle.

Some form of bread, bread mixture, or cracker crumbs also typically serves as a binder. Both bread and cracker crumbs soaked up moisture, making the meatballs hard and dry. But meatballs made with bread soaked in milk, which acted more like a paste, were moist and rich. For the milk, we tried both whole milk

SPAGHETTI AND TURKEY MEATBALLS

and low-fat milk and didn't notice much of a difference in flavor, so we opted for low-fat milk. Two teaspoons, paired with half a slice of bread, provided ample binding power. Parmesan cheese and garlic added just the right classic flavors.

In search of a lighter cooking method, we tried roasting our meatballs, but they turned out dry and crumbly. Broiling was messy and also produced dry, unevenly cooked meatballs. We would have to make pan-frying work without using the usual cup of oil. Rather than frying the meatballs start to finish, we wondered if we could brown them just enough to give them some flavor and a crust and then finish cooking them in the sauce. After testing varying amounts of oil, we found we needed a mere teaspoon and a half to get a crisp crust and perfect browning. A brief stay in the refrigerator before cooking helped the meatballs firm up and stay intact when they hit the pan.

Meatballs need a thick, clingy sauce, so we began by considering our options when it came to the tomato base. Fresh tomatoes were off-limits because their quality is too variable. We tried tomato sauce combined with diced tomatoes, but the sauce elements were too distinct, even after an extended simmering time. Canned crushed tomatoes, which are a mix of tomato chunks and puree, made for an overly thick sauce. Finally, we tried whole canned tomatoes, which we processed briefly in the food processor. The processed whole tomatoes offered the freshest tomato flavor and were just the right consistency. Simmering our sauce for 20 minutes rid the tomatoes of their raw flavor and concentrated their sweetness.

We wondered if we could save cleanup time and build more flavor into the sauce by making it in the same pan we used to brown the meatballs. After browning the meatballs, we set them aside, added some onion to the skillet, then stirred in garlic and some red pepper flakes. We added the tomatoes and meatballs and simmered until the meatballs were done. Not only was this method convenient, but it also gave the sauce depth, as the browned bits on the bottom of the pan dissolved into the sauce and married the flavors for the final dish.

These guilt-free, easy-to-prepare meatballs and sauce had a rich, deep flavor that rivaled that of beefy, simmered-all-day meatballs and sauce—but they were much better for the waistline.

Spaghetti and Turkey Meatballs

SERVES 2

Do not use ground turkey breast meat (sometimes also labeled as 99 percent fat-free); it will make meatballs that are dry and grainy. The canned tomatoes are the primary source of sodium in this recipe; if you are concerned about sodium intake, use low-sodium or no-salt-added canned tomatoes. It is important to let the meatballs chill for at least 1 hour before cooking, which allows them to firm up and remain intact during cooking.

MEATBALLS

½ slice high-quality white sandwich bread, crust removed, torn into pieces
2 teaspoons low-fat milk
1 large egg yolk, lightly beaten
8 ounces 93 percent lean ground turkey (see note)
2 tablespoons grated Parmesan cheese
2 tablespoons minced fresh parsley
1 garlic clove, minced
⅛ teaspoon pepper
1½ teaspoons olive oil

SAUCE AND PASTA

1 (28-ounce) can whole peeled tomatoes (see note)
1 small onion, minced
2 garlic cloves, minced
⅛ teaspoon red pepper flakes
6 ounces spaghetti
   Salt and pepper
1 tablespoon shredded fresh basil

1. FOR THE MEATBALLS: Combine bread, milk, and egg yolk in large bowl, let soak for several minutes, then mash to smooth paste with fork. Add turkey, Parmesan, parsley, garlic, and pepper and gently knead until well incorporated. Divide meat into 8 equal portions, then form each into meatball. Place meatballs on large plate, cover with plastic wrap, and refrigerate until firm, about 1 hour.

2. Heat oil in 12-inch nonstick skillet over medium heat until just smoking. Brown meatballs well on all sides, 7 to 10 minutes, turning as needed. Transfer meatballs to paper towel–lined plate; set aside. (Do not wash skillet.)

3. FOR THE SAUCE AND PASTA: Pulse tomatoes with their juice in food processor until coarsely chopped and no large pieces remain, 6 to 8 pulses. Add onion to fat left in skillet, cover, and cook over medium-low heat, stirring occasionally, until softened, 8 to 10 minutes. Stir in garlic and red pepper flakes and cook until fragrant, about 30 seconds. Stir in processed tomatoes, bring to simmer, and cook for 10 minutes. Return meatballs to skillet, cover, and cook until meatballs are cooked through, about 10 minutes.

4. Meanwhile, bring 4 quarts water to boil in large pot. Add pasta and 1 tablespoon salt and cook, stirring often, until al dente. Reserve ½ cup cooking water, then drain pasta and return it to pot.

5. Spoon several large spoonfuls of tomato sauce (without meatballs) into pasta and toss to combine, adjusting sauce consistency with reserved pasta cooking water as desired. Season with salt and pepper to taste. Divide pasta between 2 individual bowls. Top each bowl with remaining tomato sauce and meatballs, sprinkle with basil, and serve.

PER SERVING: **Cal** 670; **Fat** 15g; **Sat fat** 4.5g; **Chol** 175mg; **Carb** 90g; **Protein** 41g; **Fiber** 8g; **Sodium** 1100mg

NOTES FROM THE TEST KITCHEN

THE BEST CANNED WHOLE TOMATOES
A ripe, fresh tomato should balance elements of sweetness and tangy acidity. Its texture should be somewhere between firm and pliant—certainly not mushy. Ideally, canned tomatoes, which are packed at the height of ripeness, should reflect the same combination of characteristics. But with so many brands of canned tomatoes available, which one tastes best?

First we looked at how canned tomatoes are processed; they are steamed to remove their skins, then they are packed in tomato juice or puree. Overall, we prefer tomatoes packed in juice, because they generally have a fresher, livelier flavor than tomatoes packed in puree, which imparts a slightly stale taste. We tasted whole tomatoes both straight from the can and in a simple tomato sauce. **Progresso Whole Peeled Tomatoes with Basil** finished at the head of the pack, with a bright flavor and firm texture. Be sure to buy the tomatoes packed in juice; Progresso has another, similar-looking can of whole peeled tomatoes packed in puree.

CHICKEN SOFT TACOS

CHICKEN SOFT TACOS ARE EVERYWHERE, FROM THE 99-cent paper-wrapped ones at the food court to more satisfying versions at Mexican restaurants. The chicken filling can range from underseasoned, seared, and chopped white meat so bland it demands a smothering blanket of cheese to whole chicken that's been broken down and poached to tender, fall-off-the-bone perfection. We wanted our tacos to be flavorful enough on their own that fatty garnishes were not required, but we didn't want tacos that would take hours to make and require a mile-long list of exotic ingredients. We were in need of a healthy chicken soft taco recipe, one that offered the ease of the drive-through but the complex flavors and juicy texture of the real deal.

We looked at a variety of recipes and immediately crossed off those calling for 24-hour marinades and obscure ingredients. Some of the quick-cooking recipes we found called for briefly marinating boneless chicken breasts in lime juice, cilantro, garlic, and spices like chili powder and cumin, cooking them over high heat, chopping up the meat, then stuffing it into a tortilla. To begin our testing, we put together a simplified working marinade and moved ahead to settle on the cooking method. We soon learned that a quick marinade and a hot, fast sear wouldn't do—our chicken ended up with a leathery exterior and a dried-out interior.

In the test kitchen we often brine chicken in salt water to keep it juicy, but this extra step takes at least half an hour and didn't fit into our short time frame. We considered another test kitchen technique: reserving a few tablespoons of marinade to toss with the seared and chopped chicken, almost like a dressing. We tested this idea, but if the goal was juicy chicken, we'd need more than a splash of liquid to disguise dry meat.

We also realized, inevitably, that sautéing the chicken would lead to a browned exterior and add texture that, while appreciated on simple sautéed breasts, wasn't something we wanted in our tacos. We reconsidered the elaborate Mexican recipes where whole chickens are slowly simmered in flavored broths and wondered if we could borrow the technique. Poaching our chicken breasts would also have the added benefit of requiring no oil. We simmered chicken broth in a skillet, added the breasts, and cooked them, covered, for 10 minutes.

The chicken emerged tender and moist. Unfortunately, it was also bland.

Could we use the marinade ingredients as the poaching liquid to get flavor into our chicken? The idea was good, but the flavors—garlic, lime juice, fresh jalapeños, and cilantro—were out of balance. Although brightly flavored, the chicken was also aggressively tart. We discarded the lime and reached for orange juice. It did the trick, keeping the acidity while adding a note of sweetness. We replaced the jalapeños with minced chipotle chiles for a smokier, more full-bodied flavor. Still, the meat lacked robustness.

A fellow test cook who had grown up in Latin America suggested two seemingly unlikely ingredients: Worcestershire sauce and yellow mustard. These pantry items, she told us, are a mainstay in many Latin American kitchens and frequently find their way into basic chicken and beef marinades. A touch of Worcestershire mimicked the more complex flavor of dark meat, and a teaspoon of mustard pulled the sauce together, adding a sharp tang that cut through the sweet juice and smoky chipotle.

Things were going well, but when the poaching was finished, a pool of flavorful liquid remained in the skillet. Reducing it into a sauce would add even more flavor to our tacos, so we made the recipe once more, this time sautéing the garlic and chipotle to build a base for the sauce. Fifteen minutes later, once the chicken was poached and the liquid reduced, we whisked in the mustard to help thicken and emulsify our sauce. Finally, we shredded the chicken (a side-by-side test showed that shreds absorbed more sauce than cubes) and tossed it with the sauce and more fresh cilantro.

We loved the tangy, spicy flavors of the chicken, but we felt the taco was slightly unfinished. Tasters agreed that the filling could use a little something to tame the heat and round out the dish. We liked the idea of sour cream—just enough to "finish" the taco and balance the acidity of the orange juice and Worcestershire. We found that low-fat sour cream provided rich, creamy texture, and the addition of more minced chipotle chiles and cilantro added flavor and freshness.

We reached for a steamy tortilla and tucked in chicken that was incredibly moist and laced with heat, spice, and tartness. Finished with a dollop of chipotle sour cream, our Chicken Soft Tacos were anything but ordinary.

NOTES FROM THE TEST KITCHEN

THE BEST INEXPENSIVE INSTANT-READ THERMOMETER
An instant-read thermometer is the most foolproof way to determine the doneness of meat. It should have a broad range to cover high and low temperatures; a stem long enough to reach the interior of large cuts of meat; and, above all, speed, so you don't have to keep the oven door open too long. Our favorite remains the ThermoWorks Splash-Proof Super-Fast Thermapen, which meets all of these requirements (and it's water-resistant), but the $96 price tag begs for an affordable alternative.

We tested six thermometers priced under $35. Although none of them bested the Thermapen, we did find the **ThermoWorks Super-Fast Pocket Thermometer**, $24, (shown) and CDN ProAccurate Quick-Read Thermometer, $18.99, to be reasonable stand-ins. Both gave accurate and speedy readings, and both have their advantages. The ThermoWorks has an extra-thin probe for easy temperature checks, while the CDN has a higher temperature range (up to 450 degrees; the ThermoWorks can't go above 302 degrees).

Chicken Soft Tacos

SERVES 2

To make this dish more or less spicy, adjust the amount of chipotle chiles. We don't think toppings are essential for these tacos because they are so flavorful, but you can serve them with chopped tomato, avocado, or lime wedges if you like. See page 178 for a recipe to use up the leftover sour cream. We like the flavor of soft corn tortillas with these tacos; flour tortillas can be substituted, but note that the nutritional analysis is based on corn tortillas.

- ½ teaspoon vegetable oil
- 3 garlic cloves, minced
- 1½ teaspoons minced canned chipotle chile in adobo sauce (see note)
- ½ cup minced fresh cilantro
- ½ cup orange juice
- 1 tablespoon Worcestershire sauce
- 2 (6-ounce) boneless, skinless chicken breasts, trimmed
- 1 teaspoon yellow mustard
  Salt and pepper
- ½ cup low-fat sour cream
- 6 (6-inch) corn tortillas, warmed (see page 203)

1. Heat oil in 10-inch nonstick skillet over medium heat until shimmering. Stir in garlic and 1 teaspoon chipotles and cook until fragrant, about 30 seconds. Stir in 5 tablespoons cilantro, orange juice, and Worcestershire sauce.

2. Nestle chicken into skillet and bring to simmer. Cover, reduce heat to medium-low, and cook until thickest part of breasts registers 160 to 165 degrees on

---

USE IT UP: LOW-FAT SOUR CREAM

Light Caramelized Onion Dip
MAKES ABOUT 1 CUP

Regular sour cream and mayonnaise can be substituted in this recipe. Serve with crudités and pita chips. The dip can be refrigerated in an airtight container for up to 2 days; season with additional vinegar, salt, and pepper to taste before serving.

    1 teaspoon vegetable oil
    1 onion, minced
    ¼ teaspoon brown sugar
       Salt and pepper
    ½ cup low-fat sour cream (see note)
    ⅓ cup light mayonnaise (see note)
    5 teaspoons water
    1 teaspoon cider vinegar
       Dash Worcestershire sauce (optional)

1. Heat oil in 8-inch nonstick skillet over medium-high heat until shimmering. Add onion, sugar, and ⅛ teaspoon salt and cook, stirring often, until softened, about 5 minutes. Reduce heat to medium-low and continue to cook, stirring often, until onion is golden and caramelized, about 20 minutes longer. Set aside to cool slightly.

2. Stir caramelized onion, sour cream, mayonnaise, water, vinegar, and Worcestershire sauce (if using) together in serving bowl; season with salt and pepper to taste. Cover and refrigerate until flavors meld, about 1 hour.

PER 3 TABLESPOONS: Cal 80; **Fat** 6g; **Sat fat** 0.5g; **Chol** 5mg; **Carb** 3g; **Protein** 1g; **Fiber** 1g; **Sodium** 200mg

---

instant-read thermometer, 12 to 18 minutes, flipping chicken halfway through.

3. Transfer chicken breasts to plate, let cool slightly, then shred into bite-size pieces following photo on page 71. Meanwhile, continue to simmer sauce over medium heat until slightly thickened and reduced to ⅓ cup, about 2 minutes longer. Off heat, stir in mustard, 2 more tablespoons cilantro, and shredded chicken. Season with salt and pepper to taste.

4. In small bowl, whisk sour cream, remaining ½ teaspoon chipotles, and remaining 1 tablespoon cilantro together and season with salt and pepper to taste. Spoon chicken into warm tortillas and serve with sour cream mixture.

PER SERVING: Cal 520; **Fat** 9g; **Sat fat** 0.5g; **Chol** 110mg; **Carb** 52g; **Protein** 45g; **Fiber** 3g; **Sodium** 390mg

---

PESTO PASTA SALAD WITH CHICKEN

A COOL PESTO PASTA SALAD WITH CHICKEN AND vegetables makes an appealing meal that certainly seems healthy, but take one look at the fat and calories in a typical recipe and you'll do a double-take. In addition to the basil and garlic, pesto contains nuts, cheese, and a generous amount of olive oil—it all adds up really quickly. But we couldn't resist thinking that with all its appeal, there had to be a way to lighten up this classic, so we set out to see what we could do.

Starting with the foundation, the pasta, we tried all shapes and sizes. Large and small pasta either disappeared or dominated the dish, whereas medium-size pasta stood up well and didn't fall to the background or take over once pieces of vegetables and chicken were added. As for shape, tasters preferred farfalle, or bow tie pasta, which trapped the pesto and held on to it. After a few trial runs, we noticed that the texture of the pasta changed between the time it finished cooking and when it was cooled and on the plate. Pasta cooked to al dente took on a tough, chewy texture once it had cooled to room temperature. Completely tender pasta, on the other hand, cooled to a pleasant, bouncy texture. We knew from previous experience that rinsing the pasta to cool it would make the surface too slick for the pesto to take hold, so we tossed it with olive oil to prevent sticking and spread it out in an even layer on a baking sheet to cool. This worked perfectly.

We moved on to the chicken and vegetables. Tasters preferred shredded chicken to sliced or cubed chicken for the way it blended into the salad. Heartier vegetables, such as broccoli and beans, lent an unappealing toughness, and delicate vegetables like zucchini were disliked whether uncooked (they tasted too raw) or slightly cooked (too spongy). In the end, we liked the crisp texture (and bright colors) of bell pepper, shredded carrot, and cherry tomatoes. We stirred the pepper, carrot, and chicken into the pasta before adding the dressing, but we found that it was best to wait until the end to gently fold in the tomatoes to prevent them from getting smashed from all the stirring.

Finally, we turned to the pesto. Most recipes rely on anywhere from ¼ cup to ½ cup of oil to emulsify and blend the sauce, but we wanted a pesto that wasn't fat-laden, so we began thinking about creative ways to reduce the amount of oil without taking away from pesto's trademark consistency. We decided we should give our Italian sauce a little hometown flair, borrowing a standard ingredient used in many American pasta salads: mayonnaise. We tried multiple batches with varying amounts of light mayo and thought the idea was getting there, but regardless of the amount, on its own the mayo was too rich and thick. We found that 3 tablespoons of mayonnaise mixed with 1 tablespoon of lemon juice gave us a pesto with just the right consistency and that wasn't too rich—and we cut about 20 grams of fat and almost 200 calories in the process.

Our pesto was on track, but now the flavors needed to come into balance. Garlic is a hallmark ingredient, but even a single clove created an overpowering raw flavor. Toasting the garlic worked wonders to tame the harshness, allowing us to double the amount of garlic, and adding a minced shallot further complemented the flavor. Pesto traditionally contains pine nuts and/or walnuts, but we decided to try leaving them out since they add so much fat. Tasters didn't have any problem with the flavor of our nutless pesto, but since the nuts did contribute bulk, we increased the amount of basil to compensate. Bruising the basil with a meat pounder helped release its oils and intensify its flavor.

Once the salad was tossed together, we found that it quickly became too dry. Simply adding more pesto didn't solve the problem; it just made the salad heavy, and the pesto overwhelmed the other ingredients. To add moisture to the salad without ruining the balance, we reserved some of the pasta cooking water and stirred it in. Just ¼ cup loosened our pesto and kept our salad bright, fresh, and flavorful.

Pesto Pasta Salad with Chicken and Vegetables
SERVES 2

Other pasta shapes can be substituted for the farfalle; however, their cup measurements may vary (see page 85).

DRESSING
- 2 garlic cloves, unpeeled
- 1½ cups lightly packed basil leaves
- ¼ cup grated Parmesan cheese
- 3 tablespoons light mayonnaise
- 1 small shallot, minced
- 1 tablespoon fresh lemon juice
- Salt and pepper

SALAD
- 4 ounces farfalle (about 1¾ cups; see note)
- Salt and pepper
- 2 teaspoons olive oil
- 1 (8-ounce) boneless, skinless chicken breast, trimmed
- 1 carrot, peeled and shredded
- ½ red bell pepper, stemmed, seeded, and cut into ½-inch pieces
- 6 ounces cherry tomatoes (about 1 cup), quartered

1. FOR THE DRESSING: Toast garlic in small skillet over medium heat, shaking pan occasionally, until fragrant and color of cloves deepens slightly, about 7 minutes. Let garlic cool slightly, then peel and chop. Meanwhile, place basil in heavy-duty gallon-size zipper-lock bag and pound with rolling pin until leaves are lightly bruised.

2. Process toasted garlic, bruised basil, Parmesan, mayonnaise, shallot, lemon juice, and ¼ teaspoon salt in food processor until smooth, about 30 seconds, scraping down sides as needed. Transfer mixture to small bowl and season with salt and pepper to taste.

3. FOR THE SALAD: Bring 4 quarts water to boil in large pot. Add pasta and 1 tablespoon salt and cook, stirring often, until tender. Reserve ½ cup cooking water, then drain pasta and return it to pot; toss with 1 teaspoon oil. Spread pasta on rimmed baking sheet and cool to room temperature, about 30 minutes.

4. Meanwhile, pat chicken breast dry with paper towels and season with salt and pepper. Heat remaining 1 teaspoon oil in 10-inch nonstick skillet over medium-high heat until just smoking. Carefully lay chicken in skillet and cook until well browned on first side, 6 to 8 minutes.

5. Flip chicken, add ½ cup water, and reduce heat to medium-low. Cover and continue to cook until thickest part of breast registers 160 to 165 degrees on instant-read thermometer, 5 to 7 minutes longer. Transfer chicken to carving board, let cool slightly, then shred into bite-size pieces following photo on page 71.

6. Whisk dressing to recombine. In large bowl, toss pasta, chicken, carrot, and bell pepper with dressing, adjusting consistency with reserved pasta cooking water as needed. Fold in tomatoes, season with salt and pepper to taste, and serve.

PER SERVING: Cal 510; **Fat** 14g; **Sat fat** 3g; **Chol** 75mg; **Carb** 56g; **Protein** 39g; **Fiber** 5g; **Sodium** 1130mg

---

NOTES FROM THE TEST KITCHEN

BRING OUT THE HELLMANN'S
Because mayonnaise is fatty by definition (it's mostly oil and egg yolks), low-fat mayonnaise is a popular product among the diet-conscious. In the past, Hellmann's Light Mayonnaise has been the winner of taste tests here in the test kitchen among leading brands of low-fat mayonnaise. (And among leading brands of full-fat mayos, Hellmann's Real Mayonnaise has also come in first.) Nowadays Hellmann's also makes a version with canola oil. We wondered how these two lighter versions would stack up against each other and the original, so we lined up all three for a test to find out, tasting them first plain and then in macaroni salad. The outcome? While the full-fat version remains our favorite, at 90 calories, 10 grams of fat, and 1.5 grams of saturated fat per tablespoon, it's not ideal for a lightened diet. Of the two lighter versions, tasters preferred **Hellmann's Light Mayonnaise** (35 calories, 3.5 grams of fat, 0 grams of saturated fat per tablespoon), finding it slightly sweeter than the original and praising its thick texture. Hellmann's Canola Cholesterol Free Mayonnaise (45 calories, 4.5 grams of fat, 0 grams of saturated fat per tablespoon) had a "tangier" flavor that some tasters disliked, though there were those who liked its bright flavor.

CHICKEN CAESAR SALAD

MANY PEOPLE ASSUME THAT HAVING A SALAD FOR dinner is a safe bet when watching fat and calories. Think again. Consider one of the most celebrated dinner salads of all: chicken Caesar. The ideal version is made with crisp romaine lettuce and juicy chicken breast meat topped with grated Parmesan cheese and garlic croutons. And then there's the dressing: a mix of garlic, anchovy, lemon juice, and Worcestershire sauce bound by a rich emulsion of egg yolks and olive oil. When you consider the dressing, the cheese, the croutons, and sometimes even the chicken, this salad can add up to about 660 calories and 40 grams of fat per serving. We knew we could do better, but having tried existing recipes for light Caesar salads, we also knew it wouldn't be easy.

The dressing is one of the most crucial components of this salad, and many low-fat versions fall short because when the egg yolk and most of the oil are omitted, the creamy character of the dressing is lost. What's left is an out-of-balance dressing without enough body to cling to the romaine. In addition, it's awfully difficult to scale down a recipe that calls for one egg yolk (using half a yolk seemed ridiculous). So we started by looking for a way to omit the egg and reduce the amount of oil without compromising taste or richness. Some low-fat recipes use ingredients like sour cream, yogurt, tofu, and buttermilk to emulsify the dressing. We found that sour cream and yogurt were too tart and dairy-rich. Soft tofu added a nice creamy texture but was too bland. Tasters, however, were impressed with buttermilk's tang and its silkiness, which was close to that of the egg yolk. Some complained that the dressing was still missing richness, so we added just over a tablespoon of light mayonnaise. Now we were able to decrease the amount of olive oil to 1 tablespoon, easily half as much as is called for in the classic recipe.

Our dressing had perfectly balanced richness, so next we looked at finessing its flavor. Tasters liked 1 tablespoon of lemon juice, a modest ½ teaspoon of Worcestershire sauce, and just one small clove of garlic. Anchovy fillets contributed a classic flavor, and Dijon mustard—an untraditional ingredient—added depth and helped further emulsify the ingredients. And instead of tossing the romaine with all of the grated Parmesan before dressing the salad (the traditional method), we found that stirring

CHICKEN CAESAR SALAD

a portion of the Parmesan into the dressing itself spread the flavor of the cheese further and added good intensity to the dressing. With only ¼ cup of cheese (many recipes called for twice that), our dressing now had big Parmesan flavor without unnecessary fat and calories.

For the lettuce, romaine is standard, its fresh crunch a good match for the flavorful dressing. Some Caesar salads sport whole leaves of romaine, but tasters found these unwieldy on the plate, so we tore the leaves into bite-size pieces.

We wanted the chicken in our salad to be fresh and moist, so relying on leftover roast or grilled chicken was not an option. At the same time, we didn't want to make preparing the chicken a production. We wanted the flavor and color of lightly browned chicken breasts, but achieving this goal required more oil than we wanted to use. We turned to a half-sautéing, half-poaching method that required very little fat. First we browned the chicken on just one side in half a teaspoon of oil, then we flipped the chicken over, added water to the skillet, reduced the heat, and covered the skillet until the chicken was cooked through. This method yielded moist, flavorful, and lightly browned (albeit on one side only) chicken breasts.

Caesar salad wouldn't be complete without the crunch of croutons, and we found a way to make our croutons lighter than store-bought varieties (and those made with most traditional methods) by using vegetable oil spray and garlic powder rather than the traditional garlic oil. At last, we had a zesty main-course salad we could really dig into.

NOTES FROM THE TEST KITCHEN

STORING EXTRA ANCHOVIES

Unless you plan on making Caesar salad, anchovy pizza, and pasta puttanesca all on the same day, you'd be hard-pressed to use up an entire tin of anchovies without having to store them. We tested multiple ways of storing anchovies and found that coiling them up individually, then freezing them on a plate before transferring them to a zipper-lock bag was the way to go. These frozen-and-thawed anchovies tasted nearly as good as the fresh fillets and were easier to handle than those we kept in the refrigerator beneath a blanket of olive oil.

Chicken Caesar Salad

SERVES 2

Parmesan cheese is a key ingredient in this classic salad, so be sure to use authentic Parmigiano-Reggiano and grate it yourself. Olive oil spray can be substituted for the vegetable oil spray in step 2. To ensure that the dressing will cling to the lettuce, make sure the lettuce is fully dry before tossing.

DRESSING

- **3** tablespoons buttermilk
- **4** teaspoons light mayonnaise
- **1** tablespoon fresh lemon juice
- **1** tablespoon water
- **1½** anchovy fillets, rinsed and patted dry
- **1** teaspoon Dijon mustard
- **½** teaspoon Worcestershire sauce
- **1** small garlic clove, minced
- **1** tablespoon extra-virgin olive oil
- **¼** cup grated Parmesan cheese (see note)
-   Salt and pepper

SALAD

- **1** slice high-quality white sandwich bread, cut into ½-inch cubes
-   Vegetable oil spray (see note)
-   Salt and pepper
-   Pinch garlic powder
- **2** (6-ounce) boneless, skinless chicken breasts, trimmed
- **½** teaspoon vegetable oil
- **2** romaine lettuce hearts (about 12 ounces), torn into bite-size pieces (see note)

1. FOR THE DRESSING: Process buttermilk, mayonnaise, lemon juice, water, anchovies, mustard, Worcestershire sauce, and garlic together in blender until smooth, about 30 seconds, scraping down sides as needed. With motor running, add olive oil in steady stream and process until incorporated, about 10 seconds. Transfer to small bowl, stir in 3 tablespoons Parmesan, and season with salt and pepper to taste.

2. FOR THE SALAD: Adjust oven rack to middle position and heat oven to 350 degrees. Spread bread cubes on baking sheet, generously coat cubes with vegetable oil spray, and toss with pinch salt and garlic powder. Bake, stirring occasionally, until golden brown, 10 to 15 minutes; let cool completely.

3. Meanwhile, pat chicken breasts dry with paper towels and season with salt and pepper. Heat vegetable oil in 10-inch nonstick skillet over medium-high heat until just smoking. Carefully lay chicken in skillet and cook until well browned on first side, 6 to 8 minutes.

4. Flip chicken, add ½ cup water, and reduce heat to medium-low. Cover and continue to cook until thickest part of breasts registers 160 to 165 degrees on instant-read thermometer, 5 to 7 minutes longer. Transfer chicken to carving board, let rest for 5 minutes, and slice crosswise into ½-inch-thick pieces.

5. Whisk dressing to recombine. In large bowl, toss lettuce with all but 1 tablespoon dressing and divide between 2 plates. Toss chicken with remaining 1 tablespoon dressing and arrange over lettuce. Sprinkle with croutons and remaining 1 tablespoon Parmesan and serve.

PER SERVING: **Cal** 410; **Fat** 17g; **Sat fat** 3.5g; **Chol** 110mg; **Carb** 17g; **Protein** 47g; **Fiber** 3g; **Sodium** 950mg

POACHED SHRIMP SALAD

POACHED SHRIMP SALADS ARE A SPA MENU STAPLE, since seafood is a lean protein and poaching is one of the healthiest cooking techniques around. For these salads, shrimp is gently poached in an aromatic liquid, cooled, and tossed with a light vinaigrette and vegetables. But too many modern renditions have gone overboard with this classic's signature lightness, leaving us hungry for more. And all too often, the salad consists of tough, tiny shrimp plopped onto lifeless lettuce leaves. We wanted to develop a for-two main-course salad featuring properly cooked shrimp, fresh vegetables, and a flavorful dressing.

We started by exploring the poaching method. We brought a mixture of water, lemon juice, bay leaf, and whole black peppercorns to a bare simmer, then added the shrimp and cooked them for several minutes. Though this classic technique works well with fish fillets, it didn't quite pan out for our shrimp, which are smaller and more delicate. The result was chewy, overcooked shrimp. Our solution was to bring the poaching liquid to a boil, then turn off the heat before adding the shrimp and covering the pot. The shrimp picked up flavor from the liquid and cooked through gently, without any danger of overcooking.

Pleased with our tasty crustaceans, we moved on to the salad itself. With the poached shrimp anchoring the dish, we tried adding a variety of ingredients to incorporate different flavors and textures. Seafood often pairs well with citrus, so we tried grapefruit and oranges; tasters liked both, so we included ruby-red grapefruit segments in our master recipe and orange in a variation. While we wanted to keep the salad on the lighter side, it begged for balance in the form of fat. Buttery but heart-healthy avocado was just the thing we were looking for, and we found that half an avocado added a creamy richness to the salad without sending our fat count off the charts. Thinly sliced snow peas, added raw, brought a welcome crispness, and we found that chopped mint added a freshness that nicely rounded out the salad.

With all of our salad components assembled, it was time to move on to the dressing. We briefly considered straying from tradition and tested creamy dressings, but even with low-fat products they were just too heavy for our delicate salad. Tasters much preferred olive oil–based vinaigrettes. So that the mild flavor of the poached shrimp wasn't overwhelmed, we made a light vinaigrette using lime juice, a little honey, and some

NOTES FROM THE TEST KITCHEN

SEGMENTING CITRUS FRUIT

1. Slice a ½-inch piece from the top and bottom of the fruit. Then use a sharp knife to slice off the rind, including the bitter pith, following the contours of the fruit.

2. Working over a bowl, cut between a section of fruit and the membrane to the center of the fruit. Then turn the blade so it is facing out and slide it from the center out along the membrane to free the section.

PREPARING AVOCADOS

1. After slicing the avocado in half around the pit, lodge the edge of the knife blade into the pit and twist to remove. Use a large wooden spoon to pry the pit safely off the knife.

2. Use a dish towel to hold the avocado steady. Make ½-inch crosshatch incisions in the flesh of each avocado half with a knife, cutting down to but not through the skin.

3. Separate the diced flesh from the skin with a soup spoon inserted between the skin and the flesh, gently scooping out the avocado cubes.

HOW TO RIPEN AVOCADOS

Avocados have a notoriously small window of perfect ripeness. To see if we could broaden this time frame, we bought a case of unripe avocados and ripened them at room temperature and in the refrigerator three ways: on the counter (or refrigerator shelf), enclosed in a paper bag, and enclosed in a paper bag with pieces of green apple, which gives off ethylene gas that helps many fruits and vegetables ripen more quickly. We also tried two more esoteric techniques: burying the avocados at room temperature in flour and in rice. In the end, the only thing that mattered was the storing temperature.

At room temperature, rock-hard avocados ripened within two days, but many ripened unevenly, developing soft spots on one side just as the other side was ripening. After completely ripening, they lasted two days on average if kept at room temperature (stored in the fridge after ripening, they lasted five days). Avocados ripened in the refrigerator, whether in a bag or not, took longer to soften but did so evenly. Stored in the fridge, they lasted five days before overripening.

So if you need your avocados to ripen sooner rather than later, keep them on the counter. Otherwise, put them in the fridge and allow them to ripen slowly. In either case, store the ripened fruit in the fridge to extend shelf life.

grated ginger. In order to scale back the amount of oil to the absolute minimum necessary, we incorporated the juice we reserved while segmenting the grapefruit. Just half a teaspoon of Dijon mustard emulsified the dressing and helped achieve a balance of sweet, tart, and tangy flavors.

The salad was an instant success in the test kitchen; tasters commented on how flavorful our shrimp salad was—and how surprisingly easy it was to prepare.

Poached Shrimp Salad with Avocado and Grapefruit

SERVES 2

If your grapefruit tastes especially tart, add ¼ teaspoon more honey to the dressing. If you are short on grapefruit juice, substitute water.

SHRIMP

- ½ lemon
- ¼ teaspoon black peppercorns
- 1 bay leaf
- 12 ounces extra-large shrimp (21 to 25 per pound), peeled, tails removed, and deveined (see page 78)

SALAD AND VINAIGRETTE

- ½ ruby-red grapefruit, peeled, pith removed, segmented (see page 183), and 2 tablespoons juice reserved (see note)
- 1 small shallot, minced
- 1 tablespoon fresh lime juice
- 2 teaspoons extra-virgin olive oil
- ¾ teaspoon minced or grated fresh ginger
- ¾ teaspoon honey (see note)
- ½ teaspoon Dijon mustard
  Salt and pepper
- ½ ripe avocado, pitted and cut into ½-inch pieces (see photos)
- 1 ounce snow peas (about ½ cup), ends trimmed and strings removed (see page 72), sliced thin on bias
- 1 tablespoon minced fresh mint
- 1 head Bibb lettuce (about ½ pound), leaves separated

1. FOR THE SHRIMP: Place 3 cups water in medium saucepan. Squeeze juice of lemon half into water, then add lemon half, peppercorns, and bay leaf to pot. Bring to boil over high heat and boil for 2 minutes.

2. Remove pan from heat and add shrimp. Cover and steep until shrimp are firm and pink, about 7 minutes. Drain shrimp, discarding lemon half, peppercorns, and bay leaf, and plunge immediately into ice water. Drain and refrigerate shrimp until slightly chilled, about 30 minutes.

3. FOR THE SALAD AND VINAIGRETTE: Whisk reserved grapefruit juice, shallot, lime juice, oil, ginger, honey, mustard, ¼ teaspoon salt, and ⅛ teaspoon pepper together in medium bowl.

4. Toss chilled shrimp with grapefruit segments, avocado, snow peas, and mint. Pour dressing over mixture and toss gently to coat. Season with salt and pepper to taste. Arrange lettuce leaves on 2 plates and top with shrimp mixture. Drizzle with any dressing left in bowl and serve.

PER SERVING: **Cal** 370; **Fat** 15g; **Sat fat** 2.5g; **Chol** 260mg; **Carb** 22g; **Protein** 38g; **Fiber** 8g; **Sodium** 580mg

VARIATION

Poached Shrimp Salad with Avocado, Orange, and Arugula

Follow recipe for Poached Shrimp Salad with Avocado and Grapefruit, substituting 1 whole orange for grapefruit and 2 tablespoons reserved orange juice for grapefruit juice. Reduce amount of honey to ¼ teaspoon. Substitute 3 ounces baby arugula (about 3 cups) for Bibb lettuce.

PER SERVING: **Cal** 360; **Fat** 15g; **Sat fat** 2.5g; **Chol** 260mg; **Carb** 19g; **Protein** 38g; **Fiber** 6g; **Sodium** 590mg

BAKED SCALLOPS

WHILE PAN-SEARED SCALLOPS, GARNISHED WITH A simple pan sauce, are delicious and easy to prepare, they require close monitoring of the pan to prevent the scallops from burning. For a more indulgent, yet hands-off, treat, we prefer scallops baked in cream sauce, a comforting yet rich New England dish reminiscent of the classic French *coquilles St. Jacques*, scallops baked with cheese, cream, and buttery bread crumbs. While incredibly easy to make, it is also laden with fat and calories; it is so rich that we usually have to put our forks down after a few bites. We wanted to develop

a recipe for perfectly cooked, tender baked scallops prepared in a creamy sauce that tasted luxurious and hinted at richness but didn't weigh us down. And since leftover scallops are hardly haute cuisine, we needed to scale down the dish for two.

We began our testing by lightening up a basic cream sauce, swapping in low-fat milk for the cream. We added the milk with some sliced leek, garlic, thyme, and white wine to an 8-inch baking dish, followed by the scallops, then popped the whole thing into the oven. After a few tests, we knew we had our work cut out for us. While we were encouraged by the tender texture and sweet flavor of the scallops, the sauce was another story. It was thin, watery, and flavorless.

For our next test we precooked our sauce on the stovetop so it could partially reduce; we assumed it would continue to reduce in the oven and reach the proper consistency by the time the scallops were done. After cooking the sauce for just a few minutes on the stovetop, we poured it over the scallops set in a baking dish and baked them in a 450-degree oven for about 15 minutes. The scallops once again looked good, but still, our sauce was too thin.

Maybe using a thickener was a better bet. In our next test, we added a few teaspoons of flour to the pan after sautéing the garlic and thyme, then slowly whisked in the wine and milk. After about a minute our sauce was nicely thickened, so we poured it over the scallops and moved the dish to the oven. By the time the scallops had finished cooking, the sauce wasn't nearly as thin and watery as it had been previously, but it was still a far cry from the thickened sauce that had gone into the oven.

Clearly the issue wasn't just the sauce; the scallops were releasing water as they cooked. For our next test, we made a batch of sauce as usual, but this time we also pressed the scallops dry before placing them in the dish. Once again, our sauce was too thin. We then tried letting the scallops drain for 30 minutes on kitchen towels, but this didn't work much better. We obviously couldn't control how much water the scallops released, so we went back to tweaking our sauce.

Back at the stovetop, for our next test we tried taking thickening the sauce a step too far, overthickening it before we poured it over the scallops. Before going into the oven it didn't look at all like the light yet creamy sauce we were after, but after a short stint in the oven—eureka! As the scallops released their moisture, the sauce thinned out to just the right consistency by the time the scallops were cooked through. All it needed before serving was a quick whip with a whisk to incorporate the water the scallops had released. To fine-tune the ratios, a few more tests proved that 1 cup of milk, 2 tablespoons of wine, and 2 teaspoons of flour were just right. The length of time we cooked the sauce to overthicken it was crucial as well. Two to three minutes did the trick.

It was time to focus on finessing the flavors of the sauce. Lemon zest and lemon juice added a needed brightness and balance, and a little parsley rounded out the flavors of the dish. Finally, we had a foolproof method for baked scallops that were infused with flavor and perfectly cooked every time, and were coated with a smooth, luxurious sauce that wasn't so heavy we couldn't devour the whole thing.

Baked Scallops with Lemon and Herbs

SERVES 2

Do not use more than ½ cup sliced leek or the sauce will be too chunky. For this recipe, we prefer using large sea scallops. Depending on the size of your scallops, the cooking time may vary slightly. Try to buy "dry" scallops for this dish, but if you cannot find them, see our quick-soak solution (see box at right). Dry scallops will look ivory or pinkish and feel sticky or flabby, whereas processed scallops are bright white, slippery, and swollen.

- 1 **very small leek, white and light green parts only, halved lengthwise, sliced ¼ inch thick, and rinsed thoroughly (about ½ cup; see note)**
- 2 **teaspoons vegetable oil**
  Salt and pepper
- 1 **garlic clove, minced**
- ½ **teaspoon minced fresh thyme or ⅛ teaspoon dried**
- 2 **teaspoons unbleached all-purpose flour**
- 2 **tablespoons dry white wine**
- 1 **cup 1 percent low-fat milk**
- ¼ **teaspoon grated lemon zest plus 2 teaspoons fresh lemon juice**
- 12 **ounces large sea scallops (about 8 scallops) (see note), muscle removed (see photo)**
- 1 **teaspoon minced fresh parsley**

1. Adjust oven rack to middle position and heat oven to 450 degrees. Combine leek, oil, and pinch salt in medium saucepan. Cover and cook over medium-low heat, stirring occasionally, until softened, 8 to 10 minutes.

NOTES FROM THE TEST KITCHEN

PREPARING SCALLOPS

The small crescent-shaped tendon that is sometimes attached to the scallop will be inedibly tough when cooked. Use your fingers to peel it away from the side of each scallop before cooking.

QUICK SOAK FOR WET SCALLOPS

We prefer untreated "dry" scallops to treated, or "wet," scallops, but if you cannot find them, a simple soaking in a solution of 2 cups of cold water, 2 tablespoons of lemon juice, and 1 tablespoon of table salt for 30 minutes will mask the off-putting taste of the chemicals that have been added to these scallops to increase their shelf life.

BUYING AND STORING LEEKS

We try to buy leeks with the longest white stems, the most tender and usable part of a leek, but don't be fooled by supermarkets that sell leeks that are already trimmed down to the lighter base part. This may seem like a good deal because you aren't paying for the upper leaves, which are discarded anyway, but the truth is that the actual purpose of this procedure is to trim away aging leaves and make tough, old leeks look fresher to the unwary consumer.

Once at home, store your leeks in a partially open plastic bag in your refrigerator's crisper drawer, which provides a humid environment, keeping the leeks from shriveling.

WASHING LEEKS

To remove sand and dirt, rinse the sliced leeks thoroughly in a bowl of water. Dirt will settle to the bottom and the clean leeks can be lifted out.

2. Stir in garlic and thyme and cook until fragrant, about 30 seconds. Stir in flour and cook for 30 seconds. Slowly whisk in wine, then milk. Bring to simmer and cook until sauce is thickened, 2 to 3 minutes. Off heat, stir in lemon zest and season with salt and pepper to taste.

3. Pat scallops dry with paper towels and season with salt and pepper. Arrange scallops in single layer in 8-inch square baking dish and pour sauce over top. Bake until scallops are cooked through and their sides feel firm, about 10 minutes.

4. Carefully transfer scallops to platter, leaving sauce behind in dish. Whisk lemon juice and parsley into sauce, pour sauce over scallops, and serve.

PER SERVING: **Cal** 300; **Fat** 7g; **Sat fat** 1.5g; **Chol** 60mg; **Carb** 21g; **Protein** 34g; **Fiber** 1g; **Sodium** 700mg

VARIATION

Baked Scallops with Leek and Saffron
Follow recipe for Baked Scallops with Lemon and Herbs, adding ⅛ teaspoon saffron threads, crumbled, with garlic. Omit lemon zest and reduce amount of lemon juice to 1 teaspoon.

PER SERVING: **Cal** 300; **Fat** 7g; **Sat fat** 1.5g; **Chol** 60mg; **Carb** 21g; **Protein** 34g; **Fiber** 1g; **Sodium** 700mg

OVEN-FRIED FISH

FISH, ESPECIALLY WHITE FISH, IS A STANDARD GO-TO main ingredient when trying to eat healthier; it's naturally high in protein and low in fat, plus many preparations, such as poaching and baking, call on mostly good-for-you ingredients (such as citrus, herbs, and olive oil, the latter in sparing amounts) to create a flavorful dish. Frying, however, is one notable exception; in this common preparation, battered fish is dipped in a pool of hot oil until crisp, then partnered with creamy tartar sauce. We wondered if we could lighten up this seaside favorite, which can top more than 30 grams of fat per serving, and turn it into a (mostly) guilt-free weeknight supper for two.

From the get-go we knew that to make a significant dent in the fat count, we would have to relinquish the deep-fryer in favor of the oven and drastically lighten up the tartar sauce. Since just about every diet guru, low-cal website, and low-fat cookbook had an oven-baked fish recipe, we decided to start with the fish and work on the tartar sauce later. Recipes we considered fell into two camps: battered and breaded. Thin batters slid down the sides of the fish fillets, and thick batters slumped into soft heaps, so we opted for breaded fish. But after reluctantly pecking at a few mushy, waterlogged, and bland breaded samples, we knew this option wouldn't be easy either.

The first task was to select the right fish. After we tested several varieties with a simple egg wash and bread-crumb coating, it was immediately clear that delicate, flaky fish, such as cod or haddock, released too much liquid during cooking for the crumbs to crisp. Thin fillets, such as sole or flounder, overcooked and fell apart before the crumbs had a chance to brown. However, firm, meaty fresh halibut held its shape and stayed comparatively dry. We had good luck with frozen halibut, too, thawing and blotting it dry before cooking. Cutting each 6-ounce portion in two allowed for more surface area on which to layer the crunchy coating.

Now we looked for ways to get a crisper, more flavorful crumb coating. We tried making crumbs from three dry, crunchy ingredients—Melba toast, saltines, and rice puffs. These experiments stayed crunchy; in fact, they bordered on tough. Next, we toasted fresh bread crumbs, which added an appreciably nutty flavor. But the crumbs on the bottom of the fish became soggy as the fish cooked, as did those on the top and sides after the fish rested out of the oven. Placing the fish on a wire rack set inside a rimmed baking sheet helped (accumulated juice could escape), but not enough.

If we could just form a barrier between the crumbs and the fish, the juice might be contained. Could we make some sort of paste to block escaping juice and also make the crumbs adhere? After dusting the fish in flour, which created a dry surface to which the topping could bond, we smoothed on a thick paste of egg white and flour. Next we applied the toasted crumbs and gave the fish a light misting with vegetable oil spray to keep everything in place before putting it in a 450-degree oven. The tops and sides of the fish stayed crisp, but the coating on the bottom peeled off. Right there we decided to do away with the bottom coating. Tasters never missed it, and it saved a few calories. We turned our attention to the tartar sauce, hoping it would jazz up the crisp but woefully bland fish.

Our goal was to replicate a classic sweet-tangy sauce made with mayonnaise, pickles, and capers. We picked a favorite full-fat version, determined to shave fat grams where possible. Replacing the full-fat mayonnaise would be the first step. We tested Greek and regular yogurt, low-fat sour cream, light mayonnaise, and cottage cheese that we put through the blender; light mayo worked best. The tangy pickles, a bit of minced shallot, and a teaspoonful of salty capers offset the sweetness of the mayo. Worcestershire sauce added some savory depth, and lemon juice added brightness.

The tartar sauce disguised some of the fish's shortcomings, but surely the fish ought to have flavor on its own. We revisited the egg-white-and-flour paste, which perked right up when we added Dijon mustard, cayenne, and fresh parsley. But the paste—and thus the fish—truly came into its own when we made extra tartar sauce and mixed some of it into the coating, adding flavor and richness.

Lean and flavorful, our "fried" fish slimmed the original recipe by over 15 grams of fat—making this classic something we'd be able to enjoy more often.

NOTES FROM THE TEST KITCHEN

KEYS TO CRISPY OVEN-FRIED FISH

1. First, process the bread into coarse crumbs, then bake the crumbs, which maximizes crunch.

2. Next, after dredging the fish in seasoned flour, dip it in the egg white paste before coating it with bread crumbs. The paste helps the bread crumbs adhere to the fish and provides flavor.

3. Finally, bake the fish on a wire rack set in a baking sheet to allow air to circulate underneath.

OUR FAVORITE SANDWICH BREAD

Picking a high-quality loaf is key if you want to have a great crust on our Oven-Fried Fish. We gathered eight leading brands of white sandwich bread, in country styles with larger slices whenever possible, and held a blind tasting. Tasters sampled the bread plain, in grilled cheese sandwiches, and prepared as croutons seasoned only with olive oil and salt. They gave top marks to the hearty texture of **Arnold Country Classics Country White** (left) and **Pepperidge Farm Farmhouse Hearty White** (right).

Oven-Fried Fish with Tartar Sauce

SERVES 2

If using frozen fillets, press them dry with paper towels. If your fillets have skin on them, follow the instructions on page 39 to remove it.

TARTAR SAUCE
- ⅓ **cup light mayonnaise**
- 1 **tablespoon minced sweet pickles plus**
  1 teaspoon juice
- 1 **teaspoon drained capers, rinsed and minced**
- 1 **teaspoon fresh lemon juice**
- ½ **teaspoon minced shallot**
- ¼ **teaspoon Worcestershire sauce**
  Salt and pepper

FISH
- 1½ **slices high-quality white sandwich bread,**
  torn into pieces
- ¼ **cup unbleached all-purpose flour**
- 1 **large egg white**
- 2 **teaspoons Dijon mustard**
- 1 **teaspoon minced fresh parsley**
  Pinch cayenne pepper
  Pinch salt
  Pinch pepper
- 2 **(6-ounce) skinless halibut fillets (see note),**
  1 to 1½ inches thick, each fillet cut in half
  Vegetable oil spray

OVEN-FRIED FISH WITH TARTAR SAUCE

1. FOR THE TARTAR SAUCE: Whisk mayonnaise, pickles, pickle juice, capers, lemon juice, shallot, and Worcestershire sauce together in bowl and season with salt and pepper to taste.

2. FOR THE FISH: Adjust oven rack to middle position and heat oven to 400 degrees. Pulse bread in food processor to coarse crumbs, about 6 pulses. Bake bread crumbs on rimmed baking sheet, stirring occasionally, until golden, 8 to 10 minutes. Transfer toasted bread crumbs to shallow dish. Combine 2 tablespoons tartar sauce, 2 tablespoons flour, egg white, mustard, parsley, and cayenne in second shallow dish. Place remaining 2 tablespoons flour, salt, and pepper in third shallow dish.

3. Increase oven temperature to 450 degrees. Set wire rack inside rimmed baking sheet and lightly grease with vegetable oil spray. Pat fish dry with paper towels. Working with 1 fish fillet at a time, dredge fillets lightly in seasoned flour, shaking off excess. Dip top and sides of fillets in egg white mixture, allowing excess to drip back into dish, then coat top and sides evenly with bread crumbs, pressing to adhere. Transfer breaded fish to prepared rack.

4. Spray each fillet lightly with vegetable oil spray. Bake until crumbs are golden brown and fish registers 135 degrees on instant-read thermometer, 6 to 10 minutes. Serve with remaining tartar sauce.

PER SERVING: Cal 400; **Fat** 14g; **Sat fat** 2.5g; **Chol** 60mg; **Carb** 25g; **Protein** 40g; **Fiber** 1g; **Sodium** 970mg

HALIBUT EN PAPILLOTE

THERE'S A REASON THE CLASSIC FRENCH TECH-nique of cooking fish *en papillote*—baking in a tightly sealed parchment paper packet—has held its own through countless culinary fads and fashions. It's an easy, mess-free way to obtain perfectly moist, flaky, and flavorful pieces of fish. Best of all, it requires little additional fat, and by including vegetables, it becomes a well-rounded "one-pouch" meal—making a light and healthy supper for two a snap. We set out to make our own recipe that would give us perfectly moist and tender pieces of fish, well-seasoned vegetables, and flavorful juices.

All the classic recipes we found for fish en papillote called for cutting parchment paper into attractive shapes such as teardrops, hearts, or even butterflies, then creasing the seams into painstakingly precise little folds. Sure, it would make an impressive presentation, but we wanted to get dinner on the table as quickly as possible, not create origami. So we immediately turned to aluminum foil, sandwiching the fish between two 12-inch squares, then crimping the edges to create an airtight seal that would lock in steam. This was admittedly not as glamorous as an intricately folded parchment packet, but it would definitely do the job.

We decided to start by determining the best vegetables for the situation. Since the fish and vegetables would have to cook at the same rate, we knew there would be some limitations. Dense vegetables like potatoes were immediately out of the running because they took far too long to cook through, as were absorbent vegetables like eggplant, which would simply cook to mush. Broccoli seemed a little bold for an otherwise light dish. Light, clean-tasting zucchini, sliced into thin rounds, was a winner. For sweetness, color, and some moisture that would encourage steaming, we also settled on chopped tomatoes.

Our next step was to figure out what type of fish worked best and how long it would take to cook. After trying a variety of fish fillets, we determined that tasters favored flaky, mild white fish, like halibut and cod, over more assertively flavored fish like salmon or tuna. In the moist atmosphere of the foil pouch, these oilier fish had a more concentrated flavor that would overpower the flavors of the milder vegetables; better to save them for poaching or grilling.

Determining when the fish was done proved more challenging: It was hard to nick and peek inside to determine doneness when the fish was sealed tightly in foil. The old rule of thumb for fish—10 minutes of cooking time per inch of thickness—failed in this case, as the fish was barely opaque within that period. After experimenting with oven temperatures, we found that 1- to 1½-inch-thick fillets cooked best at 450 degrees for 12 minutes. While this seemed like an excessive length of time at such high heat, the fish was well insulated within the sealed packets and was flaky and moist.

But now we were ending up with diluted flavor by the end of cooking. The solution was to salt and drain the zucchini in a colander before assembling the packet—the moisture from the tomatoes was all we needed for the perfect steamy environment. Cooking the packets on the lower-middle rack of the oven helped concentrate the exuded liquid, further ensuring that neither the fish nor the vegetables became waterlogged and that the flavors were maximized.

For seasoning, we turned to garlic, red pepper flakes, and oregano for an assertive kick and to intensify the mild flavor of the fish. A dash of white wine along with some extra-virgin olive oil also helped boost flavor, and for a finishing touch, a sprinkling of chopped basil lent a pleasant fragrance.

Halibut en Papillote with Zucchini and Tomatoes

SERVES 2

Cod and haddock are good alternatives for the halibut. If your fillets have skin on them, follow the instructions on page 39 to remove it. Cooking time may vary depending on the thickness of the fish; thinner fish may require slightly less time in the oven. The packets can be assembled several hours ahead of time and refrigerated, but they should be baked just before serving. To prevent overcooking, open each packet promptly and remove from the hot sheet pan after baking.

- 1 zucchini (about 8 ounces), sliced ¼ inch thick
  Salt and pepper
- 2 plum tomatoes, cored, seeded, and chopped medium
- 1 tablespoon extra-virgin olive oil
- 1 garlic clove, minced
- ½ teaspoon minced fresh oregano or ⅛ teaspoon dried
  Pinch red pepper flakes
- 2 (6-ounce) skinless halibut fillets, 1 to 1½ inches thick (see note)
- 2 tablespoons dry white wine
- 2 tablespoons chopped fresh basil
  Lemon wedges, for serving

1. Adjust oven rack to lower-middle position and heat oven to 450 degrees. Toss zucchini with ¼ teaspoon salt, place in colander, and let drain for 30 minutes. Spread zucchini evenly on double layer of paper towels and pat dry with additional paper towels, wiping off any residual salt.

2. Combine tomatoes, oil, garlic, oregano, red pepper flakes, ¼ teaspoon salt, and pinch pepper in medium bowl. Pat halibut dry with paper towels and season with salt and pepper.

3. Cut four 12-inch sheets of heavy-duty aluminum foil. Following photos, shingle zucchini down center of 2 foil pieces. Sprinkle zucchini with 1 tablespoon wine, then lay halibut on top. Spoon tomato mixture on top of fish. Place second square of foil on top of each stack and fold edges over several times to seal.

4. Lay packets on rimmed baking sheet and bake for 12 minutes. Carefully open packets, allowing steam to escape away from you, and remove packets from hot sheet pan. Smooth out edges of foil and, using spatula, gently transfer halibut and vegetables, along with any accumulated juices, to individual plates. Sprinkle with basil and serve with lemon wedges.

PER SERVING: Cal 300; Fat 11g; Sat fat 1.5g; Chol 55mg; Carb 7g; Protein 38g; Fiber 2g; Sodium 980mg

NOTES FROM THE TEST KITCHEN

ASSEMBLING FOIL PACKETS

1. On a 12-inch square of heavy-duty aluminum foil, shingle half of the zucchini in the center, then sprinkle with 1 tablespoon of the wine. Place a halibut fillet on top of the zucchini and top with half of the tomato mixture.

2. Place a second square of foil on top of the tomato mixture. Crimp the edges together in a ½-inch fold, then fold over three more times to create an airtight packet.

LAMB SHAWARMA

ONE BIG ROAST, THREE GREAT MEALS

SLOW-ROASTED PORK

MOST COOKS NOWADAYS KNOW "ROAST PORK" AS the lean loin. While we love a perfectly roasted pork loin, sometimes we want a richer, more flavorful (read: less lean) pork roast. So we set our sights on a favorite cut for slow-cooked pulled pork: pork butt (also known as Boston butt). Loaded with flavorful intramuscular fat, it also boasts a thick fat cap that bastes the meat while it renders and crisps. True, it would take a little longer (several hours compared with just an hour for a loin) to turn the well-worked shoulder muscle fork-tender, but we'd be rewarded with enough meat for a few more meals, so it seemed well worth the wait. We sought to pair our pork with a fruity sauce that would cut through the dish's richness. With the meat left over from our large roast, we could then come up with a few creative supper ideas.

We started at the butcher case. The rectangular slab known as pork butt—not to be confused with the cone-shaped, more sinewy "picnic" roast from just below the shoulder blade—can be purchased two ways: boneless or bone-in. Boneless cuts typically cook faster than bone-in cuts and come partially butterflied, which leaves plenty of interior meat exposed and available for seasoning. Bone-in roasts take longer to cook, and the bone restricts seasoning to just the exterior of the roast, but they retain more moisture and cook more evenly. We conducted a few tests to find out which candidate would remain juicier, and the bone-in pork butt won the day. We decided to stick with the bone-in option and would find another way to season the interior of the meat.

In the test kitchen we often brine or salt poultry and pork to keep them moist during prolonged cooking and to season them. Because soaking a 6- to 8-pound pork butt can take up serious fridge space (it requires a tall container larger than the roast itself), we opted for salting our roast. After rubbing a few roasts with salt, we rested them in the fridge for various lengths of time. An overnight rest (versus two, four, or even six hours) proved the ideal amount of time to fully season our roast. It was time to start cooking.

Following our standard barbecue pork butt protocol, we set the oven to 275 degrees; covered the roast with aluminum foil to trap the damp, collagen-melting heat; and let the meat cook until supremely tender. Our roast reached this level of tenderness right around the

seven-hour mark, and the results weren't bad for a first stab. The pork, which registered 190 degrees, was tender and juicy. Just as with barbecue, slowly and gently taking the pork well beyond its 145-degree "done" stage not only melts fat but also breaks down collagen and tenderizes the meat. Yet for all the time this meat had spent in the oven, it actually tasted more steamed than roasted. Predictably, given the aluminum foil shield, the exterior was also pale and soggy.

First things first: The aluminum foil cover had to go. It was preventing the fat cap from crisping, and with so much fat marbling, there seemed little risk that the pork would dry out without its protection. Since we wanted our pork to taste rich and roasted, we spent our next several tests turning the oven dial up notch by notch to instill oven-concentrated, meaty flavor and boost browning. At 325 degrees, it took about five hours for the meat's collagen to break down and render the interior meltingly tender yet sliceable. The higher heat also crisped the crust—though not quite as much as we'd hoped. While decently rendered and copper-colored, the exterior fat was not sufficiently crunchy and brittle. We wondered if we should be rubbing the roast's exterior with more than just a handful of salt. To encourage caramelization and the development of a crackly-crisp, salty-sweet crust, we rubbed sugar over the salted pork butt just before putting it in the oven. As expected, the sugar caramelized and helped crisp the fat cap. We got even deeper browning when we replaced the sugar with brown sugar, rubbed it onto the meat together with the salt, and left it to rest overnight. To ensure that the meat didn't get too dark, we brushed off the excess sugar and salt before roasting.

To prevent the sweet pork drippings from burning onto the bottom of the roasting pan during the meat's long stay in the oven, we elevated the roast on a V-rack and added some water to the bottom of the pan. While the pork rested, we defatted this flavorful liquid and set about making a simple sauce.

To offset the richness of the meat, we created a fruity sauce with sweet and sour elements. For the main ingredient, peaches seemed a good choice; when cooked, they boast a distinctly jammy flavor. We combined a small amount of the defatted pork jus with a cup of frozen peaches cut into chunks, white wine, sugar, vinegar, and a sprig of fresh thyme and reduced the mixture to a thin syrup. To round out the sweetness, we finished our sauce with a spoonful of whole-grain mustard.

SLOW-ROASTED PORK WITH PEACH SAUCE

After finishing our pork tests, we set about developing a few exciting recipes to use up the rest of the roast, starting with pressed Cuban sandwiches. A popular street food in Miami, Cubanos are a savory combination of slow-roasted pork, ham, pickles, cheese, and mustard, stacked on Cuban bread and pressed like panini. We found a suitable stand-in for the Cuban bread with soft sub rolls. Spread with a thin layer of Dijon mustard, our rolls were ready to be topped. We layered each with shredded Gruyère, a few thick slices of our slow-roasted pork, thin deli ham, and thinly sliced pickle. While a panini press works great, not everyone has one at home. We made do with a 12-inch nonstick skillet and a heavy Dutch oven; after preheating the skillet, we placed our sandwiches in the pan and pressed them under the weight of the Dutch oven. Five minutes per side was sufficient to lightly brown the exterior and melt the cheese. Our sandwiches were spot-on when it came to flavor, but some tasters found them slightly dry. Combining the mustard with a tablespoon of mayonnaise quickly fixed the moisture issue, and our sandwiches were a hit.

Next, we set about developing a spicy Mexican pork stew. We wanted a rich broth redolent of the flavor and aroma of smoky chiles, roasted pork, and fresh cilantro. By using a handful of potent ingredients—garlic, chipotle chiles in adobo sauce, and chili powder—we were able to build a flavorful stew base in little time. We cut our pork into substantial ¾-inch pieces and looked to a few more ingredients to add heft. Tasters heartily endorsed adding ¾ cup of hominy, which stayed true to the Mexican identity of our stew; also, half a red bell pepper contributed color and substance. To ensure that our stew had sufficient body, we stirred in a little flour for thickening. Garnished with diced avocado and toasted sesame seeds, our pork stew tasted like it had simmered on the stove all day long—but it was ready in just 15 minutes.

For our final recipe, we decided to make a classic Chinese takeout dish, pork fried rice. Our salty-sweet roast pork seemed a fine substitute for the lacquered pork traditionally used in this recipe, but what about the rice? Fried rice is almost always made from day-old cooked rice that has had a chance to dry out. That's because dry rice fries more quickly, absorbs flavors better, and is less likely to clump in the pan. But we didn't want to have to plan and cook a day in advance for such a simple dinner, so we tried substituting freshly cooked rice. So that our rice would cool completely, we spread it out on a baking sheet. To our delight, this rice behaved much like its day-old counterpart, quickly frying to a golden patina. To give our dish authentic flavor, we included garlic, ginger, scallions, and shallot and built our sauce with hoisin, oyster sauce, soy sauce, and a touch of sriracha (for heat). Scrambled egg and sautéed shiitake mushrooms completed our take-in dinner that was head and shoulders above anything we'd get from a restaurant.

Slow-Roasted Pork with Peach Sauce

SERVES 2, WITH LEFTOVERS

You can use the leftovers to make all three of the following recipes: Cuban Sandwiches (page 197), Spicy Mexican Pork Stew with Hominy (page 197), and Pork Fried Rice (page 198). We prefer natural to "enhanced" pork (see page 14 for more information), though both will work in this recipe. Add more water to the roasting pan as necessary during the last hours of cooking to prevent the fond from burning.

PORK ROAST

1	(6- to 8-pound) bone-in pork butt (see note)
⅓	cup brown sugar
	Kosher salt and pepper

PEACH SAUCE

5	ounces frozen peaches (about 1 cup), cut into ½-inch chunks, or 1 fresh peach, cut into ½-inch wedges
1	cup dry white wine
¼	cup granulated sugar
2	tablespoons plus ½ teaspoon rice vinegar
1	sprig fresh thyme
¾	teaspoon whole-grain mustard

NOTES FROM THE TEST KITCHEN

RUBBING THE ROAST

For a flavorful, crisp crust, after cutting slits into the pork roast, rub it with a mixture of salt and brown sugar and let it rest overnight. The salt seasons the meat, while the brown sugar caramelizes, creating a crisp crust.

1. FOR THE PORK ROAST: Using sharp knife, cut slits 1 inch apart in crosshatch pattern in fat cap of roast, being careful not to cut into meat. Combine brown sugar and ⅓ cup kosher salt, then rub mixture over entire roast and into slits. Wrap roast tightly in double layer of plastic wrap, place on rimmed baking sheet, and refrigerate for at least 12 hours or up to 24 hours.

2. Adjust oven rack to lowest position and heat oven to 325 degrees. Coat V-rack with vegetable oil spray and set inside large roasting pan. Unwrap roast, brush any excess salt mixture from surface, and season with pepper. Place roast on prepared V-rack and pour 1 quart water into roasting pan.

3. Cook roast, basting twice during cooking, until meat is extremely tender and registers 190 degrees on instant-read thermometer, 5 to 6 hours. Transfer roast to carving board, tent loosely with foil, and let rest for 1 hour. Pour liquid from roasting pan into fat separator. Let jus settle for 5 minutes, then pour off and reserve 2 tablespoons defatted jus.

4. FOR THE PEACH SAUCE: Bring reserved 2 tablespoons defatted jus, peaches, wine, granulated sugar, 2 tablespoons vinegar, and thyme to simmer in small saucepan over medium-high heat. Cook, stirring occasionally, until reduced to ¾ cup, 20 to 30 minutes. Stir in remaining ½ teaspoon vinegar and mustard. Off heat, remove thyme and cover sauce to keep warm.

5. Using sharp paring knife, cut around inverted-T-shaped bone and, using clean kitchen towel, pull free from roast. Using serrated knife, slice roast. Serve, passing sauce separately.

Cuban Sandwiches

SERVES 2

The cooked pork in this recipe is from Slow-Roasted Pork with Peach Sauce on page 196.

1 tablespoon mayonnaise

1 tablespoon Dijon mustard

2 (6-inch) sub rolls, split partially open lengthwise

2 ounces Gruyère cheese, shredded (about ½ cup)

6 ounces cooked pork (see note), sliced ¼ inch thick (about 4 slices)

2 thin slices deli ham

1 sweet or dill pickle, sliced thin lengthwise

NOTES FROM THE TEST KITCHEN

PRESSING CUBAN SANDWICHES

If you don't have a sandwich press, simply place the sandwiches in a 12-inch nonstick skillet over medium heat and weight them with a Dutch oven.

1. Combine mayonnaise and mustard in small bowl and spread evenly inside each roll. Sprinkle 2 tablespoons cheese on 1 side of each roll, then top with cooked pork, ham, pickle slices, and remaining cheese. Fold over top of roll and press gently to flatten.

2. Heat 12-inch nonstick skillet over medium heat for 1 minute. Following photo, place sandwiches in pan and set Dutch oven on top. Cook sandwiches until golden brown and cheese is melted, about 5 minutes per side. Serve.

Spicy Mexican Pork Stew with Hominy

SERVES 2

The cooked pork in this recipe is from Slow-Roasted Pork with Peach Sauce on page 196. If you have leftover pork jus, you can stir in a tablespoon with the chicken broth for added richness.

1 tablespoon vegetable oil

1 shallot, minced

2 garlic cloves, minced

2 teaspoons chili powder

1½ teaspoons minced canned chipotle chile in adobo sauce

⅛ teaspoon dried oregano

1 tablespoon unbleached all-purpose flour

2 cups low-sodium chicken broth

¾ cup drained and rinsed canned hominy

½ red bell pepper, stemmed, seeded, and cut into ½-inch pieces

7½ ounces cooked pork (see note), cut into ¾-inch pieces (about 1½ cups)

2 tablespoons minced fresh cilantro

Salt and pepper

½ ripe avocado, pitted and cut into ½-inch pieces (see page 184) (optional)

2 teaspoons sesame seeds, toasted (see page 240) (optional)

1. Heat oil in medium saucepan over medium heat until shimmering. Stir in shallot and cook until softened, 2 to 3 minutes. Stir in garlic, chili powder, chipotles, and oregano and cook until fragrant, about 30 seconds. Stir in flour and cook 1 minute.

2. Stir in chicken broth and bring to simmer over medium-high heat. Stir in hominy and bell pepper, reduce heat to medium-low, and simmer until bell pepper is just tender, 5 to 10 minutes.

3. Stir in pork and continue to cook until heated through, about 2 minutes. Off heat, stir in cilantro and season with salt and pepper to taste. Garnish individual bowls with avocado and sesame seeds (if using) and serve.

Pork Fried Rice

SERVES 2

The cooked pork in this recipe is from Slow-Roasted Pork with Peach Sauce on page 196. You will need a small saucepan with a tight-fitting lid to make this recipe. You can substitute 3 cups cooked long-grain rice for the raw rice; omit steps 1 and 2.

4 teaspoons vegetable oil

¾ cup long-grain rice (see note), rinsed (see page 118)

1¼ cups water

¼ teaspoon salt

1 large egg, lightly beaten

1 tablespoon hoisin sauce

2 teaspoons oyster sauce

1 teaspoon soy sauce, plus extra for seasoning

½ teaspoon sriracha sauce

4 ounces shiitake mushrooms, stemmed and quartered

4 scallions, white and green parts separated, whites minced and greens sliced thin

1 shallot, sliced thin

2 teaspoons minced or grated fresh ginger

1 garlic clove, minced

½ teaspoon sugar

7½ ounces cooked pork (see note), cut into ½-inch pieces (about 1½ cups)

1. Heat 1 teaspoon oil in small saucepan over medium heat until shimmering. Stir in rice and cook until edges of grains begin to turn translucent, about 2 minutes. Stir in water and salt, increase heat to high, and bring to boil. Reduce heat to low, cover, and simmer until all liquid is absorbed, 18 to 22 minutes.

2. Off heat, uncover saucepan and place clean kitchen towel folded in half over pan, then replace lid. Let rice stand for 10 minutes, then spread on baking sheet and let cool to room temperature, about 20 minutes.

3. Heat 1 teaspoon more oil in 12-inch nonstick skillet over medium heat until shimmering. Add egg and cook, without stirring, until just beginning to set, about 20 seconds, then scramble until egg is cooked through but not browned, about 1 minute longer. Transfer egg to small bowl. Wipe out skillet with paper towels.

4. Combine hoisin sauce, oyster sauce, soy sauce, and sriracha in small bowl. Heat remaining 2 teaspoons oil in skillet over medium heat until shimmering. Stir in mushrooms and cook until golden brown, about 5 minutes. Stir in scallion whites, shallot, ginger, garlic, and sugar and cook until fragrant, about 30 seconds. Stir in rice and cook until fragrant, about 30 seconds. Stir in pork and hoisin mixture and continue to cook until rice is coated in sauce and pork is warmed through, 2 to 4 minutes longer.

5. Off heat, stir in scallion greens and scrambled egg, season with soy sauce to taste, and serve.

NOTES FROM THE TEST KITCHEN

STORING SCALLIONS
Too often we find that scallions go limp after just a few days in the fridge. To prolong their shelf life, we tried several different storage methods, from wrapping them in moistened paper towels placed inside an open zipper-lock bag to tossing them naked into the crisper drawer. We found that standing the scallions in an inch of water in a tall container covered loosely with a zipper-lock bag worked best. Stored this way (with the water refreshed every three days), our scallions lasted for well over a week with very little loss in quality.

CHICKEN IN A POT

POULET EN COCOTTE, OR CHICKEN IN A POT, IS A French bistro classic. But in spite of its fancy pedigree, it is a fairly straightforward recipe: Place a seasoned bird in a pot, scatter in some aromatics, cover, and bake. What emerges from this simple method is surprisingly special—an incredibly tender and juicy chicken with rich, soul-satisfying flavor. To make our chicken en cocotte a true dinner in a pot, we wanted to add vegetables to the mix, and we hoped we could completely cook our chicken and vegetables in about an hour. And since a whole bird leaves you with a good amount of leftover meat, we knew the moist, tender chicken would make for a few more great meals.

Before we could address vegetables or additional flavorings, we had to determine the ideal temperature at which to bake our bird. We seasoned half a dozen 4½- to 5-pound chickens, placed them in large Dutch ovens, popped on the lids, and baked them at temperatures ranging from 200 to 400 degrees, until the breast meat registered 160 degrees and the legs hit 175 degrees. There were drastic differences among these chickens. The birds baked at 375 degrees and 400 degrees cooked too rapidly, resulting in an overcooked, dry layer of breast meat just under the skin. Birds baked at the low end of the temperature range stayed moist and juicy but took up to two hours to cook through—taking this supper out of the weeknight lineup. Between these extremes we found our sweet spot, a moderate 350-degree oven. At this temperature, our bird emerged supremely juicy and tender in just under an hour. Although we usually brine poultry to prevent it from drying out, we discovered that this gentle en cocotte cooking method made brining unnecessary. With our oven temperature set, we addressed the vegetables.

Since we wanted our chicken in a pot to be a complete one-pot supper, we decided to include both red potatoes and carrots. We cut three red potatoes and two carrots into 1-inch pieces and scattered them around the chicken, covered the pot, and baked it just as before. Unfortunately, after an hour in the oven, a few of the potatoes and carrots were still raw in the middle. Up to this point, we had been following traditional chicken en cocotte doctrine, which forbids adding liquid to the pot lest flavors become washed out. Suspecting that a little more braising liquid might help the vegetables cook more evenly, we broke with tradition and added just

¼ cup of chicken broth to the pot. When we removed the lid, we were met with a plume of steam and a mix of perfectly cooked vegetables. Having determined the best way to cook our chicken and vegetables, we focused on building our sauce and developing flavor.

To add back some of the concentrated chicken flavor that had dissipated now that we were adding liquid to the pot, we decided to brown the breast and back of the chicken on the stovetop before adding the vegetables and transferring the pot to the oven. Tasters liked this version better, but now the top layer of breast meat was slightly dry. Browning the chicken back, which is composed of fatty dark meat, for a few extra minutes (and only lightly browning the breast) solved this problem and also produced a rich, full-bodied braising liquid.

Since we were now browning the chicken on the stovetop, we wondered if our vegetables would benefit from the same treatment. After removing the browned chicken, we sautéed the potatoes and carrots, along with a halved onion, crushed garlic, and thyme, until well browned. This was by far our best batch yet, boasting rich meatiness and complex flavor. With such flavorful braising liquid left behind in the pot after cooking our chicken and vegetables, we decided to create a simple sauce to coat our meat. We defatted the liquid and stirred in butter for richness and lemon juice for brightness and acidity. Now that we had successfully reinvented this rustic classic for the modern-day American table, we focused on our spin-off meals, which would make use of the juicy, tender extras.

The first thing that came to mind was chicken salad—but we didn't want any ordinary chicken salad. Instead of focusing on the familiar mayonnaise-based sandwich salad, we created a dinner salad with Spanish flavors. We started with a potent dressing, made with roasted red peppers and sherry vinegar; swapping the mayo for extra-virgin olive oil allowed the bright, clean flavors to shine through, and pureeing the ingredients ensured that the dressing was emulsified. For more texture and Spanish flavor, we stirred in more roasted peppers and chopped green olives. We also added some thinly sliced celery for crunch. After tossing our shredded chicken with this vibrant dressing, we sprinkled it with toasted sliced almonds and plated it atop a bed of salad greens for a hearty yet refreshing take on chicken salad.

In Southeast Asia, Thai cooks turn leftover cooked chicken into a light and lively meal by tossing shredded pieces of chicken with a piquant dressing of fish sauce, lime juice, sugar, pepper flakes, and fresh herbs, before wrapping the chicken in lettuce leaves. We decided to follow suit. To begin, we created a simple dressing using the same ingredients; for the herbs, we used fresh mint and cilantro. Tasters loved this combination of flavors but felt something was missing. Authentic recipes rely on toasted rice powder for nuttiness and texture; although this ingredient can be tough to find at the supermarket, it's easy enough to make at home. We toasted 2 teaspoons of white rice until golden, then ground it to a powder in a spice mill before mixing it with the dressing. We tossed the chicken in the dressing and let the mixture sit for 15 minutes to absorb the flavors. Tasters heartily approved of the brightly flavored, tender shreds of chicken, which were perfectly matched by the clean flavor of the Bibb lettuce "wrappers."

For our final recipe, we tackled a Chinese favorite, moo shu chicken. In moo shu, the meat, shredded cabbage, and other assorted vegetables are rolled up in a thin crepe. We shredded 7½ ounces of chicken (for 1½ cups of meat), then cooked it briefly with some shredded cabbage to warm the chicken and slightly wilt the cabbage. To make prep work even easier for this quick weeknight meal, we swapped the cabbage for a 10-ounce bag of coleslaw mix. To amp up the flavor of the dish, we sautéed thinly sliced shiitake mushrooms, along with the classic Chinese aromatics of ginger, garlic, and scallions. The filling was ready to go; now we just had to tackle the sauce, which we decided to keep on the light side so as not to make our crepes soggy. A simple mixture of chicken broth, soy sauce, cornstarch, and hoisin sauce provided just the right sweetness and depth. While Chinese crepes are available at specialty Asian markets, we were happy to roll up our moo shu in easy-to-find flour tortillas, which we softened in the microwave while preparing the filling.

With one simple French recipe, we had enjoyed three great meals—and traveled the globe, too.

NOTES FROM THE TEST KITCHEN

TUCKING THE WINGS

After removing the neck and giblets, twist the wingtips back behind the bird—they should stay in place by themselves.

THE BEST INEXPENSIVE DUTCH OVEN

Dutch ovens are kitchen workhorses, useful for making not only Chicken in a Pot but also other roasts, stews, and soups and for deep-frying. We tested several inexpensive Dutch ovens by making stew, rice, and french fries, hoping to find a more affordable alternative to our favorites by Le Creuset and All-Clad (which run roughly $230 and $280, respectively). The **Tramontina 6.5-Quart Cast Iron Dutch Oven**, crafted from enameled cast iron, passed all our tests with flying colors. Comparable in size to our pricier favorites and performing almost as well, it's hard to beat with its price tag of $50.

CARVING A CHICKEN

1. Cut the chicken where the leg meets the breast and pull the leg quarter away. Push up on the joint, then carefully cut through it to remove the leg quarter.

2. Cut through the joint that connects the drumstick to the thigh. Repeat on the second side to remove the other leg.

3. Cut down along one side of the breastbone, pulling the breast meat away from the bone. Then cut the breast into attractive slices.

Chicken in a Pot with Red Potatoes and Carrots

SERVES 2, WITH LEFTOVERS

You can use the leftovers to make two of the following recipes: Spanish-Style Chicken Salad with Roasted Red Peppers (page 201), Chicken Lettuce Wraps (page 203), and/or Moo Shu Chicken (page 203). If using kosher chicken, do not season with salt in step 1. Be sure to use a Dutch oven with a tight-fitting lid.

1 (4½- to 5-pound) whole chicken, giblets removed, wings tucked (see page 200) (see note)
  Salt and pepper
2 tablespoons vegetable oil
12 ounces red potatoes (2 to 3 medium), cut into 1-inch pieces
2 carrots, peeled and cut into 1-inch pieces
1 onion, peeled and halved, root end left intact
3 garlic cloves, peeled and crushed
½ teaspoon minced fresh thyme or ⅛ teaspoon dried
¼ cup low-sodium chicken broth
1 bay leaf
1 tablespoon unsalted butter
1 teaspoon fresh lemon juice

1. Adjust oven rack to lower-middle position and heat oven to 350 degrees. Pat chicken dry with paper towels and season with salt and pepper.

2. Heat oil in large Dutch oven over medium-high heat until just smoking. Add chicken, breast side down, and cook until lightly browned, about 5 minutes. Flip chicken and continue to cook until back of chicken is well browned, 6 to 8 minutes. Transfer chicken to large plate.

3. Add potatoes, carrots, onion, and garlic to fat left in pot and cook over medium heat until browned, 8 to 10 minutes. Stir in thyme and cook until fragrant, about 30 seconds. Stir in broth and bay leaf, scraping up any browned bits.

4. Off heat, place chicken, breast side up, on top of vegetables. Place large sheet of foil over pot and press to seal, then cover tightly with lid. Transfer pot to oven and cook until breast registers 160 to 165 degrees and thighs register 175 degrees on instant-read thermometer, 50 to 60 minutes.

5. Remove pot from oven. Transfer chicken to carving board, tent loosely with foil, and let rest for 20 minutes.

Using slotted spoon, transfer vegetables to large bowl, discarding onion and bay leaf. Season with salt and pepper to taste and cover to keep warm.

6. Strain cooking liquid through fine-mesh strainer into fat separator. Let jus settle for 5 minutes, then pour defatted jus back into pot. Bring jus to simmer over medium-high heat and whisk in butter. Off heat, stir in lemon juice and season with salt and pepper to taste. Following photos on page 200, carve chicken and serve with vegetables and sauce.

Spanish-Style Chicken Salad with Roasted Red Peppers

SERVES 2

The cooked chicken in this recipe is from Chicken in a Pot with Red Potatoes and Carrots. You can use most any type of lettuce, but we particularly like mesclun mix.

8 ounces jarred roasted red peppers, drained, patted dry, and chopped coarse (about 1 cup)
3 tablespoons extra-virgin olive oil
1 tablespoon sherry vinegar
1 small garlic clove, minced
  Salt and pepper
1 celery rib, sliced thin
3 tablespoons pitted green olives, chopped coarse
2 tablespoons minced fresh parsley
1 small shallot, minced
10 ounces cooked chicken (see note), shredded (about 2 cups)
4 ounces salad greens (about 4 cups) (see note)
3 tablespoons sliced almonds, toasted (see page 240)

1. Puree ½ cup roasted peppers, oil, vinegar, garlic, ¼ teaspoon salt, and ¼ teaspoon pepper together in blender until smooth, about 30 seconds. Transfer to large bowl.

2. Stir in remaining ½ cup roasted peppers, celery, olives, parsley, and shallot. Add chicken and toss to coat evenly. Let sit at room temperature until flavors meld, about 15 minutes.

3. Season chicken salad with salt and pepper to taste, mound on salad greens on individual plates, sprinkle with almonds, and serve.

CHICKEN LETTUCE WRAPS

Chicken Lettuce Wraps

SERVES 2

The cooked chicken in this recipe is from Chicken in a Pot with Red Potatoes and Carrots on page 201. Don't skip the toasted rice; it's integral to the texture and flavor of the dish. Any style of white rice can be used. Serve with sticky rice and steamed vegetables.

- 2 teaspoons white rice (see note)
- 2 tablespoons fresh lime juice, plus extra for seasoning
- 2 tablespoons coarsely chopped fresh mint
- 2 tablespoons coarsely chopped fresh cilantro
- 1 small shallot, sliced into thin rings
- 1 tablespoon fish sauce, plus extra for seasoning
- 1 tablespoon sugar, plus extra for seasoning
- ¼ teaspoon red pepper flakes
- 10 ounces cooked chicken (see note), shredded (about 2 cups)
- ½ head Bibb lettuce, washed and dried, leaves separated and left whole

1. Cook rice in 8-inch skillet over medium-high heat, stirring constantly, until deep golden brown, 3 to 5 minutes. Transfer to bowl and cool for 5 minutes. Grind rice with spice grinder, mini food processor, or mortar and pestle until it resembles fine meal, 10 to 40 seconds (you should have about 2 teaspoons rice powder).

2. Stir together rice powder, lime juice, mint, cilantro, shallot, fish sauce, sugar, and red pepper flakes in medium bowl. Add chicken; toss to coat evenly. Let sit at room temperature until flavors meld, about 15 minutes.

3. Season chicken mixture with lime juice, fish sauce, and sugar to taste and serve with lettuce leaves.

Moo Shu Chicken

SERVES 2

The cooked chicken in this recipe is from Chicken in a Pot with Red Potatoes and Carrots on page 201. Shredded carrots, bean sprouts, or thinly sliced bamboo shoots can be stirred into the pan with the cabbage.

- ⅓ cup low-sodium chicken broth
- 2 tablespoons hoisin sauce, plus extra for serving
- 2 tablespoons soy sauce
- 2 teaspoons cornstarch
- 1 tablespoon vegetable oil
- 4 ounces shiitake mushrooms, stemmed and sliced thin
- 3 garlic cloves, minced
- 1 tablespoon minced or grated fresh ginger
- 1 (10-ounce) bag coleslaw mix
- 7½ ounces cooked chicken (see note), shredded (about 1½ cups)
- 5 scallions, sliced thin on bias
- 6 (6-inch) flour tortillas, warmed (see below)

1. Stir broth, hoisin sauce, soy sauce, and cornstarch together in bowl until well combined.

2. Heat oil in 12-inch nonstick skillet over medium heat until shimmering. Stir in mushrooms and cook until golden brown, about 5 minutes.

3. Stir in garlic and ginger and cook until fragrant, about 30 seconds. Stir in coleslaw mix, chicken, and scallions and cook until cabbage begins to wilt, about 2 minutes.

4. Whisk sauce to recombine, then stir into pan and cook until mixture is thickened and hot, about 2 minutes. Serve with warm tortillas, passing additional hoisin sauce separately.

NOTES FROM THE TEST KITCHEN

WARMING TORTILLAS AND PITAS

Warming tortillas and pitas over the open flame of a gas burner or in a skillet gives them a toasted flavor, but the oven or microwave also works. If your tortillas or pitas are dry, pat them with a little water first.

If using a gas stove, toast the tortillas or pitas, one at a time, directly on the cooking grate over a medium flame until slightly charred around the edges, about 30 seconds per side. If using a skillet, toast the tortillas or pitas, one at a time, over medium-high heat until softened and speckled with brown, 20 to 30 seconds per side. Wrap the warmed tortillas or pitas in foil or a kitchen towel to keep them warm and soft until serving time.

If using an oven, stack the tortillas or pitas in a foil packet and heat at 350 degrees until warm and soft, about 5 minutes. Keep them in the foil until serving time.

To use a microwave, stack the tortillas or pitas on a plate, cover with microwave-safe plastic wrap, and heat on high until warm and soft, 1 to 2 minutes. Remove the plastic wrap and cover the tortillas or pitas with a kitchen towel or foil to keep them warm.

CLASSIC POT ROAST

IF YOU'RE LOOKING FOR A RICH, HEARTY, EASY-TO-prepare roast that also happens to be affordable and offers extras for a few more meals, look no further than the classic pot roast. A genuinely good pot roast transforms a tough (aka cheap), nearly unpalatable cut of meat into a tender, juicy, flavorful roast. Unfortunately, pot roast has garnered a rather dubious reputation for delivering stringy, dry meat, insipid flavor, and mushy vegetables. In the hope of earning this dish a place on the dinner table for two, we set about determining the right cut of beef, the ideal braising liquid, a superlative mix of vegetables to add to the pot, and a few enticing dinner ideas for the days following.

The meat for pot roast should be well marbled with fat and connective tissue in order to provide the dish with necessary flavor and moisture. Recipes typically call for roasts from the sirloin (rump), round (leg), or chuck (shoulder), so we began by cooking cuts from these three sections in order to find the right one. The lean sirloin cuts packed great beefy flavor but lacked richness. The slightly fattier round cuts never quite achieved the fall-apart tenderness we were after. In the end, we found that the high proportion of fat and connective tissue in chuck cuts (boneless chuck-eye roast, seven-bone roast, and top blade roast) gave the meat much-needed moisture as well as superior flavor. Ultimately, we crowned the boneless chuck-eye roast our winner because it is easy to find in supermarkets and requires minimal preparation.

But even with the right cut, we still had problems. Following the direction of a few recipes, we braised our chuck-eye roast for four hours. While the meat was certainly tender, there were still undesirable pockets of fat and connective tissue throughout. We wondered what would happen if we split the large cylindrical roast into two sleeker halves. This process was easy, since the seam of fat that runs down the center of the roast acted as a built-in guide. We trimmed the obvious pieces of fat from each lobe, leaving a thin layer of fat on top, and tied each piece to keep it from falling apart during braising. With less extraneous fat, these two roasts definitely cooked up better than one. To further improve our humble chuck-eye roasts, we decided to first sear them on the stovetop. This step developed a well-caramelized exterior and left us with flavorful fond (the browned bits stuck to the bottom of the pot) that we could use to build our braising liquid.

We chose to cook the pot roast in the oven since it was too difficult to maintain a steady temperature on the stove. After fiddling with the oven temperature, we found 300 degrees to be the magic number—anything above turned the meat stringy, and anything below gave us inconsistently cooked results.

Initially, we were using a modest ¼ cup of water for our braising liquid. But this produced a roast that was fibrous, even after hours of cooking. After increasing the amount of liquid incrementally, we found we ultimately needed enough liquid to come halfway up the sides of the roast (about 3 cups). To give our roast a flavor boost, we chose to use a combination of equal parts beef broth, chicken broth, and water added to sautéed onion, celery, and garlic for our final braising liquid. Flipping the meat once during cooking ensured that the roast cooked evenly and became tender throughout.

One of the basic tenets of good pot roast is that it is well-done meat—it should be cooked to an internal temperature well above 165 degrees. Up to this point, we had been bringing the meat to an internal temperature of 200 to 210 degrees, the point at which the fat and connective tissue begin to melt. In a 300-degree oven, the roast hit that temperature in about 2½ hours, but the meat was still not fall-apart tender. Slowly increasing the cooking time to 3 to 3½ hours, we found that the internal temperature of the roast stayed at 210 degrees, but the meat had a substantially different appearance and texture. The roast was so tender that a fork poked into the meat met with no resistance and nearly disappeared into the flesh. We took the roast out of the pot and sliced into it. Nearly all the fat and connective tissue had dissolved into the meat, giving each bite a soft, silky texture and rich flavor. It was clear that not only was it important to cook the roast until it reached 210 degrees, but the meat had to remain at that temperature for a full hour. In other words, we cooked the pot roast until it was done—and then we kept on cooking.

To create a sauce from the braising liquid, many recipes use a thickener (either a roux or a slurry of cornstarch mixed with some braising liquid). Both techniques made the sauce more gravylike than we wanted.

Instead, we chose to remove the roast from the pot once it had finished cooking, then stirred in a bit of red wine for acidity and reduced the liquid until the flavors were concentrated and the sauce thickened naturally.

While we were more than happy with our fall-apart roast and intensely flavored sauce, we still wanted a mix of hearty vegetables that would help round out our supper into a complete meal. Since pot roast is often served with either mashed or boiled potatoes, spuds seemed like a good place to start. Skin-on red potatoes held their shape beautifully and provided welcome creamy bites. In addition to the potatoes, we looked to some of the sweeter root vegetables; carrots and parsnips fit the bill. When we cut the carrots and parsnips into big chunks and added them after the roast had cooked for two hours, both meat and vegetables emerged tender at the same time.

With lots of tender, fall-apart meat ready to be put to good use, we considered our secondary recipes. A hearty, ultra-meaty, Texas-style chili came to mind first. Traditional Texas chili simmers for hours on the stovetop, but we wanted to create a dish that showcased all the spicy, beefy flavor of the classic yet didn't take nearly as long to make. Using chicken broth alone for the chili base gave us a chili with zero flavor, so we supplemented the broth with canned tomato sauce, which thickened our chili and added long-simmered flavor and pleasant acidity. Chili powder and chipotle chiles contributed some heat, and cumin, oregano, and garlic provided quintessential chili flavor. Kidney beans, though a blasphemous addition among chili purists, balanced the heaviness of the beef. Brown sugar and lime juice rounded out the flavor of the sauce, providing much-needed brightness and sweetness. Since our beef was already cooked, we simply stirred it in after finishing our sauce and cooked it until it was just heated through. Stirring the pot gently ensured that the meat remained in Texas-size chunks.

Next, we hit on the notion of making cheesy, saucy enchiladas. After shredding some of our pot roast meat, we combined it with enchilada sauce and shredded Monterey Jack cheese, then rolled the mixture up in 6-inch corn tortillas. After 20 minutes in the oven, our speedy Mexican-inspired supper was good, but not great. Swapping out the Monterey Jack cheese for spicy pepper Jack added a welcome punch of flavor and

heat, and minced cilantro brought some freshness and citrusy notes to the filling. Sprinkled with more cheese and garnished with lime wedges, our gooey, saucy beef enchiladas made it to the table in record time.

Finally, we looked to the British Isles for inspiration for our last recipe. Hand pies have long been a popular way to both use up extra meat and provide a hearty, filling meal. To give this traditionally casual meal a gourmet touch, we began by caramelizing an onion, to which we added garlic, thyme, and Dijon mustard. After stirring in our leftover beef, we wrapped the mixture in buttery pie dough and baked the pies until they emerged golden brown. Although they were nice to look at, our pies were dry on the inside. We tried a variety of additions. Beer, though traditional, was too astringent; cheese seemed out of place. However, heavy cream added just the right amount of creaminess to bind the filling and keep it from drying out in the oven. To counter the richness of the cream and to add some visual interest, we added frozen peas to the filling just before forming the pies. After 25 minutes in the oven, the pies were toasty and golden brown, with a rich, meaty filling and tender, flaky crust.

With one succulent, juicy pot roast, we were able to create two more speedy yet satisfying suppers—not bad for a day's work.

NOTES FROM THE TEST KITCHEN

PREPARING A POT ROAST

1. Pull the roast apart at its major seams (delineated by lines of fat) into two pieces, using a sharp knife if necessary.

2. Using a knife, remove the large knobs of fat from each piece, leaving a thin layer of fat on the meat.

Classic Pot Roast with Root Vegetables

SERVES 2, WITH LEFTOVERS

You can use the leftovers to make two of the following recipes: Quick Texas Chili (page 206), Beef Enchiladas (page 207), and/or Beef Hand Pies (page 209). Use a good-quality, medium-bodied wine, such as a Côtes du Rhône or Pinot Noir, for this dish.

- 1 (3½- to 4-pound) boneless beef chuck-eye roast, pulled apart into 2 roasts and trimmed (see page 205)
  Salt and pepper
- 3 tablespoons vegetable oil
- 1 onion, chopped medium
- 1 celery rib, chopped medium
- 4 garlic cloves, minced
- 2 teaspoons sugar
- 1 teaspoon minced fresh thyme or ¼ teaspoon dried
- 1 cup low-sodium chicken broth
- 1 cup beef broth
- 1 cup water
- 8 ounces red potatoes (1 to 2 medium), cut into 1½-inch pieces
- 2 carrots, peeled and cut into 3- to 4-inch lengths
- 2 parsnips, peeled and cut into 3- to 4-inch lengths
- ⅓ cup dry red wine (see note)

1. Adjust oven rack to lower-middle position and heat oven to 300 degrees. Tie 3 pieces of butcher's twine around each piece of beef to prevent them from falling apart. Pat beef dry with paper towels and season with salt and pepper. Heat 2 tablespoons oil in large Dutch oven over medium-high heat until just smoking. Brown both roasts on all sides, 7 to 10 minutes; transfer to large plate.

2. Add remaining 1 tablespoon oil, onion, and celery to pot and cook over medium heat until softened, about 5 minutes. Stir in garlic, sugar, and thyme and cook until fragrant, about 30 seconds. Stir in chicken broth, beef broth, and water, scraping up any browned bits.

3. Add browned roasts with any accumulated juice to pot and bring to simmer. Cover, transfer pot to oven, and cook for 2 hours, turning roasts over halfway through.

NOTES FROM THE TEST KITCHEN

ARE YOUR DRIED HERBS FRESH?

Even if you're not cooking for two, it may take a while to get through a jar of dried herbs. For this reason, we recommend replacement of dried herbs after about 12 months. If you are questioning the age and freshness of an open jar, crumble a small amount between your fingers and take a whiff. If it releases a lively aroma, it's good to use. If it doesn't, it's best to get a new jar. Or better yet, skip committing to a whole jar, and instead look for a shop that offers dried herbs (and spices) in bulk so you can purchase just what you need.

To track the ages of the dried herbs stored in your pantry or spice drawer, write the purchase date on an adhesive dot and place the dot on the lid. That way, you'll know when your herbs need to be replaced.

---

4. Nestle potatoes, carrots, and parsnips in pot around meat. Continue to cook, covered, until meat and vegetables are very tender, 1 to 1½ hours longer.

5. Remove pot from oven. Transfer vegetables to bowl, season with salt and pepper to taste, and cover to keep warm. Transfer roasts to carving board, tent loosely with foil, and let rest while finishing sauce.

6. Strain braising liquid through fine-mesh strainer into fat separator; discard aromatics. Let jus settle for 5 minutes, then pour defatted jus back into pot. Stir in wine and simmer over medium heat until sauce measures 1 cup, 8 to 10 minutes. Season with salt and pepper to taste.

7. Remove twine from roasts, cut meat against grain into ¼-inch-thick slices, and serve with vegetables and sauce.

Quick Texas Chili

SERVES 2

The cooked beef in this recipe is from Classic Pot Roast with Root Vegetables. Be sure to stir in the beef gently in step 2 so that it remains in large pieces. Serve with sour cream, shredded cheddar or Monterey Jack cheese, chopped tomatoes, minced cilantro, and/or minced onion. The chili can be refrigerated in an airtight container for up to 4 days or frozen for up to 1 month. Reheat over low heat, adding water or broth to adjust the consistency.

3 slices bacon, minced

1 small onion, chopped medium

4 teaspoons chili powder

1 teaspoon minced canned chipotle chile in adobo sauce

1 teaspoon cumin

½ teaspoon dried oregano

3 garlic cloves, minced

1¼ cups low-sodium chicken broth

1 (8-ounce) can tomato sauce

¾ cup drained and rinsed dark red kidney beans

7½ ounces cooked beef (see note),
chopped into ½-inch pieces (about 1½ cups)

1 teaspoon brown sugar

2 teaspoons fresh lime juice

Salt and pepper

1. Cook bacon in medium saucepan over medium-low heat until crisp and rendered, 5 to 7 minutes. Add onion, chili powder, chipotles, cumin, and oregano and cook until onion is softened, about 5 minutes. Stir in garlic and cook until fragrant, about 30 seconds.

2. Stir in broth, tomato sauce, and beans, bring to simmer, and cook until sauce thickens, about 30 minutes. Gently stir in beef and sugar and continue to simmer until beef is heated through, about 2 minutes longer. Off heat, stir in lime juice, season with salt and pepper to taste, and serve.

Beef Enchiladas

SERVES 2

The cooked beef in this recipe is from Classic Pot Roast with Root Vegetables on page 206. Enchilada sauce is sold in cans of various sizes; you'll need 14 ounces (1¾ cups) for this recipe, or try our recipe for Fast Enchilada Sauce (recipe follows).

7½ ounces cooked beef (see note),
shredded (about 1½ cups)

1¾ cups enchilada sauce (see note)

4 ounces pepper Jack cheese, shredded (about 1 cup)

1 tablespoon minced fresh cilantro

6 (6-inch) corn tortillas, warmed (see page 203)

Vegetable oil spray

Lime wedges, for serving

1. Adjust oven rack to middle position and heat oven to 350 degrees. Combine shredded beef, ½ cup sauce, ½ cup cheese, and cilantro in bowl.

2. Spread ¼ cup more sauce in 8-inch square baking dish. Spread tortillas on clean counter and spoon ⅓ cup beef filling down center of each tortilla. Tightly roll tortillas around filling and lay them, seam side down, in baking dish.

3. Lightly coat tops of enchiladas with vegetable oil spray. Pour ¾ cup more sauce evenly over enchiladas. Sprinkle remaining ½ cup cheese down center of enchiladas.

4. Cover baking dish tightly with foil. Bake until enchiladas are heated through, about 15 minutes. Remove foil and continue to bake until cheese is lightly browned, 5 to 10 minutes longer. Serve with lime wedges, passing remaining ¼ cup sauce separately.

Fast Enchilada Sauce

MAKES 1¾ CUPS

This sauce can be refrigerated in an airtight container for up to 1 week.

1 tablespoon vegetable oil

1 small onion, minced

Salt and pepper

2 tablespoons chili powder

2 garlic cloves, minced

1½ teaspoons cumin

1½ teaspoons sugar

1½ cups canned tomato sauce

¼ cup water

Heat oil in 10-inch skillet over medium heat until shimmering. Add onion and ½ teaspoon salt and cook until softened, about 5 minutes. Stir in chili powder, garlic, cumin, and sugar and cook until fragrant, about 30 seconds. Stir in tomato sauce and water, bring to simmer, and cook until slightly thickened, about 3 minutes. Season with salt and pepper to taste.

BEEF HAND PIES

Beef Hand Pies

MAKES 2 HAND PIES

The cooked beef in this recipe is from Classic Pot Roast with Root Vegetables on page 206. You can substitute store-bought pie dough for the Savory Pie Dough if desired (see page 62). These hand pies are good both hot and at room temperature. Once cooled, the baked hand pies can be refrigerated in a zipper-lock bag for up to 2 days.

      1   tablespoon olive oil
      1   onion, halved and sliced thin
      ½   teaspoon brown sugar
          Salt and pepper
      4   garlic cloves, minced
      2   teaspoons minced fresh thyme or ½ teaspoon dried
      ⅓   cup heavy cream
    7½   ounces cooked beef (see note), shredded
          (about 1½ cups)
      2   teaspoons Dijon mustard
      ¼   cup frozen peas
      1   recipe Savory Pie Dough (see page 62; see note)
      1   large egg, lightly beaten

1. Adjust oven rack to middle position and heat oven to 425 degrees. Heat oil in 10-inch skillet over medium-high heat until shimmering. Add onion, sugar, and ¼ teaspoon salt and cook until softened, about 5 minutes. Reduce heat to medium-low and continue to cook, stirring often, until onion is dark golden and caramelized, 15 to 20 minutes longer.

2. Stir in garlic and thyme and cook until fragrant, about 1 minute. Stir in cream and simmer until thickened, about 1 minute. Off heat, stir in beef and mustard and season with salt and pepper to taste. Transfer to bowl, cover, and refrigerate until mixture is at room temperature, 25 to 30 minutes. Stir in peas.

3. Line baking sheet with parchment paper and set aside. Roll out dough on lightly floured counter to 12-inch round, about ¼ inch thick. Following photos, cut dough round in half and arrange one half of cooled filling on 1 side of each dough half, leaving ½-inch border around edges. Brush edges of dough with water, fold over filling, and crimp edges to seal. Transfer hand pies to prepared baking sheet. Using fork, pierce dough.

4. Brush hand pies with egg and bake until golden brown, 25 to 30 minutes, rotating sheet halfway through baking. Let hand pies cool for 5 minutes before serving.

SHAPING HAND PIES

1. Cut the dough round in half and arrange half of the cooled filling on one side of each dough half, leaving a ½-inch border around the edges.

2. Brush the edges with water, then fold the dough over the filling and crimp the edges to seal.

3. Transfer the pies to the parchment paper–lined baking sheet and pierce the dough at 2-inch intervals.

ROAST BONELESS LEG OF LAMB

AT ITS BEST, ROAST BONELESS LEG OF LAMB IS pleasantly tender and juicy, with a deeply browned crust that is the perfect contrast to the rosy-pink interior. But all too often it emerges from the oven overcooked and tough, with a rubbery texture and "gamy" flavor—hardly appealing. We wanted a roasted leg of lamb with a tender, juicy interior and a well-seasoned crust, both complemented by a brightly flavored glaze.

We started by considering the cut. Whole boneless legs of lamb can weigh 8 to 9 pounds—great for a crowd, but impractical for two, even when planning for additional meals. More suitable were boneless half legs, which weigh 3 to 5 pounds. These gave us plenty of meat for dinner, as well as enough leftovers for a couple of subsequent meals. We found the sirloin (top) to be more tender than the shank (lower) end, but both roasts work well. Since boneless legs are already butterflied when purchased, we knew that for an evenly cooked roast we needed to pound the meat to an even thickness before rolling it into a tight cylinder. This

NOTES FROM THE TEST KITCHEN

PREPARING ROAST BONELESS LEG OF LAMB

1. Place the lamb on a cutting board with its rough side facing up. Cover the lamb with plastic wrap and pound to a uniform 1-inch thickness. Season the lamb and spread the herb mixture over it.

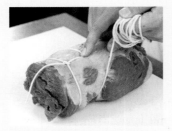

2. Roll the roast lengthwise into a tight cylinder. Slip a 6-foot piece of butcher's twine under the lamb and tie a double knot, then loop the long end of the twine under and around the roast.

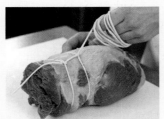

3. Run the long end of the twine through the loop and tighten around the roast. Repeat this procedure down the length of the roast, spacing the loops an inch apart.

4. Then roll the roast over and run the twine under and around each loop.

5. Once you reach the end of the roast, tie the end of the twine to the original knot.

procedure ensured that we had a roast of even width on all sides—the first step to a perfectly cooked roast.

To cook the meat, we started with the easiest method possible—we seasoned the lamb, put it in the oven, and checked on it occasionally. But the roast, to our disappointment, cooked to a brown, rubbery mass. Even worse, the outer layer of fat began to smoke, filling the kitchen with an odious aroma that penetrated the meat, giving it that familiar and offensive gamy flavor.

The first step in fixing our gamy roast was to adjust the oven temperature. We started at the low end, thinking that a low temperature might yield the most evenly cooked meat. Unfortunately, our lamb cooked at 250 degrees became mushy; a talk with our science editor made it clear that this was because of certain enzymes breaking down too much. After this disappointment, we swung in the opposite direction, roasting the lamb in a 450-degree oven. The high heat kept the lamb from disintegrating, but it also drastically overcooked the exterior portions of the roast. The middle ground—375 degrees—was our best bet, giving us evenly cooked and tender (not mushy) meat.

While the roast was now a perfect medium-rare, the exterior fat on the leg still smoked in the oven and gave the meat that unwanted gamy flavor. So we tried pan-searing the lamb on the stovetop before putting it into the oven to finish. The results were perfect. The direct heat jump-started the cooking of the lamb's exterior, producing a crisp crust in a matter of minutes. The interior, meanwhile, remained tender, and although there was still a little smoke, the meat picked up none of the gamy flavor produced with a straight roasting method. Using a wire rack to elevate the lamb above the baking sheet in which it cooked allowed the lamb to cook evenly on all sides once transferred to the oven.

With our cooking method of choice established, we were ready to test flavorings. It turned out that a simple rub of aromatics worked best—just enough herbs and garlic to enhance but not overpower the flavor of the lamb. Furthermore, the herb rub worked perfectly with our rolling and tying method. The aromatics spiraled evenly throughout the roast, lending herbal flavor to every bite. To counter the richness of the meat, we chose pomegranate juice as the main ingredient in the glaze. Glazing the lamb intermittently during cooking—when it went into the oven, halfway through cooking, when we pulled the roast from the oven, and right before serving—ensured that a sweet and distinctive tang was noticeable throughout, brightening the flavor of our dish.

With our lamb roasted, we began to develop our follow-up recipes. First, we looked to the Middle East, where lamb is very popular, for ideas. Lamb shawarma, a sandwichlike wrap, is traditionally made with spiced, spit-roasted lamb, which is shaved thin, wrapped in pita bread, and topped with a yogurt-tahini sauce. For our interpretation, we shaved our lamb as thinly as possible (briefly chilling it in the freezer helped it firm up and made it easier to slice). For flavor, we cooked, or bloomed, a mixture of cumin, coriander, and cardamom in olive oil to bring out their flavors, then added our lamb shavings. We cooked the lamb quickly, over medium-high heat, just until it heated through and began to crisp around the edges. For our sauce, we followed tradition and stirred together tahini, garlic, yogurt, lemon juice, and parsley. A whole pita bread, unsplit and rolled like a soft taco, closely approximated the traditional thin flatbread used in authentic lamb shawarma. We spread our yogurt-tahini sauce on the pita, layered the crispy lamb on top, then topped it off with thinly sliced shallot, chopped lettuce, and diced tomato. In just minutes, we had two flavorful, exotic sandwiches on the table.

Next, we borrowed flavors from Ireland and created a hearty stew perfect for a cold winter night. Traditionally, Irish stew contains little more than lamb, potatoes, and water. While certainly economical, this type of stew boasts very little in terms of flavor. To up the appeal, we began by swapping out the water in favor of chicken broth—an easy fix—and added a bit of flour for thickening. We bulked up the vegetables, adding a carrot and turnip along with the potato. Since our lamb was already cooked, we simply stirred it in at the end. Unfortunately, because we weren't cooking the lamb directly in the stew, the broth still lacked the meaty flavor we desired. Although not traditional, we added a bit of tomato paste, soy sauce, and thyme to our broth in the hope of developing a rich, savory flavor. These touches added just the right amount of meatiness. A bit of parsley stirred in at the end added herbal freshness, and our lamb stew was complete.

For our final recipe, we traveled across the Mediterranean to Greece for a refreshing salad. Traditional Greek salad is a lettuce-free mixture of chopped vegetables tossed in an herby vinaigrette with creamy, briny feta cheese and meaty olives. For a dinner-size, filling salad, we decided to take a cue from American-style Greek restaurants and add lettuce back to the mix. First, we assembled our dressing, combining olive oil, red wine vinegar, oregano, and garlic, and used this to marinate a thinly sliced cucumber and shallot. The dressing added tang to the cucumber and mellowed the bite of the shallot. To our dressing, cucumber, and shallot we added the lamb, chopped romaine, halved cherry tomatoes, and fresh mint. A sprinkling of crumbled feta and some chopped kalamata olives were the final touches on our lamb-enhanced Greek salad.

Roast Boneless Leg of Lamb with Pomegranate Glaze

SERVES 2, WITH LEFTOVERS

You can use the leftovers to make two of the following recipes: Lamb Shawarma (page 212), Irish Stew (page 213), and/or Greek Salad with Lamb (page 213). We prefer to use the sirloin end of the leg for this recipe, although the shank end can be used as well. We found that leaving a ⅛-inch-thick layer of fat on top of the leg of lamb is ideal; if your leg of lamb has a thicker fat cap, trim it to be about ⅛ inch thick. These two roasts are usually sold in elastic netting that must be removed before cooking. We prefer this roast cooked to medium-rare, but if you prefer it more or less done, see our guidelines in "Testing Meat for Doneness" on page 149.

 2 **cups pomegranate juice**
 ⅓ **cup sugar**
 3 **sprigs fresh thyme**
 2 **tablespoons olive oil**
 2 **tablespoons minced fresh parsley**
 1 **tablespoon minced fresh rosemary or**
    1 teaspoon dried
 2 **garlic cloves, minced**
 1 **(3¾-pound) butterflied boneless half leg of lamb**
    (see note)
    Salt and pepper

1. Adjust oven rack to lower-middle position and heat oven to 375 degrees. Simmer pomegranate juice, sugar, and thyme together in small saucepan over medium heat until thickened and reduced to ½ cup, about 20 minutes. Discard thyme and reserve half of glaze separately for serving.

2. Combine 1 tablespoon oil, parsley, rosemary, and garlic in bowl. Following photos on page 210, lay lamb with rough, boned side facing up and pound to uniform 1-inch thickness. Season with salt and pepper and spread herb mixture evenly over lamb. Roll and tie roast.

3. Set wire rack inside large rimmed baking sheet lined with aluminum foil. Pat roast dry with paper towels and season with salt and pepper. Heat remaining 1 tablespoon oil in 12-inch skillet over medium-high heat until just smoking. Brown roast well on all sides, about 10 minutes.

4. Transfer roast to prepared wire rack, seam side down, and brush with about half of glaze reserved for cooking. Roast until very center of meat registers 100 degrees on instant-read thermometer, 20 to 30 minutes.

5. Brush lamb with remaining glaze reserved for cooking and pour ¼ cup water into baking sheet. Continue to roast lamb until center of meat registers 125 degrees (for medium-rare), 25 to 35 minutes longer.

6. Transfer lamb to carving board and brush with half of glaze reserved for serving. Tent lamb loosely with foil and let rest for 20 minutes. Remove twine and brush with remaining glaze reserved for serving. (If glaze has solidified, microwave for 10 to 30 seconds to melt.) Slice lamb thin and serve.

Lamb Shawarma

SERVES 2

The cooked lamb in this dish comes from Roast Boneless Leg of Lamb with Pomegranate Glaze on page 211. For easier slicing, place the lamb in the freezer for 15 minutes before slicing. If you don't have tahini, you can make the sauce without it, but you may need to increase the amount of seasonings.

YOGURT-TAHINI SAUCE
- 2 tablespoons yogurt
- 1 tablespoon tahini
- 1 tablespoon lemon juice
- 1 teaspoon minced fresh parsley
- 1 small garlic clove, minced
- Salt and pepper

SANDWICHES
- 1 tablespoon olive oil
- ½ teaspoon ground cumin
- ½ teaspoon ground coriander
- ¼ teaspoon ground cardamom
- 8 ounces cooked lamb (see note), shaved thin (about 1¾ cups) (see photo)
- 2 tablespoons minced fresh parsley
- Salt and pepper
- 2 (8-inch) pita breads, warmed (see page 203)
- 1 cup chopped lettuce
- 1 plum tomato, chopped
- 1 shallot, sliced thin

1. FOR THE YOGURT-TAHINI SAUCE: Combine yogurt, tahini, lemon juice, parsley, garlic, and ⅛ teaspoon salt in bowl. Season with salt and pepper to taste, cover, and refrigerate until needed.

2. FOR THE SANDWICHES: Heat oil in 10-inch non-stick skillet over medium-high heat until shimmering. Add cumin, coriander, and cardamom and cook, stirring constantly, until fragrant and just beginning to brown, about 1 minute. Add lamb and cook until pieces begin to crisp, 3 to 5 minutes. Off heat, stir in 1 tablespoon parsley and season with salt and pepper to taste.

3. Spread 2 tablespoons yogurt-tahini sauce in center of each warmed pita. Divide lamb mixture evenly between 2 pitas. Top with remaining 1 tablespoon parsley, lettuce, tomato, and shallot. Wrap pitas around filling and serve.

NOTES FROM THE TEST KITCHEN

SHAVING LAMB

For easier slicing, place the lamb in the freezer for 15 minutes. Then, using a sharp knife, shave thin slices off the roast.

Irish Stew

SERVES 2

The cooked lamb for this recipe comes from Roast Boneless Leg of Lamb with Pomegranate Glaze on page 211. Be sure to stir in the lamb gently in step 3 so that the pieces remain intact and cook it only until heated through.

 1 tablespoon vegetable oil
 1 onion, chopped medium
   Salt and pepper
 1 tablespoon flour
 2 teaspoons tomato paste
 1 teaspoon soy sauce
 ½ teaspoon dried thyme
1½ cups low-sodium chicken broth
 1 small Yukon Gold potato (about 6 ounces),
   peeled and cut into 1-inch pieces
 1 carrot, peeled, halved, and cut into
   1-inch pieces
 1 turnip, peeled and cut into 1-inch pieces
7½ ounces cooked lamb (see note), chopped into 1-inch
   pieces (about 1½ cups)
 2 tablespoons minced fresh parsley

1. Heat oil in medium saucepan over medium-high heat until shimmering. Add onion and ¼ teaspoon salt and cook until softened and browned, 8 to 10 minutes. Add flour, tomato paste, soy sauce, and thyme and cook until fragrant, about 1 minute.

2. Stir in broth, scraping up any browned bits, and bring to simmer. Add potato, carrot, and turnip, reduce heat to low, and simmer, covered, until vegetables are tender, 25 to 35 minutes.

3. Gently stir in lamb and continue to simmer, covered, until heated through, about 2 minutes longer. Off heat, stir in parsley, season with salt and pepper to taste, and serve.

Greek Salad with Lamb

SERVES 2

The cooked lamb for this recipe comes from Roast Boneless Leg of Lamb with Pomegranate Glaze on page 211. While the onion and cucumber marinate in the dressing, prepare the other salad ingredients. See page 163 for a recipe to use up the leftover feta cheese.

DRESSING

 5 tablespoons extra-virgin olive oil
 2 tablespoons red wine vinegar
 1 small garlic clove, minced
 ½ teaspoon minced fresh oregano or
   ⅛ teaspoon dried
   Salt and pepper
   Pinch sugar

SALAD

 1 cucumber, peeled, halved lengthwise, seeded
   (see photo), and sliced ⅛ inch thick
 1 shallot, sliced thin
10 ounces cooked lamb (see note), sliced ⅛ inch thick
   (about 2 cups)
 1 heart romaine lettuce (about 6 ounces),
   torn into bite-size pieces
 6 ounces grape or cherry tomatoes (about 1 cup),
   halved
 1 tablespoon minced fresh mint or parsley
 3 ounces feta cheese, crumbled (about ¾ cup)
 ¼ cup kalamata olives, pitted and quartered

1. FOR THE DRESSING: Whisk olive oil, vinegar, garlic, oregano, ¼ teaspoon salt, and sugar together in large bowl. Season with salt and pepper to taste.

2. FOR THE SALAD: Add cucumber and shallot to bowl with dressing and toss to combine. Let sit at room temperature until flavors blend, about 20 minutes. Add lamb, romaine, tomatoes, and mint and gently toss to combine. Divide salad between 2 plates, sprinkle with feta and olives, and serve.

NOTES FROM THE TEST KITCHEN

SEEDING A CUCUMBER

Peel and halve the cucumber lengthwise. Run a small spoon inside each cucumber half to scoop out the seeds and surrounding liquid.

SLOW-COOKER BEEF CHILI

CHAPTER 8

SLOW-COOKER FAVORITES

SLOW-COOKER LEMONY CHICKEN AND POTATOES

A CLASSIC COMBINATION, CHICKEN AND POTATOES can be prepared in a multitude of ways. One stellar example is a version from Chicago known as chicken Vesuvio, which consists of bone-in chicken and potatoes smothered in a garlicky white wine sauce, brightened by lemon and garnished with peas. Typically, the chicken and potatoes are browned, then a sauce is built by sautéing aromatics in the rendered fat and deglazing with white wine. Finally, everything is combined in a roasting pan and baked in the oven before the sauce is reduced even further. We thought this regional favorite would be a perfect candidate for our slow cooker, cutting down on both dishwashing and time spent in the kitchen. The challenge would lie in keeping the flavors bold and multi-dimensional, because the moist heat of the slow cooker tends to mute flavors. We addressed the chicken first.

Initial testing showed us that bone-in chicken pieces were the best choice, as the bones helped to keep the chicken moist during the long cooking time. Chicken breasts proved a good cut and are a reliable option when cooking for two. Additionally, two breasts left plenty of available real estate for the potatoes.

Many slow-cooker recipes claim to save time by having you throw raw chicken into the slow cooker, so we decided to test this and find out if we could skip the browning as well. We placed two unbrowned chicken breasts in one slow cooker. In a second cooker we placed two breasts that we'd seared in a skillet. Both were covered with a basic sauce of wine, chicken broth, and sautéed aromatics. A few hours later, tasters got out their forks. After sampling both, we found that the browned chicken boasted richer, deeper flavor than the unbrowned chicken. Why? Sautéing the breasts had led to the development of a rich, flavorful fond on the bottom of the skillet that we could then use to sauté the aromatics, thereby giving some depth to our white wine sauce. To ensure that the finished dish wasn't greasy, we removed the skin from the browned chicken before we placed it in the slow cooker.

NOTES FROM THE TEST KITCHEN

SLOW-COOKING FOR TWO

Using a slow cooker is a great way for the time-pressed cook to get supper on the table—no close monitoring of the stovetop or oven necessary. But most slow-cooker recipes make enough food to feed a crowd. In this chapter, you'll find an array of slow-cooker recipes scaled down to serve just two. We developed these recipes with an oval 3- to 3½-quart slow cooker because we found it to be easier to maneuver and clean, more affordable, and less space-hogging than larger slow cookers, but this collection of recipes works equally well in a standard 6-quart slow cooker. After developing lots of slow-cooker recipes over the years, we've learned a few tricks for ensuring success, no matter the size of your slow cooker.

SPRAY YOUR SLOW COOKER: Spraying the sides of the insert with vegetable oil spray, before adding food, eliminates any sticking (or burning) and makes cleanup easier.

USE THE MICROWAVE: When there is no need to get out a skillet to brown meat, use the microwave to cook the aromatics and bloom the flavors of any spices. We also use the microwave to jump-start the cooking of vegetables and render excess fat from meat, as with our Pesto Meatballs and Marinara (see page 225).

BROWN YOUR MEAT—SOMETIMES: In recipes that use a lot of spicy or aromatic ingredients, we've found that we can get away with not browning. But when a deep flavor base is required, we need to get out the skillet and brown the meat. When it comes to ground beef, we found that browning is important for meat that is tender and not grainy at the end of the long cooking time.

KEEP GROUND BEEF TENDER WITH A PANADE: Ground beef can become tough and sandy after hours in the slow cooker. To keep ground beef tender, we use a panade, a mixture of bread and dairy, which we mix with the meat before cooking.

INCLUDE FLAVOR-AMPLIFYING INGREDIENTS FOR DEPTH: We've found that a handful of key ingredients, such as tomato paste and soy sauce, can increase meaty richness and depth of flavor substantially, especially when we're not browning the meat.

MAKE A FOIL PACKET: Depending on the cooking time and how the vegetables are cut, it is sometimes necessary to wrap vegetables in an aluminum foil packet to keep them from overcooking. The packet helps keep them out of the cooking liquid and slows down their cooking, protecting their flavors from fading.

To prevent the delicate white meat of our chicken breasts from overcooking, we set our cooker to the low setting, which allows the chicken time to gradually cook through without drying out. We also found that laying the chicken on the bottom of the slow cooker, so that it was covered by the liquid and potatoes as much as possible, insulated the chicken, helping to keep it moist.

As for the potatoes, waxy red potatoes were the best choice; they held their shape and texture during cooking and also contributed some color. Fluffy russets broke down too much, and Yukon Golds stayed too firm. We cut our potatoes into 1-inch chunks and parcooked them in the microwave for a few minutes, until they were just beginning to soften, to jump-start their cooking.

Finally, we zeroed in on the flavor of the sauce, which we prepared using the rich, flavorful bits left behind from browning the chicken. For the aromatics, we stayed true to tradition, sautéing plenty of garlic and oregano with the onion, as well as a pinch of red pepper flakes. We then added flour to thicken the sauce before deglazing the pan with white wine and chicken broth. (We waited until the end of cooking to add the peas and lemon juice to retain their vibrancy.)

This sauce tasted promising going into the slow cooker, but even after the relatively short cooking time (about three hours proved sufficient for our chicken), it tasted a little flat. For more assertive flavor, we decided to add a little rosemary. If added at the beginning of cooking, the rosemary tasted medicinal and overbearing. Chopped raw rosemary stirred in at the end tasted raw and harsh, and the rosemary speckled the dish like grass clippings. To tame this woodsy herb, we steeped a small sprig of it in the sauce during the last 15 minutes of cooking, which permeated the dish with a marked but mellow rosemary flavor. Using a sprig, which we then discarded, avoided the distracting look of chopped rosemary and happily reduced prep time.

A little lemon zest, in addition to the juice, further brightened the dish. To enhance the garlic flavor, we stirred in an additional clove of raw garlic with the lemon juice and zest, to release its perfume and sharpness. Employing this one-two garlic punch (both cooked and raw) created layers of flavor and imparted both piquancy and depth. Finally, this Chicago favorite was now easy enough to prepare as a weeknight dinner for two—and it didn't require an army of dishwashers.

NOTES FROM THE TEST KITCHEN

MINCING GARLIC TO A PASTE

In some recipes that use garlic raw, the minced garlic must be smooth for even distribution. Adding a pinch of salt, then dragging a chef's knife over the top to make a fine paste, helps break down the garlic further.

Slow-Cooker Lemony Chicken and Potatoes
SERVES 2

Make sure to use a small sprig of rosemary or else its flavor will be overpowering. *Cooking time: 3 to 4 hours on low*

- 2 (12-ounce) bone-in, skin-on split chicken breasts, trimmed (see page 63)
  Salt and pepper
- 4 teaspoons extra-virgin olive oil
- 1 small onion, minced
- 3 garlic cloves, minced to a paste (see photo)
- 1 teaspoon minced fresh oregano or
  ¼ teaspoon dried
  Pinch red pepper flakes
- 1 tablespoon unbleached all-purpose flour
- ¼ cup dry white wine
- ½ cup low-sodium chicken broth
- 12 ounces red potatoes (about 2 medium), cut into 1-inch chunks
- 1 small sprig fresh rosemary (see note)
- ½ cup frozen peas, thawed
- ⅛ teaspoon grated lemon zest plus 1½ teaspoons fresh lemon juice

1. Lightly spray inside of slow cooker with vegetable oil spray. Pat chicken dry with paper towels and season with salt and pepper. Heat 2 teaspoons oil in 10-inch skillet over medium-high heat until just smoking. Add chicken, skin side down, and brown lightly, about 5 minutes. Transfer chicken to plate, let cool slightly, then remove and discard skin; transfer chicken to slow cooker with any accumulated juice.

2. Add onion to fat left in pan and cook over medium heat until softened and lightly browned, 5 to 7 minutes. Stir in two-thirds of garlic, oregano, and red pepper flakes and cook until fragrant, about 30 seconds. Stir in flour and cook for 1 minute. Slowly whisk in wine, scraping up any browned bits and smoothing out any lumps. Off heat, whisk in broth until combined and transfer to slow cooker.

3. Toss potatoes with remaining 2 teaspoons oil in microwave-safe bowl and season with salt and pepper. Cover and microwave, stirring occasionally, until potatoes are nearly tender, about 5 minutes. Transfer to slow cooker. Cover and cook until chicken is tender, 3 to 4 hours on low.

4. Add rosemary sprig, cover, and cook on high until rosemary is fragrant, about 15 minutes. Transfer chicken and potatoes to serving platter and tent loosely with foil. Remove and discard rosemary. Stir in peas and let sit until heated through, about 5 minutes. Stir in remaining garlic, lemon zest, and lemon juice and season with salt and pepper to taste. Spoon ½ cup sauce over chicken and serve, passing remaining sauce separately.

SLOW-COOKER CURRIED CHICKEN BREASTS

WHEN MADE WELL, CURRY DISHES SHOWCASE complex layers of flavor, yet at the same time are light and clean-tasting. It is this intricate, deep flavor that makes curries well suited to the slow cooker—their strong and complex flavors hold up well even after hours of cooking. Following up on the success of our lemony chicken (see page 217), we decided to add chicken curry to our slow-cooker repertoire.

Authentic Indian curries can be notoriously complicated affairs, with lengthy ingredient lists and fussy techniques. Most streamlined recipes we tried, however, were uninspired, and others, overloaded with spices, were harsh and overpowering. We wanted to create a chicken curry dish that was mild but flavor-packed, with a light but substantial sauce that would hold its own when served over couscous or rice. And perhaps most important, we wanted to keep things simple by preparing our recipe in the slow cooker.

For the chicken, we started with two bone-in split breasts, which have a milder flavor than dark meat, making them the perfect neutral palette on which we could showcase bold curry flavor. We hoped that for this potently flavored dish, browning would not be necessary. For our Lemony Chicken and Potatoes, we browned the chicken, but we suspected that in our curry dish, the spices would more than make up for any flavor lost by not browning. Before adding the breasts to the slow cooker, we simply removed the skin (to prevent the final sauce from becoming overly greasy) and seasoned the meat with salt and pepper.

Next, we considered the spices and aromatics. We debated making our own curry powder, but we thought it would be silly to do this when we needed only a small amount; in the end, store-bought curry powder worked fine. For aromatics, we found that a traditional combination of onion, garlic, and ginger worked well and provided a great flavor base for our curry. Since we didn't have fond left over from browning the chicken in which to sauté and flavor our aromatics, we wondered if we could just add them raw to the slow cooker. The result was, unsurprisingly, crunchy, sour onions. In lieu of sautéing, we settled on microwaving the aromatics with a little bit of oil to soften them and bring out their flavors.

Thinking we needed to use a heavy hand with the spices, we started with a full tablespoon of curry powder, but tasters complained that the resulting dish tasted harsh and dusty. We backed down on the curry powder, finally settling on a teaspoon. Coaxing the maximum flavor from dried spices typically requires blooming them in hot oil; for our recipe we achieved similar results by microwaving the curry powder along with the aromatics. We added the microwaved mixture to the slow cooker with some chicken broth, which provided the liquid component for the sauce.

So far this curry was promising, but tasters complained that something was missing. We wondered if tomatoes would brighten the overall flavor of our dish. We tried adding diced tomatoes with their juice, but the resulting sauce was watery. Next we tried crushed tomatoes and microwaved them along with the aromatics with the hope of coaxing out more flavor. This, too, fell short of our expectations. The solution turned out to be as simple as adding tomato paste to the rest of the

SLOW-COOKER CURRIED CHICKEN BREASTS

aromatics. The tomato paste lent flavor and body to the dish, and cooking the paste in the microwave intensified its flavor, but we found the sauce was still on the thin side and not clinging to the chicken.

For thickening, many slow-cooker recipes turn to flour or cornstarch, mixed with a small amount of liquid to create a slurry, which is stirred in at the end of the cooking time. While both of these options worked, the flour imparted a raw taste and the cornstarch required at least a little extra cooking time to properly thicken the liquid. We found a substitute, however, in instant tapioca; this ingredient was ideal because it imparted no off-flavors and it could be added to the slow cooker with the broth, no extra steps required. Two teaspoons gave our curry just the right amount of body.

Finally, most curry recipes also include yogurt or coconut milk to add richness. Though we liked both, tasters felt yogurt had a cleaner flavor. A few tablespoons of plain yogurt stirred into the finished sauce added a creamy, tangy richness that brought the dish together. Tempering the yogurt with some of the hot sauce ensured that it didn't curdle.

A few final additions rounded out the dish. Toward the end of cooking, we added raisins for a subtle sweetness. A garnish of toasted sliced almonds added crunch, and minced cilantro lent a fresh touch. We had created a satisfying, potently flavored chicken curry for two—and we didn't even have to fire up a burner.

NOTES FROM THE TEST KITCHEN

THE BEST CURRY POWDER
Though blends can vary dramatically, curry powders come in two basic styles: mild or sweet, and a hotter version called Madras. The former is a combination of as many as 20 different ground spices, herbs, and seeds, the staples being turmeric (which accounts for the traditional ocher color), coriander, cumin, black and red pepper, cinnamon, cloves, fennel seeds, cardamom, ginger, and fenugreek. After tasting six curry powders—mixed into rice pilaf and in a vegetable curry—we determined our favorite: **Penzeys Sweet Curry Powder.** We found it to be neither too sweet nor too hot, while still being balanced yet complex.

Slow-Cooker Curried Chicken Breasts
SERVES 2

We prefer the richness of whole-milk yogurt for this recipe. Serve with couscous or rice. *Cooking time: 3 to 4 hours on low*

- 2 (12-ounce) bone-in split chicken breasts, skin removed, trimmed (see page 63)
  Salt and pepper
- 1 small onion, minced
- 2 garlic cloves, minced
- 2 teaspoons minced or grated fresh ginger
- 1 teaspoon curry powder
- 1 teaspoon vegetable oil
- 1 teaspoon tomato paste
- ¾ cup low-sodium chicken broth
- 2 teaspoons Minute tapioca
- 2 tablespoons raisins
- 3 tablespoons plain whole-milk yogurt (see note)
- 1 tablespoon minced fresh cilantro
- 2 tablespoons sliced almonds, toasted (see page 240)

1. Lightly spray inside of slow cooker with vegetable oil spray. Season chicken with salt and pepper and place in slow cooker.

2. Combine onion, garlic, ginger, curry powder, oil, and tomato paste in microwave-safe bowl. Microwave, stirring occasionally, until onion is softened, about 5 minutes; transfer to slow cooker. Stir in broth and tapioca. Cover and cook until chicken is tender, 3 to 4 hours on low.

3. Stir in raisins, cover, and cook on high until raisins are heated through, about 10 minutes. Transfer chicken to serving platter and tent loosely with foil.

4. In small bowl, combine ¼ cup hot braising liquid with yogurt (to temper), then stir mixture back into slow cooker. Stir in cilantro and season with salt and pepper to taste. Spoon ½ cup sauce over chicken, sprinkle with almonds, and serve, passing remaining sauce separately.

SLOW-COOKER BEEF CHILI

AMONG ALL THE RECIPES FOR SLOW-COOKER BEEF chili, not many produce a chili that's any good. Recipes we've seen tend to result in either watery, bland, Sloppy Joe–ish chili or a thick, sludgy, tarlike mixture speckled with bits of ground beef. We were looking for a hearty, all-American, ground beef chili, with rich, long-simmered flavor and a thick, substantial texture.

We started by choosing the meat. We found that 85 percent lean ground beef provided meaty flavor and ample richness; 80 percent lean ground beef gave us a greasy chili, and 90 percent lean ground beef produced a lean-tasting chili. Using a pound of beef ensured we'd have enough for a second bowl or lunch the next day (chili is a dish that tastes just as good a day later).

In some recipes we came across, the raw beef was simply tossed into the slow cooker. We decided to test this early on to see if it would work. Using a basic working recipe, we added our raw ground beef, along with a few sautéed aromatics, to the slow cooker. But the chili from this batch was, not surprisingly, lacking in flavor. For our next test, we cooked the ground beef for a few minutes, with aromatics, before transferring it all to the slow cooker. This quick step of browning the meat deepened the flavor of our chili exponentially.

With our beef at the ready, we could narrow down the aromatics. A base of onion and garlic provided a nice, savory backbone. We tried a handful of other vegetables as well, including bell pepper, celery, and carrots, but tasters felt they were distracting. Sautéing the aromatics with the ground beef helped to jump-start their cooking and made for a chili with richer flavor.

Next we considered the seasonings. After experimenting with quantities, we eventually settled on 2 tablespoons of chili powder. Though this seems like a lot, even for chili, we found that any less didn't provide potent chili flavor and noticeable heat. One and a half teaspoons each of cumin and oregano, plus a small amount of red pepper flakes, rounded out our spices. However, tasters felt something was missing. Although we didn't want a chili with killer heat, we did want real warmth and depth of flavor, so we added just a touch of cayenne pepper. Sautéing the spices with the aromatics helped develop their flavors fully.

At this point, we decided our chili could use more heft. Tasters liked the chunky, substantial bites provided by a can each of kidney beans and diced tomatoes, but the chili still needed more body. We paired the diced tomatoes with a can of tomato sauce, which provided a good balance of smooth and chunky textures. Considering other tomato products, tasters also liked the addition of a small amount of tomato paste, which we sautéed with the aromatics to give the chili a deeper, sweeter tomato flavor.

The flavor of the chili was close now, but when we removed the lid of our slow cooker, we had an unforeseen problem—our chili had a sandy, dry texture because of the long cooking time. Using a fattier cut, like 80 percent lean ground beef, would only result in greasy chili. So we looked for a different solution. When making meatballs and meatloaf, we often use

NOTES FROM THE TEST KITCHEN

THE BEST DICED TOMATOES
We rely on diced tomatoes for everything from tomato sauce to chili to soups and stews. But supermarket shelves are teeming with different brands of diced tomatoes. To make sense of the selection, we gathered 16 widely available styles and brands and tasted them plain and in tomato sauce, rating them on tomato flavor, saltiness, sweetness, texture, and overall appeal.

To our surprise, nearly half of the brands fell short. The lowest-rated tomatoes were awful, eliciting complaints like "mushy, gruel-like texture" and "rubbery and sour." We found that various factors, such as geography and additives, played into whether a sample rated highly. Our top-ranked tomatoes were grown in California, source of most of the world's tomatoes, where the dry, hot growing season develops sweet, complex flavor; the bottom-ranked brands came from the Midwest and Pennsylvania. We tasted tomatoes that were too sweet or too acidic (from not enough or too much citric acid) or bland from lack of salt. Tasters overwhelmingly favored those brands with more salt. In fact, the tomatoes with the least salt—125 mg per serving compared to 310 mg in the top-rated brand—ranked last. In the end, one can stood out from the pack. **Hunt's Diced Tomatoes** were our tasters' favorite, praised for being "fresh" and "bright," with a "sweet-tart" flavor and "juicy," "firm, crisp-tender chunks."

a panade, a mixture of milk and bread, to keep the ground beef moist. We wondered if this would work here. For our next test, we mixed a paste made from a slice of bread and a few tablespoons of milk with the raw ground beef. Though unconventional, the panade was a success, keeping the beef tender even after cooking for hours in the slow cooker.

With the core components of our recipe set, we needed to make some minor adjustments to the seasoning. The amounts of chili powder, oregano, and cumin were all fine, but the heat level wasn't translating quite right after the long cooking time. After some tinkering, we decided to decrease the amount of red pepper flakes (to ¼ teaspoon) and omit the cayenne entirely in favor of another form of heat that would also add some smokiness: canned chipotle chiles packed in adobo sauce. A single teaspoon added the complex background flavor that our slow-cooker chili had been lacking. To amp up the meaty flavor of our chili, we stirred in a small amount of soy sauce, an ingredient we have found adds meaty depth of flavor without calling attention to itself. Finally, a small amount of brown sugar lent our recipe a nice sweetness that balanced out the soy sauce and chipotles.

Though small in scale, our slow-cooker beef chili was big on meatiness and flavor.

Slow-Cooker Beef Chili

SERVES 2 WITH LEFTOVERS

Do not use beef any leaner than 85 percent or the chili will be lean and not as rich-tasting. Serve with lime wedges, minced fresh cilantro, chopped tomato, minced onion or scallions, diced avocado, shredded cheddar or Monterey Jack cheese, and/or sour cream. *Cooking time: 6 to 7 hours on low or 3 to 4 hours on high*

- 1 slice high-quality white sandwich bread, torn in half
- 3 tablespoons whole milk
- 1 pound 85 percent lean ground beef (see note)
  Salt and pepper
- 1 tablespoon vegetable oil
- 1 onion, minced
- 2 tablespoons chili powder
- 2 tablespoons tomato paste
- 3 garlic cloves, minced
- 1½ teaspoons ground cumin
- 1½ teaspoons minced fresh oregano or ½ teaspoon dried

- ¼ teaspoon red pepper flakes
- 1 (15-ounce) can tomato sauce
- 1 (15-ounce) can red kidney beans, drained and rinsed
- 1 (14.5-ounce) can diced tomatoes
- 1½ tablespoons soy sauce
- 1½ teaspoons brown sugar
- 1 teaspoon minced canned chipotle chile in adobo sauce

1. Lightly spray inside of slow cooker with vegetable oil spray. Mash bread and milk into paste in large bowl using fork. Mix in ground beef, ¼ teaspoon salt, and ¼ teaspoon pepper using hands.

2. Heat oil in 10-inch skillet over medium heat until shimmering. Add onion, chili powder, tomato paste, garlic, cumin, oregano, and red pepper flakes and cook until lightly browned, 5 to 7 minutes. Stir in beef mixture and cook, breaking up any large pieces with wooden spoon, until no longer pink, about 2 minutes. Stir in tomato sauce, scraping up any browned bits; transfer to slow cooker.

3. Stir beans, diced tomatoes with juice, soy sauce, sugar, and chipotles into slow cooker. Cover and cook until beef is tender, 6 to 7 hours on low or 3 to 4 hours on high.

4. Let chili settle for 5 minutes, then remove fat from surface using large spoon. Break up any remaining large pieces of beef with spoon. Season with salt and pepper to taste and serve.

SLOW-COOKER HEARTY BEEF STEW

RECIPES FOR SLOW-COOKER BEEF STEW CAN BE divided into two camps. In one, the meat, vegetables, and seasonings are simply dumped into a pot and left to their own devices. Effortless, yes. But flavorful? Not usually. The second type of stew, in which the meat is browned before it goes into the slow cooker, is the more flavorful stew. Here the foundation for flavor is built on the browned bits left behind (the fond), which are the backbone of the stew's sauce. But this browning can take a good chunk of time, adding precious minutes to the time it takes the hurried cook to prep the recipe and leave for work. For a simple meal for two, we wanted a faster alternative. Our goal was a richly flavored beef stew—with all the nuance of a slow-simmered beef stew, but with minimal prep and labor.

Our first decision was the cut of beef. For our standard beef stew, we usually start with a chuck-eye roast, which typically weighs about 4 or 5 pounds, clearly much more meat than we would need for a stew for two. Looking for a more appropriate option for two, we turned to blade steak. It's inexpensive, and its generous marbling of fat keeps it tender and flavorful when braised. Being that we were making a classic, ultra-satisfying stew, we wanted to have a little extra leftover and so opted to use just under 2 pounds of steaks.

We knew that in order to cut the step of browning our beef, we needed to come up with a flavor replacement for the fond. We tried an array of "browning sauces," like Gravy Master and Kitchen Bouquet, as well as bouillon cubes. In the end, the winning solution was a combination of tricks. First off, we enlisted the help of tomato paste, which we microwaved with the onion and other aromatics before adding them to the slow cooker. This step helped create a rich, complex base and also took care of the problem with throwing raw onions into the slow cooker, which tasters agreed made the stew taste vegetal; also, using the microwave ensured that we were left with no pots or pans to clean. To further pump up the meaty notes of our stew, we relied on a combination of chicken and beef broths, though it was the addition of soy sauce, which we've used before in the test kitchen to impart rich, beefy notes, that finally took this stew to the next level.

The next question was how to thicken our stew. As with our Curried Chicken Breasts (page 220), we bypassed the usual flour and cornstarch, instead selecting tapioca as the thickener. The tapioca could be added directly to the slow cooker—no precooking or extra steps needed—and it thickened our stew to just the right velvety texture.

Moving on, we wanted to find a way to perk up the vegetables that seemed to suffer dramatically in the slow cooker. Somehow we'd need to insulate our carrots and potatoes to protect them. Looking around the test kitchen, we hit on the notion of wrapping them in aluminum foil. We placed our vegetables on one half of a sheet of foil, then folded the other half over the top and crimped the edges to make sure they were sealed. We put the packet on top of the beef in the slow cooker and let the appliance do its job. When we

opened the packet and poured the tender vegetables and their juice back into the stew at the end of cooking, the results were great. The carrots were perfectly cooked and the potatoes were intact. We stirred in thawed frozen peas at the same time to ensure that they were just heated through.

Finally, we had a slow-cooker beef stew for two that was easy to make, tasted great, and left the cook with a lot of free time.

Slow-Cooker Hearty Beef Stew

SERVES 2 WITH LEFTOVERS

Wrapping the vegetables in a foil packet prevents them from falling apart during the extended time in the slow cooker. *Cooking time: 9 to 10 hours on low or 5 to 6 hours on high*

1¾	pounds blade steaks, trimmed (see page 223) and cut into 1½-inch chunks
	Salt and pepper
1	onion, minced
4	teaspoons vegetable oil
4	teaspoons tomato paste
2	garlic cloves, minced
1	teaspoon minced fresh thyme or ¼ teaspoon dried
½	cup low-sodium chicken broth, plus extra as needed
½	cup beef broth
1½	tablespoons soy sauce
1	tablespoon Minute tapioca
1	bay leaf
8	ounces red potatoes (1 to 2 medium), cut into ¾-inch chunks
2	carrots, peeled, halved lengthwise, and sliced ¾ inch thick
⅔	cup frozen peas, thawed

1. Lightly spray inside of slow cooker with vegetable oil spray. Season beef with salt and pepper and place in slow cooker.

2. Combine onion, 1 tablespoon oil, tomato paste, garlic, and thyme in microwave-safe bowl. Microwave, stirring occasionally, until onion is softened, about 5 minutes; transfer to slow cooker. Stir chicken broth, beef broth, soy sauce, tapioca, and bay leaf into slow cooker.

3. Toss potatoes and carrots with remaining 1 teaspoon oil, season with salt and pepper, and wrap in foil packet following photos on page 223. Lay foil packet on top of stew. Cover and cook until beef is tender, 9 to 10 hours on low or 5 to 6 hours on high.

4. Transfer foil packet to large plate. Let stew settle for 5 minutes, then remove fat using large spoon. Remove and discard bay leaf.

5. Carefully open foil packet (watch for steam) and stir vegetables with any accumulated juice into stew. Stir in peas and let sit until heated through, about 5 minutes. (Adjust stew consistency with additional hot broth as needed.) Season with salt and pepper to taste and serve.

SLOW-COOKER PESTO MEATBALLS AND MARINARA

MAKING MEATBALLS AND MARINARA IS USUALLY A Sunday project; preparing and shaping the meatballs, as well as slowly simmering a tomato sauce, can be an all-day affair. And if you're going to spend that much time preparing a meal, you might as well make enough to serve a crowd. We wanted to streamline this time-intensive recipe and move it to a slow cooker, so it could simmer unattended, but we still wanted moist, light meatballs, coated in a sauce that had the depth and complexity of a traditional sauce—and our recipe had to serve just two.

We focused on the meatballs first. Meatballs are often made of some combination of ground beef, pork, and often veal, but when cooking for two, it's annoying to have to buy two or three types of ground meat. We opted to use only beef and settled on half a pound of 85 percent lean ground beef (leaner beef produced dry meatballs). But without the pork and veal, our all-beef meatballs were a little bland and tough. Most meatball recipes include aromatics for flavor as well as moisture. Adding onion and garlic was an improvement, but not enough; we knew our all-beef meatballs would need big flavor that could stand up to a few hours in a slow cooker. A test kitchen colleague suggested adding pesto to the meatballs; we were excited by the notion, so we decided to give it a try. Packed with fresh basil, pine nuts, garlic, and Parmesan, pesto (just a small amount) replaced the aromatics in our working recipe, providing our meatballs with bold basil and garlic flavor. (While we prefer the flavor of homemade pesto, store-bought refrigerated pesto makes a decent substitute.)

In addition to aromatics, meatballs require a few other ingredients to keep them moist and to bind them so they don't fall apart in the tomato sauce. Eggs are commonly used to contribute moisture and provide structure. We tested meatballs made with and without egg and quickly determined that the egg was a welcome addition, giving us a more tender meatball. For the binding ingredient, we considered two common candidates: bread soaked in milk (also known as a panade) and bread crumbs. With the addition of the pesto, we thought the bread soaked in milk would result in a meatball that was too soft and wouldn't hold up in the slow cooker. One test confirmed our suspicions. We tried bread crumbs next; they proved to be the right choice. The extra moisture from the pesto hydrated the bread nicely. We found that the flavor benefit of homemade bread crumbs was difficult to detect in this case, so we opted for the ease of store-bought bread crumbs. Now, however, our meatballs were somewhat sticky. To make them easier to handle, we omitted the egg white. Finally, we added a little extra Parmesan for a nutty tang.

In most meatball recipes the meatballs are first fried to help firm them up and rid them of excess grease, and the browned bits left in the pan after frying are then used to flavor the sauce. For this streamlined recipe, we hoped to avoid the grease-splattered mess that frying leaves behind on the stovetop. We thought of baking the meatballs in the oven to release some of their fat, but waiting for the oven to heat up didn't make this recipe any more convenient. Frustrated, we turned to the microwave, which we've used to jump-start the cooking of other foods. After just five minutes in the microwave, our meatballs had released some of their fat and set up enough to spend some time simmering in the slow cooker without breaking down.

Finally, we turned our attention to the sauce. We knew that without the flavorful browned bits from frying the meatballs, we would need to find other ways to boost flavor in our sauce. We started with a heavy dose of aromatics: one minced onion, four garlic cloves, 2 teaspoons of oregano, and a pinch of red pepper flakes.

Microwaving the aromatics with some olive oil brought out their flavor. Two tablespoons of red wine and a bay leaf gave the sauce complexity, and a tablespoon of soy sauce, an ingredient we use in the test kitchen to add savory flavor, contributed meaty depth.

For the tomato aspect of our sauce, we experimented with diced tomatoes, tomato puree, and crushed tomatoes. Diced tomatoes didn't blend into the sauce as much as we would have liked, and all of our tasters agreed that tomato puree was too sweet and too thick. Crushed tomatoes gave us both the fresh flavor and smooth, light texture that we were seeking. One 28-ounce can was enough to properly cover the meatballs in the slow cooker and yielded the right amount of sauce for two.

After transferring the sauce to the slow cooker and nestling the meatballs in the sauce, we let our cooker work its magic. We found that cooking them on the low setting of the slow cooker provided sufficient heat to cook them through (being that we'd already pre-cooked them in the microwave) while also keeping them tender, and it also concentrated the flavors of our marinara sauce.

A few hours later, we had a simple-to-prepare, yet hearty and satisfying, dish of meatballs and red sauce that didn't require all day in the kitchen—or result in a full week's worth of leftovers.

Slow-Cooker Pesto Meatballs and Marinara

MAKES ABOUT 3 CUPS SAUCE AND 6 MEATBALLS,
ENOUGH TO SAUCE 6 OUNCES PASTA

We prefer the flavor of our homemade pesto (recipe follows), but you can use your favorite store-bought brand from the refrigerated section of the supermarket—avoid shelf-stable jarred pesto sold in the grocery aisles. We like spaghetti with this sauce. *Cooking time: 3 to 4 hours on low*

8   ounces 85 percent lean ground beef
⅓   cup plain bread crumbs
⅓   cup fresh basil pesto (see note)
2   tablespoons grated Parmesan cheese
1   large egg yolk
    Salt and pepper
1   onion, minced

4 garlic cloves, minced

1 tablespoon extra-virgin olive oil

2 teaspoons minced fresh oregano or ½ teaspoon dried

   Pinch red pepper flakes

1 (28-ounce) can crushed tomatoes

2 tablespoons dry red wine

1 tablespoon soy sauce

1 bay leaf

1 tablespoon chopped fresh basil

1. Lightly spray inside of slow cooker with vegetable oil spray. Mix beef, bread crumbs, pesto, Parmesan, egg yolk, ¼ teaspoon salt, and ⅛ teaspoon pepper together in bowl using hands. Divide meat into 6 equal portions, then form each portion into a meatball. Arrange meatballs on large microwave-safe plate and microwave until fat renders and meatballs are firm, 4 to 6 minutes; set aside to cool slightly.

2. Combine onion, garlic, oil, oregano, and red pepper flakes in microwave-safe bowl. Microwave, stirring occasionally, until onion is softened, about 5 minutes; transfer to slow cooker. Stir tomatoes, wine, soy sauce, and bay leaf into slow cooker. Nestle meatballs in slow cooker, discarding rendered fat. Cover and cook until meatballs are tender, 3 to 4 hours on low.

3. Remove and discard bay leaf. Before serving, stir in basil and season with salt and pepper to taste.

Basic Basil Pesto

MAKES ABOUT ⅓ CUP

The pesto can be covered with a sheet of plastic wrap pressed flush against its surface and refrigerated for up to 3 days.

1 cup packed fresh basil leaves

3 tablespoons extra-virgin olive oil

1 tablespoon pine nuts, toasted (see page 240)

½ small garlic clove, minced

2 tablespoons grated Parmesan cheese

   Salt and pepper

Process basil, oil, nuts, and garlic together in food processor until smooth, scraping down bowl as needed. Transfer pesto to bowl, stir in Parmesan, and season with salt and pepper to taste.

SLOW-COOKER MEATY TOMATO SAUCE

WHILE WE LOVE THE RICH COMPLEXITY OF Bolognese, sometimes we want a simpler, more rustic sauce that still boasts great meatiness. Enter Italian pork ragu: pork that is slow-cooked with tomatoes and wine until fall-apart tender, at which point it's shredded and returned to the sauce. Served atop a steaming bowl of al dente pasta and crowned with grated cheese, this sauce is an expressive example of Italy's deeply comforting peasant food. Given its short list of ingredients and long simmering time, we thought it would be a perfect candidate for a slow-cooker version scaled for two.

We hoped this recipe would be as easy to prepare as it is to enjoy, although we weren't surprised when recipe after recipe produced lackluster results. Most were nothing more than a glorified marinara sauce with a few stray shreds of pork, and others featured tough bites of meat in a sharp, winey sauce. None was worth the hours of simmering required. We wanted a sauce that offered rich, meaty flavor, tender pork, and a balanced tomato and wine presence.

Figuring that determining the right cut of pork for this dish was the most important matter, we decided to start there. Boston butt—a fatty, tough cut from the shoulder that becomes tender when cooked slowly—would be ideal for this recipe, but this roast is much too large. Looking for pork cuts naturally sized for two, we considered pork tenderloin. Although very lean, one 12-ounce tenderloin would be just the right size. We whipped up a quick tomato sauce consisting of onion, garlic, olive oil, red wine, and diced tomatoes, then added it to the slow cooker with the tenderloin. Once cooked, the tenderloin was dry and tough, lacking the appropriate shredding consistency as well as the richness necessary to flavor the sauce. It was clear that we needed a cut of pork with more connective tissue and fat.

We decided to try spareribs, which are even fattier than Boston butt. The braised meat from spareribs was the best yet and the sauce was really starting to taste meaty; but unfortunately, spareribs are expensive, and an entire rack weighs 3 or more pounds—still more meat than we needed. Plus, pulling the meat off the bone was a pain. Looking for a more practical way to get the flavor we were after, we took a look at boneless

SLOW-COOKER MEATY TOMATO SAUCE

country-style ribs. Country-style ribs (which are cut from the back of the pig, not the belly) are inexpensive and easy to purchase in smaller amounts. These ribs cooked up nearly as tender and rich as the spareribs. The resulting sauce had enough meatiness that we found we could forgo the step of browning and throw them into the slow cooker raw.

With a promising foundation in place, we focused on perfecting our sauce. For aromatics, in addition to onion and garlic, we added some oregano and red pepper flakes. In lieu of sautéing our aromatics in a skillet, we decided to simplify things and microwave them instead, with a little oil, to soften them and build their flavor.

So far, tasters had liked the chunks of tomato provided by the 14.5-ounce can of diced tomatoes that we had been using, but since there is very little evaporation in a slow cooker, the sauce was on the watery side. To add body, we stirred in a small can of tomato sauce, as well as some tomato paste (which we microwaved with the aromatics). Finally, a tablespoon of soy sauce enhanced the meaty, savory notes of the sauce in lieu of any fond.

This sauce was exactly what we were looking for, rich and intensely flavored. With a sprinkle of fresh parsley, our Slow-Cooker Meaty Tomato Sauce was perfect.

Slow-Cooker Meaty Tomato Sauce

MAKES ABOUT 3½ CUPS, ENOUGH TO SAUCE 6 OUNCES PASTA

Try to buy country-style pork ribs with lots of fat and dark meat, and stay away from ribs that look overly lean with pale meat. Lean country-style pork ribs will taste very dry after the extended cooking time in the slow cooker. We like ziti with this sauce. *Cooking time: 6 to 7 hours on low or 3 to 4 hours on high*

- 12 ounces boneless country-style pork ribs, trimmed and cut into 1-inch chunks (see note)
     Salt and pepper
- 1 small onion, minced
- 3 garlic cloves, minced
- 1 tablespoon extra-virgin olive oil
- 2 teaspoons tomato paste
- 1½ teaspoons minced fresh oregano or ¼ teaspoon dried
     Pinch red pepper flakes
- 1 (14.5-ounce) can diced tomatoes, drained
- 1 (8-ounce) can tomato sauce
- 2 tablespoons dry red wine
- 1 tablespoon soy sauce
- 1 bay leaf
- 1 tablespoon minced fresh parsley

1. Lightly spray inside of slow cooker with vegetable oil spray. Season pork with salt and pepper and place in slow cooker.

2. Combine onion, garlic, oil, tomato paste, oregano, and red pepper flakes in microwave-safe bowl. Microwave, stirring occasionally, until onion is softened, about 5 minutes; transfer to slow cooker.

3. Stir tomatoes, tomato sauce, wine, soy sauce, and bay leaf into slow cooker. Cover and cook until pork is tender, 6 to 7 hours on low or 3 to 4 hours on high.

4. Let sauce settle for 5 minutes, then remove fat from surface using large spoon. Remove and discard bay leaf and break up pieces of pork with spoon. Before serving, stir in parsley and season with salt and pepper to taste.

SLOW-COOKER NEW MEXICAN RED PORK CHILI

VARIOUS REGIONS OF THE COUNTRY HAVE THEIR own take on chili (Texas and Cincinnati come to mind almost immediately), and New Mexico is no exception. In *carne adovada*, which literally translates to "marinated meat," meltingly tender chunks of pork butt are braised in an intense, richly flavored red chile sauce with hints of oregano, onion, and garlic. There's a definite focus on the chiles, which make this New Mexican dish smoky yet bright, spicy yet sweet, all at once. In addition to the prerequisite simmering on the stovetop for hours, most recipes require toasting and grinding a pile of dried New Mexico chiles (commonly Anaheims). We typically don't mind taking this extra step, but when cooking for two, we want an easier method. Our goals were clear. We wanted a streamlined, slow-cooked route to this regional favorite—one that didn't require toasting and grinding dried chiles or standing by the stove, but that still delivered complexity and subtle heat. And our scaled-down version had to have the same balance of flavors.

The first issue was the pork. Well-marbled boneless pork butt roast stays tender in the slow cooker as the fat melts and keeps the meat moist, but it's an unwieldy size when cooking for two. Thinking back to our Meaty Tomato Sauce (page 228), we opted to again use boneless country-style pork ribs. Easy to purchase in quantities appropriate for two, these boneless ribs become incredibly tender with braising. As an added bonus, they were quick to prepare for cooking; after trimming 1½ pounds of ribs, we simply cut them into hearty 1½-inch chunks.

While typically the pork is browned before simmering, to limit our prep time as much as possible, we decided to skip this step and look for other ways to develop flavor in the absence of the fond left behind from browning the meat. We hoped to make up for the missing flavor with a generous mixture of aromatics and spices, and since New Mexican chili traditionally has both in spades, we had a hunch that our finished dish wouldn't be lacking in flavor.

We started with one onion and three cloves of garlic to build an aromatic base of flavor. While we didn't want to add them raw to the slow cooker, we knew from prior testing that we could bypass browning the onions by microwaving them with assertive spices to intensify their flavor. We tested various amounts of chili powder and found that 2 tablespoons would do the job. To deepen the meaty flavor in our slow-cooker chili, we added a tablespoon of tomato paste. A teaspoon and a half of minced fresh oregano rounded out the aromatics, and the same quantity of brown sugar tamed any bitterness.

In addition to our strong lineup of aromatics and spices, we added a cup of chicken broth to provide the cooking liquid and base of the sauce. We seasoned our cubes of pork with salt and pepper, then stirred them into the slow cooker with the microwaved aromatics and broth until well coated. We then put the cover on and let the slow cooker do its work. When we returned several hours later, the meat was tender and the sauce was an attractive rust red, but the flavor and texture of the sauce left something to be desired.

Chili powder alone wasn't doing a sufficient job of providing ample smoky, spicy notes in our chili, so we turned to canned chipotle chiles in adobo sauce. We tried various quantities before deciding that a single teaspoon brought the right amount of complexity

and heat. In addition to being spicy, dried chiles also boast a rich, fruity side. Wondering how to replicate the fruity quality of dried chiles here, it occurred to us that we could use actual fruit. Since the flavor of chiles is sometimes described as raisin-y, we hoped raisins might supply that nuance, but we were afraid the raisin texture would seem jarring in the slow-cooker chili. Happily, after just 10 minutes in the slow cooker, the raisins softened enough to be unobtrusive and provided the subtle, fruity notes we were after.

To replicate the slightly bitter quality of freshly ground dried chiles, we tried stirring in cocoa powder and unsweetened chocolate. In this dish, however, they tasted out of place. A colleague suggested trying coffee; indeed, replacing ¼ cup of the chicken broth with coffee brought the flavors into robust, bittersweet balance.

Finally, we needed to find a way to thicken the sauce without sacrificing flavor. We found a solution in instant tapioca, which thickened the broth perfectly without contributing any obtrusive flavors.

At the last minute, we stirred in lime juice, lime zest, and cilantro to brighten our hearty, earthy dish. When we tucked into the fragrant red chili, we were happy to find that it hit the spot—and it took a minimum of effort to get there.

Slow-Cooker New Mexican Red Pork Chili

SERVES 2

Try to buy country-style pork ribs with lots of fat and dark meat, and stay away from ribs that look overly lean with pale meat. Lean country-style pork ribs will taste very dry after the extended cooking time in the slow cooker. You can substitute ¾ teaspoon ground espresso powder dissolved in ¼ cup boiling water for the brewed coffee if desired. Serve with lime wedges, minced fresh cilantro, minced onion or scallions, diced avocado, shredded cheddar or Monterey Jack cheese, and/or sour cream. *Cooking time: 6 to 7 hours on low or 3 to 4 hours on high*

1½ **pounds boneless country-style pork ribs, trimmed and cut into 1½-inch chunks (see note)**
 Salt and pepper
1 **onion, minced**
2 **tablespoons chili powder**
1 **tablespoon vegetable oil**

1 tablespoon tomato paste

3 garlic cloves, minced

1½ teaspoons minced fresh oregano or
   ½ teaspoon dried

¾ cup low-sodium chicken broth

¼ cup brewed coffee (see note)

1 tablespoon Minute tapioca

1½ teaspoons brown sugar

1 teaspoon minced canned chipotle chile in
   adobo sauce

1 bay leaf

¼ cup raisins

2 tablespoons minced fresh cilantro

½ teaspoon grated lime zest plus 1½ teaspoons
   fresh lime juice

1. Lightly spray inside of slow cooker with vegetable oil spray. Season pork with salt and pepper and place in slow cooker.

2. Combine onion, chili powder, oil, tomato paste, garlic, and oregano in microwave-safe bowl. Microwave, stirring occasionally, until onion is softened, about 5 minutes; transfer to slow cooker. Stir broth, coffee, tapioca, sugar, chipotles, and bay leaf into slow cooker. Cover and cook until pork is tender, 6 to 7 hours on low or 3 to 4 hours on high.

3. Add raisins, cover, and cook on high until raisins are heated through, about 10 minutes. Let chili settle for 5 minutes, then remove fat from surface using large spoon. Remove and discard bay leaf. Stir in cilantro, lime zest, and lime juice. Season with salt and pepper to taste and serve.

SLOW-COOKER SMOTHERED PORK CHOPS

PORK CHOPS ARE A CONVENIENT CUT OF PORK when cooking for two. But given that chops are fairly lean, they often need a rich, velvety sauce to round them out. We set our sights on pairing our chops with a flavorful gravy, for a slow-cooker take on the classic, homey dish, smothered pork chops. We wanted pork chops that were fall-off-the-bone tender, covered with caramelized onions, and enriched with deeply flavored onion gravy.

First we had to figure out which cut of chop would stay tender in the slow cooker. We began our testing with ¾-inch rib chops, thinking that any chops under ½ inch thick would overcook quickly in our cooker. After just one test, we knew that these chops were also too thin—after six hours in the slow cooker, they were dry and stringy. It appeared that thin was not in, so we moved to thicker chops. We were certain that huge 2-inch-thick chops, which unfortunately had to be special-ordered from the butcher, were going to be the answer. We just had to determine which was better, rib or center cut.

To our dismay, both of these cuts also overcooked in six hours. We were thinking about cutting back on the cooking time when a test kitchen colleague suggested blade chops, which are cut from the shoulder end of the loin and contain a significant amount of fat and connective tissue. When we tried them, the fat melted into the meat, keeping it moist and tender, and the connective tissue all but disappeared over the course of six hours. Best of all, there was no need to special-order extra-thick chops, since ¾-inch pork blade chops worked perfectly and were readily available.

We knew that searing the chops would provide deeper flavor to our dish, but it also sped up the cooking time of the pork. While jump-starting cooking is typically a desirable thing, in this case it resulted in drier pork chops, so we opted to skip this step and find other ways to develop rich flavor in our dish.

To make up for the loss of flavor from not browning the chops, we turned to bacon fat to provide a smoky flavor base, and included the cooked bacon in the dish. Using the bacon fat to sauté our onion and some garlic further intensified the flavor of the sauce. Thyme and a bay leaf gave it aroma, and a healthy shot of soy sauce acted as a fond replacement in the absence of searing the meat. Our slow-cooker smothered chops were turning a corner.

Our last challenge was to get the texture of the onions and gravy just right—the sauce was still too watery. Currently we were using one large onion, cut into ½-inch slices. More onions thickened the sauce, but they also threw off the balance of flavors. Instead we added a couple of tablespoons of flour to the skillet with the sautéed onion and bacon fat; sautéing it briefly worked to rid the flour of its raw flavor. The resulting gravy was thick and rich—and it truly smothered each chop.

We finished the sauce with a splash of vinegar to brighten up the flavor profile, then garnished the chops with some fresh parsley.

Slow-Cooker Smothered Pork Chops with Onion and Bacon

SERVES 2

Be sure to use blade-cut pork chops, which are cut from the shoulder end of the loin and contain a significant amount of fat and connective tissue. *Cooking time: 6 to 7 hours on low or 3 to 4 hours on high*

- 2 (7-ounce) bone-in blade-cut pork chops, about ¾ inch thick, sides slit (see page 152)
  Salt and pepper
- 2 slices bacon, chopped
- 1 large onion, halved and sliced pole to pole into ½-inch-thick pieces
- 2 teaspoons brown sugar
- 2 garlic cloves, minced
- 1 teaspoon minced fresh thyme or ¼ teaspoon dried
- 7½ teaspoons unbleached all-purpose flour
- ½ cup low-sodium chicken broth
- 1 tablespoon soy sauce
- 1 bay leaf
- 1 tablespoon minced fresh parsley
- 1½ teaspoons cider vinegar

1. Lightly spray inside of slow cooker with vegetable oil spray. Season chops with salt and pepper and place in slow cooker.

2. Cook bacon in 10-inch skillet over medium heat until crisp, 5 to 7 minutes. Using slotted spoon, transfer bacon to slow cooker, leaving fat behind.

3. Add onion and ½ teaspoon sugar to fat in skillet and cook over medium-high heat until onion is softened and well browned, 8 to 10 minutes. Stir in garlic and thyme and cook until fragrant, about 30 seconds. Stir in flour and cook for 1 minute. Slowly whisk in broth, scraping up any browned bits and smoothing out any lumps.

4. Off heat, stir in soy sauce and remaining 1½ teaspoons sugar until combined; transfer to slow cooker. Add bay leaf. Cover and cook until pork is tender, 6 to 7 hours on low or 3 to 4 hours on high.

5. Transfer pork chops to serving platter, tent loosely with foil, and let rest for 10 minutes. Let braising liquid settle for 5 minutes, then remove fat from surface using large spoon. Remove and discard bay leaf. Stir in parsley and vinegar and season with salt and pepper to taste. Spoon ½ cup sauce over chops and serve, passing remaining sauce separately.

SLOW-COOKER SWEET AND SOUR STICKY RIBS

SWEET AND SOUR STICKY RIBS, WITH THEIR RICH, succulent meat and potent mahogany-colored sauce, have long been staples on bar menus and at parties. But we saw no reason we had to wait for Friday night and a fiesta to enjoy them. We decided to scale down this recipe and move it to the slow cooker at the same time. After all, sweet and sour ribs already require a lengthy cooking time, plus they're regularly basted in a sweet, tangy sauce that cooks down and reduces in the oven. We thought the slow cooker would be the perfect vessel to provide our ribs with this concentrated flavor.

After trying a few slow-cooker recipes, we realized that creating traditional sticky ribs in the moist slow-cooker environment would be a challenge. Most versions came out gray and flavorless with a watery sauce. We knew we could do better.

We started by considering the popular rib choices: whole spareribs, St. Louis–style spareribs, and baby back ribs. We eliminated whole spareribs right off the bat—a typical 5-pound rack is too much for two people. St. Louis–style spareribs usually weigh about 3 pounds—more manageable, but still too much meat for this recipe. One rack of baby back ribs, however, was

SLOW-COOKER SWEET AND SOUR STICKY RIBS WITH THAI CABBAGE SLAW

about 1½ to 2 pounds—the perfect size to serve two.

There are three basic components to the sweet and sour sauce: the sweetener, the aromatics, and the fruit. In most recipes we researched, sugar, honey, or even jam was dumped on top of the ribs, followed by a heaping handful of onions, peppers, and sometimes pineapple. In search of a fresher, more cohesive flavor, we started our own sauce from the ground up. We sautéed onion and red bell pepper with a hefty amount of garlic, ginger, and tomato paste (the last of these helped with browning and flavor development). For sweetness we added brown sugar and jam, settling on apricot because of its bright, fruity flavor. To incorporate pineapple flavor we tried both canned and fresh pineapple. The canned was basically flavorless and added little to the sauce. Fresh pineapple's contribution was only as good as its ripeness, which was inconsistent at best. In the end we opted to omit the pineapple and increase the amount of apricot jam to bump up the fruity notes. The last touches to the sauce were soy sauce for depth and rice vinegar for brightness. Armed with a cohesive, flavorful sauce recipe, we headed back to the slow cooker.

To fit the ribs in the slow cooker, we cut the rack in half and stacked the two pieces on top of each other before pouring our sauce over the top. But stacking them left us with unevenly cooked ribs because only the bottom rack was touching the sauce and the bottom of the slow cooker. Lining the whole rack across the bottom of the slow cooker allowed more contact with the sauce so that the ribs could properly absorb more of the sauce's flavors.

Most rib recipes call for removing the thin, chewy membrane from the back of the ribs, which is a great idea if you plan on grilling or roasting them. But we found that after hours of cooking in the moist environment of the slow cooker, the racks without the membrane fell apart when we tried to remove them. Leaving the membrane attached for this recipe held the ribs together during cooking.

When the ribs were tender, we transferred them to a carving board to rest and returned our attention to the sauce. The basic flavors were there now, but so much moisture had leached from the ribs as they cooked that the sauce was diluted and not thick enough to coat the ribs. We decided to finish the sauce on the stovetop and simmered it, adding a little cornstarch to help it thicken, until it reduced to a gooey, syrupy glaze. Simply tossing the ribs with this thickened sauce was good,

but we knew we could do better without too much more effort. We transferred the ribs to a baking sheet, brushed the rack with the sauce, and threw it under the broiler, basting every few minutes until we achieved the ultimate lacquered, sticky perfection.

Slow-Cooker Sweet and Sour Sticky Ribs
SERVES 2

Leaving the membrane on the underside of the ribs attached helps the rack stay together in the slow cooker. Avoid buying a rack of ribs larger than 2 pounds as it will be difficult to maneuver into the slow cooker. Serve with Thai Cabbage Slaw (page 131). *Cooking time: 6 to 7 hours on low*

- 1   rack baby back ribs (about 1½ pounds) (see note)
     Salt and pepper
- 2   teaspoons vegetable oil
- 1   small onion, minced
- ½   red bell pepper, stemmed, seeded, and chopped fine
- 1   tablespoon minced or grated fresh ginger
- 2   garlic cloves, minced
- 2   teaspoons tomato paste
     Pinch red pepper flakes
- 8   ounces apricot jam or preserves (about ⅔ cup)
- 2   tablespoons soy sauce
- 2   tablespoons rice vinegar
- 3   tablespoons brown sugar
- 1   teaspoon cornstarch
- 1   teaspoon water
- 1   tablespoon minced fresh cilantro

1. Lightly spray inside of slow cooker with vegetable oil spray. Season ribs with salt and pepper and arrange along bottom and sides of slow cooker, with meaty side facing down, following photo on page 234.

2. Heat oil in 10-inch nonstick skillet over medium-high heat until shimmering. Add onion and bell pepper and cook until vegetables are softened and lightly browned, 5 to 7 minutes. Stir in ginger, garlic, tomato paste, and red pepper flakes and cook until fragrant, about 30 seconds. Stir in apricot jam, soy sauce, 5 teaspoons vinegar, and sugar and bring to simmer; spoon mixture over ribs in slow cooker. Cover and cook until ribs are tender, 6 to 7 hours on low.

3. Position oven rack 10 inches from broiler element and heat broiler. Place wire rack in large foil-lined

ARRANGING A RACK OF RIBS IN THE SLOW COOKER

To ensure that the ribs are covered in sauce, arrange the rack with the meaty side down across the bottom of the slow cooker. The ends of the rack will come up against the sides.

rimmed baking sheet and coat with vegetable oil spray. Carefully transfer ribs, meaty side down, to prepared baking sheet and tent with foil. Let braising liquid settle for 5 minutes; remove fat from surface using large spoon.

4. Strain sauce through fine-mesh strainer into small saucepan. Whisk cornstarch and water together in small bowl, then whisk into sauce. Bring to simmer, whisking constantly, and cook until sauce is thickened and measures ⅔ cup, about 10 minutes. Stir in remaining 1 teaspoon vinegar and cilantro and season with salt and pepper to taste.

5. Brush ribs with sauce and broil until beginning to brown, 2 to 4 minutes. Flip ribs over, brush with more sauce, and continue to broil until ribs are well browned and sticky, 9 to 12 minutes longer, brushing with additional sauce every few minutes. Transfer ribs to cutting board, tent with foil, and let rest for 10 minutes. Slice ribs between bones and serve, passing remaining sauce separately.

SLOW-COOKER KOREAN BRAISED SHORT RIBS

WE LOVE THE MARRIAGE OF SWEET AND SAVORY flavors found in Korean cuisine. One of our favorite dishes making use of this match is *kalbi*, beef short ribs marinated in a sweet soy mixture with garlic, scallions, and pears. Although this dish is usually grilled, we saw no reason it couldn't be revamped to work in the slow cooker; short ribs are well suited to braising, so we thought that they would do fine after a stint in our favorite countertop appliance. But while the texture of the ribs would benefit from the slow, moist heat of the slow cooker, we were concerned that the bold flavor of the marinade would be diluted by the cooking liquid. Could we find the secret for tender braised ribs with intense Korean barbecued flavor—all prepared in the slow cooker?

Short ribs are a tough cut of meat, usually requiring a long, slow braise to achieve melting, fork-tender perfection, making them ideal for the slow cooker. In the test kitchen, we usually turn to English-style ribs for braises. Their single bone and thick layer of meat make for hefty, uniform portions. Browning the ribs in a skillet first is standard protocol to intensify the meat's flavor, but we wanted to avoid the mess and cleanup of this added step. While we were interested in saving time, we didn't want to do so at the expense of flavor. We looked at the bones sticking out of the ribs and wondered if they could be the key to increasing flavor in our slow-cooker braise.

Restaurant chefs know that roasting bones is key to making flavorful stock, since bones carry lots of flavor and roasted bones carry even more. Could we remove the meat from the rib bones and brown the bones to add flavor to our braise? Roasting the bones in the oven would take more time than we wanted, but we wondered if we could "roast" them in the microwave. We sliced the meat off the bones from our pile of short ribs for two (about 2½ pounds), laid the bones on a large plate, popped them in the microwave, and hit the start button. After about 10 minutes, the bones looked as if they'd spent hours in an oven, and indeed, they added unequivocal depth to the sauce.

Now that we had found a way to add flavor to our dish without browning the meat, we focused on the liquid component. We started with the most common marinade ingredients in kalbi. For the soy sauce, ¼ cup, once reduced in the slow cooker, provided the right level of salty, savory flavor. For aromatics, tasters liked the addition of ginger to a base of garlic and scallions. A little rice vinegar provided an acidic component. Finally, we added the "secret" ingredient: pureed pear. Many kalbi recipes claim it acts as a tenderizer. Although our ribs didn't need any assistance in the tenderness department, we included the pear nonetheless for the authentic touch it provided and the sweetness and fruity flavor it imparted to our sauce; we found that a single pear was enough for our scaled-down recipe.

After we processed the aromatics and liquid ingredients with the pear in the food processor, our sauce was plenty smooth, but it didn't have that rich, glossy sheen we wanted. For a glossy, velvety consistency, we turned to tapioca, which we could simply add to the slow cooker with the other ingredients; just a tablespoon and a half produced a smooth, slightly thickened sauce.

By the end of the cooking time, the sauce boasted great flavor—but we found there wasn't quite enough of it to cover the meat and bones adequately. Though not a traditional marinade ingredient, chicken broth gave the cooking liquid sufficient volume without making the sauce overly salty or diluting its flavor.

At this point, only one problem remained: Short ribs ooze fat as they cook. To remedy this, many recipes include the step of chilling the cooked ribs overnight so that the gelled fat can be scraped from the cooking liquid and discarded. We didn't want to add a day to our cooking, so we simply fished out the ribs and set them aside, discarded the bones, let the sauce settle, and skimmed as much fat as we could from the top. At last our sauce had sheen, body, and layers of flavor.

After hours of cooking, we were amazed by the richness of the sauce and the depth of flavors. The short ribs were unbelievably tender, smothered in a sauce with just the right balance of salty soy and sweet pear notes. For a final touch, we sprinkled minced cilantro over the sauce for a bright, fresh accent. Without lighting a burner or grill, we had successfully combined the flavors of tangy Korean barbecue with the ease of slow-cooker braising in one satisfying dish.

Slow-Cooker Korean Braised Short Ribs

SERVES 2

Buy English-style short ribs that have at least 1 inch of meat on top of the bone; avoid ribs that have little meat or large bones. Because the soy sauce contributes a fair amount of salt, it is best not to season the ribs before adding them to the slow cooker to prevent an overly salty dish. *Cooking time: 9 to 10 hours on low or 5 to 6 hours on high*

- 2½ **pounds bone-in English-style short ribs (see note), meat and bones separated (see photo)**
- 1 **pear, peeled, cored, and chopped coarse**
- ½ **cup low-sodium chicken broth**
- ¼ **cup soy sauce**
- 3 **garlic cloves, minced**
- 2 **scallions, sliced thin**
- 2 **teaspoons minced or grated fresh ginger**
- 1½ **teaspoons rice vinegar**
- 1½ **tablespoons Minute tapioca**
- 1 **tablespoon minced fresh cilantro**
  Salt and pepper

1. Lightly spray inside of slow cooker with vegetable oil spray. Arrange beef bones on large microwave-safe plate and microwave until well browned, 8 to 10 minutes, turning as needed. Place browned bones and meat in slow cooker.

2. Process pear, broth, soy sauce, garlic, scallions, ginger, and vinegar together in food processor until smooth, about 1 minute; transfer to slow cooker. Stir in tapioca. Cover and cook until beef is tender, 9 to 10 hours on low or 5 to 6 hours on high.

3. Transfer short ribs to serving platter and tent loosely with foil. Remove and discard bones. Let braising liquid settle for 5 minutes, then remove fat from surface using large spoon. Stir in cilantro and season with salt and pepper to taste. Spoon ½ cup sauce over ribs and serve, passing remaining sauce separately.

NOTES FROM THE TEST KITCHEN

BUYING BEEF SHORT RIBS

Short ribs are just that: fatty ribs (cut from any location along the length of the cow's ribs) that are shorter than the more common, larger beef ribs. Short ribs come in two styles: "English," which contain a single rib bone, and "flanken," which have several smaller bones. After cooking both, we found the two options to be equally tender and flavorful. However, the flanken-style ribs are more expensive, and you typically have to buy them from a butcher. We prefer the cheaper and more readily available English-style ribs.

ENGLISH

FLANKEN

PREPARING SHORT RIBS FOR THE SLOW COOKER

Insert a knife between the rib and meat and, staying as close to the bone as possible, saw the meat off the bone.

BABY SPINACH SALAD WITH CARROT, ORANGE, AND SESAME

CHAPTER 9

SIDE DISHES

BABY SPINACH SALADS

WHEN YOU'RE BROWSING THE PRODUCE AISLE FOR salad greens, baby spinach seems like the light at the end of the tunnel. After all, there's zero washing to be done, and no fancy knife work is needed. But let's face it—as a salad choice, this green is never as flavorful as it is convenient. Unlike sturdier, more mature spinach, the tender, delicate leaves of baby spinach can't support hefty mix-ins like hard-cooked eggs, bacon, or avocado. Worse yet, their smooth, flat surfaces tend to cling together, leaving olives, tomatoes, and nuts drowning in dressing at the bottom of the bowl. Rather than resign ourselves to an endless rotation of hardy romaine and red leaf blends, we were determined to make the most of the ultimate convenience product, baby spinach, to create a variety of interesting salads for two.

Our first move was to rethink how we were cutting our vegetables. Just about any ingredient can overwhelm baby spinach when chopped into heavy chunks. Thinly slicing the vegetables (or at least tearing them into small pieces) allowed us to introduce harder, crunchier produce. We thinly sliced fennel, tore frisée, and shaved carrot ribbons with a vegetable peeler. Added to individual salads, each fluffed up the spinach leaves considerably and worked in welcome crunch and varying textures.

These salads were shaping up nicely, although they were a bit one-dimensional. While cheese often works well in green salads, we had little luck incorporating it with the spinach. Firmer, denser varieties like pecorino and feta sank to the bottom of the bowl, and goat cheese and blue cheese glued the leaves together. For brighter, cleaner flavors and textural appeal we decided to try adding fresh fruits instead. Orange segments enlivened one of our salads with acidity and juicy sweetness. Thinly sliced strawberries paired nicely with assertive frisée, and crisp apple wedges blended in naturally with fennel. A final flourish of sesame seeds or fresh herbs served to complement the fruit in our salad creations.

All that was left to do was whisk up a dressing. Anything creamy bogged down the greens, so a light vinaigrette was the way to go. For an Asian-inspired salad with carrot, orange, and sesame seeds, we chose a vinaigrette made with rice vinegar, vegetable oil, and sesame oil. Our next spinach salad with strawberries and basil paired well with a balsamic vinaigrette, and a third salad that included fennel and apples benefited from a bright, lemony dressing.

To emulsify the vinaigrettes, we relied on mustard as well as mayonnaise, both of which we've found work to keep the vinegar and oil well combined and the dressing's consistency light and clean. While standard vinaigrettes call for a 3-to-1 ratio of oil to acid, our tasters were asking for more brightness in all three salads. Bumping up the acid, we settled on a 2-to-1 ratio, giving our otherwise mellow spinach a welcoming bite.

Baby Spinach Salad with Carrot, Orange, and Sesame

SERVES 2

Slicing the vegetables as thinly as possible is important in order to separate the clingy spinach leaves, and to ensure that the vegetables don't sink to the bottom of the bowl.

- 3 ounces baby spinach (about 3 cups)
- ½ carrot, peeled and shaved with vegetable peeler lengthwise into ribbons (about ½ cup) (see note)
- ¼ teaspoon grated orange zest plus one orange, peeled and segmented (see page 183)
- 1 scallion, sliced thin (see note)
- 3½ teaspoons rice vinegar
- 1 small shallot, minced
- ½ teaspoon mayonnaise
- ½ teaspoon Dijon mustard
- ⅛ teaspoon salt
- 4½ teaspoons vegetable oil
- 2 teaspoons toasted sesame oil
- 2 teaspoons sesame seeds, toasted (see page 240)

1. Place spinach, carrot, orange segments, and scallion in large bowl.

2. In separate bowl, whisk orange zest, vinegar, shallot, mayonnaise, mustard, and salt together until well combined. Whisking constantly, very slowly drizzle oils into mixture until glossy and lightly thickened. Pour dressing over spinach mixture and toss to coat. Sprinkle with sesame seeds and serve.

VARIATIONS
Baby Spinach Salad with Frisée and Strawberries

SERVES 2

Slicing the berries as thinly as possible is important in order to separate the clingy spinach leaves, and to ensure that the fruit doesn't sink to the bottom of the bowl.

3 ounces baby spinach (about 3 cups)

½ medium head frisée, washed, dried, and torn into 2-inch pieces

1 cup (about 5 ounces) strawberries, hulled and sliced thin (see note)

1 tablespoon chopped fresh basil

4 teaspoons balsamic vinegar

1 small shallot, minced

½ teaspoon mayonnaise

½ teaspoon Dijon mustard

⅛ teaspoon salt

¼ teaspoon pepper

6½ teaspoons extra-virgin olive oil

1. Place spinach, frisée, strawberries, and basil in large bowl.

2. In separate bowl, whisk vinegar, shallot, mayonnaise, mustard, salt, and pepper together until well combined. Whisking constantly, very slowly drizzle oil into mixture until glossy and lightly thickened. Pour dressing over spinach mixture, toss to coat, and serve.

Baby Spinach Salad with Fennel and Apple

SERVES 2

If your fennel bulb does not come with fronds, substitute 1 tablespoon coarsely chopped tarragon. Slicing the fennel and apple as thinly as possible is important in order to separate the clingy spinach leaves, and to ensure that they don't sink to the bottom of the bowl. See page 123 for a recipe to use up the leftover fennel.

3 ounces baby spinach (about 3 cups)

½ fennel bulb (about 6 ounces), cored and sliced thin (see page 92), plus 2 tablespoons coarsely chopped fennel fronds (see note)

1 Golden Delicious apple, cored, quartered lengthwise, and sliced thin (see note)

½ teaspoon grated lemon zest plus 4 teaspoons fresh lemon juice

1 small shallot, minced

1½ teaspoons honey

½ teaspoon mayonnaise

½ teaspoon whole grain mustard

⅛ teaspoon salt

6½ teaspoons extra-virgin olive oil

1. Place spinach, fennel, fennel fronds, and apple in large bowl.

2. In separate bowl, whisk lemon zest, lemon juice, shallot, honey, mayonnaise, mustard, and salt together until well combined. Whisking constantly, very slowly drizzle oil into mixture until glossy and lightly thickened. Pour dressing over spinach mixture, toss to coat, and serve.

ROASTED BEET SALAD

TODAY, YOU'LL FIND SOME VARIATION OF BEET salad on the menu of almost every chic bistro and trendy gastropub—and it is no mystery why: With their unique, sweet flavor, firm, juicy texture, and ruby-red hue, beets are a bona fide showstopper. But what's the best way to prepare beets for a salad? And is there any way to make peeling them a less messy endeavor? We wanted to find a way to bring this bistro favorite home, and to make it the centerpiece for an elegant, yet effortless, salad for two.

To find the best way to cook the beets, we tried three different methods: boiling, steaming, and roasting. Boiled beets were diluted in flavor. Steaming was slightly better, but the flavor wasn't as concentrated as we would have liked. Roasting was the next option. We tried wrapping the beets in foil as well as leaving them unwrapped. The unwrapped beets dried out and became leathery, but the wrapped beets were juicy and tender with the concentrated sweetness we were looking for. There was another significant advantage with the wrapped beets: The baking sheet remained mess-free. So far, so good.

Although roasting hadn't made a mess, we suspected peeling would, as beet juice is notorious for its staining power. To bypass the usual stained cutting boards and blotchy dish towels that normally accompany peeling beets, we simply held each beet using layers of paper towels, then used another paper towel to wipe away the skin. When we were done, we simply pitched the stained paper towels into the trash. Peeling the beets while they were still slightly warm ensured that the skin was easy to remove. With our beets peeled, we sliced them into attractive wedges and turned our attention to the rest of the salad.

For the greens, we settled on baby arugula, which offered a sharp, peppery edge that played nicely off the sweetness of the beets. Cheese, especially crumbly varieties like blue cheese, feta, and goat cheese, are a popular component of beet salads, and we tested them all. Blue cheese was far too bold for our salad and overpowered the flavor of the beets, and feta wasn't potent enough to establish its own presence. Goat cheese proved best, with both a creaminess and tang that tasters appreciated.

At this point, we still needed to dress the salad. Tasters liked the idea of a simple vinaigrette; extra-virgin olive oil and sherry vinegar paired well, creating a rich vinaigrette with deep, complex flavor. Dressing the beets while they were still warm enabled them to absorb the vinaigrette's flavors, but we waited until the beets had cooled down to add the arugula, lest our greens become drab and wilted from the warm beets.

For the perfect finishing touch to our bistro-style salad, we sprinkled toasted pistachios over the top, which added crunch and richness.

NOTES FROM THE TEST KITCHEN

TOASTING NUTS AND SEEDS

Toasting nuts and seeds maximizes their flavor, so whether you are adding them to a salad or tossing them into a pasta dish, it pays to spend a few minutes toasting them. To toast a small amount of nuts or seeds, put them in a dry skillet over medium heat. Shake the skillet occasionally to prevent scorching and toast until they are lightly browned and fragrant, 3 to 8 minutes. Watch the nuts closely because they can go from golden to burnt very quickly.

CUTTING ORANGES INTO PIECES

1. Slice off the top and bottom of the orange, then cut away the rind and pith using a paring knife.

2. Quarter the peeled orange, then slice each quarter crosswise into ½-inch-thick pieces.

Roasted Beet Salad with Goat Cheese and Pistachios

SERVES 2

When buying beets, look for bunches that have the most uniformly sized beets so that they will roast in the same amount of time. If the beets are different sizes, remove the smaller ones from the oven as they become tender. You can use either golden or red beets or a mix of each in this recipe.

- 1 **pound beets (about 4), greens discarded (see note)**
- 2 **tablespoons extra-virgin olive oil**
- 5 **teaspoons sherry vinegar**
  Salt and pepper
- 1 **ounce baby arugula (about 1 cup)**
- 1 **ounce goat cheese, crumbled (about ¼ cup)**
- 2 **tablespoons chopped unsalted pistachios, toasted**

1. Adjust oven rack to middle position and heat oven to 400 degrees. Wrap beets individually in foil and place in rimmed baking sheet. Roast beets until skewer inserted into center meets little resistance (you will need to unwrap beets to test them), 45 to 60 minutes.

2. Remove beets from oven and carefully open foil packets (watch for escaping steam). When beets are cool enough to handle, carefully and gently rub off skins using several layers of paper towels. Slice beets into ½-inch-thick wedges; if large, then cut in half crosswise.

3. Meanwhile, whisk oil, vinegar, ¼ teaspoon salt, and ¼ teaspoon pepper together in large bowl. Add sliced beets to dressing, toss to coat, and let cool to room temperature, about 20 minutes.

4. Add arugula to beets and gently toss to coat greens. Season with salt and pepper to taste. Sprinkle with goat cheese and pistachios and serve.

VARIATION

Roasted Beet Salad with Blood Orange and Almonds

A navel orange can be substituted for the blood orange.

Follow recipe for Roasted Beet Salad with Goat Cheese and Pistachios, reducing amount of sherry vinegar to 4 teaspoons. Substitute 1 ounce ricotta salata, shaved (about ½ cup), for goat cheese and 2 tablespoons toasted sliced almonds for pistachios. Add 1 blood orange, peeled and cut into ½-inch pieces (see photos), with arugula.

ROASTED BEET SALAD WITH GOAT CHEESE AND PISTACHIOS

BRAISED HEARTY GREENS

BRAISED GREENS ARE A STAPLE IN SOUTHERN cuisine, both in restaurants and in home kitchens. The traditional method—simmering the greens with a ham hock for hours—results in a rich and tasty dish, but because the greens are essentially overcooked, they lose their deep color, fleshy texture, and earthy flavor. We wanted braised greens for today's table.

Alternatives to the traditional hours-long, pork-infused simmering method call for blanching and sauté-ing the greens. This method is quicker and yields greens with texture, but blanching, draining, squeezing—and then sautéing? No way. We were after a one-pot recipe that wouldn't require parcooking or take so long.

We began by prepping a single pound of greens (collards, kale, mustard, or turnip greens work well), removing the tough center ribs and chopping the leaves into 1-inch pieces, which would still be sizable bites once cooked. Our first thought was to treat them like tender spinach or chard—skip blanching and go directly to sautéing. Starting with a bit of vegetable oil in the pan, we added a shallot and then began tossing in the greens.

We'd added only about half of the greens when it became clear that sautéing alone wasn't going to work: The greens took so long to soften that the leaves on the bottom of the pot started to scorch while the leaves on top remained virtually raw. Adding a few tablespoons of water helped—but not enough. It was clear we needed more cooking liquid, but how much? We didn't want to end up submerging our greens—that would just produce the soupy greens we were trying to avoid. We went up gradually and found that just ½ cup of water was sufficient. To ensure that the liquid didn't cook off too quickly, we covered the pot. Once the greens were softened, about 10 minutes later, we uncovered the pot and allowed the remaining liquid to cook off. Success! We had found a way to avoid waterlogged greens, and the texture was spot-on, but now we had to work on the flavor of our dish, which was a little one-dimensional.

First, we found that some brown sugar helped to soften the greens' peppery bite, and a bit of cayenne pepper added a subtle heat. For savory depth, we replaced the water with chicken broth. Swapping the oil for butter added richness, as did tossing the cooked greens with more butter. Finally, we finished our greens with a little cider vinegar for brightness.

Our braised greens were fresh, flavorful, and done in no time—and they were so satisfying that even our most steadfast Southern critics were pleased.

Braised Hearty Greens

SERVES 2

Don't dry the greens completely after washing; a little extra water clinging to the leaves will help them wilt when cooking. If using collard greens, allow 2 to 3 extra minutes of cooking time in step 1.

- 2 **tablespoons unsalted butter**
- 1 **shallot, sliced thin**
- 1 **pound hearty greens (kale, mustard, turnip, or collards), stemmed, leaves chopped into 1-inch pieces (see page 125)**
- ½ **cup low-sodium chicken broth**
- 1½ **teaspoons brown sugar**
   Salt and pepper
- ⅛ **teaspoon cayenne pepper**
- 1½ **teaspoons cider vinegar**

1. Melt 1 tablespoon butter in medium saucepan over medium heat. Add shallot and cook until softened, 2 to 3 minutes. Add greens, broth, sugar, ¼ teaspoon salt, and cayenne. Cover, reduce heat to medium-low, and cook, stirring occasionally, until completely tender, about 10 minutes.

2. Uncover and increase heat to medium-high, stirring occasionally until liquid is nearly evaporated. Off heat, stir in remaining 1 tablespoon butter and vinegar. Season with salt and pepper to taste and serve.

NOTES FROM THE TEST KITCHEN

THE BEST CHICKEN BROTH

Store-bought chicken broth is a real time-saver, but which brand is best? Our winning broth, **Swanson Certified Organic Free Range Chicken Broth**, has two important characteristics: less than 700 milligrams of sodium per serving (others contain up to 1,350 milligrams per serving) and a short ingredient list that includes vegetables such as carrots, celery, and onions. Don't be intimidated by the large 32-ounce carton; extra chicken broth can be used in many applications, from cooking rice and grains to making soups and stews.

STIR-FRIED BROCCOLI

CRISP-TENDER BITES OF STIR-FRIED BROCCOLI accented with a lively sauce sound appealing. The quick blast of high heat should coax out the vegetable's sweetness before it has a chance to overcook, and the broccoli should be cooked through yet still retain its character. However, Chinese takeout containers—and our own pans—too often contain limp florets weighed down by sauce, or broccoli so undercooked it's practically crunchy. What would it take to perfect this simple side and restore its fresh, vibrant appeal?

For starters, we swapped the wok for a 12-inch non-stick skillet, which we've found works better on the American stovetop. We proceeded with the simplest stir-fry method we came across, which called for broccoli florets only—stalks cook at a different rate. We cut 12 ounces of broccoli florets into smaller pieces, tossed them into the skillet with neutral vegetable oil and some minced garlic, and cooked everything over high heat for a few minutes. Yes, this method was simple—to a fault. Tossing everything into the pan at once rendered burnt aromatics and charred yet crunchy florets.

We reviewed a few basic tenets of successful stir-frying. Not only is it crucial to have all the ingredients prepped and ready to go before heating up the pan, but it is equally important to know when to add each component to the heat. The garlic, for example, was added to the pan too early, causing it to scorch; we found that adding it toward the end of cooking still extracted flavor but kept it from burning. But this still didn't solve the problem of practically raw—yet torched—broccoli.

For the next tests, we meticulously extended the cooking time minute by minute, but even then we couldn't consistently achieve the texture we wanted. The blistering heat was simply too hard to control. Maybe the problem was the heat itself.

Traditional Chinese stir-fries call for blazing heat, but we were beginning to believe this method is better suited to quick-cooking vegetables like onions and snow peas than to thick, stubby broccoli. Taking down the heat—from high to medium-high—turned out to be a dramatic turn for the better. A longer cooking time (roughly five to seven minutes over more moderate heat) slowed things down enough that it was easy to cook the florets just until they were perfectly crisp-tender and nicely browned. A little sugar sprinkled over the broccoli deepened the caramelization even further.

With our cooking technique settled, the broccoli just needed a few Asian-inspired sauces to dress it up. Our first attempt, made with chicken broth, spicy Asian chili-garlic sauce, sherry, and soy sauce, went overboard; even though we added it to the skillet at the last minute, all the liquid undid our hard work, rendering the broccoli soggy and drowning its flavor. The answer was ½ teaspoon of cornstarch, which thickened the sauce just enough to prevent it from bogging down the florets. In fact, chicken broth and cornstarch worked well as a base for a few more variations—one with oyster sauce, another with hoisin sauce, and a final one flavored with orange juice and fresh ginger. These options were so quick and flavorful, we suspected takeout night would be a thing of the past.

Stir-Fried Broccoli with Chili-Garlic Sauce
SERVES 2

Look for precut broccoli florets in your supermarket's produce department or at the salad bar to cut down on prep time.

- 2 tablespoons low-sodium chicken broth
- 2 teaspoons soy sauce
- 1½ teaspoons dry sherry
- 1 teaspoon Asian chili-garlic sauce
- ½ teaspoon toasted sesame oil
- ½ teaspoon cornstarch
- 3½ teaspoons vegetable oil
- 1 garlic clove, minced
  Pinch red pepper flakes
- 12 ounces broccoli florets (about 5 cups), cut into ¾-inch pieces (see note)
- ⅛ teaspoon sugar

1. In small bowl, whisk broth, soy sauce, sherry, chili-garlic sauce, sesame oil, and cornstarch together until well combined. In second small bowl, combine ½ teaspoon vegetable oil, garlic, and red pepper flakes.

2. Heat remaining 1 tablespoon vegetable oil in 12-inch nonstick skillet over medium-high heat until just smoking. Add broccoli and sugar and cook, stirring frequently, until broccoli is well browned, 5 to 7 minutes.

3. Stir in garlic-oil mixture and cook until fragrant, about 15 seconds. Add broth–soy sauce mixture and toss until broccoli is evenly coated. Serve.

Stir-Fried Broccoli with Oyster Sauce

Follow recipe for Stir-Fried Broccoli with Chili-Garlic Sauce, reducing amount of chicken broth to 1 tablespoon and substituting 5 teaspoons oyster sauce for soy sauce and ½ teaspoon brown sugar for chili-garlic sauce.

Stir-Fried Broccoli with Hoisin and Five-Spice Powder

Follow recipe for Stir-Fried Broccoli with Chili-Garlic Sauce, substituting 4½ teaspoons hoisin sauce for sherry and pinch five-spice powder for chili-garlic sauce.

Stir-Fried Broccoli with Orange and Ginger

Follow recipe for Stir-Fried Broccoli with Chili-Garlic Sauce, substituting 2 tablespoons fresh orange juice for sherry and omitting toasted sesame oil and chili-garlic sauce. Increase amount of red pepper flakes to ⅛ teaspoon and add 1½ teaspoons minced or grated fresh ginger to garlic-oil mixture.

NOTES FROM THE TEST KITCHEN

ALL ABOUT ASIAN CHILE SAUCES

Used both in cooking and as a condiment, each of these chile-based sauces has a slightly different character. Sriracha (left), the spiciest of the three, is made from garlic and chiles that are ground into a smooth paste. Chili-garlic sauce (middle) also contains garlic and is similar to sriracha except that the chiles are coarsely ground, giving it a chunkier texture, and we have found that it has a rounder flavor than sriracha. Sambal oelek (right) is made purely from ground chiles, without the addition of garlic or other spices, thus adding heat but not additional flavor. Once opened, these sauces will keep for several months in the refrigerator.

SRIRACHA **CHILI-GARLIC SAUCE** **SAMBAL OELEK CHILI PASTE**

SAUTÉED PEAS

YOU WON'T FIND US PROMOTING THE FRESH-tasting flavor of frozen broccoli, or reaching into our freezer for precut frozen vegetable medleys, but frozen peas are a different story. Not only are they convenient and quick-cooking, but they're also usually sweeter and more tender than fresh-picked peas, which can turn starchy and bland a mere 24 hours after harvest. What is even better is the versatility that peas have; it doesn't take too many supporting ingredients to bring out their natural clean sweetness. And when cooking for two, a bag of peas stashed in the back of the freezer makes for the perfect last-minute side when the meaty main dish is already in the works. We wanted a few flavorful, easy side dishes of peas with fresh add-ins like herbs, aromatics, and quick-sautéed complementary ingredients.

Since all frozen peas have already been blanched, we quickly learned that the key was not overdoing it—five minutes of simmering to heat them through was all they needed. The peas didn't even need to be thawed; they went straight from freezer to stovetop. And the less liquid the better; we settled on a couple of tablespoons for 1½ cups of peas.

To build up their sweet, grassy taste, we turned to aromatics, sweating a minced shallot and garlic in the saucepan with olive oil before adding the peas with a little water. This proved to be only a slight improvement; we realized that a good bit of flavor was being poured down the sink when we drained the peas. There wasn't that much cooking liquid as it was, so for our next go-round we treated the cooking liquid like a sauce and served it with the peas.

We were getting closer, but tasters complained that this sauce was too thin and bland. Swapping the water for chicken broth was a step in the right direction, adding depth and flavor. A small amount of butter stirred in after the peas finished simmering contributed body, and a dose of minced fresh mint provided a nice aromatic complement. Still, something was missing. A smidge of sugar added to the broth and a healthy squirt of lemon juice stirred into the peas just before serving were all it took to bring everything into balance.

We thought we were finished when a fellow test cook suggested switching from a saucepan to a skillet to ensure that the peas heated a tad more quickly and evenly across the larger surface area. Now our peas were ready in as little as four minutes.

With our method established, we developed a few easy variations. We found that the peas paired nicely with a leek and a little cream in one variation, and fennel contributed its sweet, licorice-y notes in another. One last variation with thyme and mushrooms delivered an earthy, woodsy flavor. Not only were these recipes easy; they were also so flavorful that no one would ever guess these peas weren't fresh from the garden.

Sautéed Peas with Shallot and Mint

SERVES 2

Do not thaw the peas before cooking. Regular-size frozen peas can be used in place of baby peas; increase the cooking time in step 2 by 1 to 2 minutes. Add the lemon juice right before serving, or the peas will turn brown.

- 2 teaspoons olive oil
- 1 shallot, minced
- 1 garlic clove, minced
- 1½ cups frozen baby peas (see note)
- 2 tablespoons low-sodium chicken broth
- ⅛ teaspoon sugar
- 2 tablespoons minced fresh mint
- 1 tablespoon unsalted butter
- 1½ teaspoons fresh lemon juice
  Salt and pepper

1. Heat oil in 10-inch skillet over medium heat until shimmering. Add shallot and cook until softened, 2 to 3 minutes. Stir in garlic and cook until fragrant, about 30 seconds.

2. Stir in peas, broth, and sugar. Cover and cook until peas are bright green and just heated through, 2 to 4 minutes. Add mint and butter and toss until incorporated. Off heat, stir in lemon juice, season with salt and pepper to taste, and serve.

VARIATIONS

Sautéed Peas with Leek and Tarragon

Follow recipe for Sautéed Peas with Shallot and Mint, substituting 1 small leek, white and light green parts only, halved lengthwise, sliced thin, and rinsed thoroughly (see page 186), for shallot and increasing cooking time in step 1 to 3 to 5 minutes. Substitute 2 tablespoons heavy cream for chicken broth, 1 tablespoon minced fresh tarragon for mint, and 1½ teaspoons white wine vinegar for lemon juice.

Sautéed Peas with Fennel

If your fennel bulb does not come with fronds, you can substitute 1 tablespoon minced fresh tarragon. See page 123 for a recipe to use up the leftover fennel.

Follow recipe for Sautéed Peas with Shallot and Mint, substituting ½ small fennel bulb, trimmed of stalks, cored, and chopped fine (about ½ cup) (see page 92), for shallot and increasing cooking time in step 1 to 3 to 5 minutes. Substitute 2 tablespoons minced fennel fronds for mint.

Sautéed Peas with Mushrooms and Thyme

Follow recipe for Sautéed Peas with Shallot and Mint, substituting 3 ounces white mushrooms, quartered, for shallot and increasing cooking time in step 1 to 3 to 5 minutes. Substitute 1 tablespoon minced fresh thyme for mint.

PAN-ROASTED CHICKPEAS

LET'S FACE IT: MOST OF US EAT CHICKPEAS IN THE form of hummus, or maybe when tossed into a salad. But humble canned chickpeas, with their buttery, nutty flavor, can also make a terrific, easy-to-prepare side dish when paired with a few well-chosen ingredients.

To start, we added rinsed canned chickpeas to a skillet with water and a sautéed shallot. We brought everything to a simmer, then covered the pan for a few minutes, just until everything was heated all the way through. While the water kept our chickpeas moist and tender, the taste was a little flat. In addition, we had hoped for a saucy dish, but our first trial was looking a little soupy. We'd need to find a way to reduce the liquid to a light, saucy glaze and to amp up the flavor of our dish.

Reducing the liquid to the right consistency was a simple fix: After simmering our chickpeas covered, we uncovered the pan and cooked them for a few minutes longer. Though the legumes were now coated in a light sauce, the flavor was still bland.

Looking for kitchen staples that would turn our sauté-and-serve chickpeas into a flavorful side dish, we reached for garlic and red pepper flakes. Instead of mincing the garlic, we sliced it thin before sautéing it in extra-virgin olive oil. The thin slivers maintained their presence in the finished dish, and a pinch of red pepper flakes provided a bit of heat. While these additions were an improvement, we knew we could do even better.

One quick flavor fix was swapping in chicken broth for water. The chicken broth imparted a rich, deep flavor backbone to the dish, without overpowering the nutty flavor of the chickpeas themselves. And as final touches, parsley and lemon juice gave our canned beans a burst of freshness. Given that chickpeas are so versatile, we created two more variations with distinct flavor profiles. In one variation, sautéed red bell pepper lent a subtle sweetness, and basil made for a bolder, more aromatic dish. For another variation, smoked paprika and cilantro added warmth and citrusy undertones.

Pan-Roasted Chickpeas with Garlic and Parsley

SERVES 2

Make sure you rinse the chickpeas thoroughly before adding them to the pan to get rid of excess salt. This side dish can easily be transformed into dinner when paired with Couscous with Tomato, Scallion, and Lemon (page 254).

   2   **tablespoons extra-virgin olive oil**
   2   **garlic cloves, sliced thin**
       Pinch red pepper flakes
   1   **large shallot, minced**
   1   **(15-ounce) can chickpeas, drained and rinsed (see note)**
  ½   **cup low-sodium chicken broth**
   1   **tablespoon minced fresh parsley**
   1   **teaspoon fresh lemon juice**
       Salt and pepper

1. Combine oil, garlic, and red pepper flakes in 10-inch skillet and cook over medium heat, gently shaking pan to prevent garlic from sticking, until garlic turns pale gold, about 1 minute.

2. Stir in shallot and cook, stirring often, until softened and lightly browned, about 3 minutes. Stir in chickpeas and broth and bring to simmer.

3. Cover and cook until chickpeas are hot and flavors have blended, about 2 minutes. Uncover, increase heat to high, and simmer until liquid has reduced to light coating on bottom of pan, about 3 minutes. Off heat, stir in parsley and lemon juice. Season with salt and pepper to taste and serve.

VARIATIONS

Pan-Roasted Chickpeas with Red Bell Pepper and Basil

Follow recipe for Pan-Roasted Chickpeas with Garlic and Parsley, adding ½ red bell pepper, stemmed, seeded, and chopped, to pan with shallot. Cook until softened, about 5 minutes. Substitute 1 tablespoon chopped fresh basil for parsley.

Pan-Roasted Chickpeas with Smoked Paprika and Cilantro

Follow recipe for Pan-Roasted Chickpeas with Garlic and Parsley, omitting red pepper flakes and adding ¼ teaspoon smoked paprika to pan once shallot has softened. Substitute 1 tablespoon minced fresh cilantro for parsley and ½ teaspoon sherry vinegar for lemon juice.

PAN-ROASTED CARROTS AND PARSNIPS

WHEN IT COMES TO PREPARING ROOT VEGETABLES like carrots and parsnips, nothing coaxes out the naturally sweet and earthy flavors more than roasting. But when you're cooking a side dish for two, the hassle of turning your oven on and waiting for it to preheat just so you can roast a few vegetables doesn't seem worth the bother. Enter pan-roasting, which (as its name implies) relies on a skillet and the stovetop to deliver oven-roasted results in a lot less time. It was easy enough to find recipes for pan-roasted vegetables; the hard part started when we tried making them.

Many recipes instructed us to cook the carrots and parsnips in a nonstick skillet in oil over medium or high heat, covered, to simulate oven-roasting. While this method proved to be good in theory, it gave us burned exteriors with raw centers. The only tip we picked up was using a nonstick skillet, which helped keep the pan surface mess-free as the natural sugars of the carrots and parsnips were released. Other recipes had us steam the vegetables first, then sauté them in butter or oil for color, but the vegetables became too tender toward the end and fell apart. Ever optimistic, we continued on in the hope that our oven would be able to stay off for the evening.

We knew that we would have to cook these vegetables in fat in order to jump-start the browning, so we started by testing both butter and oil to see which would work better. While butter won out on the flavor front, it burned too easily. Using just vegetable oil, we were able to successfully brown the carrots and parsnips, and then turn down the heat and cover the pan so that they could steam and cook through. This gave us evenly browned, tender vegetables, but by the time they were tender, they were also dry and wrinkled. To correct the moisture loss, we added ½ cup of water to the pan before covering, which created a more gentle steaming effect. We knew we were getting somewhere with this approach, but it also washed away the caramelized coating on the vegetables that we had worked so hard to achieve. Maybe switching around the cooking order would help—we'd simmer the vegetables first, then brown them.

We heated the oil in the skillet, then added our carrots, parsnips, and water and covered them. Putting the oil in at the beginning kept the vegetables from sticking to the pan as the water evaporated. Once the vegetables were almost cooked, we removed the lid and reduced the water. When the water was evaporated, our vegetables could sauté until they were well browned and tender. While we were happy with the color we got on the carrots and parsnips, the parsnips had become too mushy in the time it took the carrots to become tender. We wondered if maybe these family members were not created equal after all.

After several tests, we determined that a staggering method worked better. We started by steaming the heartier carrots and then adding the parsnips once the lid was removed. This gave the carrots a head start and the parsnips just the right amount of time to cook all the way through and still caramelize.

Now that we were satisfied with the method, we had to address the complaints we were receiving about the overall "flat" flavor of the dish. Adding a little sugar to enhance the natural sweetness of the vegetables worked like a charm, and adding it at the beginning with the water avoided any burnt sugar disasters. Last, with a little help from our pepper mill and a sprinkling of fresh parsley, we infused our vegetables with a zesty bite. For a more piquant variation, we replaced the sugar with a generous amount of maple syrup and added cayenne at the end for a spicy edge.

NOTES FROM THE TEST KITCHEN

CARROTS' PERFECT MATCH: PARSNIPS

Recipes for roasted carrots pair the vegetable with any one (or more) of a smattering of other root vegetables, from rutabagas to turnips, but we prefer matching carrots with parsnips. Because they are similar in shape to carrots, parsnips allow for evenly cooked vegetables, and their flavor is also the perfect match for that of their perhaps better-known cousin. Tasters have described the flavor of pan-roasted parsnips as "sugary and floral," like "a carrot doused in perfume." Since older, larger parsnips can be tough and fibrous, look for parsnips that are no more than 1 inch in diameter.

SLICING CARROTS AND PARSNIPS ON THE BIAS

For an elegant presentation, slice the carrots and parsnips on the bias into pieces that are ½ inch thick and approximately 2 inches long.

Pan-Roasted Carrots and Parsnips
SERVES 2

When buying parsnips, choose those that are no wider than 1 inch—larger parsnips are likely to have tough, fibrous cores.

- **4 teaspoons vegetable oil**
- **3 small carrots, peeled and sliced ½ inch thick on bias (see photo)**
- **½ cup warm water**
- **½ teaspoon sugar**
- **Salt and pepper**
- **3 small parsnips (see note), peeled and sliced ½ inch thick on bias (see photo)**
- **1 tablespoon minced fresh parsley**

1. Heat oil in 10-inch nonstick skillet over medium heat until shimmering. Stir in carrots, water, sugar, and ¼ teaspoon salt and cover. Cook, stirring occasionally, until carrots begin to soften but substantial amount of water remains in skillet, about 5 minutes.

2. Uncover, add parsnips, and increase heat to high. Cook, stirring occasionally, until water has completely evaporated and vegetables are well browned, 6 to 8 minutes. Off heat, stir in parsley, season with salt and pepper to taste, and serve.

VARIATION

Maple-Cayenne Pan-Roasted Carrots and Parsnips
Follow recipe for Pan-Roasted Carrots and Parsnips, substituting 3 tablespoons maple syrup for sugar and pinch cayenne for parsley.

BUTTERMILK MASHED POTATOES

GENERALLY, MASHED POTATOES SEEM TO BE reserved for a table of hungry diners, whether it's Thanksgiving or a Sunday dinner. But cooking for two doesn't mean you don't also crave a creamy mound of spuds. We particularly like the tang and deceptive richness of buttermilk mashed potatoes, so we set out to develop a recipe for two.

We started by choosing the right potatoes. In the test kitchen, we've found that simmering whole russet potatoes in their jackets yields a true potato flavor and a rich, silky texture. But simmering whole potatoes until tender can take some time. Peeling and cutting up the russets into smaller pieces cut down on cooking time, but the resulting potatoes had too thin a texture and a weak taste. We wondered if switching the variety of potato we were using would make a difference.

After a few more tests, we found that red potatoes made for a dense, gluey, and pasty mash, but peeled and cut Yukon Golds made for creamy, smooth mashed potatoes. Why did the Yukon Golds behave so differently from the russets? Russet potatoes have more starch than Yukon Golds and therefore absorb a lot more water. So while mashed russets became soggy and bland if peeled before cooking, Yukon Golds turned out just right.

During our testing, we examined plate after plate of mashed potatoes, trying to gauge the ideal amount of mash for two. Ultimately, we decided that a pound of potatoes yielded two generous servings; a pound and change provided way too much food for two, while 12 ounces gave us two skimpy portions.

The next hurdle to jump was figuring out the right amount of buttermilk. We started out with a cup of buttermilk, but the tanginess came on way too strong and gave the potatoes a loose consistency. Reducing the amount to ⅓ cup turned out potatoes with a mildly tangy taste that kept every bite interesting. But at this point, with only buttermilk added to our mashed potatoes, they tasted lean. Butter was the solution—just 3 tablespoons provided adequate richness and creaminess. But now we had a new problem on our hands; our mashed potatoes were curdled, crumbly, and dry.

Buttermilk curdles at 160 degrees, a temperature reached almost instantly when the cold liquid hits steaming-hot potatoes. For our next test, we melted the butter and added it to room-temperature (not cold) buttermilk, thereby coating the proteins in the buttermilk and protecting them from the heat shock that causes curdling. Now we had perfectly creamy spuds. Not only that, but they were also perfectly portioned for two—and they still met all of our comfort-food expectations.

Buttermilk Mashed Potatoes
SERVES 2

To achieve the proper texture, it is important to cook the potatoes thoroughly; they are done if they break apart when a knife is inserted and gently wiggled. To reduce the chance of curdling, make sure the buttermilk is at room temperature when mixed with the cooled melted butter.

1 **pound Yukon Gold potatoes (about 2 medium), peeled and sliced ½ inch thick**
  Salt and pepper
⅓ **cup buttermilk, room temperature (see note)**
3 **tablespoons unsalted butter, melted and cooled**

1. Place potatoes and ½ teaspoon salt in medium saucepan, add enough cold water to cover potatoes by 1 inch, and bring to boil over high heat. Reduce heat to medium-low and simmer until potatoes break apart when pierced with knife, 12 to 15 minutes.

2. Drain potatoes and return to saucepan set on still-hot burner. Using potato masher, mash potatoes until few small lumps remain. Gently stir buttermilk and cooled butter together in small bowl until combined. Fold buttermilk mixture into potatoes until just incorporated. Season with salt and pepper to taste and serve.

BUTTERMILK MASHED POTATOES

AUSTRIAN-STYLE POTATO SALAD

POTATO SALAD ALMOST ALWAYS CONJURES UP images of fork-friendly chunks of potato in a mayonnaise dressing or German-style sliced potatoes tossed with a warm bacon vinaigrette. Less familiar, but no less tasty, is creamy, yet light, Austrian-style potato salad. We set out to bring this elegant version of potato salad to the for-two table.

Austrian potato salad is served either warm or at room temperature and relies on a vinaigrette that includes white wine vinegar, chicken broth, pickles, and herbs. We started by testing the most popular method for making the dish: Boil whole potatoes in their jackets, peel and slice them while hot, then toss in dressing until the starch from the potatoes turns the dressing creamy. This sounded simple enough, but we found that the line between creamy and soupy was too thin, and our window for perfectly cooked potatoes was too small to ensure that this recipe would work every time. If we cooked the potatoes for too long, they fell apart when combined with the dressing; all that work and we just ended up with mashed potatoes. Undercooking our potatoes meant they wouldn't release enough starch to thicken the dressing, leaving us with room-temperature potato soup. Last, there was the issue of stirring: Too much mixing turned the potatoes gluey, and with not enough stirring the creamy consistency we wanted was nonexistent.

We decided to tackle the variety of potato first. Traditionally, the choice of potato for this dish is the starchy Austrian fingerling known as the crescent potato. We were right in guessing that they wouldn't be available at our local supermarket, so we wanted to find a more widely available potato that would work just as well. We found that starchy russets disintegrated too much, and waxy reds didn't have enough starch and left the sauce too thin. We finally found a winner with Yukon Golds. They had just enough starch to help deliver creaminess while still holding their shape when it came time to mix everything together. Two potatoes provided two ample servings of potato salad.

Though many recipes called for cooking the potatoes in their skins to improve flavor, tasters found it made very little difference. This method may have worked fine for smaller fingerling potatoes, but Yukon Golds needed a different method. Peeling and cutting them into thin slices before cooking avoided the consequence of uneven cooking and also saved us from burning our fingers trying to get the hot skins off.

Since we were dealing with such a small amount of potatoes, we had to be sure they wouldn't overcook. Adding a little acid in the form of vinegar to the cooking liquid helped keep the potatoes' structure intact by slowing down the rate at which the starches were released. As an added bonus, the vinegar permeated the potatoes as they cooked, giving the finished dish an even tangier flavor. Discovering the pleasant side effect of the vinegar had made us wonder what would happen if we used the chicken broth, traditionally reserved for the dressing, as part of the cooking liquid. This hunch proved to be successful because it imparted a subtle complexity that is usually not found in potato salads.

The only remaining barrier to making this recipe foolproof was the mixing. Even when the potatoes were cooked perfectly, stirring too much led to an excess of starch that turned the potatoes from creamy to gluey. In order to ensure that the same amount of starch was released each time, we incorporated a measured amount of cooked potatoes with the reserved cooking liquid and mashed them until the mixture became thick and creamy. Only then were we able to gently fold in the remaining potatoes without running the risk of them falling apart. We were happy with the consistent results that came from using a portion of the potatoes as our thickener.

Our last task was to examine the flavorings that go into an authentic Austrian potato salad. The traditional choice is a lightly pickled cucumber known as *sauergurken*, but we wanted an easy-to-find alternative. We tried a range of pickles to find the perfect substitute, quickly dismissing varieties such as bread-and-butter pickles, because of the cloying sweetness they gave the salad. Kosher dills were OK, but our tasters thought that cornichons—just three were sufficient—were the undisputed winners. Their sharp, salty flavor and notable crunch went perfectly with our mellow and tender potatoes. All we needed now was a little Dijon mustard for depth and a sprinkling of minced chives, and our flavorful, creamy, not-so-traditional potato salad was complete.

Austrian-Style Potato Salad

SERVES 2

The finished salad should be creamy and loose, with chunks of potato that keep their shape but are very tender. To maintain its consistency, don't refrigerate the potato salad; it should be served within 4 hours of preparation.

- 1 **pound Yukon Gold potatoes (about 2 medium), peeled, quartered lengthwise, and cut into ½-inch-thick slices**
- ½ **cup low-sodium chicken broth**
- ½ **cup water**
- 1 **tablespoon white wine vinegar**
- 1½ **teaspoons sugar**
  Salt and pepper
- 2 **tablespoons vegetable oil**
- 1½ **teaspoons Dijon mustard**
- 3 **cornichons, minced**
- 1 **shallot, minced**
- 1 **tablespoon minced fresh chives**

1. Bring potatoes, broth, water, 1½ teaspoons vinegar, sugar, and ½ teaspoon salt to boil in 10-inch skillet over high heat. Reduce heat to medium-low, cover, and cook until potatoes are tender but not falling apart, about 15 minutes. Uncover, increase heat to high, and cook until liquid reduces and thickens slightly, about 2 minutes.

2. Drain potatoes in colander set over large bowl, reserving cooking liquid. Set drained potatoes aside. Pour off and discard all but ¼ cup cooking liquid (if there is not enough to make ¼ cup, add water). Whisk remaining 1½ teaspoons vinegar, oil, and mustard into cooking liquid.

3. Add ¼ cup cooked potatoes to bowl with dressing and mash with potato masher or fork until a thick and chunky sauce forms. Gently fold in remaining potatoes, cornichons, shallot, and chives. Season with salt and pepper to taste and serve warm or at room temperature.

QUINOA SALAD

WITH ITS HEARTY FLAVOR, UNIQUE CHEWY TEXture, and complete protein properties, quinoa has increasingly become a popular side dish. Quinoa is also easy to prepare, making it a great choice for weeknight cooking. It was settled—we set out to develop our own quinoa side dish. And because quinoa is often used as the base of a salad, not unlike couscous, we started there.

Almost every recipe we looked at called for the same cooking method: Rinse the quinoa to wash off the bitter protective layer (called saponin), bring it to a boil in either water or broth, and simmer over low heat, covered, for 15 minutes. We found that this basic method worked pretty well to get the quinoa cooked; however, it made for a wet, dense salad, so we decided to make a pilaf-style quinoa that would be lighter, drier, and fluffier. After rinsing the quinoa, we let it dry on a towel and then transferred it to a saucepan to toast (drying the quinoa was an important step if we wanted it to toast properly). Toasting grains before adding liquid is standard pilaf procedure because it ensures plumped, individual grains. After the quinoa became lightly toasted and aromatic, we added water and salt and brought it to a simmer. Once it was simmering, we covered it and let it cook until it had absorbed most of the water and was just about tender. Because the quinoa cooks further while it cools, it was important to make sure we didn't let it overcook. By using a baking sheet, we were able to spread the quinoa out evenly, which ensured a quicker cool-down.

This pilaf method dramatically improved the quinoa's texture, ensuring the dry, separate grains we sought. With our cooking method squared away, we started creating a flavorful vinaigrette and appropriate additions for our quinoa salad. Simplicity was the best way to go for adding flavor. The grain's down-to-earth flavor paired well with jalapeño and cilantro, and our tasters thought we should build on the Latin flavor profile a little more by making a zesty lime vinaigrette. Crisp red bell pepper added a much-needed sweetness and crunch, and a little cumin gave an extra layer of complexity and warmth to our bright and delectable salad.

QUINOA SALAD WITH RED BELL PEPPER AND CILANTRO

Quinoa Salad with Red Bell Pepper and Cilantro
SERVES 2

To make this dish spicier, add the jalapeño seeds. After 12 minutes of cooking, there will still be a little bit of water in the pan, but this will evaporate as the quinoa cools. The quinoa can be made ahead and refrigerated in an airtight container for up to 2 days. See page 41 for a recipe to use up the leftover jalapeño.

NOTES FROM THE TEST KITCHEN

ALL ABOUT QUINOA
Quinoa originated in the Andes Mountains of South America, and while it is generally treated as a grain, it is actually the seed of the goosefoot plant. Quinoa has gained in popularity in recent years, in part because of its reputation as a "supergrain." This moniker refers to the fact that quinoa is high in protein, and its protein is complete—that is, quinoa possesses all of the amino acids in the balanced amounts that our bodies require. Beyond its nutritional prowess, we love quinoa for its addictive crunch, nutty taste, and ease of preparation. Note that unless it is labeled as "prewashed," quinoa should always be rinsed before cooking to remove its protective layer (called saponin), which is unpleasantly bitter.

RINSING AND DRYING QUINOA

1. Rinse the quinoa in a fine-mesh strainer until the water runs clear, and let it drain briefly.

2. Then spread the grains on a kitchen towel–lined rimmed baking sheet and let them dry for 15 minutes.

3. To remove the grains from the towel, pick up the towel by the corners and gently shake the grains into a bowl.

⅔ cup quinoa, rinsed and dried on towel (see photos)

1 cup water

Salt and pepper

2 tablespoons finely chopped red bell pepper

¼ jalapeño chile, stemmed, seeded, and minced

1 shallot, minced

1 tablespoon minced fresh cilantro

2 tablespoons extra-virgin olive oil

2 teaspoons fresh lime juice

1 teaspoon Dijon mustard

1 small garlic clove, minced

¼ teaspoon ground cumin

1. Toast quinoa in small saucepan over medium heat, stirring often, until lightly toasted and aromatic, about 5 minutes. Stir in water and ⅛ teaspoon salt and bring to simmer. Reduce heat to low, cover, and continue to simmer until quinoa has absorbed most of water and is just tender, 12 to 14 minutes longer. Spread quinoa on rimmed baking sheet lined with towel and set aside until tender and cool, about 20 minutes.

2. When quinoa is cool, transfer to serving bowl. Stir in bell pepper, jalapeño, shallot, and cilantro. In separate bowl, whisk oil, lime juice, mustard, garlic, and cumin together until well combined. Pour over quinoa and toss to coat. Season with salt and pepper to taste and serve.

COUSCOUS

NOWADAYS, JUST ABOUT EVERY SUPERMARKET SELLS boxes of quick-cooking flavored couscous. But the seasoning packets in these boxes never manage to impress, instead infusing the couscous with a dry, powdery, processed flavor. We set out to make our own couscous side dish—it had to be just as easy and speedy, but it had to be fresh and flavorful, and nothing like the dusty, stale-tasting side dish solutions sold at the grocery store.

We started our recipe following basic couscous cooking procedure: We put our couscous in a bowl, boiled water, poured it over the bowl, and covered the bowl tightly with plastic wrap. Once it was steamed and completely tender, we fluffed up the couscous with a fork and tasted it. Though it was cooked to perfection, we knew we could do better in the flavor department. Taking a cue from our quinoa salad (see page 253), we decided to first toast our couscous in a saucepan until a portion of the grains began to brown slightly. After transferring the couscous to a bowl, we used the same saucepan to sauté a single shallot and garlic clove in some olive oil, before adding our water to the pan. Once the liquid came to a boil, we poured it over our toasted couscous and wrapped it tightly once more.

After just 12 minutes we had the same tender and fluffy grains but with a stronger foundation of flavor. However, our side dish still needed a flavor boost. For more savory depth, we decided to replace some of the water with chicken broth. Adding some lemon zest and a pinch of cayenne pepper to our aromatics made for a more flavorful dish overall.

At this point, what was lacking was a bright, fresh punch. After the couscous had cooked, we stirred in lemon juice for brightness and sliced scallions and chopped tomato for crunch and texture. Finally, a little more olive oil added moisture and flavor to our quick and easy couscous side dish—no spice packet needed.

Couscous with Tomato, Scallion, and Lemon
SERVES 2

Do not use Israeli couscous in this recipe; its larger size requires a different cooking method. Whole wheat couscous can be substituted for regular couscous.

- ⅓ cup couscous (see note)
- 1 tablespoon extra-virgin olive oil
- 1 shallot, minced
- 1 garlic clove, minced
- ¼ teaspoon grated lemon zest plus 1 teaspoon fresh lemon juice
- Pinch cayenne pepper
- ¼ cup water
- ¼ cup low-sodium chicken broth
- 1 plum tomato, cored, seeded, and chopped fine
- ½ scallion, sliced thin
- Salt and pepper

1. Toast couscous in small saucepan over medium-high heat, stirring often, until some grains begin to brown, about 3 minutes. Transfer couscous to medium bowl and set aside.

2. Heat 1½ teaspoons oil in saucepan over medium heat until shimmering. Add shallot and cook until softened, 2 to 3 minutes. Stir in garlic, lemon zest, and cayenne and cook until fragrant, about 30 seconds. Stir in water and broth and bring to boil.

3. Stir boiling liquid into couscous, cover bowl tightly with plastic wrap, and let sit until grains are tender, about 12 minutes. Uncover bowl and fluff grains with fork. Stir in remaining 1½ teaspoons oil, lemon juice, tomato, and scallion. Season with salt and pepper to taste and serve.

VARIATION

Couscous with Saffron, Raisins, and Toasted Almonds
Follow recipe for Couscous with Tomato, Scallion, and Lemon, substituting pinch crumbled saffron threads for garlic and pinch ground cinnamon for lemon zest. Substitute ¼ cup raisins for tomato and 2 tablespoons toasted sliced almonds for scallion.

CREAMY PARMESAN POLENTA

OFTEN REGARDED AS ITALY'S OTHER NATIONAL dish, polenta has been a staple in northern Italy for centuries. And we can see why: It's simple, versatile, satisfying, and thrifty. Unfortunately, its long and fussy preparation time keeps this timeless dish off the weeknight supper rotation. We wanted to have all of the spoils of a creamy, slow-cooked polenta without the steep time commitment, but we also hoped we didn't have to resort to instant brands, which we've historically found result in a gluey, bland dish. With instant brands off the table, we considered our options when it came to types of cornmeal.

First, we considered whole grain cornmeal, which we prepared following the traditional (read: time-consuming and arm ache–inducing) method. Though the whole grain cornmeal boasted a full-corn flavor, we couldn't get over its grittiness, and no matter how long we cooked the cornmeal, its texture didn't get any better. Next, we tried degerminated cornmeal, in which the hard hull and the germ have been removed from each kernel. After a few tests, we found that this was the way to go. Degerminated cornmeal can be found in a variety of grinds; we preferred coarse-ground cornmeal (about the size of couscous) for the way it stayed soft yet hearty after cooking. (In supermarkets, this is usually labeled as traditional polenta.)

Before we could refine our cooking method, we needed to understand the overall process. After a discussion with our science editor, we had a clear picture of what was happening in a pot of polenta: When the starchy part of the corn kernel comes in contact with hot water, it eventually absorbs the liquid, swells, and then bursts, releasing starch. At the same time, the grains soften and lose their gritty texture. While the explanation is simple, it takes a long time for the water to crack open the kernel. Also, the pot must be stirred constantly; otherwise the polenta will heat unevenly, causing lumps. Although we understood the chemistry, we still weren't any closer to having a fast and stir-free side dish; we wondered if thinking outside the box would help.

After consulting numerous recipes and cookbooks, we found our answer in a bean recipe, of all places, which advocated adding a little baking soda in order to accelerate the cooking process and soften the bean skins. We decided to see if this same ingredient would work for our cornmeal, so we started another batch and added ⅛ teaspoon of baking soda to the water as soon as it came to a boil. To our surprise and delight, the cornmeal cooked up in less than 10 minutes, but the baking soda had worked so effectively that the porridge turned gluey and had a weird chemical flavor. We lowered the amount and tried just a pinch, which produced a polenta that still cooked in about 15 minutes, without any gluey texture or foreign flavors.

To eliminate the need for constant stirring, we decided to try covering the pot in our next test, basically steaming the grains. We covered the polenta after stirring it into the boiling water, baking soda, and salt solution, then reduced the heat to the lowest level. To see how far we could push it, we didn't uncover the pot for the entire 15 minutes. With bated breath, we lifted the lid and found that the baking soda helped break down the granules so efficiently and uniformly that the bottom and top cooked through at the same time. But also, we found that the low, gentle heat facilitated even cooking and lump-free cornmeal, no stirring required.

We repeated our recipe one last time to work out any small kinks and found that all it needed was a brief whisking as we added our polenta to the boiling water, and then another short stir about five minutes later to smooth out any lumps that had formed. Other than that, we didn't even have to lift the lid until it was time to finish the dish with cheese and butter. High-quality Parmesan cheese, folded in, gave this humble classic a nutty tang, and just a tablespoon of butter added a layer of richness to make it a satisfying dish with an impressive lack of effort.

Creamy Parmesan Polenta
SERVES 2

Be sure to use traditional dried polenta here, not instant polenta or precooked logs of polenta; dried polenta can be found alongside cornmeal or pasta in the supermarket (it looks like large-ground cornmeal). Do not omit the baking soda—it reduces the cooking time and makes for a creamier polenta. It is important to cook the polenta over very low heat; if your stovetop runs hot, and you do not have a flame tamer, see page 133 for how to make one.

1⅔ cups water
    Salt and pepper
    Pinch baking soda (see note)
⅓ cup polenta (see note)
1 tablespoon unsalted butter
1 ounce Parmesan cheese, grated (about ½ cup), plus extra for serving

1. Bring water to boil in small, heavy-bottomed saucepan over medium-high heat. Stir in ¼ teaspoon salt and baking soda. Slowly pour cornmeal into water in steady stream, stirring constantly with wooden spoon or rubber spatula. Bring mixture to boil, stirring constantly, about 30 seconds. Reduce heat to lowest possible setting and cover.

2. After 5 minutes, whisk polenta to smooth out any lumps that may have formed, making sure to scrape down sides and bottom of pan. Cover and continue to cook, without stirring, until grains of cornmeal are tender but slightly al dente, 8 to 10 minutes longer. (The polenta should be loose and barely hold its shape; it will continue to thicken as it cools.)

3. Off heat, stir in butter and Parmesan and season with salt and pepper to taste. Let stand, covered, about 5 minutes. Serve, passing extra Parmesan separately.

WHITE WINE–POACHED PEARS

BAKED GOODS & DESSERTS

COFFEE CAKE MUFFINS

A TRANSFORMATION OF THE ULTIMATE AMERICAN breakfast treat, the perfect coffee cake muffin has the best features of coffee cake—rich, buttery cake and crunchy, sweet streusel—in an abbreviated form. Its texture should lie somewhere between the delicate, fine crumb of coffee cake and the slightly coarser, chewier crumb of a muffin. Too often, however, coffee cake muffins fall terribly short of their potential. Cloyingly sweet and pasty or dry and leaden, these muffins are often a disappointment. We knew we could do much better—and we were encouraged by the fact that households of two would appreciate not being left with most of a 9-inch coffee cake hogging counter space.

We began our testing by trying comparable recipes we unearthed in our research. Many recipes opted for sour cream over butter, but sour cream alone made our muffins greasy. It was clear we'd need to use both sour cream and butter for muffins (we settled on four muffins as the optimum yield) with a rich, buttery flavor. For the butter, we started at a meager 2 tablespoons and went up a teaspoon at a time until we were satisfied with the buttery-rich flavor that 4 tablespoons provided.

We then moved on to the sour cream. We started with 1 tablespoon and tested all the way up to ¼ cup. Somewhere in between—at 2 tablespoons plus 2 teaspoons—we found success. In addition to the moisture and richness the sour cream contributed, it also worked to provide the perfect light texture and kept our muffins from being overly sweet.

For the streusel topping, the combination of nuts, sugar, and cinnamon used in many recipes results in a sandy mixture that slides off the top of the muffin and winds up on a plate, napkin, or the floor. We wondered what would happen if we put the streusel inside the muffin, rather than on top. We combined granulated sugar, brown sugar (which added a deeper flavor than white sugar alone), flour, and cinnamon. After filling the muffin cups partway with batter, we sprinkled on some of the streusel mixture and added more batter. Now the streusel stayed in place. Not only did we have a more flavorful muffin, but it was also more attractive, with an appealing swirl floating through it.

We were ready to bake our coffee cake muffins but wondered about batter placement. Whether we were using a 6-cup or a 12-cup muffin tin, there would be empty muffin cups left after we filled 4 cups with our batter. Did it matter which cups were filled? Our tests revealed that placement didn't matter at all; all the muffins, regardless of placement, rose and browned equally. Since the streusel filling stuck to the tins, we used cupcake liners to make muffin removal easier.

After 20 minutes in a 350-degree oven, our muffins were subtly sweet with a warm, cinnamon-sugar center. But while our finished muffins were full of streusel flavor, their tops were now woefully bare. A light dusting of confectioners' sugar remedied this and added a perfectly sweet finish.

Coffee Cake Muffins

MAKES 4 MUFFINS

Any size muffin tin will work here, and the batter can be placed in any of the muffin cups. See page 178 for a recipe to use up the leftover sour cream.

⅓ cup (2⅓ ounces) granulated sugar
½ cup (2½ ounces) unbleached all-purpose flour
2 tablespoons plus 2 teaspoons dark brown sugar
1 teaspoon ground cinnamon
⅛ teaspoon baking powder
⅛ teaspoon baking soda
⅛ teaspoon salt
4 tablespoons (½ stick) unsalted butter, cut into 4 pieces and chilled
1 large egg
2 tablespoons plus 2 teaspoons sour cream
Confectioners' sugar, for dusting

1. Adjust oven rack to middle position and heat oven to 350 degrees. Place 4 paper or foil liners in 4 cups of muffin tin.

2. Pulse granulated sugar, 8 teaspoons flour, and 4 teaspoons brown sugar together in food processor to combine, about 3 pulses. Transfer 2 tablespoons processed sugar mixture to small bowl (leaving rest in food processor) and whisk in remaining 4 teaspoons brown sugar and cinnamon to make streusel; set aside.

3. Add remaining flour, baking powder, baking soda, and salt to sugar mixture left in food processor and pulse to combine, about 5 pulses. Scatter butter evenly over top and pulse until mixture breaks down into small pebbly pieces, about 8 pulses. Add egg and sour cream and pulse until batter is well combined and thick, about 8 pulses.

4. Portion generous tablespoon batter into each muffin cup, then sprinkle each with scant 1 tablespoon streusel mixture. Spoon remaining batter over streusel. Bake until muffin tops are golden and toothpick inserted into center of muffin comes out with few crumbs attached, 20 to 24 minutes, rotating pan halfway through baking.

5. Cool muffins in tin for 5 minutes, then turn out onto wire rack and let cool for 5 minutes. Dust lightly with confectioners' sugar before serving.

CHEDDAR CHEESE BREAD

CHEESE BREAD IS THE PERFECT ACCOMPANIMENT to chili and soup or a nice change from the usual toast alongside eggs. Using a mini loaf pan, we aimed to develop a for-two version that was richly flavored, moist, and satisfying.

We began by reviewing the test kitchen's established recipe for cheese bread. Since this recipe yields a 9-inch loaf and our goal was to produce a single 5½ by 3-inch loaf, we had quite a bit of trimming to do. For our first test, we cut the recipe in half, but there was so much batter, it overflowed in the oven. We found that reducing the original recipe's ingredient amounts by two-thirds worked much better, and the batter stayed put, rising slightly over the rim once baked (but not spilling over).

As for the cheese, earlier tests for our published recipe showed that small chunks of cheese, not shreds, were best, as they melted into luscious, cheesy pockets. Parmesan and cheddar were the two cheeses tasters preferred, as they provided a nice balance of intense cheesiness and nutty flavor. We cut our cheddar into ½-inch chunks and shredded the Parmesan, then mixed both into our batter. While the cheese didn't inhibit the bread's rise—which indicated that our scaled-down amounts of cheese and baking powder were in balance—it did give us bread with an overly dense texture and pockets of cheese that were too big. Tasters agreed that the large chunks of cheese were taking up too much space in our smaller loaf pan.

Cutting the cheddar into smaller, ¼-inch pieces made for a less dense bread, but a few slices revealed an interior that was more moist than it should have been. We found that decreasing the amount of liquid (milk, per the original recipe) in the batter helped, but the bread still seemed just a bit too moist. We couldn't decrease the liquid any further for fear our batter wouldn't hold together, so instead we tried increasing the amount of flour. By adding just 2 more tablespoons, we were able to get the texture of our cheese bread in balance, leaving us with a rich, tender crumb and pockets of gooey sharp cheddar.

For an ultra-cheesy finish, we coated the interior of our mini loaf pan with shredded Parmesan before filling it with batter. A final sprinkling of Parmesan over the top ensured that when we pulled our mini cheese bread from the oven, it had a crispy, bronzed crust.

Cheddar Cheese Bread

MAKES ONE 5½ BY 3-INCH LOAF

You will need a 5½ by 3-inch loaf pan or a pan of similar size for this recipe (see page 3). Shredding the Parmesan on the large holes of a box grater and sprinkling it over the top of the bread adds a nice texture and helps prevent the cheese from burning; do not grate it fine or use pregrated Parmesan. A mild, soft Asiago cheese, crumbled into ¼-inch pieces, is a nice substitute for the cheddar. The texture of the bread improves as it cools, so resist the urge to slice the loaf while it is piping hot. The bread can be wrapped tightly in plastic wrap and stored at room temperature for up to 3 days. See page 178 for a recipe to use up the leftover sour cream.

1 ounce Parmesan cheese, shredded on large holes of box grater (about ⅓ cup; see note)

¾ cup (3¾ ounces) plus 2 tablespoons unbleached all-purpose flour

1 teaspoon baking powder

¼ teaspoon salt

Pinch cayenne pepper

Pinch pepper

2 ounces extra-sharp cheddar cheese (see note), cut into ¼-inch cubes (½ cup)

¼ cup whole milk

3 tablespoons sour cream

1 tablespoon unsalted butter, melted and cooled

1 large egg

1. Adjust oven rack to middle position and heat oven to 350 degrees. Grease 5½ by 3-inch loaf pan, then sprinkle 2 tablespoons plus 1 teaspoon Parmesan evenly over bottom of pan.

2. Whisk flour, baking powder, salt, cayenne, and pepper together in medium bowl. Fold in cheddar, breaking up clumps, until it is coated with flour mixture. In separate bowl, whisk milk, sour cream, melted butter, and egg together until smooth. Gently fold milk mixture into flour mixture with rubber spatula until just combined. (Do not overmix.) Batter will be heavy and thick.

3. Scrape batter into prepared pan and smooth top. Sprinkle remaining 3 tablespoons Parmesan evenly over top. Bake until golden brown and toothpick inserted into center comes out with few crumbs attached, 30 to 40 minutes, rotating pan halfway through baking.

4. Let bread cool in pan for 5 minutes, then turn it out onto wire rack and let cool for 1 hour before serving.

SIMPLE DROP BISCUITS

CUT-OUT BAKING POWDER BISCUITS HAVE THEIR place, but you can't beat the ease of a drop biscuit. With their crisp and craggy golden brown exteriors full of hills and valleys, and their tender, fluffy interiors, drop biscuits are both eye-catching and incredibly satisfying. And unlike baking powder biscuits that are split in half and buttered, drop biscuits are meant to be broken apart and eaten as is, piece by buttery piece. Since a standard recipe yields too many biscuits for most households of two, we decided to scale down the recipe without sacrificing any of the satisfaction.

While both types of biscuit use the same handful of ingredients, drop biscuits don't rely on any of the finicky steps rolled biscuits require. There's no need to cut super-cold butter into the dry ingredients, and kneading and rolling aren't necessary. Drop biscuits barely require a recipe: Flour, leavener, and salt are combined in a bowl; the wet ingredients (milk or buttermilk and melted butter or vegetable oil) are stirred together in a measuring cup; the wet ingredients are stirred into the dry; and the resulting batter (which is wetter than traditional biscuit dough) is scooped up and dropped onto a baking sheet. We hoped that developing a recipe for four drop biscuits would be as simple as it sounded.

Using the test kitchen's standard formula for drop biscuits, we came up with a working recipe. We settled on ⅔ cup of all-purpose flour, ¾ teaspoon of baking powder, ¼ teaspoon of baking soda, ¼ teaspoon of sugar, ⅛ teaspoon of salt, ½ cup of buttermilk, and 2 tablespoons of melted butter. A few preliminary tests had told us that butter was the way to go, as it provided more flavor than vegetable oil. Once the wet and dry ingredients were just combined, we used a ¼-cup dry measure to scoop the batter onto a parchment-lined baking sheet and baked the biscuits in a 450-degree oven. Both the texture and flavor of our biscuits needed some improvement—the biscuits were slightly heavy and denser than we wanted, and the flavor was on the sweet side. It was clear we had some rejiggering of our recipe to do.

The biscuits' texture indicated that there was too much buttermilk in the dough. Cutting the amount by half (from ½ cup to ¼ cup) was too drastic—now our biscuits were dry and crumbly. We found that the middle ground—⅓ cup—provided a tender, buttery interior and a craggy, crunchy exterior.

As for the sweetness of the biscuits, a quick fix—cutting the amount of sugar by half, to ⅛ teaspoon—kept the biscuits from tasting as if they were destined for the dessert table (with berries and whipped cream piled on top).

There was just one aspect of the recipe that seemed slightly finicky. For the buttermilk and melted butter to emulsify properly, the buttermilk had to come to room temperature (which involved some waiting on our part), and the melted butter had to cool down (requiring more waiting). For a quick and simple recipe, this waiting seemed like a hassle. We wondered what would happen if we let our impetuous sides get the best of us and combined the melted butter with straight-from-the-refrigerator buttermilk. The first thing we noticed was that the butter formed clumps in the buttermilk. While this didn't look promising, we held our breath as we mixed the rest of the dough, suspecting this misstep would lead to flat biscuits. Fortunately, this misstep turned out to be the final secret to our recipe. The lumps of butter turned to steam in the oven and helped create more rise. The clumpy buttermilk seemed to mimic the positive effects of making biscuits the old-fashioned way—with bits of cold butter left in the dough—but this method was better on two counts: It was more reliable and less messy. The only hard part was having the patience to wait for the biscuits to cool down before devouring them.

Simple Drop Biscuits

A ¼-cup spring-loaded ice cream scoop (also called a #16 scoop) makes portioning these biscuits particularly easy. You will need about 1 teaspoon melted butter for brushing the tops of the biscuits.

- ⅔ **cup (3⅓ ounces) unbleached all-purpose flour**
- ¾ **teaspoon baking powder**
- ¼ **teaspoon baking soda**
- ⅛ **teaspoon sugar**
- ⅛ **teaspoon salt**
- ⅓ **cup buttermilk, chilled**
- 2 **tablespoons unsalted butter, melted and slightly cooled, plus extra for brushing (see note)**

1. Adjust oven rack to middle position and heat oven to 450 degrees. Line baking sheet with parchment paper.

2. Whisk flour, baking powder, baking soda, sugar, and salt together in medium bowl. In small bowl, stir chilled buttermilk and melted butter together until butter forms small clumps. Stir buttermilk mixture into flour mixture with rubber spatula until just incorporated and dough pulls away from sides of bowl.

3. Using greased ¼-cup measure, scoop out and drop four mounds of dough onto prepared baking sheet, spacing them about 1½ inches apart. Bake until tops are golden brown and crisp, 12 to 15 minutes, rotating pan halfway through baking.

4. Brush baked biscuits with extra melted butter, transfer to wire rack, and let cool for 5 minutes. Serve warm.

NOTES FROM THE TEST KITCHEN

THE KEY TO LIGHT AND FLUFFY BISCUITS

When slightly cooled melted butter is stirred into cold buttermilk, the butter clumps. Although it looks like a mistake, it's not; the clumps of butter turn to steam in the oven, ensuring a light and fluffy interior.

CREAM AND CURRANT SCONES

SCONES ARE A POPULAR COFFEEHOUSE OFFERING, but order one and you'll wonder why; most of the ones we've sampled were dry, crumbly, or bland. We wanted scones that were light and delicate, with a tender crumb and an ever-so-slightly browned top. We set out to develop a recipe for scones for two; four seemed like a good number, providing enough for breakfast and to satisfy an afternoon craving.

Most recipes we surveyed used similar amounts of flour—about 2 cups—to produce eight scones, but they used different types of flour. We figured we'd need to cut the amount of flour down to 1 cup for our batch of four scones, but we'd have to do some legwork to figure out which type of flour to use. We tested bread flour, cake flour, and all-purpose flour, and the differences in outcome were astonishing. The scones made with bread flour were heavy and tough. Cake flour produced scones that were doughy in the center, with a raw taste and poor texture. All-purpose flour was the clear winner, resulting in scones that were light and tender.

For the butter, we tested varying amounts, ending up at 3 tablespoons for rich scones with a tender texture. Any more butter, and the dough was too soft; any less, and the scones baked up dry and tough.

Not surprisingly, the choice of liquid also profoundly affected the flavor of our scones. Scones made with milk were bland and dry. Buttermilk gave us scones with plenty of flavor, but they were too flaky and biscuitlike. Scones made with cream were both light in texture and flavorful.

Conventional recipes tend to call for ⅓ cup or ½ cup of sugar for eight scones. Cutting the amount to ¼ cup gave us toothache-inducing scones; half that amount (2 tablespoons) worked much better.

To enhance their appeal, scones are often coated with a sweet glaze or filled with dried fruit or chocolate. Chocolate scones had their proponents in the test kitchen, but we were after a morning or teatime treat, not dessert. We opted for fruit and tried raisins, cranberries, and currants. The currants won out, providing a slightly sweet-tart flavor that didn't overwhelm the scones.

The quickest and easiest way we found to mix the dough was in a food processor. We found the food processor to be more reliable than hand mixing, which can overheat the butter and soften it. For shaping the scones, many recipes suggest using a 9-inch round cake pan as a mold before cutting the dough into wedges. But with so little dough, we did away with the cake pan entirely and simply pressed the dough into a 5-inch circle of even thickness before cutting it into four wedges.

The biggest problem we encountered in our scaled-down recipe arose when we put the scones in the oven. Without the extra scones to absorb the heat from our 450-degree oven (the temperature stipulated by a number of recipes), our scones began to darken before they completely baked through, resulting in moist, gummy centers. Reducing the heat to 425 degrees merely bought us a few more minutes before the scones began to burn—but it still wasn't enough to fully bake them. We turned the oven knob down to 400 degrees—still no luck. Finally, at the gentler temperature of 375 degrees, we were able to bake the scones for a full 20 minutes, long enough to ensure that the centers were fully baked and the crusts were just the right shade of light golden brown.

Cream and Currant Scones

MAKES 4 SCONES

Resist the urge to eat the scones hot out of the oven, as letting them cool for at least 10 minutes allows them to firm up and improves their texture.

- 1 cup (5 ounces) unbleached all-purpose flour
- 2 tablespoons sugar
- 1½ teaspoons baking powder
- ¼ teaspoon salt
- 3 tablespoons unsalted butter, cut into ¼-inch pieces and chilled
- ¼ cup dried currants
- ½ cup heavy cream

1. Adjust oven rack to middle position and heat oven to 375 degrees. Line rimmed baking sheet with parchment paper.

2. Pulse flour, sugar, baking powder, and salt together in food processor to combine, about 3 pulses. Scatter butter evenly over top and pulse until mixture resembles coarse cornmeal with some slightly larger butter lumps, about 6 pulses. Transfer mixture to large bowl and stir in currants. Stir in cream with rubber spatula until dough begins to form, about 30 seconds.

3. Turn out dough and any floury bits onto floured counter and knead until rough, slightly sticky ball forms, 5 to 10 seconds. Following photos, shape dough into 5-inch round of even ¾-inch thickness and cut into 4 wedges.

4. Place wedges on prepared baking sheet. Bake until tops are light golden brown, 18 to 22 minutes, rotating pan halfway through baking. Transfer scones to wire rack and let cool for at least 10 minutes. Serve warm or at room temperature.

NOTES FROM THE TEST KITCHEN

MAKING SIMPLE CREAM SCONES

1. Pat the dough into a 5-inch round, about ¾ inch thick.

2. Using a metal bench scraper or knife, cut the dough into four evenly sized wedges.

OUR FAVORITE BENCH SCRAPER

Here in the test kitchen, we find that there is one incredibly simple and inexpensive piece of equipment that is invaluable for baking: a bench scraper. A bench scraper is a rectangular blade with a wood or plastic handle affixed to one side. Bench scrapers are ideal for countless baking tasks, like dividing dough for scones or cleaning up a messy counter. Our favorite bench scraper is the **OXO Good Grips Stainless Steel Multi-Purpose Scraper and Chopper**, $8.95, which has a sturdy blade and comfortable handle. We also like the ruler marked along the blade, which is helpful for accurate measuring.

CREAM AND CURRANT SCONES

QUICK APPLE STRUDEL

CLASSIC STRUDEL INVOLVES HOURS OF HANDS-ON preparation, rolling and pulling the dough until it is so thin you can read a newspaper through it. But when you're making dessert for two, the effort and time investment doesn't seem worth it. Chucking the notion of homemade strudel dough, we started with a simpler option—store-bought phyllo dough—which would make it much easier to both dramatically simplify this classic dessert and bring it to the table for two. We hoped to keep the rich apple filling and as much of the crisp, flaky texture as possible, but to speed up the process so this could be a satisfying finish to any weeknight supper.

A classic apple strudel contains apples, bread crumbs, sugar, cinnamon, and raisins. Although this combination sounds great, some recipes yield dry, bready fillings overpowered by the flavor of the spices, and leathery, bland crusts that separate from the filling as soon as a fork comes near. We wanted our filling and pastry to come together as a unified whole, with a crust that was crisp and flaky yet still held its shape. The filling had to be moist but not wet, and the flavor of apple needed to shine through.

Our first strudels threatened to shatter to bits if we so much as looked at them funny. Butter is usually brushed between the layers of phyllo dough to help keep them crisp and flaky, so we thought that by eliminating the butter we might get a more cohesive crust. But the phyllo crust without butter was still crisp, only now it was also dry and unappealing. We tried adding a bit of milk to the butter, in the hope that the added moisture might add flavor while creating cohesive layers, but that strudel was simply soggy. Then a test cook recalled a method she used while working as a pastry chef that called for sprinkling sugar with the butter on each layer of phyllo. The melted sugar acted as a glue between the layers and added flavor to an otherwise bland dough. Finally, we were on the right track.

Phyllo is notorious for drying out and cracking when it sits out; to prevent this from happening, we kept the layers of phyllo covered with damp towels while we were layering the sheets. Once they were layered and filled with a working apple mixture, we baked them for 40 minutes in a 400-degree oven. With sugar between the layers, the strudel held its shape better, but as it cooled on the rack, the outer layers curled and flaked. We thought the long time in the oven might be drying out the phyllo, so we tried baking the strudel at a higher temperature—450 degrees—for a lot less time. After just 15 minutes, the crust was perfect: toothsome yet slightly yielding, with a deeply caramelized exterior. And it could be cut into clean, solid slices. There was only one problem: The apple was still raw.

It was time to address the filling. Up until this point, we had been using a sliced Granny Smith, figuring that a firm, tart apple would be best. The quick blast of heat was perfect for the phyllo, but the apple never had a chance to cook and soften. We tried slicing the apple thinner, but it was still too firm. Switching to a McIntosh apple worked better, and our strudel now had body and apple flavor, plus a yielding yet firm texture.

To replace some of the tartness of the Granny Smith that was lost, we added some lemon juice. A scant ⅛ teaspoon of cinnamon added some warmth and ensured the filling was well rounded. After testing various combinations of brown and granulated sugars, we discovered that less was more—just 2 tablespoons of granulated sugar added a clean sweetness that tasters liked.

Almost every recipe we'd seen called for raisins of some kind, and tasters preferred milder golden raisins to dark ones. Added straight to the apples, the raisins were a bit dry and chewy, but we found that simmering them in liquid plumped them up in no time. For the liquid, we tried Calvados (apple brandy), which added a great layer of sweet apple flavor that everyone liked.

We knew that the bread crumbs, a classic component of strudel, were there to absorb the juice from the apples and prevent a damp crust, but we weren't completely convinced they were necessary. We were wrong; strudel made without bread crumbs was soggy. But the amount we were working with (¼ cup, based on other recipes) resulted in a strudel with a dry, pasty filling. We settled on 2 tablespoons of dried bread crumbs (making such a small amount of fresh bread crumbs seemed silly), which gave us a strudel that was moist without being too wet. The flavor, however, was too lean. We browned the crumbs in butter, and tasters loved the results. The filling was now buttery, rich, and moist.

While not very classic in preparation, our apple strudel still delivered on all the rich flavors and crispy texture of an authentic version—but it was ready in a fraction of the time.

Quick Apple Strudel

SERVES 2

Make sure the phyllo is fully thawed before using. To thaw frozen phyllo, let it sit in the refrigerator overnight or on the counter for several hours; don't thaw it in the microwave or it will turn into an unusable, soggy mess.

¼ **cup golden raisins**

1 **tablespoon Calvados, applejack, or apple cider**

2 **tablespoons dried bread crumbs or panko**

4 **tablespoons (½ stick) unsalted butter, melted and cooled**

1 **medium McIntosh apple, peeled, cored, quartered, and sliced ¼ inch thick crosswise**

3 **tablespoons granulated sugar**

½ **teaspoon fresh lemon juice**

⅛ **teaspoon ground cinnamon**

   Pinch salt

5 **(14 by 9-inch) sheets phyllo dough, thawed (see note)**

   Confectioners' sugar, for dusting

1. Adjust oven rack to lower-middle position and heat oven to 450 degrees. Line baking sheet with parchment paper. Combine raisins and Calvados in small microwave-safe bowl; cover tightly and microwave until simmering, 30 seconds to 1 minute. Set aside, covered.

2. Toast bread crumbs with 1 tablespoon melted butter in small skillet over medium heat, stirring frequently, until golden brown, about 2 minutes. Transfer crumbs to large bowl.

3. Drain raisins, discarding liquid. Stir raisins, apple, 2 tablespoons granulated sugar, lemon juice, cinnamon, and salt into bread crumbs until thoroughly combined.

4. Place large piece of parchment paper on counter. Following photos, lay one sheet of phyllo on parchment with short side facing you, then brush with melted butter and sprinkle with ½ teaspoon granulated sugar. Repeat and layer with 4 more phyllo sheets, brushing each with butter and sprinkling each with ½ teaspoon granulated sugar.

5. Mound filling along bottom edge of phyllo, leaving 2½-inch border at bottom and 2-inch border on sides. Fold dough on sides over apples. Fold dough on bottom over apples and continue to roll dough around filling into log.

6. Gently transfer strudel, seam side down, to prepared baking sheet. Brush with remaining melted butter and sprinkle with remaining ½ teaspoon granulated sugar. Cut four 1-inch vents across top of strudel.

7. Bake strudel until golden brown, 12 to 15 minutes, rotating baking sheet halfway through baking. Let strudel cool on baking sheet until warm, about 20 minutes. Dust with confectioners' sugar before serving. Serve warm or at room temperature.

NOTES FROM THE TEST KITCHEN

ASSEMBLING QUICK APPLE STRUDEL

1. On a large piece of parchment paper, layer the phyllo sheets on top of one another, brushing each sheet with melted butter and sprinkling it with ½ teaspoon of granulated sugar.

2. Mound the filling along the bottom edge of the phyllo, leaving a 2½-inch border on the bottom and a 2-inch border on the sides.

3. Fold the dough in on the sides over the apples. Fold the dough in on the bottom over the apples and continue to roll the dough around the filling to form the strudel.

4. Brush the strudel with the remaining butter and sprinkle with the remaining granulated sugar, then cut four 1-inch vents across the top of the strudel with a small knife.

APPLE UPSIDE-DOWN CAKE

PINEAPPLE AND UPSIDE-DOWN CAKE ARE JUST about synonymous. But long before the introduction of canned pineapple in the early 1900s sparked a craze for pineapple in baked goods, upside-down cakes were made with seasonal fruit such as apples. The technique was straightforward: Pour melted butter and brown sugar into a pan or skillet, add sliced apples, spread cake batter over them, and bake. The apples caramelize on the bottom of the pan, revealing a layer of burnished amber fruit when the cake is upturned. After testing a few recipes, however, we understood why sweet, juicy pineapple had overshadowed the humble apple. Rather than a luscious topping full of deeply fruity, caramelized flavor, the apple slices tasted bland and watery and seemed more garnish than topping. Our challenge was not only to restore rich, apple-y flavor to this upside-down cake, but also to downsize it for two.

We started by tinkering with the apple topping, trying several varieties, including Golden Delicious apples, Braeburns, Cortlands, and Granny Smiths. Tasters liked Granny Smiths' sharper flavor but also praised sweet Golden Delicious apples—we leave the choice up to you. Our apple of choice in hand, we turned to the rest of the topping. The ingredients and method were roughly the same in most recipes: Melt half a stick of butter and ⅔ cup of light brown sugar in a saucepan, pour the mixture into a 9-inch round cake pan, fan two sliced apples across the top, spread cake batter over them, and slide the pan into the oven. We figured that we'd need to cut those amounts almost in half to accommodate our 6-inch cake pan. But when we inverted our baked cake onto a plate, we found that the single apple in our mini cake had cooked down to a shriveled layer, with patches of cake peeking through.

The obvious solution? Add another apple. We expected a substantial topping steeped with fruit flavor but instead got a cake jammed with unevenly cooked apples—some slices made contact with the pan and caramelized; the rest just steamed, and their surplus moisture left the cake gummy. We needed to get rid of the excess moisture, or we could give up our dream of caramelized apple goodness. We wondered if precooking the apples in a skillet would solve two problems at once: First, precooking the apples would draw out moisture; second, if we added some butter and brown sugar to the skillet, we could get the apples

to caramelize before they reached the cake pan. There was just one problem: Precooking meant sacrificing fresh apple flavor.

Hoping to strike a compromise, we tried cooking half of the apples, then folding in the remainder before turning the topping into the pan. This was an improvement. A few more tests revealed that slicing the uncooked apples thinner (to about ¼-inch thickness) let them bake in the same amount of time as the apples that had been sliced ½ inch thick and sautéed. All this full-flavored topping needed was a squirt of fresh lemon juice to add brightness and balance.

There was still the cake to contend with. We had been scaling down the standard butter cake called for in the typical pineapple version of the recipe. After numerous tests, we cut the yield of the batter by about half, which fit nicely in our 6-inch round cake pan. For the main players in our cake, we settled on ½ cup each of flour and sugar, an egg, and ¼ cup milk. To keep with the rustic nature of this cake, we opted for an easy mixing method—nothing is easier than the quick-bread method, in which the butter is melted and the liquid and dry ingredients are mixed separately before being combined. After 40 minutes in a 350-degree oven, the cake was an attractive golden brown.

Although our cake now had the ideal tender texture, it tasted a little lackluster. Trading the milk for subtly tangy sour cream balanced the sweetness of the cake and complemented the caramelized apple. For another dimension to the sweetness, we swapped 2 tablespoons of granulated sugar for brown sugar, which offered a hint of molasses.

This apple cake was perfect—until the upside-down part came in. Most recipes call for a stay of 5 or 10 minutes in the pan before the cake is inverted onto a serving plate, but this caused the bottom of the cake to steam, resulting in a gummy base. In addition, the apples slid off, and the piping-hot caramel dripped down the sides of the cake like sauce over ice cream. By mustering a little more patience, we found a remedy: letting the cake rest in the pan for a good 20 minutes, which allowed the apple topping to set. Afterward, turning the cake out onto a rack to finish cooling let the bottom of the cake breathe, avoiding sogginess. We reluctantly bided our time while the cake cooled, then cut a piece. Our patience was rewarded—the buttery, moist cake was perfectly matched by the fruity, deeply caramelized flavor of the topping.

Apple Upside-Down Cake

SERVES 2

You will need a 6-inch round cake pan for this recipe (see page 3). Be careful not to burn the apples while caramelizing them in step 2. To ensure a clean release, cool the cake in the pan for 20 minutes before inverting it onto a wire rack; using a rack prevents trapped steam from making the cake bottom gummy. See page 178 for a recipe to use up the leftover sour cream.

TOPPING

- 2 **Granny Smith or Golden Delicious apples (about 1 pound), peeled and cored**
- 2 **tablespoons unsalted butter, cut into 2 pieces**
- ⅓ **cup packed (2⅓ ounces) brown sugar**
- 1 **teaspoon fresh lemon juice**

CAKE

- ½ **cup (2½ ounces) unbleached all-purpose flour**
- ½ **teaspoon baking powder**
- ¼ **teaspoon salt**
- 6 **tablespoons granulated sugar**
- 2 **tablespoons brown sugar**
- 1 **large egg**
- 2 **tablespoons unsalted butter, melted and cooled**
- ¼ **cup sour cream**
- ½ **teaspoon vanilla extract**

1. Adjust oven rack to lowest position and heat oven to 350 degrees. Grease 6-inch round cake pan and set aside.

2. FOR THE TOPPING: Halve apples from pole to pole. Cut 1 apple into ¼-inch-thick slices; set aside. Cut remaining apple into ½-inch-thick slices. Melt butter in 10-inch skillet over medium-high heat. Add ½-inch-thick apple slices and cook, stirring 2 or 3 times, until apples begin to caramelize, 3 to 4 minutes. (Do not fully cook apples.) Add ¼-inch-thick apple slices, brown sugar, and lemon juice and continue to cook, stirring constantly, until sugar dissolves and apples are coated, about 1 minute longer. Transfer apple mixture to prepared pan and lightly press into even layer. Set aside while preparing cake.

3. FOR THE CAKE: Whisk flour, baking powder, and salt together in bowl; set aside. In separate bowl, whisk granulated sugar, brown sugar, and egg together until thick and homogeneous, about 45 seconds. Slowly whisk in butter until combined. Whisk in sour cream and vanilla until combined. Gently whisk in flour mixture until just incorporated.

4. Give batter final stir with rubber spatula to make sure it is thoroughly combined. Scrape batter into prepared pan over apples and smooth top. Bake until cake is golden brown and toothpick inserted into center comes out clean, 35 to 40 minutes.

5. Transfer cake to wire rack and let cool for 20 minutes. Run paring knife around sides of cake to loosen. Place wire rack over top of cake pan, invert cake pan and wire rack together, and let sit over baking sheet or large plate until cake releases itself from pan (do not shake or tap pan), about 1 minute. Gently remove cake pan, replacing any apple slices that fall off or stick to pan bottom. Cool cake completely, about 1 hour, before serving.

SUMMER BERRY SNACK CAKES

UNLIKE FANCY LAYER CAKES, SNACK CAKES COME together in just minutes with little effort—no complicated mixing techniques involved, and no fussy frosting required. We thought our for-two dessert repertoire was begging for a simple yellow snack cake dotted with juicy bites of berries, perfect for a coffee-time offering or last-minute finale to tonight's dinner. And so that both diners wouldn't be fighting for the last bit of cake in the pan, we wanted to make two individual cakes.

To start, we needed to find just the right bakeware. A bit of digging at our local kitchen supply shop turned up small (1-cup) Bundt pans. With their ridges and curves, these two pans, we hoped, would turn out enticing, golden cakes.

We started out by scaling down a fairly basic yellow cake recipe, with the goal of trimming the batter to yield just under 2 cups. The ingredient list included the standard roster of players: flour, sugar, butter, milk, and an egg for structure and moisture, vanilla and salt for flavor, and baking powder for height. Since we wanted to give our cakes a light and airy crumb to balance the berries (blueberries to start), we would first cream the sugar and butter until the mixture was light and fluffy; then the egg and dry ingredients could be incorporated. For our first test, we creamed 3 tablespoons of softened butter with 3 tablespoons of sugar, then beat in the lone egg. We mixed in the dry ingredients (½ cup of flour, ½ teaspoon of baking powder, and ⅛ teaspoon

SUMMER BERRY SNACK CAKES

of salt), alternating with 2 tablespoons of whole milk, before folding in ⅔ cup of blueberries. We poured the batter into our Bundt pans, then baked the cakes at 350 degrees for about 30 minutes.

Although our cakes looked great on the plate, the texture and flavor were lacking. It was clear we had way too much fruit in our cakes—they were overly wet and dense, not fluffy and tender, and the bites of cake were overpowered by the fruit. Also, the cake itself didn't taste sweet enough when compared with the slightly tart fruit.

Our first order of business was cutting down on the amount of fruit. Reducing the amount of blueberries from ⅔ cup to ½ cup made quite an impact; now the berries were an accent, not a scene-stealer, and there were more bites of tender, moist cake. Subsequent tests told us that raspberries were a great substitute for the blueberries; strawberries, on the other hand, contributed too much moisture and made the cakes wet and dense.

Next we addressed the lack of sweetness in the cake. Just 1 more tablespoon of sugar brought the sweetness into balance.

After baking our snack cakes in the Bundt pans, we let them cool for half an hour before dusting them with confectioners' sugar. With the light and tender crumb and bites of sweet berries in our cakes, it was clear we'd be enjoying snack time a lot more around here.

Summer Berry Snack Cakes

SERVES 2

You will need two 1-cup Bundt pans for this recipe (see page 3). Since this recipe involves very small quantities of ingredients, we recommend using a hand-held electric mixer for thorough mixing. The cakes can be served warm or at room temperature.

½ cup (2½ ounces) unbleached all-purpose flour

½ teaspoon baking powder

⅛ teaspoon salt

3 tablespoons unsalted butter, softened

¼ cup (1¾ ounces) granulated sugar

1 large egg, room temperature

¼ teaspoon vanilla extract

2 tablespoons whole milk, room temperature

½ cup ripe blueberries or raspberries

Confectioners' sugar, for dusting

1. Adjust oven rack to middle position and heat oven to 350 degrees. Grease two 1-cup Bundt pans. Whisk flour, baking powder, and salt together in small bowl.

2. In medium bowl, beat butter and granulated sugar together with electric mixer on medium speed until light and fluffy, about 3 minutes. Beat in egg until combined, about 30 seconds. Beat in vanilla until incorporated.

3. Reduce mixer speed to low and beat in one-third of flour mixture, followed by 1 tablespoon milk. Repeat with half of remaining flour mixture and remaining 1 tablespoon milk. Beat in remaining flour mixture until just incorporated (batter will be quite thick). Gently fold in fruit with rubber spatula.

4. Divide batter evenly between prepared pans, smooth tops, and gently tap each pan on counter to settle batter. Wipe any drops of batter off sides of pans. Place pans on rimmed baking sheet and bake cakes until toothpick inserted into centers comes out clean, 20 to 30 minutes, rotating pans halfway through baking.

5. Let cakes cool in pans for 10 minutes, then flip them out onto wire rack. Let cakes cool completely, about 30 minutes. Dust with confectioners' sugar and serve.

NOTES FROM THE TEST KITCHEN

THE BEST HAND-HELD MIXER
Stand mixers are a pricey purchase—around $300 for our top-rated model. But we've found that a hand mixer can be a good alternative, especially when baking for two and working with small amounts of ingredients, which can get lost at the bottom of a stand mixer's large mixing bowl. Besides being more affordable, hand mixers take up less counter space and are easier to clean, too. But it's important to invest in a good one; in the past, we've found too many hand mixers with lousy designs and weak motors. We recently gathered seven models, priced from $15.99 to $79.99, to see if any could meet our standards. We beat egg whites to stiff peaks, creamed butter and sugar, whipped cream, and mixed flour and peanuts into thick peanut butter cookie dough. One mixer aced every test: The **Cuisinart Power Advantage 7-Speed Hand Mixer** offered excellent control with gentle low speeds and powerful high speeds that nearly matched those of a stand mixer. We also liked its digital display and quiet motor. And at $49.95, it's a fraction of the cost of a stand mixer.

WHITE WINE–POACHED PEARS

ALTHOUGH WE'RE NEVER ONES TO SHUN A PIECE OF cake or pie, some dinners call for a lighter, more refreshing finale. Enter pears poached in wine, a classic French dessert. Though this stunner might look like it belongs on a white tablecloth at a four-star establishment, it's actually quick-cooking and easy to prepare, and it requires few ingredients. We set out to develop a recipe for poached pears that were soft and tender and infused with aromatics. Served chilled with the poaching liquid as the sauce, our pears would provide an elegant finish to any special-occasion meal.

Poaching is a particularly apt way to cook fruit. Unlike other cooking methods, poaching allows the shape, texture, and inherent flavor of the fruit to remain intact, while improving its tenderness and enhancing, rather than masking, its flavor. We tested poaching pears in varying states of ripeness. Perfectly ripe fruit poached quickly and easily. But we found that poaching is also a perfect remedy for underripe or bland fruit, rendering it sweet and tender. Rock-hard pears, however, never attained a tender texture no matter how long they simmered, and if the pears were too ripe, they were difficult to handle and easily cooked to mush. Moderately ripe pears, which gave slightly when pressed with a finger, became our favorites to work with.

We next focused our attention on which pear to use. We immediately narrowed our choice to the readily available varieties: Bosc, d'Anjou, Comice, and Bartlett. Our favorite varieties were the Bartlett, for its floral, honeyed notes, and the Bosc, because it tasted like a sweet, ripe pear should taste. With our pear varieties selected, we went about trying to bolster their flavor by testing different poaching mediums. Most of the recipes we came across in our research involved poaching the pears in sugar-sweetened white wine, which resulted in bright, clean flavor. To customize the recipe to serve two, we would need less than the entire 750-milliliter bottle of wine usually required to poach six to eight pears. But while we needed less wine, we still needed enough to cover the pears in a small saucepan. Reducing the amount of wine to 2 cups worked well.

After testing both red and white wine, we preferred the milder, floral flavors in the pears poached in white wine, which lent itself to additional poaching aromatics such as herbs and lemon. We also liked the added flavors of cinnamon and vanilla in the poaching liquid as well as the resulting sauce. Unfortunately, when we went to scale the amounts for our pair of pears, we found the cinnamon—even a quarter of a stick—

NOTES FROM THE TEST KITCHEN

REMOVING SEEDS FROM A VANILLA BEAN

1. Use a small knife to cut the piece of vanilla bean in half lengthwise.

2. Then scrape the vanilla seeds out of the bean using the blade of the knife.

HOW TO CORE PEARS

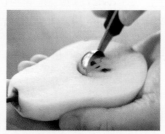

1. Halve the pears from stem to blossom end and then remove the core using a melon baller for a clean look.

2. After removing the core, use the edge of the melon baller to scrape away the interior stem of the pear, from the core to the stem end.

to be overwhelming, obliterating the more subtle flavors of the lemon and herbs. We decided to omit the cinnamon, leaving the vanilla bean alone to balance the citrusy, herbal notes.

Poaching took about 20 minutes more or less, depending on the ripeness of the pears; cooking the pears covered at a gentle simmer ensured that they were evenly cooked. Cutting the pears in half and using a melon baller to scoop out the core also helped to guarantee that the pears cooked through evenly and scored presentation points.

Once the pears are tender, recipes often recommend that they be allowed to cool in the poaching liquid. This, we found after a few tests, proved to be good advice. If the pears were plucked from the hot poaching liquid, the syrup did not have a chance to be absorbed into the flesh of the fruit, resulting in a drier texture. If left to cool in the liquid, the pears absorbed some syrup, took on a candied translucency, and became plump, sweet, and spicy.

Finally, we tested sugar amounts. Most of the recipes for poached pears that we researched made saccharine-sweet poaching liquids. After extensive testing, however, we chose a lighter syrup made with just ⅓ cup of sugar to 2 cups of wine, as opposed to the typical ratio of ½ cup of sugar to 2 cups of wine. The drawback, however, was that this less-sweet syrup didn't have the consistency of sweeter poaching liquids. To thicken the liquid slightly, we removed the pears and reduced the liquid until it was saucy and clingy. We then poured the hot, thickened syrup over the pears and allowed it to cool. Once cooled, the syrup napped the pears in a thin coat that was at once bright and refreshing, yet luscious and velvety.

White Wine–Poached Pears

SERVES 2

For the best texture, try to buy pears that yield just slightly when pressed; they should be ripe but still firm. Use a vegetable peeler to peel strips of zest, but take care to avoid the bitter pith beneath the skin. For the white wine, we recommend a medium-bodied dry white wine such as Sauvignon Blanc or Chardonnay. Serve with ice cream, if desired.

USE IT UP: VANILLA BEAN

Vanilla Syrup
MAKES ABOUT 1 CUP

Stir vanilla syrup into your morning coffee, toss it with fruit, or drizzle it over pound cake. The syrup can be refrigerated in an airtight container for up to two weeks.

- 1 **cup water**
- 1 **cup (7 ounces) sugar**
- ½ **vanilla bean (about 3-inch piece), halved lengthwise, seeds removed and reserved (see page 270)**

1. Combine water, sugar, and vanilla bean seeds and pod in small saucepan. Bring to simmer over medium heat, whisking frequently, until sugar dissolves completely. Simmer, uncovered, about 4 minutes.

2. Remove from heat and cool. Remove and discard vanilla bean pod.

- 2 **cups dry white wine (see note)**
- ⅓ **cup (2⅓ ounces) sugar**
- 5 **(1½-inch) strips lemon zest (see page 68) plus 2 teaspoons fresh lemon juice**
- 4 **sprigs fresh mint**
- 3 **sprigs fresh thyme**
- ½ **vanilla bean (about 3-inch piece), halved lengthwise, seeds removed and reserved (see page 270)**
  Pinch salt
- 2 **ripe but firm Bosc or Bartlett pears (see note)**

1. Combine wine, sugar, lemon zest, mint, thyme, vanilla seeds and pod, and salt in small saucepan. Bring mixture to simmer over medium heat and cook, stirring occasionally, until sugar dissolves completely, about 5 minutes; cover and set aside.

2. Meanwhile, fill medium bowl with water and add lemon juice. Peel, halve, and core pears, following photos on page 270, and add to lemon water to prevent browning.

3. Drain pears, discarding lemon water, and add to wine mixture. Bring mixture to boil, then reduce heat to low, cover, and simmer until pears are tender and toothpick can be inserted with very little resistance, 15 to 25 minutes, gently turning pears over every 5 minutes.

4. Using slotted spoon, transfer pears to shallow casserole dish. Return syrup to simmer and cook until thickened and reduced to ½ cup, about 20 minutes. Strain syrup through fine-mesh strainer, then pour over pears, discarding strained solids. Refrigerate pears until well chilled, at least 2 hours or up to 3 days. To serve, spoon portions of fruit and syrup into individual bowls.

PEACH BROWN BETTY

DATING BACK TO COLONIAL TIMES, BROWN BETTY is a homey sweet traditionally made by layering fruit and buttery bread crumbs in a deep dish and baking until the fruit is tender and the crumb topping is crisp. Apples are the usual star of brown betty, but we wanted something different (apples get enough attention as it is) and thought juicy, ripe peaches would make for a brightly flavored yet still old-fashioned dessert.

Even though we were dealing with only a few peaches, we knew that what made our ripe, in-season peaches so satisfying—that rich juice that drips off the chin when enjoying the fruit out of hand—would make our betty too watery if we weren't careful. We tried the usual tactics for dealing with excess fruit juice but didn't have much luck. Adding cornstarch or flour to the peaches dulled their flavor. Tossing the peaches with sugar to draw out their liquid and draining them worked but took about an hour, more time than we were willing to devote to what should be an uncomplicated dessert.

Casting about for another solution, we thought maybe easiest would prove best and simply precooked our peaches in a skillet. As fast as they released their juice into the pan, the juice evaporated. Even better, the natural sugars began to deepen and caramelize, intensifying the peach flavor. We wondered if sprinkling in more sugar would magnify the effect. It did just that. In fact, without constant stirring, the juice on the bottom of the skillet began to scorch. So we opted to wait until after the sauté to add sugar (granulated for pure sweetness, brown for deeper flavor).

Although brown betty is usually made in a baking dish, we thought our skillet would work just as nicely (and cut down on extra dishes). We sprinkled fresh bread crumbs over the fruit and put the skillet into the oven to brown them. However, when we pulled the pan out of the oven, we found that the topping had drowned in the bubbling juice, rendering a mushy, bland mess. We had to find a way to get rid of the moisture released by the peaches during baking and decided to stir in a portion of the bread crumbs to absorb the liquid. Happily, the filling thickened nicely. To brighten the flavor, we

NOTES FROM THE TEST KITCHEN

PEELING PEACHES

1. With a paring knife, score a small *X* at the base of each peach.

2. Lower the peaches into boiling water and simmer until the skins loosen, 30 to 60 seconds.

3. Transfer the peaches immediately to ice water and let cool for about 1 minute.

4. Finally, use a paring knife to remove strips of loosened peel, starting at the *X* on the base of each peach.

added a little lemon juice; a splash of vanilla extract brought the flavor of the peaches into focus.

Now, with the peach juice reined in, the topping was dry enough to turn golden brown, but it still wasn't crisp enough for contrast with the tender peaches. A sprinkling of cinnamon sugar improved the situation slightly, but it was clear we had to revisit the bread-crumb issue. Up to this point, we'd been tossing fresh bread crumbs (made in the food processor) with melted butter. We tried using dried crumbs, but they were too fine and sank into the peaches in seconds. Toasting the fresh crumbs first made the topping too dark and the filling too dry. Going back to untoasted bread crumbs, we wondered if the melted butter was weighing them down. Next time around, we processed the crumbs with cold butter, stirred some of the coarse, shaggy mixture into the peaches, sprinkled the rest on top, then placed our betty in the oven. About a half-hour and one bowl of peach brown betty later, we were thrilled—our super-crisp topping was a suitable match for the juicy, fragrant peach filling.

Peach Brown Betty

SERVES 2

You can substitute 1 pound frozen sliced peaches, thawed and drained, for the fresh peaches. If you don't own an ovensafe skillet, transfer the peach filling to a 3-cup baking dish at the end of step 2 and bake as directed.

TOPPING

- 1 **slice high-quality white sandwich bread, torn into 1-inch pieces**
- 1 **tablespoon unsalted butter, cut into ½-inch pieces and chilled**
- 1 **teaspoon granulated sugar**
  Pinch ground cinnamon

PEACH FILLING

- 1 **tablespoon unsalted butter**
- 1 **pound peaches (2 to 3), peeled (see page 272), pitted, and cut into ½-inch wedges (see note)**
- 2 **tablespoons granulated sugar**
- 2 **tablespoons brown sugar**
- 1 **teaspoon fresh lemon juice**
- ½ **teaspoon vanilla extract**
  Pinch salt

1. FOR THE TOPPING: Adjust oven rack to middle position and heat oven to 400 degrees. Pulse bread and butter in food processor to coarse crumbs, 6 to 8 pulses. Set aside. Combine sugar and cinnamon in small bowl.

2. FOR THE PEACH FILLING: Melt butter in 8-inch nonstick ovensafe skillet over medium heat. Add peaches and cook, stirring occasionally, until they begin to caramelize, 6 to 9 minutes. Off heat, stir in ¼ cup bread-crumb mixture, granulated sugar, brown sugar, lemon juice, vanilla, and salt.

3. Top peach mixture with remaining crumbs. Sprinkle with cinnamon sugar and bake until topping is golden brown and juice is bubbling, 15 to 20 minutes. Cool for 10 minutes and serve warm.

SWEET CHERRY PIE

GREAT CHERRY PIE IS JUICY AND FULL OF BRIGHT berry flavor. But to get this luscious flavor and texture, most recipes call for sour cherries—their soft, juicy flesh and bright, punchy flavor aren't dulled by oven heat or sugar. But sour cherries can be tough to find, even during cherry season. Sweet cherries have a mellower flavor and meaty, firm flesh—traits that make them ideal for eating straight off the stem but don't translate well to baking. Our challenge was obvious: Develop a sweet cherry pie with all the intense, jammy flavor and soft-ened but still intact fruit texture of the best sour cherry pie. As if that wasn't already a tall order, we wanted our pie to serve just two.

We settled on using a 6-inch pie plate for our small pie. For the pie dough, we followed the standard formula of flour, fat, and water, ultimately settling on 5 tablespoons of butter and 3 tablespoons of shortening to 1¼ cups of flour; these amounts provided the most buttery flavor and tender texture. After rolling out the dough into two rounds, one for the top crust and one for the bottom crust, we allowed the dough to chill for half an hour while we prepared the filling.

In order to make our sweet cherry pie behave like a sour cherry pie, we had two issues to resolve: taming the cherries' sweetness, and getting them to break down to the lovely juicy texture of baked sour cherries. To get our bearings, we conducted a preliminary test in an effort to nail down the right quantity of cherries for our 6-inch pie plate and gauge their sweetness level. We began with 3 cups (about 1 pound) of sweet cherries and ½ cup of sugar, plus 1 tablespoon of ground instant tapioca (the test kitchen's preferred thickener for juicy fruit pies). As soon as we poured the filling into the pie crust, we knew we were in trouble—the filling was threatening to overflow the crust. Reducing the amount of cherries by half provided the right amount of filling.

After we baked our pie, it was clear we had our work cut out for us. No one could taste past the filling's sweetness, and its texture was unappealingly clumpy. It seemed that 1 tablespoon of tapioca was more than we needed to thicken the fruit, especially after cutting back on the amount of cherries; reducing the amount to 2 teaspoons was an easy fix.

Adjusting the sugar level was more difficult, since we needed the sugar to draw out the moisture in the cherries and keep the filling juicy. We found that cutting the sugar amount in half and adding some lemon juice helped, but not enough. As a last-ditch effort, we tried introducing alternative fruits: super-tart cranberries (too bitter), tangy red grapes (too musty), and dried sour cherries (too chewy). Although none of these ideas panned out, the concept did get us to thinking about other types of fruit—especially stone fruits. Cherries fall into the stone fruit category, along with nectarines, peaches, and plums. Sweet nectarines and peaches wouldn't help here, but tart plums just might. For our next pie, we sliced a plum and added it to our filling. Mixed with the cherries, the plum flavor was undetectable, yet the tartness was just right, perfectly toning down the sweetness of the filling. Now we had the cherries' overly firm texture to deal with.

A closer analysis revealed that the problem was twofold: Not only were the cherries refusing to break down, but as a result of not breaking down, they also weren't

NOTES FROM THE TEST KITCHEN

MAKING SWEET CHERRY PIE

1. Using scissors, trim all but ½ inch of the dough overhanging the edge of the pie plate.

2. Press the top and bottom crusts together, then tuck the edges underneath.

3. Crimp the dough evenly around the edge of the pie, using your fingers. Then cut five vent holes attractively in the center of the top crust with a paring knife.

THE BEST FROZEN SWEET CHERRIES

Cherry season is a mere blip on the summer produce radar, so a good brand of frozen cherries can come in handy. In the three brands we tasted (first plain, then baked in pie), appearance was a good predictor of quality: Darker color corresponds to greater ripeness in many sweet cherry varietals (yellow-red Rainier cherries are an exception), and the best frozen cherries were uniformly maroon and tangy-sweet, while lighter-colored fruits tasted washed out and harshly sour. Besides differences in appearance, there was also a discrepancy in overall quality: Two of the brands contained lots of blemished, mushy fruit; in one bag we even found pits and stems. Though we chose only brands that had been individually quick frozen, or IQF—a system of rapidly freezing individual items at extremely low temperatures to help prevent the formation of water crystals that can rupture cells and compromise texture—the squishiness of some cherries could have been caused by improper handling. If fruit partially thaws and refreezes, water crystals can still form and severely damage texture. The best of the three brands we sampled was **Cascadian Farm Premium Organic Sweet Cherries**. These large, glossy, dark cherries were consistent in both size and appearance— and they tasted as good as they looked, with tasters describing them as "sweet, ripe, and fruity."

releasing enough juice to provide sufficient moisture to the filling. A chat with our science editor revealed that the culprit was cellulose, the main structural component of fruit cells. Compared to sour cherries, the sweet variety contains a full 30 percent more cellulose, making the flesh more rigid.

Without a way to rid the cherries of that extra structure, we'd have to rely on more conventional techniques to soften the flesh. Halving the cherries helped considerably, since their juice was very easily drawn out of the exposed fleshy centers. Even better, the cut cherries collapsed more readily and turned out markedly softer in the finished pie, save for a few too many solid chunks. Taking this one step further, we got out the food processor and tossed in ½ cup of our cherries along with the plum. From the resulting pulp, we strained out the chewy skins and added the remaining puree to the filling. Our baked pie finally had the texture we wanted—the filling was ideally soft and studded with a few still-intact cherry pieces.

We found that baking our pie on a preheated baking sheet guaranteed that the bottom crust crisped up before the fruit filling could seep through and make it soggy. A little less than an hour later, we were rewarded with a light golden, crispy crust, packed to the brim with a perfectly juicy (but not runny) sweet cherry filling. Only one question remained: What if we wanted to get our cherry pie fix in the dead of winter? Luckily, a few more tests told us we could achieve the same flavor and texture using frozen sweet cherries—making cherry pie a dessert option all year long.

Sweet Cherry Pie
SERVES 2

We prefer the buttery flavor and flaky texture of homemade pie dough here; however, you can substitute store-bought pie dough if desired. You will need a 6-inch pie plate for this recipe (see page 3). Make sure not to use more than 14 ounces of cherries, or your pie will overflow. If you are using frozen cherries, do not let them thaw completely before using; they should be measured, prepped, and used in a semifrozen state in order to preserve their juice. The tapioca should be measured first, then ground in a spice grinder for 30 seconds or in a mortar and pestle to a fine powder.

1 recipe Sweet Pie Dough (recipe follows;
   see note)
2¾ cups (about 14 ounces) pitted sweet cherries
   or 2¾ cups pitted frozen cherries, halved
   (see note)
1 red plum, quartered and pitted
¼ cup (1¾ ounces) sugar
2 teaspoons instant tapioca, ground (see note)
1½ teaspoons fresh lemon juice
   Pinch salt
   Pinch ground cinnamon (optional)
1 tablespoon unsalted butter, cut into ¼-inch pieces
1 large egg, lightly beaten with 1 teaspoon water

1. Adjust oven rack to lowest position, place aluminum foil–lined rimmed baking sheet on rack, and heat oven to 425 degrees. Roll out 1 disk of dough into 9-inch circle on lightly floured counter, then fit into 6-inch pie plate, letting excess dough hang over edge; cover with plastic wrap and refrigerate until firm, about 30 minutes. Roll out other disk of dough into 9-inch circle on lightly floured counter, then transfer to parchment paper–lined plate; cover with plastic wrap and refrigerate until firm, about 30 minutes.

2. Process ½ cup cherries and plum together in food processor until smooth, about 1 minute, scraping down sides of bowl as necessary. Strain puree through fine-mesh strainer into large bowl, pressing on solids to extract liquid; discard solids. Stir remaining halved cherries, sugar, ground tapioca, lemon juice, salt, and cinnamon (if using) into puree and let stand for 15 minutes.

3. Transfer cherry mixture, including all juices, to dough-lined pie plate (pie plate will be very full). Scatter butter pieces over fruit. Following photos on page 274, gently arrange second piece of pie dough over pie. Trim, fold, and crimp edges and cut 5 evenly spaced 1-inch-long vents in top. Brush crust with egg and freeze pie for 20 minutes.

4. Place pie on heated baking sheet and bake until top is golden brown, about 20 minutes. Reduce oven temperature to 350 degrees, rotate baking sheet, and continue to bake until juices are bubbling and crust is deep golden brown, 25 to 35 minutes longer.

5. Let pie cool on wire rack until filling has set, about 2 hours. Serve slightly warm or at room temperature.

Sweet Pie Dough

MAKES ENOUGH FOR ONE DOUBLE-CRUST 6-INCH PIE

If you don't have a food processor, see the hand-mixing instructions on page 60; add the sugar along with the flour and salt.

- 1¼ cups (6¼ ounces) unbleached all-purpose flour
- 1 tablespoon sugar
- ½ teaspoon salt
- 3 tablespoons vegetable shortening, cut into ½-inch pieces and chilled
- 5 tablespoons unsalted butter, cut into ¼-inch pieces and chilled
- 4-6 tablespoons ice water

1. Process flour, sugar, and salt together in food processor until combined. Scatter shortening over top and process until mixture resembles coarse cornmeal, about 10 seconds. Scatter butter pieces over top and pulse until mixture resembles coarse crumbs, about 10 pulses. Transfer mixture to medium bowl.

2. Sprinkle 4 tablespoons water over mixture. Using stiff rubber spatula, stir and press dough until it sticks together. If dough does not come together, stir in remaining water, 1 tablespoon at a time, until it does.

3. Turn out dough onto counter. Divide dough into 2 equal pieces, shape each into ball, and flatten to 3-inch disk; wrap each piece in plastic wrap and refrigerate for 1 hour. Before rolling out dough, let sit on counter to soften slightly, about 10 minutes. (Dough can be refrigerated for up to 2 days or frozen for up to 1 month. If frozen, let dough thaw completely on counter before rolling out.)

KEY LIME PIE

WE'VE BEEN SERVED COUNTLESS KEY LIME PIES AT restaurants where the cook seemed to get carried away with the artificial coloring—and not only was the resulting dessert as green as Kermit, but the citrus flavor was noticeably artificial-tasting and harshly acidic as well. We wanted to bring Key lime pie back to what it should be: brightly flavored, with both the sweet and tart notes perfectly in balance, and boasting a subtle pale green hue.

We started our quest for the perfect scaled-down Key lime pie by reviewing the test kitchen's standard recipe. To make the filling, four egg yolks are beaten with a 14-ounce can of sweetened condensed milk, half a cup of lime juice, and a tablespoon of lime zest. The filling is then poured into a prebaked graham cracker crust and the pie is baked, chilled until firm, and topped with whipped cream. To make the dessert work with only two diners in mind, we would need to scale down the recipe to fit a 6-inch pie plate.

We began with the graham cracker crust. Our 9-inch crust called for eight graham crackers, 5 tablespoons of melted butter, and 3 tablespoons of sugar. The graham crackers are processed in a food processor until broken down into fine, even crumbs before being mixed with the butter and sugar and pressed into a pie plate. For our 6-incher, we reduced the amounts of ingredients to five graham crackers, 3 tablespoons of butter, and 5 teaspoons of sugar. While the crust was plenty rich and lightly sweetened, we found that it was just too thick for the delicate, creamy filling of Key lime pie. We decided to try cutting down further on the graham crackers (to four) and sugar (to 4 teaspoons), but we were hesitant to reduce the amount of butter, fearing the ingredients wouldn't hold together with less. When the next test yielded a decidedly greasy crust, we reduced the amount of butter to 2 tablespoons. Baked at 325 degrees for 15 minutes, our crust was ready to be filled.

Since the creamy custard of Key lime pie relies on egg yolks as its thickener, we knew we couldn't cut too many from the original recipe without sacrificing texture. We began with two, hoping the other ingredients would keep the filling from tasting eggy.

Sweetened condensed milk provides the bulk of the filling; its sweet and creamy richness helps balance the tartness of the lime juice. Our full-size recipe called for an entire 14-ounce can; we opted to use 1 cup in our first test, combined with ¼ cup of lime juice. For more lime flavor without adding more moisture or tart flavor, we included 3 teaspoons of lime zest.

While our pie looked appealing, our tasters were dismayed; they agreed that the sweetened condensed milk was overwhelming the lime flavor. In addition, we had a very full pie crust that left little room for the whipped cream topping that traditionally accompanies Key lime pie. We cut down on the sweetened condensed milk

KEY LIME PIE

(to ⅔ cup) and found the flavor greatly improved, but now that the lime flavor could shine through that of the sweetened condensed milk, we found the lime zest a bit aggressive. Reducing the amount to 2 teaspoons ensured that our creamy filling had the perfect balance of sweet and tart.

As for baking, we found it was important to bake the custard in a warm pie crust; this way, the filling would adhere to the crust, rather than separating from it as soon as the pie was sliced. After 15 minutes in the oven to set the custard, we let the pie cool for an hour, then refrigerated it for a few more hours to make sure the filling was completely set.

The finishing touch on Key lime pie is sweetened whipped cream, which cuts the tartness of the limes. Since we didn't come this far just to pull out a can of Reddi-wip, we combined heavy cream, confectioners' sugar, and vanilla in a small bowl and whipped until soft, cloudlike peaks had formed. We spread the creamy topping over the pie and sliced. Our tasters were thrilled

by the fresh lime flavor of our creamy, luscious, lightly sweetened pie—and those who didn't get a bite were green with envy.

Key Lime Pie
SERVES 2

The timing here is a bit different from that of other pies; you need to make the filling first, then prepare the crust (the crust must still be warm when the filling is added). Feel free to use Key limes if desired; note that you'll need about 10 Key limes to yield ¼ cup juice. You will need a 6-inch pie plate for this recipe (see page 3).

FILLING
- **2 large egg yolks**
- **2 teaspoons grated lime zest plus ¼ cup fresh lime juice from 2 to 3 limes (see note)**
- **⅔ cup sweetened condensed milk**

CRUST
- **4 whole graham crackers, broken into 1-inch pieces**
- **2 tablespoons unsalted butter, melted and cooled**
- **4 teaspoons granulated sugar**

TOPPING
- **¼ cup heavy cream, chilled**
- **2 teaspoons confectioners' sugar**
- **⅛ teaspoon vanilla extract**

1. FOR THE FILLING: Whisk egg yolks and lime zest together in medium bowl until mixture has light green tint, about 1 minute. Whisk in condensed milk until smooth, then whisk in lime juice. Cover mixture and set aside at room temperature until thickened, about 30 minutes.

2. FOR THE CRUST: Meanwhile, adjust oven rack to middle position and heat oven to 325 degrees. Process graham cracker pieces in food processor to fine, even crumbs, about 30 seconds. Sprinkle butter and granulated sugar over crumbs and pulse to incorporate. Sprinkle mixture into 6-inch pie plate. Following photo on page 279, use bottom of measuring cup to press crumbs into even layer on bottom and sides of pie plate.

3. Bake until crust is fragrant and beginning to brown,

USE IT UP: SWEETENED CONDENSED MILK

Caramel Dip
MAKES ½ CUP

Serve with sliced apples or pears, or spread on toast for a special treat.

- **½ cup sweetened condensed milk**
- **2 tablespoons heavy cream or half-and-half, room temperature**
- **¼ teaspoon vanilla extract**
- **⅛ teaspoon salt**

1. Pour milk into medium microwave-safe bowl and cover tightly with plastic wrap. Microwave on medium-low power, stirring and replacing plastic every 3 to 5 minutes, until slightly darkened and thickened, 10 to 20 minutes.

2. Remove from microwave and whisk in cream, vanilla, and salt until smooth. Let cool to room temperature. Serve at room temperature or warmed slightly in microwave.

MAKING A GRAHAM CRACKER CRUST

To make the graham cracker crust, press the crumb mixture firmly and evenly across the bottom and up the sides of the pie plate, using the bottom of a measuring cup.

13 to 18 minutes. Transfer pie plate to wire rack; do not turn oven off.

4. Pour thickened filling into warm pie crust. Bake pie until center is firm but jiggles slightly when shaken, 15 to 20 minutes. Let pie cool slightly on wire rack, about 1 hour, then cover loosely with plastic wrap and refrigerate until filling is chilled and set, about 3 hours.

5. FOR THE TOPPING: Before serving, whisk cream, confectioners' sugar, and vanilla together until cream forms soft peaks. Spread whipped cream attractively over top of pie and serve.

EASY LEMON SOUFFLÉ

MANY HOME COOKS RELEGATE SOUFFLÉS TO THE category of "restaurant desserts"—those that are impossibly difficult to make for the average layperson. But the truth is, although soufflés can be finicky and fussy, requiring stiffly beaten egg whites and a clean bowl (more on this later), they're not that daunting to make. Our hope was that in scaling this recipe down for two, we'd make the mythical soufflé—with its unique, ethereal, airy texture—more accessible and less intimidating for the home cook.

Our first move was to swap out the typical tall soufflé dish in favor of a small skillet. Not only would this help us cut back on leftover soufflé (which isn't terribly appetizing), but we suspected it would help make our soufflé foolproof and streamlined: We could utilize heat from the stovetop to activate the batter and ensure a

tall, sturdy rise, allowing us to nix the more labor- and time-intensive traditional French cooking methods. The traditional methods call for either a béchamel base, which is a classic French sauce made from butter, flour, and milk, or a *bouillie* base, which is a paste made from flour and milk, to help stabilize the whipped egg whites. Indeed, one test pitting these two methods against a streamlined soufflé, with raw whipped egg yolks as the base, confirmed we were right. Lemon, a common dessert soufflé variation, was the flavor we chose because the bright, citrus notes burst through the eggy base especially well. Of the three, the soufflé with a whipped egg yolk base boasted the cleanest, freshest lemon flavor and was the easiest to make—we didn't have to cook anything in advance. Theory confirmed, we began to tweak the ratios of soufflé batter ingredients in search of the ultimate soufflé texture.

We started with the eggs, which give the soufflé its delicate and lofty texture, using a simple ingredient list: egg whites, egg yolks, and sugar. To determine the proper ratio of egg whites to egg yolks, we tried several variations, whipping whites and yolks separately, then folding the egg whites into the whipped yolk base. We found that too many egg whites resulted in a foamy but stiff soufflé; an equal number of yolks and whites worked better. Scaling the eggs to just two seemed logical, but we found that this small quantity didn't achieve the rise we were hoping for. In the end, three eggs gave us a supremely rich and creamy soufflé.

The technique used to beat the egg whites is crucial to a successful soufflé—its structure comes solely from the aerated eggs. The objective is to create a strong, stable foam that rises well and doesn't collapse during either folding or baking. We knew that adding sugar to the whites during beating would result in stable whites that would be more resilient when it came time to fold them into the yolks, and the soufflé would be less apt to fall quickly after baking. We made sure our mixing bowl was clean—even the tiniest speck of oil in a bowl can prevent the whites from rising well—and began whipping our whites, adding sugar after the whites were broken and foamy. Dumping in the sugar all at once produced a soufflé with an uneven, shorter rise and an overly sweet taste, so we added the sugar gradually. Adding an acid (we used cream of tartar) to the whites as they were whipped also helped them build to a sturdy texture and retain their shape.

At this point, our soufflé was slightly foamier than we wanted. We followed the lead of many classic soufflé recipes and added a tablespoon of flour, which turned our foamy soufflé perfectly creamy.

We had the great texture of a first-class soufflé but now had to work on the flavor. A good lemon soufflé should burst with bright, citrus flavors, instead of being overly eggy. We wanted a clean, natural lemon flavor, so we added a mixture of lemon juice and lemon zest.

NOTES FROM THE TEST KITCHEN

PROPERLY WHIPPED EGG WHITES

Soufflés rely on perfectly whipped whites for their lightness, so it's important to whip them right. Egg whites whipped to soft peaks (top), drooping slightly from the tip of the whisk or beater, will not have the structure to properly support the soufflé. Overwhipped egg whites (center), looking curdled and separated, will not incorporate well into the soufflé base and often result in flat soufflés. (If your whites are overwhipped, start over with new whites and a clean bowl.) Egg whites whipped to stiff peaks (bottom), standing up tall on their own on the tip of the whisk or beater, have the ideal structure to support a light-as-air soufflé.

PROBLEM:
Soft Peaks

PROBLEM:
Overwhipped Whites

PERFECT:
Stiff Peaks

Ultimately, it took ¾ teaspoon of zest and 3 tablespoons of juice to make us happy with the lemony flavor and zing.

With our whites sturdily whipped and the egg yolk base brightly flavored, we folded the whites gently into the yolks, being careful not to overmix and therefore deflate the whites. We poured all of the batter into a buttered 8-inch skillet and let it cook for a minute over medium-low heat until just set around the edges and on the bottom, setting up the base for the soufflé to rise in the oven.

Almost there, we moved the soufflé into the oven to finish cooking. An oven temperature of 375 degrees worked well, producing a dramatic rise. We expected the soufflé to be done quickly and started checking on it after six minutes—just one extra minute in the oven makes all the difference between a perfectly cooked soufflé and one that's overdone. Looking through the oven window, we saw that the top was lightly golden. We dipped into the soufflé with our spoons and found that it was ethereally creamy and moist in the middle with bright, balanced lemon flavor.

Easy Lemon Soufflé

SERVES 2

Don't open the oven door during the first 5 minutes of baking, but do check the soufflé regularly for doneness during the final few minutes in the oven. Be ready to serve the soufflé immediately after removing it from the oven. The center of the soufflé should be creamy and slightly liquid. Since the recipe involves such a small quantity of ingredients, we recommend using a hand-held electric mixer for thorough mixing. Using an 8-inch traditional (not nonstick) skillet is essential to getting the right texture and height in the soufflé.

- **3 large eggs, separated**
- **⅛ teaspoon cream of tartar**
- **6 tablespoons granulated sugar**
- **⅛ teaspoon salt**
- **¾ teaspoon grated lemon zest plus 3 tablespoons fresh lemon juice**
- **1 tablespoon unbleached all-purpose flour**
- **2 teaspoons unsalted butter**
- **Confectioners' sugar, for dusting**

1. Adjust oven rack to middle position and heat oven to 375 degrees. In large bowl, whip egg whites and cream of tartar together with electric mixer on medium-low speed until foamy, about 1 minute. Slowly add 2 tablespoons granulated sugar and salt, then increase mixer speed to medium-high and continue to whip until whites are glossy and stiff peaks form, 2 to 3 minutes longer.

2. In separate bowl, whip egg yolks and remaining ¼ cup granulated sugar together using electric mixer on medium-high speed until pale and thick, about 1 minute. Beat in lemon zest, lemon juice, and flour until incorporated, about 30 seconds.

3. Fold one-quarter of whipped egg whites into yolk mixture until almost no white streaks remain. Gently fold in remaining egg whites until just incorporated.

4. Melt butter in 8-inch ovenproof skillet over medium-low heat. Swirl pan to coat evenly with melted butter, then gently scrape soufflé batter into skillet and cook until edges begin to set, about 1 minute.

5. Transfer skillet to oven and bake soufflé until puffed, center jiggles slightly when shaken, and surface is golden, 6 to 8 minutes. Using potholder (skillet handle will be hot), remove skillet from oven. Dust soufflé with confectioners' sugar and serve immediately.

CHOCOLATE POTS DE CRÈME

LITERALLY TRANSLATED, *POTS DE CRÈME* MEANS "pots of cream," but "cream" in this case refers to custard, a word the French simply don't have a translation for. Once we tasted our first pots de crème, we understood exactly why tiny Limoges china pots were commissioned especially for this exotic puddinglike dessert. The custard is so remarkably rich, so intensely flavored, that just a small amount satisfies. When properly made, this rich custard boasts a satiny texture and intense chocolate flavor, but we've had other versions that are no better than cafeteria pudding. We set out to develop an authentic recipe for this dessert that was not only authentic, but foolproof.

We started with a handful of existing recipes. Not surprisingly, the ingredients were more or less the same across the board: chocolate, eggs, sugar, and cream (or other dairy). The differences lay in the ratios of ingredients and the way the custard was cooked. Most of the recipes employed the usual treatment for baked custard: a hot water bath and a moderately low oven. But two out of the 20 or so recipes we found employed an unconventional method in which the custard is cooked on the stovetop in a saucepan until thickened, combined with the chocolate, then poured into ramekins and chilled. Since we wanted just two servings, a hot water bath seemed like a lot of fuss; it would be stovetop all the way for our little custards.

In the pot de crème recipes we came across, about 2 cups of dairy were required to yield eight servings; the richest recipes used heavy cream exclusively, but some called for a combination of heavy cream and half-and-half to give the custard a balance of richness and body. Five to six egg yolks helped to enrich and thicken the custard. For our initial test, we tried combining ½ cup of heavy cream, ¼ cup of half-and-half, and one egg yolk, but this gave us a loose custard. Adding another egg yolk helped the custard set up, but it was still thinner than it should have been. Since fat contributes to the thickness of the custard, we decided to omit the half-and-half altogether and increase the amount of heavy cream to ¾ cup. Sure enough, the heavy cream improved the texture of our dessert.

Since we were making chocolate pots de crème, we knew it was important to get intense chocolate flavor that could stand up to all that heavy cream. With that in mind, we passed over milk chocolate and semisweet chocolate; they would be too mild and, we suspected, would make our custards cloyingly sweet (4 teaspoons of granulated sugar had provided ample sweetness in our recipe thus far). We tested cocoa powder and unsweetened chocolate, but they were too gritty, so we focused on bittersweet chocolate. We found that 2½ ounces delivered just the intensity and rich flavor our tasters desired, and a small amount of instant espresso, dissolved in water, added some complexity and deepened the overall flavor of our pots de crème.

After chilling the filled ramekins and counting down the minutes (no less than four hours), we garnished our pots de crème with dollops of whipped cream and chocolate shavings and sampled the rich, creamy, uberchocolaty custard. To our delight, not only had we made this refined French classic fantastic and foolproof, we'd simplified it as well.

CHOCOLATE POTS DE CRÈME

Chocolate Pots de Crème

SERVES 2

You will need two 5-ounce ramekins for this recipe (see page 3). We prefer pots de crème made with 60 percent cocoa bittersweet chocolate (our favorite brands are Ghirardelli and Callebaut). A teaspoon of strong brewed coffee may be substituted for the instant espresso and water. Covered tightly with plastic wrap, the pots de crème will keep for up to 3 days in the refrigerator, but the whipped cream must be made just before serving.

POTS DE CRÈME

- 2½ ounces bittersweet chocolate (see note), chopped fine
- 2 large egg yolks
- 4 teaspoons granulated sugar
- Pinch salt
- ¾ cup heavy cream
- 1 teaspoon vanilla extract
- ⅛ teaspoon instant espresso dissolved in 1 teaspoon water (see note)

WHIPPED CREAM AND GARNISH

- ¼ cup heavy cream, chilled
- 2 teaspoons confectioners' sugar
- ⅛ teaspoon vanilla extract
- Cocoa powder, for dusting (optional)
- Chocolate shavings, for sprinkling (optional)

1. FOR THE POTS DE CRÈME: Place chocolate in heatproof bowl; set fine-mesh strainer over bowl and set aside.

2. Whisk egg yolks, granulated sugar, and salt together in medium bowl until combined, then whisk in heavy cream. Transfer mixture to small saucepan. Cook mixture over medium-low heat, stirring constantly and scraping bottom of pot with wooden spoon, until it is thickened and silky and registers 175 to 180 degrees on instant-read thermometer, 3 to 6 minutes. (Do not let custard overcook or simmer.)

3. Immediately pour custard through strainer over chocolate. Let mixture stand to melt chocolate, about 5 minutes. Whisk gently until smooth, then whisk in vanilla and espresso. Divide mixture evenly between two 5-ounce ramekins. Gently tap ramekins against counter to remove any air bubbles.

4. Cool pots de crème to room temperature, about 1 hour. Cover ramekins tightly with plastic wrap and refrigerate until chilled, at least 4 hours or up to 3 days. Before serving, let pots de crème stand at room temperature for 20 to 30 minutes.

5. FOR THE WHIPPED CREAM AND GARNISH: Before serving, whisk cream, confectioners' sugar, and vanilla together until cream forms soft peaks. Dollop each pot de crème with about 2 tablespoons whipped cream and garnish with cocoa powder and/or chocolate shavings, if desired.

TIRAMISÙ

THE NAME OF THIS CLASSIC ITALIAN DESSERT translates literally as "pick me up"—a reference to the invigorating qualities of the dish's espresso, sugar, and alcohol. In tiramisù, store-bought ladyfingers (sponge-cakelike cookies) are dipped into alcohol-spiked espresso and then layered into a dish along with a thick, creamy mixture of buttery mascarpone (an Italian creamy cheese), sugar, and eggs. Finally, the dish is dusted with cocoa or sprinkled with chocolate and served chilled. Since tiramisù is usually made in a 13 by 9-inch baking dish, it's not exactly an option when cooking for two, which we felt was a tragedy. We said *arrivederci* to the huge baking dish and set out to scale down the recipe so that even tables of two could enjoy the luxurious combination of flavors and textures that have made this dessert so popular.

Finding the right vessel to hold our scaled-down dessert was the first challenge. We knew that an 8-inch square baking dish, though almost half the size of our 13 by 9-inch dish, would still be far too big for two people. A scan of our bakeware led us to a mini loaf pan and a 3-cup baking dish. But after preparing preliminary batches of tiramisù in both vessels, we decided the loaf pan was out (these skimpy portions would have diners fighting over the last dollop of mascarpone) and the baking dish was in.

Using an established test kitchen recipe as our foundation, we began by working on the filling, for which raw egg yolks are combined with sugar and rum before mascarpone cheese and whipped heavy cream are incorporated. We first considered the amount of mascarpone we'd need. The full-size recipe called for a pound and a half of mascarpone to create a dessert for 10 or more. But when cut back proportionately, to about 4 ounces of mascarpone, our two servings of tiramisù were minuscule. We decided to double the amount of cheese; the servings were now generous, but we figured that for this once-in-a-while indulgence we could deal (not very reluctantly) with a few extra spoonfuls of tiramisù.

Now we could consider the remaining filling ingredients. Two egg yolks made the filling silky and suave, with a round, rich flavor. (For those wary of desserts made with raw eggs, we also created a slightly more involved variation in which the yolks are cooked.) As for the sugar, ¼ cup provided the perfect amount of sweetness for our 8 ounces of mascarpone; the same amount of cream, whipped, lightened the texture of the filling without affecting the mascarpone's delicate flavor. A single tablespoon of dark rum gave us a filling with added richness and a slightly boozy backbone.

Traditionally, in tiramisù, ladyfingers are dipped in espresso spiked with alcohol so that the dry, plain cookies soften and take on some flavor. Since brewed espresso is not practical for many home cooks, we opted for instant espresso, dissolved in water and flavored with more rum, which complemented the rich, deep, toasty qualities of the coffee.

After assembling batch upon batch of tiramisù, we can say with confidence that the technique for dipping or soaking the ladyfingers greatly affects the outcome. A quick in-and-out dip wasn't adequate for moistening the cookies, and the result was a dry, crumbly tiramisù. Fully submerging or otherwise saturating the ladyfingers yielded a wet, squishy tiramisù. To achieve the best results, we dropped the ladyfingers, one at a time, into the liquid so that they floated on the surface, then we rolled them over to moisten the other side. This middle ground of soaking ensured that the ladyfingers absorbed the right amount of liquid and were slightly cakey in the finished dessert.

With our soaking strategy worked out, we placed half of our dipped ladyfingers in the dish, covered them with half of the mascarpone filling, then dusted the filling with cocoa powder before repeating the layers. Finally, for a restaurant-worthy presentation, we sprinkled grated chocolate over the top. After waiting patiently for hours while the tiramisù chilled in the fridge, we dug in. The rich, creamy filling boasted a hint of rummy flavor, and the ladyfingers had softened to the perfect cakey texture—and the whole dish was accented by the bittersweet notes of the cocoa powder and grated chocolate. This was one pick-me-up we wouldn't be putting down anytime soon.

Tiramisù

SERVES 2

You will need a 3-cup baking dish measuring 7¼ by 5¼ inches for this recipe (see page 3). Since the recipe involves such a small quantity of ingredients, we recommend using a hand-held electric mixer for thorough mixing. Brandy and even whiskey can stand in for the dark rum. Do not allow the mascarpone to warm to room temperature before using it; it has a tendency to break if allowed to do so.

⅔	cup water, room temperature
2	tablespoons instant espresso
2	tablespoons dark rum (see note)
2	large egg yolks
¼	cup (1¾ ounces) sugar
	Pinch salt
8	ounces mascarpone (see note)
¼	cup heavy cream, chilled
10–15	dried ladyfingers (about 2¾ ounces)
1	tablespoon Dutch-processed cocoa powder
1	tablespoon grated semisweet or bittersweet chocolate (optional)

1. Stir water, espresso, and 1 tablespoon rum together in wide bowl or baking dish until espresso dissolves; set aside.

2. Using electric mixer, beat egg yolks at low speed until just combined. Add sugar and salt and beat on medium-high speed until pale yellow, 1 to 1½ minutes, scraping down sides of bowl with rubber spatula as needed. Add remaining 1 tablespoon rum and beat on medium speed until just combined, 15 to 30 seconds; scrape bowl. Add mascarpone and beat on low speed until no lumps remain, 15 to 30 seconds.

3. In small bowl, beat cream at medium speed until frothy, 30 seconds to 1 minute. Increase mixer speed to high and continue to beat until cream holds stiff peaks, 1 to 1½ minutes longer. Using rubber spatula, fold one-third of whipped cream into mascarpone mixture to lighten, then gently fold in remaining whipped cream until no white streaks remain.

4. Using half of ladyfingers and working with one at a time, drop ladyfingers into coffee mixture, roll, remove, and transfer to 7¼ by 5¼-inch glass or ceramic baking dish. (Do not submerge ladyfingers in coffee mixture; entire process should take no longer than 2 to 3 seconds for each cookie.) Following photos, arrange soaked cookies in single layer, breaking or trimming ladyfingers as necessary to fit. Spread half of mascarpone mixture over ladyfingers; use rubber spatula to spread mixture to sides and into corners of dish and smooth surface. Place 1½ teaspoons cocoa in fine-mesh strainer and dust cocoa over mascarpone mixture.

5. Repeat dipping and arrangement of ladyfingers; spread remaining mascarpone mixture over ladyfingers and dust with remaining 1½ teaspoons cocoa. Wipe edges of dish with dry paper towel. Cover with plastic wrap and refrigerate for at least 6 hours or up to 24 hours. Sprinkle with grated chocolate, if using; cut into pieces and serve chilled.

VARIATION

Tiramisù with Cooked Eggs

This recipe involves cooking the yolks in a double boiler, which requires a little more effort and makes for a slightly thicker mascarpone filling, but the results are just as good as with our traditional method. You will need an additional 2 tablespoons heavy cream.

Follow recipe for Tiramisù through step 1. In step 2, add 2 tablespoons cream to yolks after beating in sugar and salt; do not whisk in rum. Set bowl with yolks over medium saucepan containing 1 inch gently simmering water; cook, constantly scraping along bottom and sides of bowl with heatproof rubber spatula, until mixture coats back of spoon and registers 160 degrees on instant-read thermometer, 3 to 5 minutes. Remove from heat and stir vigorously to cool slightly, then set aside to cool to room temperature, about 15 minutes. Whisk in remaining 1 tablespoon rum until combined. Using electric mixer, add mascarpone and beat at low speed until no lumps remain, 15 to 30 seconds. Transfer mixture to large bowl and set aside. Continue with recipe from step 3, using full amount of heavy cream specified (¼ cup).

DIP, DON'T SUBMERGE

Both of the ladyfingers below were in the coffee mixture for the same amount of time, but different soaking techniques yielded very different results.

PERFECTLY SOAKED: This ladyfinger was dropped into the coffee mixture, rolled, and removed within 2 to 3 seconds. The coffee mixture has not completely saturated this cookie.

OVERSOAKED: This ladyfinger was fully submerged in the coffee mixture for 2 to 3 seconds. The coffee mixture has penetrated all the way to the center of the cookie.

ASSEMBLING TIRAMISÙ

1. Arrange soaked ladyfingers snugly in a single layer in a 3-cup baking dish measuring 7¼ by 5¼ inches.

2. Spread half of the mascarpone mixture over the ladyfingers.

3. Dust half of the cocoa over the mascarpone mixture. Repeat the layering and dusting with the remaining ladyfingers, mascarpone mixture, and cocoa.

Conversions & Equivalencies

SOME SAY COOKING IS A SCIENCE AND AN ART. We would say that geography has a hand in it, too. Flour milled in the United Kingdom and elsewhere will feel and taste different from flour milled in the United States. So, while we cannot promise that the loaf of bread you bake in Canada or England will taste the same as a loaf baked in the States, we can offer guidelines for converting weights and measures. We also recommend that you rely on your instincts when making our recipes. Refer to the visual cues provided. If the bread dough hasn't "come together in a ball," as described, you may need to add more flour—even if the recipe doesn't tell you so. You be the judge.

The recipes in this book were developed using standard U.S. measures following U.S. government guidelines. The charts below offer equivalents for U.S., metric, and Imperial (U.K.) measures. All conversions are approximate and have been rounded up or down to the nearest whole number. For example:

1 teaspoon = 4.929 milliliters, rounded up to 5 milliliters
1 ounce = 28.349 grams, rounded down to 28 grams

VOLUME CONVERSIONS

U.S.	METRIC
1 teaspoon	5 milliliters
2 teaspoons	10 milliliters
1 tablespoon	15 milliliters
2 tablespoons	30 milliliters
¼ cup	59 milliliters
⅓ cup	79 milliliters
½ cup	118 milliliters
¾ cup	177 milliliters
1 cup	237 milliliters
1¼ cups	296 milliliters
1½ cups	355 milliliters
2 cups	473 milliliters
2½ cups	592 milliliters
3 cups	710 milliliters
4 cups (1 quart)	0.946 liter
1.06 quarts	1 liter
4 quarts (1 gallon)	3.8 liters

WEIGHT CONVERSIONS

OUNCES	GRAMS
½	14
¾	21
1	28
1½	43
2	57
2½	71
3	85
3½	99
4	113
4½	128
5	142
6	170
7	198
8	227
9	255
10	283
12	340
16 (1 pound)	454

CONVERSIONS FOR INGREDIENTS COMMONLY USED IN BAKING

Baking is an exacting science. Because measuring by weight is far more accurate than measuring by volume, and thus more likely to achieve reliable results, in our recipes we provide ounce measures in addition to cup measures for many ingredients. Refer to the chart below to convert these measures into grams.

INGREDIENT	OUNCES	GRAMS
Flour		
1 cup all-purpose flour*	5	142
1 cup cake flour	4	113
1 cup whole-wheat flour	5½	156
Sugar		
1 cup granulated (white) sugar	7	198
1 cup packed brown sugar (light or dark)	7	198
1 cup confectioners' sugar	4	113
Cocoa Powder		
1 cup cocoa powder	3	85
Butter†		
4 tablespoons (½ stick, or ¼ cup)	2	57
8 tablespoons (1 stick, or ½ cup)	4	113
16 tablespoons (2 sticks, or 1 cup)	8	227

* U.S. all-purpose flour, the most frequently used flour in this book, does not contain leaveners, as some European flours do. These leavened flours are called self-rising or self-raising. If you are using self-rising flour, take this into consideration before adding leavening to a recipe.

† In the United States, butter is sold both salted and unsalted. We generally recommend unsalted butter. If you are using salted butter, take this into consideration before adding salt to a recipe.

OVEN TEMPERATURES

FAHRENHEIT	CELSIUS	GAS MARK (imperial)
225	105	¼
250	120	½
275	130	1
300	150	2
325	165	3
350	180	4
375	190	5
400	200	6
425	220	7
450	230	8
475	245	9

CONVERTING TEMPERATURES FROM AN INSTANT-READ THERMOMETER

We include doneness temperatures in many of our recipes, such as those for poultry, meat, and bread. We recommend an instant-read thermometer for the job. Refer to the table above to convert Fahrenheit degrees to Celsius. Or, for temperatures not represented in the chart, use this simple formula:

Subtract 32 degrees from the Fahrenheit reading, then divide the result by 1.8 to find the Celsius reading.

EXAMPLE:

"Roast until the thickest part of a chicken thigh registers 175 degrees on an instant-read thermometer." To convert:

175° F − 32 = 143°
143° ÷ 1.8 = 79.44°C, rounded down to 79°C

Index

Beef
blade steaks, trimming, 223
broth, taste tests on, 223
Chili, Slow-Cooker, *214,* 221–22
Classic Pot Roast with Root Vegetables, 204–6
Enchiladas, 207
Grilled Argentine Steaks with Plantains and Chimichurri
    Sauce, 144–46
Grilled Pimento Cheeseburgers and Potato Wedges with
    Garlic Mayonnaise, 149–51
Hand Pies, *208, 209*
pot roast, preparing, 205
Quick Texas Chili, 206–7
Satay with Spicy Peanut Dipping Sauce, 10–12
Sheet Pan Stir-Fried, with Snap Peas and Bell Peppers, 50–52
Short Ribs, Braised, with Potato and Carrots, 46–47
short ribs, buying, 235
short ribs, separating meat from bones, 235
slicing, for stir-fries, 52
Slow-Cooker Korean Braised Short Ribs, 234–35
Slow-Cooker Pesto Meatballs and Marinara, 224–26
Spice-Rubbed Strip Steak with Cherry Tomato and
    Black Bean Salad, 50
Spice-Rubbed Strip Steak with Toasted Corn and
    Black Bean Salad, 47–50, *49*
Steak Tips with Mushroom-Onion Gravy, 6–8, *7*
Stew, Slow-Cooker Hearty, 222–24
Stew, Weeknight, 9–10
Tenderloin, Grilled, with Green Beans and Blue Cheese
    Dressing, 146–48, *147*
testing for doneness, 149
Weeknight Bolognese with Linguine, 95–97
Beet(s)
Roasted, Salad with Blood Orange and Almonds, 240
Roasted, Salad with Goat Cheese and Pistachios, 239–40,
    241
Bench scrapers, ratings of, 262
Berry(ies)
Baby Spinach Salad with Frisée and Strawberries,
    238–39
Cranberry-Roasted Pork Tenderloin, 17–19
Summer, Snack Cakes, 267–69, *268*
**Biryani-Style Chicken and Rice with Caramelized
    Onion, Raisins, and Cardamom, 71**
Biscuits, Simple Drop, 260–61
Black Bean(s)
Burgers, 127–28
Burgers with Corn and Chipotle Chiles, 128
canned, taste tests on, 128
and Cherry Tomato Salad, Spice-Rubbed Strip Steak
    with, 50
Chili, 125–27
and Chorizo, Sopa Seca with, 108–9
and Pork Stew, Brazilian-Style, 56–58
Salsa, Smoky, 119
Skillet Brown Rice and Beans with Corn and Tomatoes,
    118–19
and Toasted Corn Salad, Spice-Rubbed Strip Steak with,
    47–50, *49*

Blue Cheese Dressing and Green Beans, Grilled
    Beef Tenderloin with, 146–48, *147*
Bok Choy Slaw and Soy-Ginger Vinaigrette,
    Grilled Tuna Steaks with, 164–66, *165*
Bouillabaisse, Chicken, *66,* 67–69
Box graters, ratings of, 82
Braised Beef Short Ribs with Potato and Carrots,
    46–47
Braised Hearty Greens, 242
Brazilian-Style Black Bean and Pork Stew, 56–58
Breads
baguettes, storing, 68
Cheddar Cheese, 259–60
Coffee Cake Muffins, 258–59
Cream and Currant Scones, 261–62, *263*
Croutons, 69
Garlic Toasts, 107
pita, warming, 203
sandwich, taste tests on, 188
Simple Drop Biscuits, 260–61
see also Tortillas
Breakfast Sausage, 23
Brining 101, 18
Broccoli
with Brown Butter, Parmesan, and Walnuts, 65
crown, preparing for roasting, 64
recipes using small amounts of, 1
Roasted, Garlic, and Almonds, Pasta with, 88
Roasted, Prosciutto and Sage "Un-Stuffed" Chicken
    Breasts with, 64–66
Stir-Fried, with Chili-Garlic Sauce, 243
Stir-Fried, with Hoisin and Five-Spice Powder, 244
Stir-Fried, with Orange and Ginger, 244
Stir-Fried, with Oyster Sauce, 244
Broccoli Rabe
and Italian Sausage, Orecchiette with, 93–95
Sautéed, with Garlic and Lemon, 94
and White Beans, Orecchiette with, 95
**Broiled Salmon with Honeydew and
    Radish Salsa, 41**
Broiled Salmon with Mango Salsa, 41
Broiled Salmon with Pineapple Salsa, 39–41, *40*
Broth, beef, taste tests on, 223
Brown Betty, Peach, 272–73
**Brussels Sprouts and Red Potatoes,
    Roasted Chicken Breasts with, 64**
Bundt pans, small, 3
Burgers
Black Bean, 127–28
Black Bean, with Corn and Chipotle Chiles, 128
Grilled Pimento Cheeseburgers and Potato Wedges
    with Garlic Mayonnaise, 149–51
Turkey, Grilled, with Warm Potato and Arugula Salad,
    156–59, *157*
Turkey, Grilled Smoky Southwestern, with Warm
    Potato and Arugula Salad, 159
Butter, Jalapeño-Garlic, 41
Buttermilk Mashed Potatoes, 248, *249*

C

S

Saffron
  and Leek, Baked Scallops with, 187
  Raisins, and Toasted Almonds, Couscous with, 254
Salads (main-dish)
  Charred Romaine and Red Onion, Grilled Pizza with, *142*, 167–69
  Cherry Tomato and Black Bean, Spice-Rubbed Strip Steak with, 50
  Chicken, Spanish-Style, with Roasted Red Peppers, 201
  Chicken Caesar, 180–83, *181*
  Dijon Potato, Warm, Bacon-Wrapped Pork Chops with, 53–54
  Greek, with Lamb, 213
  Pesto Pasta, with Chicken and Vegetables, 178–80
  Poached Shrimp, with Avocado, Orange, and Arugula, 185
  Poached Shrimp, with Avocado and Grapefruit, 183–85
  Potato, Warm, and Arugula, Grilled Smoky Southwestern Turkey Burgers with, 159
  Potato, Warm, and Arugula, Grilled Turkey Burgers with, 156–59, *157*
  Toasted Corn and Black Bean, Spice-Rubbed Strip Steak with, 47–50, *49*
  Tofu, with Vegetables, *114*, 140–41
Salads (side-dish)
  Baby Spinach, with Carrot, Orange, and Sesame, *236*, 238
  Baby Spinach, with Fennel and Apple, 239
  Baby Spinach, with Frisée and Strawberries, 238–39
  Fennel, Apple, and Shallot, 123
  Potato, Austrian-Style, 250–51
  Quinoa, with Red Bell Pepper and Cilantro, 251–53, *252*
  Roasted Beet, with Blood Orange and Almonds, 240
  Roasted Beet, with Goat Cheese and Pistachios, 239–40, *241*
Salmon
  with Asparagus and Herb Vinaigrette, 73–76, *75*
  Broiled, with Honeydew and Radish Salsa, 41
  Broiled, with Mango Salsa, 41
  Broiled, with Pineapple Salsa, 39–41, *40*
Salsa, Smoky Black Bean, 119
Sambal oelek chili paste, about, 244
Sandwiches
  Cuban, 197
  Lamb Shawarma, *192*, 212
Satay, Beef, with Spicy Peanut Dipping Sauce, 10–12
Saucepans, large, ratings of, 10
Sauces
  Chimichurri, 144–46
  Enchilada, Fast, 207
  Meaty Tomato, Slow-Cooker, 226–28
  Orange, Spicy, 52
  Oyster, 52
  Rouille, 69
  Smoky Black Bean Salsa, 119
  Tartar, 188–90, *189*
  Yogurt-Tahini, 212

Sausage(s)
  andouille, taste tests on, 25
  Baked Ziti with, 101–2
  Brazilian-Style Black Bean and Pork Stew, 56–58
  Breakfast, 23
  Cajun Red Beans and Rice, 23–26, *24*
  Italian, and Broccoli Rabe, Orecchiette with, 93–95
  Italian, and Fennel, Whole-Wheat Spaghetti with, *90*, 91–92
  Sopa Seca with Chorizo and Black Beans, 108–9
Sautéed Broccoli Rabe with Garlic and Lemon, 94
Sautéed Peas with Fennel, 245
Sautéed Peas with Leek and Tarragon, 245
Sautéed Peas with Mushrooms and Thyme, 245
Sautéed Peas with Shallot and Mint, 244–45
Savory Pie Dough, 62
Scallion(s)
  storing, 198
  Tomato, and Lemon, Couscous with, 253–54
Scallops
  Baked, with Leek and Saffron, 187
  Baked, with Lemon and Herbs, 185–87
  preparing, 186
  treated ("wet"), quick soak for, 186
Scones, Cream and Currant, 261–62, *263*
Seeds
  Baby Spinach Salad with Carrot, Orange, and Sesame, *236*, 238
  toasting, 240
Sesame, Carrot, and Orange, Baby Spinach Salad with, *236*, 238
Shallot and Mint, Sautéed Peas with, 244–45
Sheet Pan Stir-Fried Beef with Snap Peas and Bell Peppers, 50–52
Shellfish
  Baked Scallops with Leek and Saffron, 187
  Baked Scallops with Lemon and Herbs, 185–87
  mussels, debearding, 106
  mussels, selecting and storing, 106
  Mussels Marinara with Spaghetti, 106–7
  Poached Shrimp Salad with Avocado, Orange, and Arugula, 185
  Poached Shrimp Salad with Avocado and Grapefruit, 183–85
  Rice Noodles with Shrimp, Shiitakes, and Snow Peas, 112–13
  scallops, preparing, 186
  scallops, treated ("wet"), quick soak for, 186
  Thai Red Curry with Shrimp, Asparagus, and Carrots, 79
  Thai Red Curry with Shrimp, Bell Pepper, and Snap Peas, *44*, 77–79
Shrimp
  Asparagus, and Carrots, Thai Red Curry with, 79
  Bell Pepper, and Snap Peas, Thai Red Curry with, *44*, 77–79
  Poached, Salad with Avocado, Orange, and Arugula, 185
  Poached, Salad with Avocado and Grapefruit, 183–85
  Shiitakes, and Snow Peas, Rice Noodles with, 112–13